ASP
IN A NUTSHELL
A Desktop Quick Reference

ASP
IN A NUTSHELL

A Desktop Quick Reference

Second Edition

A. Keyton Weissinger

O'REILLY®

Beijing • Cambridge • Farnham • Köln • Paris • Sebastopol • Taipei • Tokyo

ASP in a Nutshell, Second Edition

by A. Keyton Weissinger

Copyright © 2000 O'Reilly & Associates, Inc. All rights reserved.
Printed in the United States of America.

Published by O'Reilly & Associates, Inc., 101 Morris Street, Sebastopol, CA 95472.

Editor: Ron Petrusha

Production Editor: Jeffrey Holcomb

Cover Designer: Edie Freedman

Printing History:

       February 1999:   First Edition.

       July 2000:   Second Edition.

Library of Congress Cataloging-in-Publication Data

Weissinger, A. Keyton.
    ASP in a nutshell : a desktop quick reference / A. Keyton Weissinger.--2nd ed.
      p. cm.
    ISBN 1-56592-843-1
    1. Acitive server pages. 2. Web sites--Design. 3. Microsoft Internet information
      server. 4. SQL server. 5. Web servers. I. Title.

TK5105.8885.A26 W45 2000
005.2'76--dc21   00-042757

ISBN: 1-56592-843-1
[VH]

Table of Contents

Part III. Installable Component Reference

Part IV. Appendixes

Preface

Active Server Pages (ASP) allows for powerful web application development. It is both simple to use and, with its extensibility through ActiveX and Java components, very powerful. But what is it? Is it a programming language? No, not exactly. Is it a Microsoft-only rapid development platform? No, not really.

Active Server Pages is a technology originally created by Microsoft as an answer to the sometimes complex problems posed by CGI application development. It allows you to use any scripting language, from VBScript to Python, to create real-world web applications.

Although originally only available for Microsoft platforms, ASP is quickly becoming available for nearly any web server on many operating systems. Microsoft suggests that there are 250,000 web developers using ASP and over 25,000 web applications built using ASP. So you're not alone.

You hold in your hands the desktop reference for this exciting technology.

Who Is This Book for?

This book is intended as a reference guide for developers who write Active Server Page web applications. Whether you are a professional developer paid to work magic with the Web or an amateur trying to figure out this web development thing, this book is for you. If you are coming to ASP from CGI, I hope this book will help make your transition from CGI to ASP an easy one.

I hope this book will be a very accessible, very convenient reference book. While I was writing this book, I envisioned myself (or one of you) with half a line of code written, trying to remember what options were available for the specific property or method I was attempting to use. I wanted a quick access book that would sit on my desk and be there when I needed it. I hope I have achieved that goal.

This book is not for the beginning programmer that knows nothing about the Web. There are already several books out there that will teach you about web applications and even how to write ASP applications specifically. Although each chapter starts with a brief overview, I have included these sections only to put the current object for that chapter in the context of Active Server Pages as a whole.

How to Use This Book

As previously mentioned, this book is a reference. Although you can read the entire book from beginning to end and understand Active Server Pages from a holistic perspective, that was not my intent. There are two ways to use this book:

- You can navigate to the particular chapter that covers the intrinsic ASP object or component in which you're interested. This method of navigating the book will help you learn more about the intrinsic object or component with which you are working.

- You can look up the particular method, property, or event with which you're working and go directly to the explanation and example code that you need.

Each chapter is divided into sections to help make reference simple. Each section covers a specific topic related to the intrinsic ASP object or component that is the focus of that chapter. The sections are:

Introduction
> This section introduces the object or component in the context of its use in ASP applications.

Summary
> This section lists the object or component's properties, methods, collections, and events. Note that not all of these elements are present for every object or component.

Comments/Troubleshooting
> This section contains my comments or experiences I have had with the specific object or component. It is here that I will talk about possible discrepancies between Microsoft's documentation and my experience.

Properties
> This section covers all the properties and their uses for the specific object or component.

Collections
> This section covers all the collections for the specific object or component.

Methods
> This section covers all the methods for the specific object or component.

Events
> This section covers all the events for the specific object or component. (Note that most objects and components don't support any events.)

Each Properties, Collections, Methods, and Events section is further divided into an introduction, an example, and comments.

How This Book Is Structured

ASP in a Nutshell is divided into three parts. Part I, *Introduction to Active Server Pages*, provides a fast-paced introduction to ASP that consists of three chapters. Chapter 1, *Active Server Pages: An Introduction*, places ASP within the broader context of the evolution of web application development, provides a quick example Active Server Page, and briefly examines the ASP object model. Chapter 2, *Active Server Pages: Server-Side Scripting*, examines the difference between client-side scripting and server-side scripting, takes a look at the structure and syntax of ASP pages, and examines the scripting languages that can be used for ASP development. Chapter 3, *Extending Active Server Pages*, examines the general mechanism for incorporating external COM components into an ASP application and lists the components that are included with Internet Information Server (IIS).

Active Server Pages is an object model that features seven intrinsic objects (Application, ASPError, ObjectContext, Request, Response, Server, and Session) that are always available to your scripts. (Actually, the ObjectContext object is a Microsoft Transaction Server object that is available only if you're using ASP 2.0 or greater.) Part II, *Object Reference*, documents each of these intrinsic objects. These chapters are arranged alphabetically by object. In addition, Chapter 11, *Preprocessing Directives, Server-Side Includes, and GLOBAL.ASA*, covers three major structural features of ASP that are not closely related to its object model.

ASP is extensible. That is, by calling the Server object's CreateObject method, you can instantiate external COM components that can be accessed programmatically just like any of the seven intrinsic objects. Part III, *Installable Component Reference*, documents the components that are included with the IIS installation. These thirteen chapters are again arranged alphabetically by component name.

Finally, *ASP in a Nutshell* includes four appendixes. Appendix A, *ASP Intrinsic Objects Member Summary*, lists the properties, methods, and events of the built-in ASP objects alphabetically. Appendix B, *Converting CGI/WinCGI Applications into ASP Applications*, shows what's involved in converting a simple application from Perl and Visual Basic to ASP and VBScript. It also includes two handy tables that list CGI and WinCGI environment variables and their equivalent ASP properties. Appendix C, *ASP on Alternative Platforms*, examines some of the beta and released software that will allow you to develop ASP applications for software other than Microsoft's. Finally, Appendix D, *Configuration of ASP Applications on IIS*, covers the configuration details that you need to know about to get your ASP application to run successfully.

Conventions Used in This Book

Throughout this book, we've used the following typographic conventions:

Constant width
> Constant width in body text indicates an HTML tag or attribute, a scripting language construct (like For or Set), an intrinsic or user-defined constant, or an expression (like dElapTime = Timer()-dStartTime). Code fragments and code examples appear exclusively in constant-width text. In syntax statements and prototypes, text in constant width indicates such language elements as the method or property name and any invariable elements required by the syntax. Constant width is also used for operators, statements, and code fragments.

Constant width italic

> Constant width italic in body text indicates parameter and variable names. In syntax statements or prototypes, constant width italic indicates replaceable parameters.

Italic

> Italicized words in the text indicate intrinsic or user-defined functions and procedure names. Many system elements, such as paths, filenames, and URLs, are also italicized. Finally, italic is used to denote a term that's used for the first time.

 This symbol indicates a tip.

 This symbol indicates a warning.

Request for Comments

The information in this book has been tested and verified, but you may find that features have changed (or even find mistakes!). You can send any errors you find, as well as suggestions for future editions, to:

> O'Reilly & Associates, Inc.
> 101 Morris Street
> Sebastopol, CA 95472
> (800) 998-9938 (in the United States or Canada)
> (707) 829-0515 (international/local)
> (707) 829-0104 (fax)

You can also send messages electronically. To be put on the mailing list or request a catalog, send email to:

> *info@oreilly.com*

To ask technical questions or comment on the book, send email to:

> *bookquestions@oreilly.com*

There is a web site for the book, where examples, errata, and any plans for future editions are listed. The site also includes a link to a forum where you can discuss the book with the author and other readers. You can access this site at:

> *http://www.oreilly.com/catalog/aspnut2*

For more information about this book and others, see the O'Reilly web site:

> *http://www.oreilly.com*

Acknowledgments for the Second Edition

As always, the first person I have to thank for all my endeavors is my wife Liticia and our daughters Mara and Hannah. Without their support this book would never have been written, much less revised.

Again, I'd like to thank Ron Petrusha, my editor at O'Reilly. He and his assistant Bob Herbstman have been instrumental in taking this book to its next level. Thank you.

Finally, I'd like to thank you for buying this book and for using it. As I said last time, I hope it helps you get home a little earlier or get a little more done in your day.

Acknowledgments from the First Edition

I'd like to start by thanking my wife, Liticia, without whose support this book would not have been written.

Next, I'd like to thank Ron Petrusha, my editor at O'Reilly. His comments and thoughtful insights have helped to make this book what it is. Also, if it weren't for the tireless efforts of his assistant editors, Tara McGoldrick and Katie Gardner, this book may not have been completed on time. Thank you.

I'd also like to personally thank Tim O'Reilly for not only publishing some of the best books in the industry, but also for going one step further and publishing several titles meant to "give back" to the community. How many technical publishers would produce the best computer documentation in the industry, support free software efforts worldwide, and still make time to publish books like *Childhood Leukemia*. Very few. Thank you, Tim.

I'd like to thank my technical reviewers, Chris Coffey, John Ternent, Matt Sargent, and Sarah Ferris. Their efforts and professional comments helped keep me focused on creating a quick reference that's useful to real-world, professional ASP developers. I'd like to especially thank Chris for helping me to focus on the details and maintain a high level of consistency.

I'd like to note my gratitude to Chris Burdett, Karen Monks, Chad Dorn, Chris Luse, and Jeff Adkisson at the technical documentation department at my last employer. Their contributions to the skills required to write this book were early but imperative.

Finally, I'd like to thank you for buying this book and for using it. I hope it helps you get home a little earlier or get a little more done in your day.

PART I

Introduction to
Active Server Pages

This part contains a brief introduction to Active Server Pages and an overview of the interaction between Active Server Pages and Microsoft's Internet Information Server. Also in this part, you will be introduced to the IIS object model and the objects that make it up and to all the installable server components that come with IIS. Part I consists of the following chapters:

Chapter 1, *Active Server Pages: An Introduction*

Chapter 2, *Active Server Pages: Server-Side Scripting*

Chapter 3, *Extending Active Server Pages*

CHAPTER 1

Active Server Pages: An Introduction

ASP is a technology that allows you to dynamically generate browser-neutral content using server-side scripting. The code for this scripting can be written in any of several languages and is embedded in special tags inside the otherwise-normal HTML code making up a page of content. This heterogeneous scripting/content page is interpreted by the web server only upon the client's request for the content.

To understand the evolution of ASP and its current capabilities, it helps to quickly review the history of web-based content and applications.

The Static Internet

In the early days of the World Wide Web, all information served to the client's browser was static. In other words, the content for page A served to client 1 was exactly the same as the content for page A served to client 2. The web server did not dynamically generate any part of the site's contents but simply served requests for static HTML pages loaded from the web server's file system and sent to the requesting client. There was no interactivity between the user and the server. The browser requested information, and the server sent it.

Although the static Internet quickly evolved to include graphics and sounds, the Web was still static, with little interactivity and very little functionality beyond that provided by simple hyperlinking.

Figure 1-1 illustrates the user's request and the web server's corresponding response for static (HTML, for example) web content.

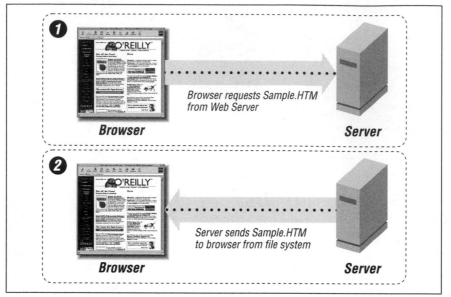

Figure 1-1: Static web content: request and delivery

The Dynamic Internet Part I: CGI Applications

One of the first extensions of the static internet was the creation of the Common Gateway Interface. The Common Gateway Interface, or CGI, provides a mechanism by which a web browser can communicate a request for the execution of an application on the web server. The result of this application is converted/formatted into a browser-readable (HTML) form and sent to the requesting browser.

CGI applications raised the bar on what was expected from a web site and transitioned the World Wide Web from an easy way to share information to a viable platform for information processing. The response to this evolution of the Web was rapidly accelerated growth and the beginning of the business world's interest in the Internet.

Part of this growth was the creation of several client-side scripting solutions that enabled the client's machine to take on part of the processing tasks. Chief among these client-side solutions are Netscape's JavaScript and Microsoft's VBScript.

During this huge growth in Internet-based technologies, Microsoft released its Internet Information Server. Touted as being easy to use, scalable, portable, secure, and extensible, it is also free and closely integrated with Microsoft's Windows NT and Windows 2000 operating systems. It quickly became very popular.

The Dynamic Internet Part II: ISAPI

In addition to supporting the CGI specification, Microsoft introduced an alternative to CGI, the Internet Server Application Programming Interface (or ISAPI). ISAPI addresses one of the most limiting features of CGI applications.

Each time a client requests the execution of a CGI application, the web server executes a separate instance of the application, sends in the user's requesting information, and serves the results of the CGI application's processing to the client. The problem with this approach is that a separate CGI application is loaded for each request. This can be quite a drain on the server's resources if there are many requests for the CGI application.

ISAPI alleviates this problem by relying on dynamic link libraries (DLLs). Each ISAPI application is in the form of a single DLL that is loaded into the same memory space as the web server upon the first request for the application. Once in memory, the DLL stays in memory, answering user requests until it is explicitly released from memory. This increased efficiency in memory usage comes at a cost. All ISAPI DLLs must be thread-safe so that multiple threads can be instantiated into the DLL without causing problems with the application's function.*

ISAPI applications are normally faster than their equivalent CGI applications because the web server does not have to instantiate a new application every time a request is made. Once the ISAPI application DLL is loaded into memory, it stays in memory. The web server does not need to load it again.

In addition to ISAPI applications, ISAPI allows for the development of ISAPI filters. An *ISAPI filter* is a custom DLL that is in the same memory space as the web server and is called by the web server in response to every HTTP request. In this way, the ISAPI filter changes the manner in which the web server itself behaves. The ISAPI filter then instructs the web server how to handle the request. ISAPI filters thus allow you to customize your web server's response to specific types of user requests. To state the difference between ISAPI filters and ISAPI applications (and CGI applications) more clearly, ISAPI filters offer three types of functionality that set them apart from ISAPI (or CGI) applications:

- An ISAPI filter allows you to provide a form of web site or page-level security by its insertion as a layer between the client and the web server.

- An ISAPI filter allows you to track more information about the requests to the web server and the content served to the requestor than a standard HTTP web server on its own can. This information can be stored in a separate format from that of the web server's logging functions.

- An ISAPI filter can serve information to clients in a different manner than the web server can by itself.

---

* As of version 4.0, Microsoft Internet Information Server allows you to load CGI applications into the same memory space as the web server, just as you can ISAPI applications.

Here are some examples of possible ISAPI filters:

- A security layer between the client and the web server. This security layer could provide for a more thorough screening of the client request than that provided for by straight username and password authentication.

- A custom filter could interpret the stream of information from the server and, based on that interpretation, present the stream in a different format than would the original web server. The *ASP.DLL* (see the following section) is an example of this type of ISAPI filter. It interprets the server code in a script requested by the client and, depending on its interpretation, serves the client customized content according to the client's request.

- A custom filter could map a client's request to a different physical location on the server. This could be used in high-volume sites where you might want to move the client onto a different server.

Active Server Pages and Active Server Pages 2.0

Late in the life of Internet Information Server 2.0, Microsoft began public beta testing of a technology whose code name was Denali. This technology is now known as Active Server Pages and is a very important aspect of Microsoft's Internet Information Server strategy.

This ASP technology is encapsulated in a single, small (~300K) DLL called *ASP. DLL*. This DLL is an ISAPI filter that resides in the same memory space as Internet Information Server. (For more about how IIS is configured to use ISAPI filters, see Appendix C, *Configuration of ASP Applications on IIS.*) Whenever a user requests a file whose file extension is *.ASP*, the ASP ISAPI filter handles the interpretation. ASP then loads any required scripting language interpreter DLLs into memory, executes any server-side code found in the Active Server Page, and passes the resulting HTML to the web server, which then sends it to the requesting browser. To reiterate this point, the output of ASP code that runs on the server is HTML (or HTML along with client-side script), which is inserted into the HTML text stream sent to the client.* Figure 1-2 illustrates this process.

ASP: A Demonstration

The actual interpretation of the web page by the *ASP.DLL* ISAPI filter is best explained by example. Example 1-1 shows a simple active server page, *Sample. ASP*. In this example, three pieces of server-side code, indicated in boldface, when executed on the server, create HTML that is sent to the client. This is a quick intro-duction. Don't worry if you don't understand exactly what is going on in this example; the details will be explained in Chapter 2, *Active Server Pages: Server-Side Scripting*.

---

* Note, however, that an Active Server Page application could just as easily send XML, for ex-ample, to the browser. HTML is only the default.

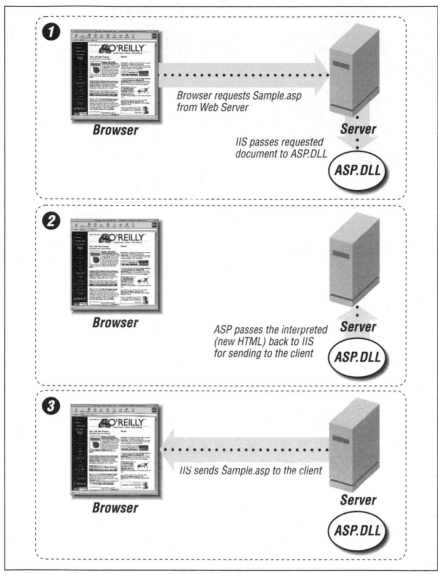

Figure 1-2: Dynamically generated web content: request and delivery

Example 1-1: Sample.ASP, an Example of Processing Server-Side Script

```
<%@ LANGUAGE="VBSCRIPT" %>

<HTML>
<HEAD>
<TITLE>Sample ASP</TITLE>
</HEAD>
<BODY>
```

```
Good afternoon.<BR>
Welcome to the sample. It is now approximately
<%=Time()%> at the server. Here are a couple of
demonstrations:<BR><BR><BR>

Some simple text formatting done using HTML:<BR>
<FONT SIZE = 1>Hello Size 1</FONT><BR>
<FONT SIZE = 2>Hello Size 2</FONT><BR>
<FONT SIZE = 3>Hello Size 3</FONT><BR>
<FONT SIZE = 4>Hello Size 4</FONT><BR>
<FONT SIZE = 5>Hello Size 5</FONT><BR>
<BR>
The same text formatting using server-side code:<BR>
<%
For intCounter = 1 to 5
%>
<FONT SIZE = <%=intCounter%>>
Hello Size <%=intCounter%></FONT><BR>
<%
Next
%>
<BR>
</BODY>
</HTML>
```

When the client receives the HTML result from the ASP script's execution, it resembles Figure 1-3.

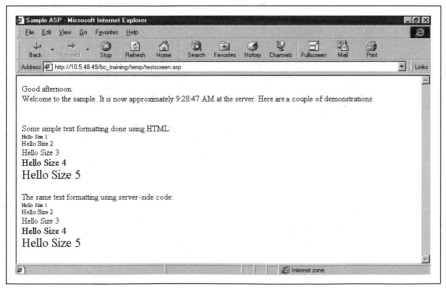

Figure 1-3: Client-side view of Sample.ASP

If you were to view the HTML source behind this HTML, you would see the output in Example 1-2.

Example 1-2: Sample.HTM, the Output of Sample.ASP

```
<HTML>
<HEAD>
<TITLE>Sample ASP</TITLE>
</HEAD>
<BODY>

Good afternoon.<BR>
Welcome to the sample. It is now approximately
9:28:47 at the server. Here are a couple of
demonstrations:<BR><BR><BR>

Some simple text formatting done using HTML:<BR>
<FONT SIZE = 1>Hello Size 1</FONT><BR>
<FONT SIZE = 2>Hello Size 2</FONT><BR>
<FONT SIZE = 3>Hello Size 3</FONT><BR>
<FONT SIZE = 4>Hello Size 4</FONT><BR>
<FONT SIZE = 5>Hello Size 5</FONT><BR>
<BR>

The same text formatting using server-side code:<BR>
<FONT SIZE = 1>Hello Size 1</FONT><BR>
<FONT SIZE = 2>Hello Size 2</FONT><BR>
<FONT SIZE = 3>Hello Size 3</FONT><BR>
<FONT SIZE = 4>Hello Size 4</FONT><BR>
<FONT SIZE = 5>Hello Size 5</FONT><BR>
<BR>

</BODY>
</HTML>
```

The server accepted the request, ASP.DLL interpreted and ran the server-side script and created HTML. The HTML is sent to the client, where it appears indistinguishable from straight HTML code.

As mentioned earlier, you will learn more about server-side scripting and how it works in Chapter 2.

The ASP Object Model

ASP encapsulates the properties and methods of the following seven built-in objects:

- Application
- ASPError
- ObjectContext
- Request
- Response

- Server

- Session

These objects are part of the *ASP.DLL* and are always available to your ASP applications.

The *Application object* represents your ASP application itself. This object is universal to all users attached to an application, and there is only one Application object for all users. The Application object has two events, Application_OnStart and Application_OnEnd, that fire when the first user requests a page from your application and when the administrator explicitly unloads the application using the Microsoft Management Console (see Chapter 4, *Application Object*), respectively. The OnStart event can be used to initialize information needed for every aspect of the application. The OnEnd event can be used to do any custom cleanup work after the end of your application. You can store any variable type (with some limitations—see Chapter 3, *Extending Active Server Pages*) with application-level scope. These variables hold the same value for every user of the site. See Chapter 4 for more information on the Application object.

 In this book, an ASP application is a group of scripts and HTML content files that together form some function.

Added in Active Server Pages 3.0, the *ASPError object* allows developers to access properties that characterize the last error that occurred in the currently executing script. It is only accessible through the Server object's GetLastError method and its properties are all read-only. The addition of the ASPError object is an important one in Active Server Pages 3.0 and significantly improves the handling of errors in Active Server Page scripts. See Chapter 5, *ASPError Object*, and Chapter 9, *Server Object*, for more information.

The *ObjectContext object* is actually part of the Microsoft Transaction Server and is only interfaced through ASP. The ObjectContext object allows you to create transactional Active Server Pages. The functions in these pages that support transactions will succeed as a single unit or fail completely. If your application requires the use of functions that do not natively support transactions (notably file access), you must write custom code to handle success or failure of these functions. See Chapter 6, *ObjectContext Object*, for more information.

The *Request object* represents the way you interact with the client's HTTP request. This is one of the most important objects in the ASP object model. It is through the use of the Request object that you access both HTML form-based data and parameters sent over the address line. In addition, you can use the Request object to receive HTTP cookie information and client certificate information from your users. Finally, the ServerVariables collection of the Request object gives you access to all the information in the HTTP request header. This information contains (in addition to the cookie information) other relevant data describing the client machine, its connection, and its actual requests. The ServerVariables collection is equivalent to environment variables in traditional CGI applications. See Chapter 7, *Request Object*, for more information.

The *Response object* represents your access/control over the HTTP response sent back to the user. Through the Response object, you can send cookies to the client and set if and when content should expire. In addition to this, the Response object is your route to completely controlling how data is sent to the client. Is it buffered before sending? Is it sent as it is constructed? Finally, the Response object allows you to seamlessly redirect the user from one URL to another. See Chapter 8, *Response Object*, for more information.

The *Server object* gives you access to the web server itself. This object contains many utility features that you use in almost every application. Through the Server object, you can set the timeout variable for your scripts (how long the web server will attempt to serve a script before serving an error note instead). You also can use the Server object to map a virtual path to a physical path or encode information for sending over the address line. The most important method of the Server object, however, is its CreateObject method, which enables you to create instances of server-side components. You will use this method any time you require functionality outside that provided by the built-in objects. Database access, for example, is handled by various ActiveX Data Objects that must be instantiated on the server before being used. See Chapter 9, *Server Object*, for more information.

Finally, the *Session object* holds information that is unique to a specific user's current session on the web server. Each user session is identifiable through the use of a unique cookie that is sent to the user every time the user makes a request. The web server starts a session for every new user that requests a page from your web application. This session stays active by default until 20 minutes after the user's last request or until the session is explicitly abandoned through code. See Chapter 10, *Session Object*, for more information.

CHAPTER 2

Active Server Pages:
Server-Side Scripting

Chapter 1, *Active Server Pages: An Introduction*, provided a brief introduction to Active Server Pages and how they can be used to dynamically create HTML content. In this chapter, you will learn more about what's going on behind the scenes. First we'll review scripting, scripting hosts, and scripting languages. You will learn about how Active Server Pages (the actual *ASP.DLL*) work to interpret your server-side code to create HTML and how IIS then inserts that dynamically created HTML into the HTML stream.

Client-Side Scripting

The Hypertext Markup Language, or HTML, provides for very detailed formatting of static textual content. This content can contain images, tables, and carefully formatted text and hyperlinks, making for a very powerful medium through which to present information. However, aside from the very low-level interactivity of hyperlinks and their ability to move the user from one page to another in a stream of information flowing from one page to another, HTML by itself allows for no true interactivity. HTML does not allow the web page to react to user input in any way beyond navigating to another page. HTML is an excellent way to allow for the presentation of information but does not allow for the interactivity required to transform web pages from an information medium to a dynamic web application solution.

Netscape Communications, along with Sun Microsystems, created a solution called LiveScript that allowed for the inclusion of limited programming instructions that reside in web pages viewed using the Netscape Navigator browser on the client machine. This programming language was limited in its ability to interact with the user's machine outside the browser and slowly over an evolving process was made safe and secure. You could not use LiveScript programming instructions on the client machine to undermine the security innate to the Netscape Navigator browser. LiveScript, in accordance with the marketing frenzy surrounding Java, was quickly renamed to JavaScript. Unfortunately, this renaming has led, erroneously, to its being thought of by many as a subset of the powerful Java language, although only its syntax is similar to that of Java.

HTML was enlivened. Using JavaScript, you could build forms and mortgage calculators and all sorts of interactive web pages. The only drawback was that your browser had to be a scripting host for this scripting language. But that being said, web content quickly went from being static and largely simple to being interactive and alive.

Before JavaScript, all interaction with the user and all reaction on the part of the web server required the use of sophisticated web server applications and higher-end web server machines. With the advent of JavaScript, the user's machine was now added to the equation, making it possible to offload some of this computational power onto the client, whereas before it had rested solely on the server.

Not to be outdone, Microsoft Corporation quickly created a scripting language of its own: Visual Basic, Scripting Edition, or VBScript for short. VBScript is a subset of the Visual Basic for Applications language and, like JavaScript, it allows for the creation of interactive web pages. Unlike JavaScript, whose syntax was similar to that of Java (and thus similar to that of C++), the syntax of VBScript was exactly that of Visual Basic. If you knew Visual Basic (and many, many people do), you already had a good grasp on VBScript. Furthermore, Microsoft also created its own version of JavaScript called JScript that was similar but not identical to its predecessor.

Today (only a few short years later), JavaScript has undergone a transformation into a new language built using submissions from both Netscape and Microsoft. This new language is called ECMAScript (from European Computer Manufacturers Association). According to David Flanagan in *JavaScript: The Definitive Guide, 3rd Edition*, this name was chosen specifically because it had no relation to either parent company and it had none of the marketing glitz of Java artificially associated with it. Both Netscape and Microsoft have continued to help ECMAScript (still called JavaScript by everyone except members of the European Computer Manufacturers Association) evolve. For more details on the different browsers' implementations, Flanagan provides excellent coverage in his book

Although the preceding discussion suggests that only JavaScript and VBScript exist, the web browser actually allows for a multitude of scripting language alternatives. You could even build your own. Some of the other languages include PerlScript, Python, and Awk, with PerlScript being the most popular after JavaScript and VBScript.

Two things all scripting languages have in common, however, is how they are included on a web page and how the browser recognizes them as script and not as HTML. All script is surrounded by matching <SCRIPT></SCRIPT> tags, as the three examples of client-side script in Example 2-1 illustrate. Each of the three routines performs exactly the same action: each displays a message box (or alert box, depending on your preference of nomenclature) on the screen containing the words "Hello world."

Example 2-1: Client-Side Scripting Using Three Scripting Languages

```
<SCRIPT LANGUAGE = "JavaScript">
<!--
Function AlertJS()
{
    alert("Hello world.")
}
-->
</SCRIPT>

<SCRIPT LANGUAGE = "VBScript">
<!--
Sub AlertVBS()
    MsgBox "Hello world."
End Sub
-->
</SCRIPT>

<SCRIPT language="PerlScript">
<!--
sub AlertPS()
{
    $window->alert("Hello world.");
}
-->
</SCRIPT>
```

There are two features in Example 2-1 to notice. The first is how the actual code is surrounded by HTML comment symbols:

```
<!--
code here
-->
```

This lets the page be shown in browsers that do not support the <SCRIPT> tag without causing problems or displaying the script on the page.

The second feature is the **LANGUAGE** attribute in each piece of sample code. The **LANGUAGE** attribute of the <SCRIPT> tag, as you've undoubtedly guessed, indicates what scripting language the browser should use to execute the included code. This can be any language that your browser supports. JavaScript is probably the safest bet for client-side scripting, since VBScript is supported only with the use of plugins in non-Microsoft browsers, and other scripting languages are not commonly installed on user machines. For more information about JavaScript, see David Flanagan's excellent book, *JavaScript: The Definitive Guide*, 3rd Edition. For more information about VBScript, see *VBScript in a Nutshell*, by Matt Childs, Paul Lomax, and Ron Petrusha. Both are published by O'Reilly & Associates. We'll revisit the question of scripting languages at the end of this chapter.

Server-Side Scripting

The last section served to introduce you to client-side scripting: how to include scripting code in the web pages that are viewed by your users. Now you will learn

---

how to bring the power of scripting to the server and harness it to dynamically create HTML in reaction to user requests.

As you will recall from the last chapter, when the browser makes a request for a file ending with the *.ASP* file extension, IIS knows to bring *ASP.DLL* into play to interpret the ASP code in the file. Once interpreted, the results of this code are placed into the document, which is a simple HTML document before it is sent to the user.

How does *ASP.DLL* know which code to interpret? The answer to this question is the key to executing code on the server. *ASP.DLL* interprets all code in a file (with the *.ASP* file extension) that's delimited with <%...%> as being ASP code. (There is another way to delineate server-side code that I'll cover in a moment.) Example 2-2 shows an active server page named *ExampleChap2.ASP*, with the VBScript code that will be interpreted by *ASP.DLL* in bold.

Example 2-2: ExampleChap2.ASP

```
<HTML>
<HEAD><TITLE>Example</TITLE></HEAD>
<BODY>
<%
' Construct a greeting string with a salutation and the
' current time on the server (retrieved from the Time()
' function) and then display that in the HTML sent to the
' client.
strGreetingMsg = "Hello. It is now " & Time() & _
                 " on the server."
Response.Write strGreetingMsg
%>
</BODY>
</HTML>
```

When a user requests *ExampleChap2.ASP*, IIS pulls the file from the file system into its memory. Recognizing the *.ASP* extension from the settings in the Management Console, it uses *ASP.DLL* to read and interpret the file. Once interpreted, IIS sends the final result down to the requesting client browser.

IIS handles all the HTTP traffic. *ASP.DLL* only interprets server-side code, pulling in the DLL of the appropriate scripting engine when necessary. Let's assume the time is 10:42:43. The previous ASP file, once interpreted, would result in the following dynamically created HTML page that will in turn be sent to the client by IIS:

```
<HTML>
<HEAD><TITLE>Example</TITLE></HEAD>
<BODY>
Hello. It is now 10:42:43 on the server.
</BODY>
</HTML>
```

You will learn more about the Write method of the Response object in Chapter 8, *Response Object*. For now, recognize it as one way of writing information from the portion of the script that is interpreted on the server to the portion of HTML that will be displayed on the browser.

It is important to recognize this for what it is. There is no magic here. We are simply capturing the HTTP request. Then *ASP.DLL* interprets some code and alters the HTTP response that is sent back to the client.

 ASP.DLL is an ISAPI filter that alters the resulting HTTP response stream in reaction to information in the HTTP request combined with code in the requested document.

The Response.Write method call is one way of inserting code into the HTML stream that is sent back to the client, but there is a shortcut for this method call: the <%=...%> delimiters. Note the inclusion of the equal sign (=). The equal sign is what differentiates this as a shortcut call to the Response.Write method and not simply more ASP code to interpret.

The <%=...%> delimiters allow for some subtle effects that can allow you to produce some powerful server-side/client-side HTML combinations. Here is Example 2-2 rewritten using the <%=...%> delimiters:

```
<HTML>
<HEAD><TITLE>Example</TITLE></HEAD>
<BODY>
Hello. It is now <%=Time()%> on the server.
</BODY>
</HTML>
```

Using the <%=...%> delimiters is the same as using the Write method of the Response object. It simply inserts into the HTML stream whatever is between the opening <%= and the closing %>. If the content between the delimiters represents a variable, that variable's value is inserted into the HTML stream. If the content is a call to a function, the result of the function call is inserted into the HTML stream.

With the careful use of these delimiters, you can dynamically construct not only HTML content but also client-side script code, as Example 2-3 demonstrates. The script is called *DynamicForm.ASP*, and it accepts a single parameter, button_Count. Based on the value of button_Count, *DynamicForm.ASP* will dynamically build between one and ten HTML submit buttons and also dynamically generate script for the onClick events for each of them. We will discuss this script in detail.

Example 2-3: DynamicForm.ASP

```
<HTML>
<HEAD><TITLE>DynamicForm.asp</TITLE></HEAD>
<BODY>
Welcome to the dynamic form!
<%
' Retrieve the number of buttons the user wishes to create.
intCmdCount = Request.QueryString("button_Count")

' Ensure that the sent parameter is within the acceptable
' limits.
```

Example 2-3: DynamicForm.ASP (continued)

```
If intCmdCount < 1 Then
    intCmdCount = 1
End If

If intCmdCount > 10 Then
    intCmdCount = 10
End If

' Create the buttons.
For intCounter = 1 to intCmdCount
%>
    <INPUT TYPE = button VALUE = Button<%=intCounter%>
    OnClick = "Button<%=intCounter%>_Click()">
<%
Next
%>

<SCRIPT LANGUAGE = "VBScript">
<%
' Create the scripts for each of the created buttons.
For intCounter = 1 to intCmdCount
%>
Sub Button<%=intCounter%>_Click()
    MsgBox "You just clicked button <%=intCounter%>."
End Sub
<%
Next
%>
</SCRIPT>

</BODY>
</HTML>
```

Suppose we call this script with the following line:

```
/DynamicForm.asp?button_Count=3
```

The result appears in Figure 2-1, and the resulting HTML source is shown in Example 2-4.

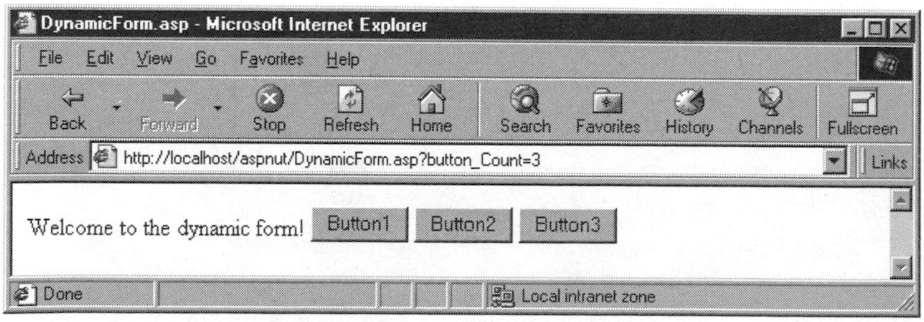

Figure 2-1: The web page that results from invoking DynamicForm.ASP

Example 2-4: HTML Source Produced by DynamicForm.ASP

```
<HTML>
<HEAD><TITLE>DynamicForm.asp</TITLE></HEAD>
<BODY>
Welcome to the dynamic form!
<INPUT TYPE = button VALUE = Button1
OnClick = "Button1_Click()">

<INPUT TYPE = button VALUE = Button2
OnClick = "Button2_Click()">

<INPUT TYPE = button VALUE = Button3
OnClick = "Button3_Click()">

<SCRIPT LANGUAGE = "VBScript">

Sub Button1_Click()
    MsgBox "You just clicked button 1."
End Sub

Sub Button2_Click()
    MsgBox "You just clicked button 2."
End Sub

Sub Button3_Click()
    MsgBox "You just clicked button 3."
End Sub

</SCRIPT>
</BODY>
</HTML>
```

The parameter *button_Count=3* translated into the construction of three HTML button elements and the corresponding code to go with them. Note the names and the onClick event procedure names for each of these buttons (in bold in the following code):

```
<INPUT TYPE = button VALUE = Button1
OnClick = "Button1_Click()">

<INPUT TYPE = button VALUE = Button2
OnClick = "Button2_Click()">

<INPUT TYPE = button VALUE = Button3
OnClick = "Button3_Click()">
```

These button element names and event procedure titles each came from the following line of code:

```
<INPUT TYPE = button VALUE = Button<%=intCounter%>
OnClick = "Button<%=intCounter%>_Click()">
```

Note that the result of <%=intCounter%> is inserted into the HTML text stream. Using ASP, we were able to dynamically generate names for each of our buttons

---

by appending the value of a counter variable onto the end of the word "Button" in the HTML stream.

This is a subtle point. One of the most common errors in ASP development is to treat the result of <%=...%> as a variable name. For example, the following line of server-side code does not result in the greeting "Hello Margaret," though some developers mistakenly believe it does:

```
<%
' INCORRECT CODE.
strUserName = "Margaret"
%>
MsgBox "Hello " & <%=strUserName%>
```

When the preceding is sent to the client, it will appear like this:

```
MsgBox "Hello " & Margaret
```

VBScript tries diligently to make something of the token `Margaret`, but the result is shown in Figure 2-2.

Figure 2-2: Treating the result of <%= . . . %> as a variable name

The correct line of code to produce the desired result is the following:

```
MsgBox "Hello <%=strUserName%>"
```

The point here is that what's in the <%=...%> delimiters comes into the HTML stream *as is, even inside a string.* Whatever the value of the content is, that is what is inserted into the HTML stream. Do not treat <%=...%> as a variable.

ASP Functions

Code reuse is as important in Active Server Pages as it is in any other form of application programming. The first example of code reuse is the ASP function or subroutine. As I mentioned in the beginning of this chapter, there is one other way to delineate server-side code: the RUNAT attribute of the <SCRIPT> tag. You can use the RUNAT attribute to specify that a particular function or subroutine is to be run (and called from) the server side. Example 2-5 demonstrates the use of the RUNAT attribute to create a simple function that uses the last three letters of the domain string to return the general type of site that it represents. This function takes a domain string such as *perl.ora.com* and returns the string "company." The RUNAT attribute instructs ASP that this is a server-side-only function. It will not be sent to the client and is a valid function to call from within the server-side code. We could now incorporate that into a script, as shown in Example 2-6.

Example 2-5: Using the RUNAT Attribute to Create a Server-Side Function

```
<SCRIPT LANGUAGE = "VBScript" RUNAT = SERVER>
Function DomainType(strDomainString)

    strPossibleDomain = Right(strDomainString, 3)

    Select Case Ucase(strPossibleDomain)
       Case "COM"
          DomainType = "company"
       Case "EDU"
          DomainType = "educational"
       Case "GOV"
          DomainType = "government_civil"
       Case "MIL"
          DomainType = "government_military"
       Case Else
          DomainType = "UNKNOWN"
    End Select

End Function
</SCRIPT>
```

Example 2-6: Including a Server-Side Function in an ASP

```
<HTML><HEAD><TITLE>Function Example</TITLE></HEAD>
<BODY>
<%
' In this script we'll simply initialize a string
' example parameter, but this value could have
' come from another script.
strDomainString = "perl.ora.com"
strDomainType = DomainType(strDomainString)
%>
<%=strDomainString%> is a <%=strDomainType%> site.
</BODY>
</HTML>

<SCRIPT LANGUAGE = "VBScript" RUNAT = SERVER>
Function DomainType(strDomainString)

    strPossibleDomain = Right(strDomainString, 3)

    Select Case Ucase(strPossibleDomain)
       Case "COM"
          DomainType = "company"
       Case "EDU"
          DomainType = "educational"
       Case "GOV"
          DomainType = "government_civil"
       Case "MIL"
          DomainType = "government_military"
       Case Else
          DomainType = "UNKNOWN"
```

Example 2-6: Including a Server-Side Function in an ASP (continued)

```
    End Select

End Function
</SCRIPT>
```

The script in Example 2-6, once interpreted, generates and sends the following script to the client:

```
<HTML>
<HEAD><TITLE>Function Example</TITLE></HEAD>
<BODY>
perl.ora.com is a company site.
</BODY>
</HTML>
```

Note that neither the text between the `<%...%>` delimiters nor the *DomainType* function is present in the resulting HTML.

The script in Example 2-6 also demonstrates that we need not place our server-side functions within the `<HTML>...</HTML>` tags. However, if we do (as in Example 2-7), the resulting HTML will be exactly the same as it was before. The server-side function is still not inserted into the HTML stream, even when we place it inside the `<BODY>` tags.

Example 2-7: Script Placed Within the <HTML>...</HTML> Tags

```
<HTML>
<HEAD><TITLE>Function Example</TITLE></HEAD>
<BODY>
<%
' In this script we'll simply initialize a string
' example parameter, but this value could have
' come from another script.
strDomainString = "perl.ora.com"
strDomainType = DomainType(strDomainString)
%>
<%=strDomainString%> is a <%=strDomainType%> site.

<SCRIPT LANGUAGE = "VBScript" RUNAT = SERVER>
Function DomainType(strDomainString)

    strPossibleDomain = Right(strDomainString, 3)

    Select Case Ucase(strPossibleDomain)
        Case "COM"
            DomainType = "company"
        Case "EDU"
            DomainType = "educational"
        Case "GOV"
            DomainType = "government_civil"
        Case "MIL"
            DomainType = "government_military"
        Case Else
```

```
            DomainType = "UNKNOWN"
    End Select

End Function
</SCRIPT>

</BODY>
</HTML>
```

Scripting Languages

You do not have to use one single language for the entire ASP application. There is no problem with mixing and matching for convenience. I typically use VBScript in server-side code and JavaScript on the client, but you are not forced to use a single language in either setting. You can, however, force ASP to default to a specific script by using the @LANGUAGE preprocessor ASP directive. ASP directives are covered in Chapter 11, *Preprocessing Directives, Server-Side Includes, and GLOBAL.ASA*. For now, know that you can use the following line of code as the first in your script to force ASP to use JScript as the default scripting language when interpreting your code:

```
<%@ LANGUAGE = JScript%>
```

If you place this line anywhere but as the first line, you will receive an error. Also note that VBScript is the default for all server-side scripts. However, you can change this in the Application options for your ASP application's virtual directory. See Appendix D, *Configuration of ASP Applications on IIS*.

CHAPTER 3

Extending Active Server Pages

Chapter 1, *Active Server Pages: An Introduction*, presented a very brief overview of the Active Server Pages application paradigm. This chapter covers the various extensions for ASP. Some of these are included with IIS 4.0 and ASP 2.0, and some are available via the World Wide Web.

Extending Active Server Pages applications usually takes the form of instantiating server-side objects that expose methods and properties that you can access through your server-side code. Microsoft includes many of these Active server components with IIS 5.0. For example, one of the server components included with IIS is the Browser Capabilities component. Once instantiated, a Browser Capabilities object allows you to discern details about the user's web browser: what scripting it supports, what platform it is running on, and so on. This component allows you to dynamically alter your site in response to the presence or absence of certain browsers.

As will be discussed in Chapter 0, *Server Object*, you use the CreateObject method of the Server object to instantiate a server component. For example, to create a *MyInfo* object in your Active Server Page, you could use code similar to the following:

```
<%
' Declare local variables.
Dim objMyInfo

' Instantiate a MyInfo object.
Set objMyInfo = Server.CreateObject("MSWC.MyInfo")

' You can now initialize the values.
objMyInfo.PersonalName = "A. Keyton Weissinger"
...[additional code]
%>
```

As you see in this example, instantiating these server components is simple. Once instantiated, you can use any of an object's exposed methods or properties to extend your web application.

Although IIS comes with several server components, you also can write your own in any development language that can create COM objects, such as Microsoft Visual Basic, Visual C++, Visual J++, or Inprise's Delphi. The details of writing server components are beyond the scope of this book, so I would encourage you to read *Developing ASP Components*, by Shelley Powers, published by O'Reilly & Associates.

The server components discussed in this book are described in Table 3-1.

Table 3-1: Server Components Discussed in ASP in a Nutshell

Server Component	Description
ADO	Adds database access to Active Server Pages applications. Through its COM interface to OLE DB data providers, you are able to access any OLE DB or ODBC compliant data source.
Ad Rotator Component	Randomly chooses one of a number of advertisements for a web page based on a weighting system.
Browser Capabilities	Easily determines the functionality supported by your user's web browser.
Collabora-tion Data Objects for NTS	Adds messaging functionality to web applications. Using the objects that make up CDONTS, you can create robust, mail-enabled groupware applications using ASP. Although not discussed at length in this book, CDONTS is a powerful extension to ASP.
Content Linking	Maintains a linked list of static content files. From within these static files, the Content Linking component allows you to set up easy-to-use navigation from one page to the next (or previous) page.
Content Rotator	Creates a schedule file containing several pieces of HTML that are alternately placed in your web site. This component is similar to the Ad Rotator component but works with straight HTML content rather than advertisements.
Counters	Maintains a collection of counters, over the scope of an entire ASP application, that can be incremented or decremented from anywhere in your web site.
File Access Components	Allows you to access your local and network file system. It's part of the scripting runtime library that's installed and registered by default when you install IIS.
Logging Utility Component	Provides programmatic access to the IIS web or FTP server log.
MyInfo	Maintains commonly accessed information, such as the webmaster's name, address, company, etc., from within your web applications.

Table 3-1: Server Components Discussed in ASP in a Nutshell (continued)

Server Component	Description
Page Counter	Creates a page counter on any page on your web site. The page count is saved regularly to a text file. This allows you to maintain page count information even if the web server is restarted.
Permission Checker	Checks the permissions on a given resource on the local machine or on the network. This allows you to determine on the fly whether the current user has permission to see a file.
Tools Component	Provides a variety of useful utility functions.

PART II

Object Reference

This part covers every aspect of the intrinsic objects that make up the IIS object model. This includes every event, method, property, and collection for the Application, ASPError, ObjectContext, Request, Response, Session, and Server objects. This part also includes a reference for all of the ASP directives and in-depth coverage of the *GLOBAL.ASA* file.

Because support for these objects, as well as for the *GLOBAL.ASA* file, is built in to Active Server Pages, you can access and take advantage of all of these components from ASP automatically; no additional components or libraries are needed.

Part II is organized into the following chapters:

Chapter 4, *Application Object*

Chapter 5, *ASPError Object*

Chapter 6, *ObjectContext Object*

Chapter 7, *Request Object*

Chapter 8, *Response Object*

Chapter 9, *Server Object*

Chapter 10, *Session Object*

Chapter 11, *Preprocessing Directives, Server-Side Includes, and GLOBAL.ASA*

CHAPTER 4

Application Object

In the context of Active Server Pages, an *application* is the sum of all the files that can be accessed through a given virtual directory and its subdirectories. This ASP application context is the same for all clients using the application. For example, a client from Thailand who requests pages from your */SearchApp* virtual directory is accessing the same "application" as a second client from Sweden who is requesting pages from the same virtual directory—regardless of which specific web page within the virtual directory each is requesting.

Just as traditional standalone applications allow you to share information throughout the application, so too do ASP applications. You can share information among all clients of a given ASP application using the *Application* object. This built-in object represents the ASP application itself and is the same regardless of the number or type of clients accessing the application and regardless of what part or parts of the application those clients are requesting.

The Application object is initialized by IIS the moment the first client requests *any* file from within the given virtual directory. It remains in the server's memory until either the web service is stopped or the application is explicitly unloaded from the web server using the Microsoft Management Console.

IIS allows you to instantiate variables and objects with application-level scope. This means that a given variable contains the same value for all clients of your application. You also can instantiate server-side objects with application-level scope that likewise contain the same values for all clients. These application-level variables and objects can be accessed and changed from the context of any user's session and from any file within the current application.

As stated earlier, the Application object's initialization occurs when the first user of your application requests any file from within the virtual directory that the ASP application encompasses. This initialization can be thought of as setting aside memory for the given ASP application. The web server instantiates and initializes the Application object for you. However, you can customize this initialization by including code in a special optional file called *GLOBAL.ASA*. Although I will discuss this file in greater depth in Chapter 11, *Preprocessing Directives, Server-Side Includes, and GLOBAL.ASA*, it is worth presenting a brief overview here.

The *GLOBAL.ASA* file exists—if it exists—at the root of the physical directory mapped to by your ASP application's virtual directory. It is processed every time a new user requests a page from within the application's virtual directory. This file contains initialization code for both the user's session and the application itself. If the user is not the first user, the application-specific sections of *GLOBAL.ASA* are not processed. If the *GLOBAL.ASA* file does not exist or does not contain any code, but the user's request is the web server's first request for files within a given application, the web server still initializes the Application object. However, the web server's initialization involves only the dimensioning of memory required for the application.

The *GLOBAL.ASA* file provides a place for you to create variables and objects that have application-level scope. This section of the *GLOBAL.ASA* file represents an event procedure. The event is the OnStart event, and its event handler is executed when the application is started. It's important to note that although the *GLOBAL.ASA* file is processed for every user that makes a request, the Application object's OnStart event is executed for only the first user. (The OnStart and the corresponding OnEnd event procedures are covered in detail later in this chapter.)

Variables and objects with application-level scope have the same value for all users at all times during the life of the application. If one user requests a page containing code that changes an application-level variable's value, then that variable's value is changed for all users. This presents a problem: potentially, two or more users could attempt to change the value of the same application-level variable at the same time. Fortunately, ASP provides the Application object's Lock and Unlock methods to avoid conflicts in these situations. Just as you must carefully consider the ramifications of using global variables in a multithreaded application, you also must consider the ramifications of using variables with application-level scope. Use application-level variables with care.

The properties, collections, methods, and events of the ASP Application object are outlined in the "Application Object Summary" sidebar.

Comments/Troubleshooting

Application-level variables are, in effect, global variables for your ASP application. The use of globals in ASP applications should be viewed with as much skepticism as the use of globals in traditional standalone applications, if not with more. The most important step is to painstakingly consider its scope before implementing any object or variable with application-level scope. There are very few instances in which using these ASP global variables is necessary.

With that warning, there are a few instances in which using application-level variables or objects is useful in creating functional ASP applications. One of the most important of these is maintaining application-specific statistics for your web site. Using application-level variables that are incremented at the beginning of each user session, for example, you could maintain a count of clients that have used

Application Object Summary

Properties
> None

Collections
> Contents
> StaticObjects

Methods
> Contents.Remove
> Contents.RemoveAll
> Lock
> Unlock

Events
> OnEnd
> OnStart

your application. Although such web management tools as Microsoft Site Server perform similar tasks, their statistics are file-specific, not application-specific.

Some ASP literature has suggested using application-level objects for maintaining open ActiveX Data Objects (ADO) database connections for all application users. (For more information on ADO, see Chapter 12, *ActiveX Data Objects 2.6.*) This is *not* a good use of application-level variables, since this approach prevents ODBC from pooling connections per individual pages.[*] However, you could use an application-level variable to maintain an application-specific connection string for that same database connection.

There is one trap that you should be aware of when considering the use of application-level variables and objects. Consider the following scenario. You have two physical directories: *c:\inetpub\wwwroot\MainApp* and *c:\inetpub\wwwroot\ MainApp\SearchApp*. These directories are mapped to the virtual directories */MainApp* and */SearchApp*, respectively. You have, in effect, an application within an application. The first client requests a page within the *c:\inetpub\wwwroot\ MainApp\SearchApp* physical directory. Which initialization code will be used to initialize the Application object—the code in the *GLOBAL.ASA* for */MainApp* or the *GLOBAL.ASA* for */SearchApp*? In this case the */SearchApp GLOBAL.ASA* is the one processed. Until a file in */MainApp* that does not exist in */SearchApp* is requested, the *GLOBAL.ASA* file for */MainApp* is not processed. If the two *GLOBAL.ASA* files define different sets of application-level variables, you have no way of knowing within your code which Application variables were properly initialized without testing them.

---

[*] ODBC connection pooling provides a method by which ODBC connections can be reused by successive users. Instead of creating a new connection each time a client requests one, the server attempts to reuse an already existing connection that is no longer in use. If unused ODBC connections reside in memory after a certain period of time (configured in the MMC), they are destroyed to free memory.

Finally, note that IIS now allows you to set ASP applications up in separate memory spaces from each other and from the web server itself by simply checking an option on the Properties panel of a given virtual directory in IIS's Microsoft Management Console. This ability is an important improvement in IIS. If your ASP application is running in a separate memory space from the web server and a server object in it (or the scripting engine itself) crashes, it will not also crash the web server or your other ASP applications.

Collections Reference

Contents Collection   Application.Contents(*Key*)

The Contents collection of the Application object contains all the application-level scoped variables and objects added to the current application through the use of scripts (*not* through the use of the <OBJECT> tag).

Before examining how elements are added to the Contents collection, you must first understand the properties of the Contents collection. The Contents collection has three properties:

Item

Retrieves the value of a specific member of the Contents collection. You specify which member using a string key (whose value is obtainable using the index through the Key property, explained later in this section) or using an index number. For example, if you wish to initialize an element in the Contents collection with the value of Pi, you might use a line of code similar to the following:

```
Application.Contents.Item("Pi") = 3.14
```

In the preceding line of code, the desired element in the collection is specified using the key value "Pi." Thus initialized, you can then retrieve the value of this element of the Contents collection using the following line of code:

```
dblMyVar = Application.Contents.Item("Pi")
```

For reasons that will become clear in a moment, let's assume that this is the first element added to the Contents collection.

You could also retrieve the value of an element in the Contents collection using its index in the collection rather than a key, as demonstrated in the following line of code:

```
dblMyVar = Application.Contents.Item(1)
```

Note that you use a 1 (one), not a 0 (zero), to represent the first element in the Contents collection. This is a subtle point, since using a zero in this line of code will result in the variable dblMyVar being initialized with an undefined value. Unfortunately, this will not result in an error. It will result only in an improperly initialized variable:

```
dblMyVar = Application.Contents.Item(0)  ' WRONG.
```

Item is the default property of the Contents collection and the Contents collection is the default collection of the Application object. This means that each of the following three lines of code is interpreted in exactly the same manner in your application:

```
Application.Contents.Item("Pi") = 3.14
Application.Contents("Pi") = 3.14
Application("Pi") = 3.14
```

Correspondingly, you would assume that the following three lines of code are also equivalent:

```
Application.Contents.Item(1) = 3.14159
Application.Contents(1) = 3.14159
Application(1) = 3.14159
```

However, this is only the case if the first element in the Contents collection has previously been defined using a key. Although not mentioned in the documentation that accompanies ASP, to use either of the preceding first two lines of code, the element must have been previously defined using a key. For example, assume you decide to add a second element to the Contents collection. You cannot initialize this element using either of the following lines of code:

```
Application.Contents.Item(2) = 3.14159      ' WRONG.
Application.Contents(2) = 3.14159           ' WRONG.
```

Unfortunately, even this exception has an exception. You *can* use the following code to initialize a second variable:

```
Application(2) = 3.14159
```

When you consider these inconsistencies, it becomes quickly apparent that it is always safest to use a key rather than an index when referencing the value of a specific element in the Contents collection.

Also, it is important to use a key when referring to a specific member of the Contents collection because that member's index may change. For example, suppose you have the following code in your application:

```
Application("strFirstName") = "Arthur"
Application("strMiddleName") = "Keyton"
Application("strLastName") = "Weissinger"
```

Assuming these variables are the first three added to the Contents collection, you could later refer to each using its index:

```
strFirst = Application(1)
strMiddle = Application(2)
strLast = Application(3)
```

However, if you use the Remove method, which completely removes a variable from the collection (see later in this chapter), to remove the strMiddleName variable, the index numbers will change:

```
Session.Contents.Remove("strMiddleName")
```

```
strFirst = Application(1)        ' Initializes to "Arthur"
strMiddle = Application(2)       ' Initializes to "Weissinger"
strLast = Application(3)         ' Initializes to Undefined.
```

Key

Represents the name of a specific element in the Contents collection. Remember from earlier that each element's value is represented by the Item property. Similarly, each element's name is represented by its Key property.

If you do not know the name of a specific key, you can obtain it using its ordinal reference. For example, assume that you want to learn the key name for the third element in the collection and, subsequently, retrieve that element's value. You could use the following code:

```
strKeyName = Application.Contents.Key(3)
strKeyValue = Application.Contents.Item(strKeyName)
```

Count

Represents the total number of elements in the Contents collection.

Notes

You can initialize application-level variables and thus add elements to the Contents collection in one of two ways. First, you can initialize Application variables in the Application_OnStart event procedure in the *GLOBAL.ASA* file, as Example 4-1 illustrates.

Example 4-1: Initializing Application-Level Variables in GLOBAL.ASA

```
' <<<<<<<<<<<<<<< FROM GLOBAL.ASA >>>>>>>>>>>>>>>>>>>
' This code resides in the GLOBAL.ASA file at the
' root of the current application.
' See Chapter 11 for more details on the GLOBAL.ASA file.

Sub Application_OnStart

   Application.Contents.Item("STATE_FIRST") = "California"
   Application.Contents("STATE_SECOND") = "Oregon"
   Application("STATE_THIRD") = "Washington"

End Sub
```

The code in Example 4-1 creates three application-scoped variables, thus adding three elements to the Contents collection. Note that these variables will be instantiated and initialized only at the start of the application, not upon every visit to the site by subsequent users. These variables maintain the same values unless another script changes them for all pages and for all users.

The previous code adds elements to the Contents collection by key. You can also add elements to the collection by using an index value, as in:

```
Application.Contents(1) = "California"
```

However, you should add elements to a collection either by key or by index, but not both. If you add elements both by index and by key, elements with keys will overwrite elements at lower ordinal positions that have not been assigned keys.

You also can create application-scoped variables and thus add elements to the Contents collection inside any script on any page. Note, however, that any variables created in this manner are created and maintained across the whole application and all its users. Example 4-2 illustrates this method of initializing application-scoped variables.

Example 4-2: Initializing Application-Level Variables in a Server-Side Script

```
<%
' This code exists in the server-side section of a script
' on the web site.
Application.Contents.Item("STATE_FOURTH") = "New York"
Application.Contents("STATE_FIFTH") = "New Jersey"
Application("STATE_SIXTH") = "Vermont"

%>
```

The code in Example 4-2 adds three more application-scoped variables to the application. Note that these variables will be reinitialized every time a user requests the page containing this code. To prevent this waste of processor power, it might be better to perform this initialization using code similar to the following:

```
<%
' A more efficient example of the creation of an
' application-scoped variable.
If IsEmpty(Application.Contents.Item(STATE_SEVENTH)) Then
    Application.Contents(STATE_SEVENTH) = "Texas"
End If

%>
```

This code creates a seventh application variable for the current application only if it has not already been created.

The Contents collection supports the For Each and For...Next constructs for iterating the collection, as Example 4-3 demonstrates.

Example 4-3: Using For Each with the Contents Collection

```
<%
For Each strKey in Application.Contents
%>
    The next item in Application's Contents collection<BR>
    has <%= strKey %> as its key and
    <%= Application.Contents(strKey) %>
    as its value.<P>
<%
Next %>
```

Note, however, that unlike most collection objects, the Contents collection does not support the Add method, and until IIS 5.0 did not support a Remove method. Unless they are explicitly removed, variables given application scope stay resident until the web server is stopped or the last user's session times out.

If you add an object to the Application's Contents collection, make sure that the threading model for the object supports its use in an application scope; use of the free-threaded model is recommended.* For more on the use of various threading models in IIS server components, see Shelley Powers' book *Developing ASP Components*, published by O'Reilly & Associates.

To access an application-scoped object's properties or methods, use an extension of the syntax you saw earlier for accessing the value of an application-scoped variable, as the following code fragment illustrates:

```
' In this example, assume you have an application-scoped Ad
' Rotator variable called MyAdRot.

' Accessing a property:
intBorder = Application.Contents("MyAdRot").Border

' Executing a method:
Application.Contents("MyAdRot").GetAdvertisement("Sched.txt")
```

 If you intend to use a given object in a transaction using the Object-Context object, do not give that object application or session scope. Objects used in transactions are destroyed at the end of the transaction and any subsequent reference to their properties or calls to their methods will result in an error.

When adding an array to the Application object's Contents collection, add the entire array as a whole. When changing an element of the array, retrieve a copy of the array, change the element, and then add the array to the Contents collection as a whole again. The code in Example 4-4 demonstrates this.

Example 4-4: Working with Arrays in the Contents Collection

```
<%
' Create an array variable and add it to Contents collection.
ReDim arystrNames(3)

arystrNames(0) = "Chris"
arystrNames(1) = "Julie"
arystrNames(2) = "Vlad"
arystrNames(3) = "Kelly"

Application("arystrUserNames") = arystrNames

%>

The second name in the User Names array is
<%= Application("arystrUserNames")(1) %>
<BR>
<%
```

---

* Free-threaded applications allow multiple user processes to access the same instance of the component simultaneously.

Example 4-4: Working with Arrays in the Contents Collection (continued)

```
' Change an element of the array being held in the
' Contents collection.
Dim arystrNamesLocal

arystrNamesLocal = Application("arystrUserNames")
arystrNamesLocal(1) = "Mark"

Application("arystrUserNames") = arystrNamesLocal
' The second name is now Mark.


%>
Now, the second name in the User Names array is
<%= Application("arystrUserNames")(1) %>
<BR>
```

Contents Collection Methods

Remove   Application.Contents.Remove(*Key*| *Index*)

Removes a specific member from the Contents collection. An addition in IIS 5.0, the Remove method allows you to remove from memory a specific variable from the Application's Contents collection without removing all the others.

Parameters

Key

    A string variable that specifies the name of the specific member of the Contents collection to be removed.

Index

    An integer variable that specifies the index of the member of the Contents collection to be removed.

Example

The following script removes two members of the Contents collection:

```
<%
' This script assumes you have set up two greeting salutations for all
' the members of your site based on time of day. You want to now
' remove these from your site.
strAppMorningGreeting = Application("strAMGreet")
strAppEveningGreeting = Application("strPMGreet")

    .
    .
    .
Application.Contents.Remove("strAMGreet")
Application.Contents.Remove("strPMGreet")
    .
    .
    .
%>
```

Notes

The Remove method is an important addition to the Contents collection because it allows for better memory control and cleanup. It allows you to remove from memory some of your collection's elements without abandoning the user's session. As discussed earlier under the Item property of the Contents collection, it is very important to use a string key instead of an index when calling the Remove method. An element's index may change over the life of the application, and then your call to Remove using a stored index value may lead to unpredictable results.

The Remove method of the Application's Contents collection allows you to remove members of the Contents collection without unloading the entire web application through the IIS web admin interface. The lack of this functionality in pre-5.0 IIS led to difficult management of application-scoped variables.

RemoveAll   `Application.Contents.RemoveAll`

Removes all members from the Contents collection. An addition in IIS 5.0, the RemoveAll method allows you to remove from memory all application-scoped variables without unloading the application itself.

Parameters

None

Example

The following script removes all members of the Contents collection:

```
<%
' This script assumes you have set up two greeting salutations for all
' the members of your site based on time of day. You want to now remove
' these from your site.
strAppMorningGreeting = Application("strAMGreet")
strAppEveningGreeting = Application("strPMGreet")

  .
  .
  .

Application.Contents.RemoveAll
  .
  .
  .
%>
```

Notes

Like the Remove method, the RemoveAll method is an important addition to the Contents collection because it allows for better memory control and cleanup. It allows you to remove all application-scoped variables without unloading the application itself.

StaticObjects

The StaticObjects collection contains all of the objects added to the application through the use of the <OBJECT> tag. You can use the Item property (discussed later) of the StaticObjects collection to retrieve properties of a specific object in the collection. You also can use the Item property of the `StaticObjects` collection to access a specific method of a given object in the collection.

You can add objects to this collection only through the use of the <OBJECT> tag in the *GLOBAL.ASA* file, as in the following example:

```
<OBJECT RUNAT=Server SCOPE=Application ID=AppInfo2
        PROGID="MSWC.MyInfo">
</OBJECT>
```

You cannot add objects to this collection anywhere else in your ASP application.

The StaticObjects collection, like other ASP collections, has the following properties:

Item

Returns a reference to a specific element in the collection. To specify an item, you can use an index number or a key.

Key

Returns the name of a specific element in the collection; the name is assigned by the ID attribute of the <OBJECT> tag. For example, you could receive the name of the first element in the collection like this:

```
objElement = Application.StaticObjects.Key(1)
```

Use the value of the Key property to retrieve the value of an element by name. For example, suppose the first object in the StaticObjects collection is named MyAdRotator. You could then use the following line of code to set (or retrieve) the value of the Border property of that object:

```
strKey = Application.StaticObjects.Key(1)
Application.StaticObjects.Item(strKey).Border = 0
```

Count

The current number of elements in the collection.

For more imformation on the Item, Key, and Count properties of a collection, see the section on the Contents collection of the Application object, earlier in this chapter.

Example

```
' <<<<<<<<<<<<<<< FROM GLOBAL.ASA >>>>>>>>>>>>>>>>>>>
' This code resides in the GLOBAL.ASA file at the root
' of the current application. The following <OBJECT>
' tag is processed only once for the current application.
' See Chapter 11 for more details on the GLOBAL.ASA file.
```

```
<OBJECT RUNAT=Server
SCOPE=Application
ID=AppInfo1
PROGID="MSWC.MyInfo">
</OBJECT>

' <<<<<<<<<<<<<<<<<<<<<<<<<<<<<>>>>>>>>>>>>>>>>>>>>>>>>>

<%
' The following code initializes the AppInfo1 component.
' This initialization code can reside anywhere.
AppInfo1.PersonalName = "Gertrude Stein"
AppInfo1.PersonalAddress = "233 Main Street"

' The following code uses the StaticObjects collection
' of the Application object to retrieve the value
' of the PersonalName property of AppInfo1.
For Each objInfo In Application.StaticObjects
%>
    The personal name is <BR>
    <%= Application.StaticObjects(objInfo).PersonalName%><P>
<%
Next
%>

There are <%= Application.StaticObjects.Count %> items
in the Application's StaticObjects collection.
```

Notes

The StaticObjects collection allows you to access any object instantiated with application-level scope through the use of an <OBJECT> tag. Objects instantiated using the Server.CreateObject method are not accessible through this collection. The nomenclature here can be a bit confusing. To reiterate: the StaticObjects collection contains those *server* objects instantiated through the use of the <OBJECT> tag, not through the CreateObject method of the Server object.

The StaticObjects example in the IIS 4.0 documentation by Microsoft suggests that if you iterate through this collection, you will be able to reference each property. This is somewhat misleading, as it suggests that the collection actually represents all the properties of the objects rather than the objects themselves. If you want to access the properties or methods of objects in the StaticObjects collection, you must use the dot operator outside of the parentheses around the Key, followed by the property or method name, as demonstrated in the preceding example.

Objects created in the *GLOBAL.ASA* file are not actually instantiated on the server until the first time a property or method of that object is called. For this reason, the StaticObjects collection cannot be used to access these objects' properties and methods until some other code in your application has caused them to be instantiated on the server.

Do not give application or session scope to an object used in a transaction using the ObjectContext object. Objects used in transactions are destroyed at the end of the transaction, and any subsequent references to their properties or calls to their methods will result in an error.

Methods Reference

Lock

The Lock method locks the Application object, preventing any other client from altering *any* variables' values in the Contents collection (not just those variables you alter before calling the Unlock method). The corresponding Unlock method is used to release the Application object so other clients can again alter the Contents collection variable values. If you fail to use the Unlock method, IIS will unlock the variable automatically at the end of the current Active Server Pages script or upon script timeout,* whichever occurs first.

Parameters

None

Example

```
<%
' This script exists on the second page of a
' multipage ASP application, so that users may
' or may not visit it. The example shows how you could
' see how many visitors the page has had.
' Assume that TotalNumPage2 starts at 0.

' Lock the Application object.
Application.Lock

intNumVisits = Application.Contents("TotalNumPage2")
intNumVisits = intNumVisits + 1
Application.Contents("TotalNumPage2") = intNumVisits

' Explicitly unlock the Application object.
Application.Unlock

' NOTE: Using the PageCounter would be a more
' efficient manner of doing this.

%>
<HTML>
<HEAD><TITLE>Home Page</TITLE></HEAD>
<BODY BGCOLOR = #ffffcc>
Welcome to our homepage. You are client number
<%= Application.Contents("TotalNumPage2")%> to our site. Thank you for
your patronage.
</BODY>
</HTML>
```

---

* The ASP script timeout is adjustable through the Properties page of the web site using the Microsoft Management Console. The default is 120 seconds.

Notes

Any client connected to your web server can call a script that potentially could alter the value of a variable in the Application Contents collection. For this reason, it is a good idea to use the Lock and Unlock methods every time you reference or alter a variable in the Contents collection. This prevents the possibility of a client attempting to change a variable's value when another client is resolving that variable's value.

Keep in mind that you cannot create a read-only variable by using a call to the Lock method without a corresponding call to Unlock, since IIS automatically unlocks the Application object.

You do not have to call the Lock and Unlock methods in the Application_OnStart event procedure (see this chapter's Events Reference for more about the Application_OnStart event). The Application_OnStart event occurs only once regardless of the number of sessions that are eventually initiated. Only the first client request triggers the Application_OnStart event and, for that reason, only that client can alter the value of the specific Application variable. Also, no other client requests will be handled until the Application_OnStart code has completed.

Unlock   `Application.Unlock`

The Unlock method releases the application variables from a Lock method call. Once Unlock has been called, other clients can again alter the values of the variables in the Application Contents collection. If you call Lock and do not provide a corresponding Unlock, IIS will automatically unlock the variables in the Application Contents collection at the end of the current active server page or when the script times out, whichever comes first.

Parameters

None

Example

See the example for Application.Lock.

Notes

See the notes for Application.Lock.

Events Reference

OnEnd   `Application_OnEnd`

The Application_OnEnd event is triggered when the ASP application itself is unloaded from the web server (using the Microsoft Management Console) or when the application is inadvertently stopped for some reason (i.e., the web service is stopped on the web server). Application_OnEnd is called only once per application. The code for this event procedure resides in the *GLOBAL.ASA* file and is processed after all other code in the file. It is in the code for the Application_OnEnd event that you will "clean up" after any application-scoped variables.

Parameters

None

Example

```
' <<<<<<<<<<<<<< FROM GLOBAL.ASA >>>>>>>>>>>>>>>>>
' This code resides in the GLOBAL.ASA file at the
' root of the current application. The following
' procedure is processed only once for the current
' application.
' See Chapter 11 for more details on the GLOBAL.ASA file.

<SCRIPT LANGUAGE="VBScript" RUNAT=Server>
Sub Application_OnEnd

' This code will run on the server when
' the application stops.
' This code saves the final count of an application
' use counter to a file.
Set filsysObj1 = _
    CreateObject("Scripting.FileSystemObject")
Set tsObj1 = filsysObj1.CreateTextFile("c:\usrcount.txt", _
            True)
tsObj1.WriteLine(Application.Contents("AppUserCount"))
tsObj1.Close

End Sub
</SCRIPT>

' <<<<<<<<<<<<<<<<<<<<<<<<<<<<<>>>>>>>>>>>>>>>>>>>>>>>>
```

Notes

The use of the Application_OnEnd event is tricky. The Microsoft documentation suggests that the OnEnd event is triggered when there are no longer any active sessions. However, this is not the case. Only when the web service is interrupted or when the administrator explicitly unloads the application from the web server's memory (using the MMC) is OnEnd executed. You cannot assume that this event will ever be called from your application without something going wrong or direct intervention on your part. This is yet another reason to very carefully consider the implications before using application-level variables of any kind.

You cannot use the Server object method MapPath (see Chapter 9, *Server Object*, for more on the Server object) to map a relative or virtual directory to a physical directory within the Application_OnEnd event procedure. Microsoft gives no reason for this limitation, though it is likely a security-related control.

OnStart   Application_OnStart

The Application_OnStart event is triggered when the first client request is received. Application_OnStart is called only once per application. The code for this event procedure resides in the *GLOBAL.ASA* file and is processed before any other code or object instantiation in the file.

Parameters

None

Example

```
' <<<<<<<<<<<<<< FROM GLOBAL.ASA >>>>>>>>>>>>>>>>>
' This code resides in the GLOBAL.ASA file at the
' root of the current application. The following
' procedure is processed only once for the current
' application.
' See Chapter 11 for more details on the GLOBAL.ASA file.

<SCRIPT LANGUAGE="VBScript" RUNAT=Server>
Sub Application_OnStart

' This code will run on the server when
' the application starts.
' This code retrieves the last final user count
' and uses it to initialize an Application
' variable.
Set filsysObj1 = CreateObject("Scripting.FileSystemObject")
Set tsObj1 = filsysObj1.OpenTextFile("c:\usrcount.txt", _
             True)
Application.Contents("AppUserCount") = tsObj1.ReadAll
tsObj1.Close

End Sub
</SCRIPT>

' <<<<<<<<<<<<<<<<<<<<<<<<<<<<<<>>>>>>>>>>>>>>>>>>>>>>>>>>>>>>>
```

Notes

The Application_OnStart event procedure, if it exists, is the first code run on the server for a given Active Server Pages application. For this reason, it is the best place to initialize application-level variables. No other code in your ASP application is guaranteed to run.

Carefully consider the use of application-level variables. Every variable with application scope that you dimension and initialize in the Application_OnStart event continues to take up memory on the server until the end of the application.

CHAPTER 5

ASPError Object

Introduced with ASP 3.0, the built-in ASPError object allows you to view detailed information about the last error that occurred in the script of an ASP page in the current session. This object, through its nine read-only properties, provides more detailed information about the type and source of errors than does the Err object provided in VBScript.

To use the ASPError object and its properties, you must call a new method of the Server object, GetLastError, which returns an ASPErrorObject with its properties' values set to reflect details about the last error that occurred in the script:

```
Dim objMyASPError
Set objMyASPError = Server.GetLastError
```

When you install IIS 5.0, by default, all preprocessing, script and runtime errors in ASP code cause IIS to stop processing the current script and redirect script execution to a custom error page named *500-100.ASP*. This redirection occurs through an internal call to the Server.Transfer method which, as detailed in Chapter 9, *Server Object*, shifts execution from one script to another while protecting all state information available in the first script.

The *500-100.ASP* script (located by default in the *C:\WINNT\Help\iisHelp\ common* directory) contains a call to the Server.GetLastError method. When this script is executed, it formats and displays the current property values of the ASPError object returned by this call to GetLastError.

You can use the default error page, *500-100.ASP*, as-is; edit it to reflect your site's look and feel; or use the Internet Services Manager snap-in to redirect IIS to a page of your choosing (see Appendix D, *Configuration of ASP Applications on IIS*).

The properties, collections, methods, and events of the ASPError object are outlined in the following box.

ASPError Object Summary

Properties
    ASPCode
    ASPDescription
    Category
    Column
    Description
    File
    Line
    Number
    Source

Collections
    None

Methods
    None

Events
    None

Comments/Troubleshooting

Many beginning ASP developers use the following code to enable debugging of their scripts using the Err object in VBScript:

```
On Error Resume Next
```

If you include this line of code in your script, then only preprocessing and script (syntax) errors will cause IIS to call the Server.Transfer method and redirect script execution to your *500-100.ASP* script (or custom error-handling script). Runtime errors will not cause IIS to transfer processing to *500-100.ASP*. For example, if you use this line of debugging code, you will not necessarily catch the error in the following block of code:

```
Dim intCounter
For intCounter = 1 to 100
    intResult = intCounter / (intCounter - 100)
Next
```

In this snippet, you would have to add code before the **Next** statement to catch the division by zero error that will arise when *intCounter* is 100. Adding these lines to catch errors throughout your code is costly in processing time and error-prone in its own right, since you have to anticipate the line on which an error is likely to occur in order to effectively trap it. As a result, and because the ASPError object provides more information than the Err object, you should not use **On Error Resume Next** if you can avoid it.

Another excellent use of the ASPError object page, *500-100.ASP* (or similar, customized scripts for errors) is to handle errors that occur in a publicly available site. For example, you could customize the *500-100.ASP* script to contain your site's color scheme and background and to include a Help phone number that could connect the user experiencing difficulty with someone who could help. And support personnel can field the call more effectively if you take advantage of the mroe extensive range of information that the ASPError object can provide to the *500-100.ASP* script.

Another possibility is to use *500-100.ASP* to route an error notification to the appropriate personnel "in the background," and to hide the details of the error from the end user. This version of *500-100.ASP* would simply display the fact that an error has occurred and that the user should try his or her action later, while—in the background—sending an error email to support personnel. An example script that performs these functions can be found at the end of this chapter.

The code examples that illustrate the properties of the ASPError object all make use of three different error-generating scripts. The first contains a syntax error, the second contains an error in a preprocessing directive, and the third generates a runtime error. While the examples all make use of the same three ASP pages to generate errors, it is the contents of the custom error page *500-100.ASP* that change to illustrate the particular property. The three ASP pages that raise errors are the following:

```
**** BEGIN Error Generating Script #1 ****
<HTML>
<HEAD> <TITLE>
Error Generation Page #1
</TITLE></HEAD>
<BODY>
<%
' This page contains a syntax error.
' In the following For...Next loop, the keyword
' "For" is mispelled.
Dim intCounter
Fir intCounter = 1 to 100
%>
Look everyone! I'm counting: <%=intCounter%><BR>
<%
Next
%>
</BODY>
</HTML>
**** END Error Generating Script #1 ****


**** BEGIN Error Generating Script #2 ****
<HTML>
<HEAD><TITLE>
Error Generation Page #2
</TITLE></HEAD>
<BODY>
<%
' This page contains a preprocessing error.
' The work "file" in the #INCLUDE preprocessor
' directive is mispelled:
%>
```

ASPError
Object

```
<!--#include fil=/headers/AdminHeader.INC -->
</BODY>
</HTML>
**** END Error Generating Script #2 ****


**** BEGIN Error Generating Script #3 ****
<HTML>
<HEAD><TITLE>
Error Generation Page #3
</TITLE></HEAD>
<BODY>
<%
' This page contains a runtime error.
' In the following For...Next loop, when the
' intCounter variable gets to zero, the result
' is a divide by zero error.
Dim intCounter
Dim dblDivResult
For intCounter = 1 to 100
    dblDivResult = intCounter / (intCounter - 100)
%>
Look everyone! I'm dividing: <%=dblDivResult%><BR>
<%
Next
%>
</BODY>
</HTML>
**** END Error Generating Script #3 ****
```

Properties Reference

ASPCode   objASPError.ASPCode

The ASPCode property holds a numeric code representing the ASP-specific error that occurred in the script that raised the error. This property is populated by IIS if the error occurred in processing the ASP script.

The ASPCode property is read-only.

Parameters

None

Example

This example assumes that the following code has been added to the default custom error script, *500-100.ASP,* and that each of the three scripts shown at the end of the Comments/Troubleshooting section is used to raise an error that invokes it:

```
**** BEGIN ASPCode Example Script ****
<%
```

```
' This script demonstrates the use of the ASPCode
' property of the ASPError object.
Dim objMyASPError

Set objMyASPError = Server.GetLastError()

Response.Write "The value of the ASPCode property is " & objMyASPError.
ASPCode
%>
**** END ASPCode Example Script ****
```

When the error-generating scripts are executed, the preceding example script generates the following three responses:

Error Generating Script #1:

```
The value of the ASPCode property is [EMPTY]
```

Error Generating Script #2:

```
The value of the ASPCode property is ASP 0128
```

Error Generating Script #3:

```
The value of the ASPCode property is [EMPTY]
```

Notes

As previously noted, the ASPCode property is not populated unless the error occurred when interpreting the ASP script itself. This covers all preprocessing directives.

ASPDescription   objASPError.ASPDescription

The ASPDescription property is a string value that IIS populates upon encountering an ASP error. It provides more descriptive data about the type of ASP error that occurred than does the ASPCode property. As with the ASPCode property, the ASPDescription property is only populated if the error that occurs is part of the interpretation of an ASP script, rather than as a result of a runtime error.

Parameters

None

Example

This example uses the error-generating scripts listed at the end of the Comments/Troubleshooting section. It assumes that the following code has been added to the default custom error script, *500-100.ASP*:

```
**** BEGIN ASPDescription Example Script ****
<%
' This script demonstrates the use of the ASPDescription
' property of the ASPError object.
Dim objMyASPError

Set objMyASPError = Server.GetLastError()
```

```
Response.Write "The value of the ASPDescription property is " & _
    objMyASPError.ASPDescription
%>
**** END ASPDescription Example Script ****
```

When the error-generating scripts are executed, the preceding ASPDescription script generates the following three responses:

Error Generating Script #1:

```
The value of the ASPDescription property is [EMPTY]
```

Error Generating Script #2:

```
The value of the ASPDescription property is The Include file name must be
specified using either the File or Virtual attribute.
```

Error Generating Script #3:

```
The value of the ASPDescription property is [EMPTY]
```

Notes

Like ASPCode, the ASPDescription property is only useful for ASP interpretation-specific errors. The Description property of the ASPError object almost always provides the same or better information about the most recent error.

Category   objASPError.Category

The Category property holds a string that specifies the type of error that has occurred: IIS-specific, scripting language specific, or component specific.

Parameters

None

Example

This example uses the error-generating scripts listed at the end of the Comments/Troubleshooting section. It assumes that the following example code has been added to the default custom error script, *500-100.ASP*:

```
**** BEGIN Category Example Script ****
<%
' This script demonstrates the use of the Category
' property of the ASPError object.
Dim objMyASPError

Set objMyASPError = Server.GetLastError()

Response.Write "The value of the Category property is " & objMyASPError.
Category
%>
**** END Category Example Script ****
```

When the error-generating scripts are executed, this script generates the following three responses:

Error Generating Script #1:

The value of the Category property is **Microsoft VBScript compilation**

Error Generating Script #2:

The value of the Category property is **Active Server Pages**

Error Generating Script #3:

The value of the Category property is **Microsoft VBScript runtime**

Notes

The Category property allows you to narrow down where to look for the error.

Column

objASPError.Column

The Column property holds a long value that specifies the specific character column containing the first character of the error-causing code.

Parameters

None

Example

This example uses the error-generating scripts listed at the end of the Comments/ Troubleshooting section. It assumes that the following code has been added to the default custom error script, *500-100.ASP*:

```
**** BEGIN Column Example Script ****
<%
' This script demonstrates the use of the Column
' property of the ASPError object.
Dim objMyASPError

Set objMyASPError = Server.GetLastError()

Response.Write "The value of the Column property is " & objMyASPError.
Column
%>
**** END Column Example Script ****
```

When the error-generating scripts are executed, the preceding Column script generates the following three responses:

Error Generating Script #1:

The value of the Column property is **19**

Error Generating Script #2:

The value of the Column property is **-1**

Error Generating Script #3:

The value of the Column property is **-1**

ASPError Object

Notes

The Column property is valuable in helping you locate erroneous syntax in your code. However, if the error is ASP-specific or the location where the error arises does not contain syntactically incorrect code, this value is –1 and, as such, is of limited use.

Description   objASPError.Description

The Description property is a string describing the last-occurring error. It is typically more descriptive and useful than the related ASPDescription property, except when the error is ASP interpretation-specific.

Parameters

None

Example

This example uses the error-generating scripts listed at the end of the Comments/ Troubleshooting section. It assumes that the following code has been added to the default custom error script, *500-100.ASP*:

```
**** BEGIN Description Example Script ****
<%
' This script demonstrates the use of the Description
' property of the ASPError object.
Dim objMyASPError

Set objMyASPError = Server.GetLastError()

Response.Write "The value of the Description property is " &
objMyASPError.Description
%>
**** END Description Example Script ****
```

When the error-generating scripts are executed, the preceding Description script generates the following three responses:

Error Generating Script #1:

```
The value of the Description property is Expected end of statement
```

Error Generating Script #2:

```
The value of the Description property is Missing File or Virtual
attribute
```

Error Generating Script #3:

```
The value of the Description property is Division by zero
```

Notes

The Description property value is typically more descriptive than the other properties of the ASPError object. However, like all the other properties, it is of very little use to the end users of your ASP application. As such, it is important that any information you display explaining the cause of the error be informative or useful to the user. At the end of this chapter is an example of a customized *500-100.ASP* script that you can use to display innocuous error information while still providing useful information to the developer of the script.

File

`objASPError.File`

The File property contains the full path to the file containing the error-producing code. This filename contains the full path of the file from the web root.

Parameters

None

Example

This example uses the error-generating scripts listed at the end of the Comments/ Troubleshooting section. It assumes that the following code has been added to the default custom error script, *500-100.ASP*:

```
**** BEGIN File Example Script ****
<%
' This script demonstrates the use of the File
' property of the ASPError object.
Dim objMyASPError

Set objMyASPError = Server.GetLastError()

Response.Write "The value of the File property is " & objMyASPError.File
%>
**** END File Example Script ****
```

When the error-generating scripts are executed, the preceding File script generates the following three responses:

Error Generating Script #1:

> The value of the File property is **/errorgen1.asp**

Error Generating Script #2:

> The value of the File property is **/errorgen2.asp**

Error Generating Script #3:

> The value of the File property is **/errorgen3.asp**

Notes

Note that the file path is listed from the web server's root path, not from the root of the current application.

Line

`objASPError.Line`

The Line property is a long value representing the line number where the error-producing code occurs.

ASPError Object

Parameters

None

Example

This example uses the error-generating scripts listed at the end of the Comments/ Troubleshooting section. It assumes that the following code has been added to the default custom error script, *500-100.ASP*:

```
**** BEGIN Line Example Script ****
<%
' This script demonstrates the use of the Line
' property of the ASPError object.
Dim objMyASPError

Set objMyASPError = Server.GetLastError()

Response.Write "The value of the Line property is " & objMyASPError.Line
%>
**** END Line Example Script ****
```

When the error-generating scripts are executed, the preceding Line script generates the following three responses:

Error Generating Script #1:

```
The value of the Line property is 11
```

Error Generating Script #2:

```
The value of the Line property is 11
```

Error Generating Script #3:

```
The value of the Line property is 14
```

Notes

The line count starts with the very first ASP line of code and begins with 1.

Number   objASPError.Number

The Number property contains a long value that represents an error code returned by a COM component. This long value will be a standard COM error code.

Parameters

None

Example

This example uses the error-generating scripts listed at the end of the Comments/ Troubleshooting section. It assumes that the following code has been added to the default custom error script, *500-100.ASP*:

```
**** BEGIN Number Example Script ****
<%
' This script demonstrates the use of the Number
' property of the ASPError object.
```

```
Dim objMyASPError

Set objMyASPError = Server.GetLastError()

Response.Write "The value of the Number property is " & objMyASPError.
Number
%>
**** END Number Example Script ****
```

When the error-generating scripts are executed, the following three responses are generated:

Error Generating Script #1:

```
The value of the Number property is -2146827263
```

Error Generating Script #2:

```
The value of the Number property is -2147467259
```

Error Generating Script #3:

```
The value of the Number property is -2146828277
```

Notes

None

Source

objASPError.Source

The Source property is a string containing the line of code that caused the most recent error, if that code was syntactically incorrect.

Parameters

None

Example

This example uses the error generating scripts listed at the end of the ASPError Troubleshooting section. It assumes that the following code has been added to the default custom error script, *500-100.ASP*:

```
**** BEGIN Source Example Script ****
<%
' This script demonstrates the use of the Source
' property of the ASPError object.
Dim objMyASPError

Set objMyASPError = Server.GetLastError()

Response.Write "The value of the Source property is " & objMyASPError.
Source
%>
**** END Source Example Script ****
```

When the error-generating scripts are executed, the preceding Source script generates the following three responses:

Error Generating Script #1:

The value of the Source property is **Fir intCounter = 1 to 100**

Error Generating Script #2:

The value of the Source property is [EMPTY]

Error Generating Script #3:

The value of the Source property is [EMPTY]

Notes

As mentioned previously, the Source property is only useful if the error produced is syntax-related. Otherwise, this property is empty.

ASPError Example

The following script could be used as a custom version of *500-100.ASP*. It demonstrates several of the items discussed in this chapter and others.

From the user's perspective, this script simply informs him or her that an error has occurred, that the developers of the application have been notified, and that the user should try his or her action again later. It also provides a number that the user can call for support. In the background, however, this script creates a mail message containing information about the offending error, the state of the application and about the specific user who was attempting the action in the application. This mail message is then routed to a developer mailbox.

Note that you could add more sophistication to the routing mechanism that could, for example, look up the appropriate recipient based on the script title. Also, you may want to log these error messages in a database for later review.

```
<%@ LANGUAGE="VBSCRIPT" %>
<%
Response.Buffer = TRUE
Response.Expires = 0

' Script Name:  500-100_Custom.ASP

' Description:  This script catches the last error and
' creates and sends a message via email
' to the responsible developer.

' Inputs: Will take whatever information was previously
' submitted into the error-raising script.

' Author: Keyton Weissinger


' Change Log:
' Date       Programmer     Notes
' -------------------------------------------------
' 3/24/2000  AKW            Created script.
```

```
' *** Dimension local variables needed for script. ***

' Vars for user and server info.
Dim strUser
Dim strRemoteAddress
Dim strServerName
Dim strServerAddress

' Vars for ASPError object property values.
Dim strASPCode
Dim strASPDescription
Dim strCategory
Dim strColumn
Dim strDescription
Dim strFile
Dim strLine
Dim strNumber
Dim strSource

' Vars for Request collection values.
Dim intKey
Dim strQueryStringElement
Dim strQueryStringValue
Dim strCurrentQueryString
Dim strFormElement
Dim strFormValue
Dim strCurrentForm

' Var for all HTTP header data.
Dim strAllHTTP

' Vars for Mail Message and sending.
Dim strErrMsgBody
Dim strRecipient
Dim strSender
Dim objNewMail

' Flush the buffer to ensure that no response information is sent to the
' client.
If Response.Buffer Then
   Response.Clear
   Response.Status = "500 Internal Server Error"
   Response.ContentType = "text/html"
   Response.Expires = 0
End If

' *** Initialize the user and server variables. ***
strUser = Request.ServerVariables("REMOTE_USER")
strRemoteAddress = Request.ServerVariables("REMOTE_HOST")
strServerName = Request.ServerVariables("SERVER_NAME")
strServerAddress = Request.ServerVariables("LOCAL_ADDR")

' *** Initialize the ASPError object. ***
Set objASPError = Server.GetLastError()
```

```
' *** Initialize the ASPError object property value variables. ***
strASPCode          = objASPError.ASPCode
strASPDescription   = objASPError.ASPDescription
strCategory         = objASPError.Category
strColumn           = objASPError.Column
strDescription      = objASPError.Description
strFile             = objASPError.File
strLine             = objASPError.Line
strNumber           = objASPError.Number
strSource           = objASPError.Source

' *** Retrieve the keys and values from the QueryString. ***
For Each intKey in Request.QueryString
     strQueryStringElement = Request.QueryString.Key(intKey)
     strQueryStringValue = Request.QueryString.Item(strQueryStringElement)
     strCurrentQueryString = strCurrentQueryString & "Element: " & _
     strQueryStringElement & ".......Value: " & strQueryStringValue & _
          Chr(10) & Chr(13)
Next

' *** Retrieve the keys and values from the Form. ***
For Each intKey in Request.Form
     strFormElement = Request.Form.Key(intKey)
     strFormValue = Request.Form.Item(strFormElement)
     strCurrentForm = strCurrentForm & "Element: " & _
     strFormElement & ".......Value: " & strFormValue & _
          Chr(10) & Chr(13)
Next

' *** Retrieve the keys and values from all HTTP headers
' sent by client. ***
strAllHTTP = Request.ServerVariables("ALL_HTTP")

' *** Construct the error email message body string. ***
strErrMsgBody = "Greetings. An error has occurred." & Chr(10) & Chr(13) & _
     Chr(10) & Chr(13)
strErrMsgBody = strErrMsgBody & _
     "Here is information that should help you debug the script."
strErrMsgBody = strErrMsgBody & Chr(10) & Chr(13) & Chr(10) & Chr(13)
strErrMsgBody = strErrMsgBody & "User: " & strUser & Chr(10) & Chr(13)
strErrMsgBody = strErrMsgBody & "User Address: " & strRemoteAddress & _
     Chr(10) & Chr(13)
strErrMsgBody = strErrMsgBody & Chr(10) & Chr(13)
strErrMsgBody = strErrMsgBody & "The error occurred on the following" _
     & "server: " & vbCrLf
strErrMsgBody = strErrMsgBody & "Server Name: " & strServerName & _
     vbCrLf
strErrMsgBody = strErrMsgBody & "Server I.P. Address: " & strServerAddress & _
     Chr(10) & Chr(13)
strErrMsgBody = strErrMsgBody & Chr(10) & Chr(13)
strErrMsgBody = strErrMsgBody & "ASP Error Information:" & Chr(10) & Chr(13)
strErrMsgBody = strErrMsgBody & "ASPCode: " & strASPCode & Chr(10) & Chr(13)
```

```
strErrMsgBody = strErrMsgBody & "ASPDescription: " & strASPDescription & _
    Chr(10) & Chr(13)
strErrMsgBody = strErrMsgBody & "Category: " & strCategory & _
    vbCrLf
strErrMsgBody = strErrMsgBody & "Column: " & strColumn & Chr(10) & Chr(13)
strErrMsgBody = strErrMsgBody & "Description: " & strDescription & _
    vbCrLf
strErrMsgBody = strErrMsgBody & "File: " & strFile & Chr(10) & Chr(13)
strErrMsgBody = strErrMsgBody & "Line: " & strLine & Chr(10) & Chr(13)
strErrMsgBody = strErrMsgBody & "Number: " & strNumber & Chr(10) & Chr(13)
strErrMsgBody = strErrMsgBody & "Source: " & strSource & Chr(10) & Chr(13)
strErrMsgBody = strErrMsgBody & Chr(10) & Chr(13) & Chr(10) & Chr(13)
strErrMsgBody = strErrMsgBody & "Request.QueryString Information:" & _
    vbCrLf
strErrMsgBody = strErrMsgBody & strCurrentQueryString & Chr(10) & Chr(13)
strErrMsgBody = strErrMsgBody & "Request.Form Information:" & _
    vbCrLf
strErrMsgBody = strErrMsgBody & strCurrentForm & Chr(10) & Chr(13)
strErrMsgBody = strErrMsgBody & Chr(10) & Chr(13)
strErrMsgBody = strErrMsgBody & Chr(10) & Chr(13)
strErrMsgBody = strErrMsgBody & "All HTTP headers sent by the client:" & _
    Chr(10) & Chr(13)
strErrMsgBody = strErrMsgBody & strALLHTTP & Chr(10) & Chr(13)

' Initialize the NewMail object and set the mail recipient, sender and body.
' Note you may want to insert your own code here to look up the specific
' developer to which you want the error message sent.
Set objNewMail = Server.CreateObject("CDONTS.NewMail")
strRecipient = "Dev1@myapp.com"
strSender = strServerName & " at " & strServerAddress
objNewMail.Body = strErrMsgBody
objNewMail.To = strRecipient
objNewMail.From = strSender

' Send the email.
objNewMail.Send

' The rest of this script generates a non-specific error message for viewing
' by the client.
' Customize its look and feel to match that of your site.
%>

<HTML>
<HEAD>
<TITLE>
Error Notice
</TITLE>
</HEAD>
<BODY>
We apologize for the inconvenience but your last action triggered an error on
the web server.<BR>
```

A message has been sent to our development group and the error should be resolved shortly.
Please contact support at 800-555-HELP for more information or try your action again later.

Thank you.
</BODY>
</HTML>

CHAPTER 6

ObjectContext Object

As of version 2.0, an important feature of Active Server Pages is the ability to create a transactional script: one whose constituent code segments all succeed completely or fail as a group. For example, using such a script, one section of code could remove a record from an inventory table, and a second section could add a record to a sales log table. However, only if both sections of code succeed does the script itself succeed. If the removal of the inventory record or the addition of the sales record fails, the script itself fails. Both processes are rolled back: the deleted record, if it was removed, is added back into the database, and the sales record, if it was added, is removed from the sales log table. This ability to wrap several functions in a single transactional unit that succeeds or fails as a whole is an important improvement in the power of ASP applications. Previously, all transactions relied on database transaction support.

ASP application transactions are controlled by Windows 2000 COM+ Component Services or Windows NT's Microsoft Transaction Server (MTS). This piece of the BackOffice suite allows control over all database actions coded to use it. Support for transactional scripts is built into IIS and Personal Web Server and does not require any special setup. Without COM+ Component Services or, in ASP 2.0, MTS transactional support, your applications would have to track all database changes manually and roll back all database actions by hand, keeping track of multiuser and concurrency issues, etc. MTS or COM+ Component Services gives this support for very little extra coding—as long as the database your application is connected to is Microsoft SQL Server or it supports the XA protocol from the X/Open consortium. Note that this means that file actions are not yet supported—or at least, not automatically.

ASP's support of transactions is coded through the use of the ObjectContext object, which represents the actual ObjectContext object of COM+ Component Services itself. By calling methods of the ObjectContext object and coding its events, you can create a transactional script with only a few more lines of code.

To declare all the script on a given page to be transactional, simply add the following line of code as the first line in your script:

```
<%@ TRANSACTION = Required %>
```

For more details on the TRANSACTION ASP directive, see Chapter 11, *Preprocessing Directives, Server-Side Includes, and GLOBAL.ASA*. Here it is important only that this line be the first in your script; including this line alerts the web server to use Component Services to ensure that the script succeeds or fails as a whole.

To commit the transaction or abort it, you simply call the SetComplete or SetAbort methods of the ObjectContext object, respectively. If you are dealing with a complex transaction containing segments of code that are not supported by Component Services (notably file actions), you can specially code for these actions in the ObjectContext events OnTransactionCommit and OnTransactionAbort. There are examples of all of these methods and event procedures in the reference section later in this chapter.

ObjectContext Object Summary

Properties
> None

Collections
> None

Methods
> SetAbort
> SetComplete

Events
> OnTransactionAbort
> OnTransactionCommit

Comments/Troubleshooting

There are currently two very important limitations in constructing transactional scripts:

- Only database actions are supported, and only SQL Server and databases that support the XA protocol are supported by COM+ Component Services or MTS.

- A transaction cannot span more than one ASP page. For this reason, you must be very careful in creating your pages: they must include all the actions required by your transactions but not be so large as to slow the processing of the page by too large a percentage.

If you write your own server components that complete some or all of the database actions in your transaction, that component must be registered in an MTS package.* MTS transactional support is provided only if the component is

---

* For more information on the ObjectContext object and server components, see *Developing ASP Components*, written by Shelley Powers and published by O'Reilly & Associates.

registered. What's more, you should create your own library packages and not include your component in the IIS in-process package. Custom library packages can be used by multiple ASP applications and are run in the same process as the ASP DLL. Setting up library packages also gives your component the ability to be pooled for reuse by your applications. This pooling is managed by MTS as well. You also can add your components to a server package, but doing so is required only for role-based transactions or transactions running on remote computers.

Note that you should not give objects functioning in transactions session- or application-level scope, since transactional objects are deactivated at the end of their transaction. If you do give such an object session or application scope, calls after the end of the transaction will fail and raise an error.

Although transactions are supported only for database actions, you can add code to the OnTransactionCommit and OnTransactionAbort event procedures to provide your own nondatabase transactional support. For example, code in these event procedures could easily be used to write or remove files from the file system upon success or failure of a given transaction.

ObjectContext exposes six methods other than the ones you can access through ASP. However, these are accessible only through code within the server components being managed by COM+ Component Services or MTS, and therefore are not documented here.

Transactional scripts are a very important addition to ASP. If you had access to database transactions only through use of ActiveX Data Objects, it would still be a very important and useful function. However, by creating custom server components, you can create complex and powerful transactions.

Methods Reference

SetAbort `ObjectContext.SetAbort`

ObjectContext
Object

Aborts the transaction as a whole. When it is called, the transaction ends unsuccessfully, regardless of code that has or has not already been processed in your script.

You can use this method in your script after testing for the completion of a given part of the transaction, or a server component managed by MTS or COM+ Component Services can call it. Calling SetAbort rolls back any parts of the transaction that have already occurred and calls the ObjectContext_OnTransactionAbort event procedure if one exists in your script.

Parameters

None

Example

```
<%

    ' The following code tests the result from a method call
    ' to a custom server component that attempts to remove
```

```
' a book from the inventory table and then tests the
' results from a credit card check.

' Based on this code and the segment that follows it, the
' script will call either the SetAbort or the SetComplete
' method of the ObjectContext object.

' Attempt to sell 2 copies of the book Animal Farm.
intBooks = MyInventory.SellBook("Animal Farm", 2)

' Check the credit card given by the client.
intCheckCC = MyCreditChecker.ChkCard("0001231234")

If intBooks = 2 And intCheckCC = 0 Then

    ' Complete the transaction. Two copies of the book
    ' are in the inventory and the credit card checks out.
    ObjectContext.SetComplete

Else

    ' Abort the transaction. Either there are not two
    ' copies of the book in the inventory or the credit
    ' card did not check out.
    ObjectContext.SetAbort

End If

%>
```

Notes

Any segment of a transactional script can call the SetAbort method. Note that if you have code that exists after the call to SetAbort, it will not be processed until after the execution of the OnTransactionAbort event procedure, if one exists. For this reason, be sure that your OnTransactionAbort event procedure performs any cleanup that is necessary for actions that are not supported in a transaction (notably file actions).

If you want some code to be processed regardless of a call to SetAbort, make sure that it is before the call to SetAbort in the script, or test for completion of the transaction after your code in the script.

SetComplete   ObjectContext.SetComplete

Signals the successful completion of a transaction. When it is called, the code in the OnTransactionCommit event procedure code is processed if it exists.

A call to the SetComplete method from within the script itself only indicates the success of the script on the page. It does not override possible failure of the code within the components referenced in the script. All transactional components in the script must signal SetComplete for the transaction to commit.

Parameters

None

Example

See the example in the previous section, "SetAbort."

Notes

Note that calling SetComplete does not necessarily mean that the entire transaction is complete. Every component called from the script also must call the SetComplete method of the ObjectContext object.

If you do not explicitly call SetComplete, the transaction is complete only after all code is processed without any calls to SetAbort. If no call to SetAbort is made by the end of the script, the OnTransactionCommit event procedure code is processed if it exists, regardless of whether SetComplete is called.

Events Reference

OnTransactionAbort OnTransactionAbort( )

The OnTransactionAbort event procedure is processed immediately if the SetAbort method of the ObjectContext object is called explicitly in scripted code or by a server component called from the scripted code. If no code calls the SetAbort method, this event procedure is never processed.

Parameters

None

Example

```
<%

' The following code procedure is processed when the code in
' the SetAbort method example is processed.
Sub OnTransactionAbort ()
%>
    Your book sales transaction could not be completed.
    Either there was not sufficient inventory for your
    sale to be processed, or your credit card did not
    go through.
<%
    ' Clean up any nontransactional actions here...

End Sub

%>
```

Notes

Use OnTransactionAbort to clean up any nonsupported actions your transaction makes that must be reversed if the transaction fails. This includes changes to variables (session- and application-level scope), the registry, and the file system. Note, however, that your server components should clean up after themselves.

You also should use the OnTransactionAbort event to inform the client that the transaction has failed.

Do not call the SetAbort or SetCommit methods from the OnTransactionAbort event procedure. Doing so may introduce a loop and result in the loss of function for your application and/or a loss of data.

OnTransactionCommit   OnTransactionCommit()

The OnTransactionCommit event procedure is processed immediately if the SetComplete method of the ObjectContext object is called explicitly in scripted code or by a server component called from the scripted code. It also is called implicitly if no script on the current page called the SetAbort method.

Parameters

None

Example

```
<%

' The following code procedure is processed when the code in
' the SetComplete method example is processed.
Sub OnTransactionCommit ()
%>
    Your book sales transaction was completed.
    Thank you for your sale.

<%
    Session("intTotalSales") = Session("intTotalSales") + 1

    ' Process any nontransactional code here...

End Sub

%>
```

Notes

The OnTransactionCommit event procedure can be used to inform the client of the success of the transaction. It also can be used for code that you want to be processed only if the transaction completes successfully.

Do not call the SetAbort or SetCommit methods from the OnTransactionCommit event procedure. Doing so may introduce a loop and result in the loss of function for your application and/or a loss of data.

CHAPTER 7

Request Object

The Request object gives you access to the user's HTTP request header and body. It is arguably the most important built-in ASP object to understand, since it is through this object that you will be able to react to the decisions made by the user. Using the Request object, you can dynamically create web pages and perform more meaningful server-side actions (such as updating a database) based on input from the user.

How HTTP Works

I will cover the Request object in detail in just a moment. First, however, it is important for you to understand the basics of the HTTP protocol. With such an introduction, use of the Request object is translated from the realm of the mysterious to the ordinary. For those of you whose eyes are beginning to glaze over, don't worry. This will be only a brief overview of the HTTP protocol.

HTTP: A Simple Example

You probably already know that HTTP is a "transaction"-style protocol. The browser (the client) sends a request to the server. The server obeys the request if it can and sends a response back to the client. The server then completely forgets about the transaction. The browser may or may not forget about it.

To illustrate the interaction between web browser and server, let's examine a fairly simple example that illustrates this exchange. Figure 7-1 shows Netscape Navigator displaying a very simple form, *HELLO.HTM*, that prompts the user for her name. When the user clicks the Submit button, a CGI application is invoked on a WebSite server that sends back the page displayed in Figure 7-2. (Although Navigator and WebSite are used for this example, the exchange between any browser and any server would be more or less identical. Also, although this example uses a CGI application, the HTTP request/response cycle is almost exactly the same as that for ASP applications. For more about CGI-to-ASP conversion, see Appendix B,

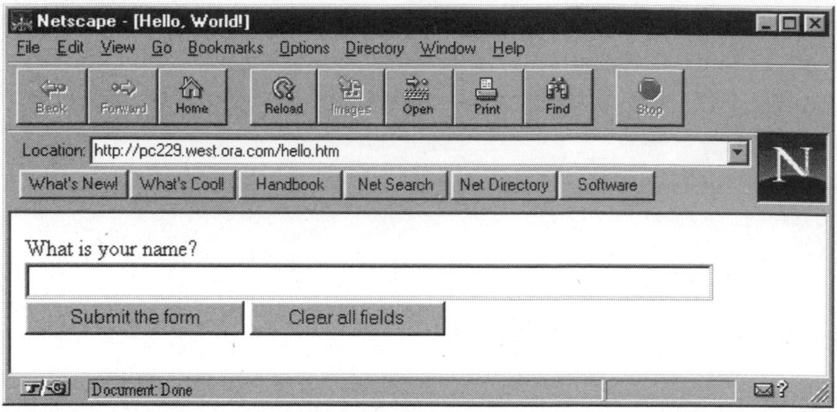

Figure 7-1: HELLO.HTM, a simple HTML form

Figure 7-2: HELLOCGI.HTM, an HTML page created by a CGI application

Converting CGI/WinCGI Applications into ASP Applications.) Let's see how this interchange between browser and server are handled by the protocol:

1. When the user finishes entering the URL for *HELLO.HTM*, Navigator sends* the following stream to the server:

```
[73:send:(179)]GET /hello.htm HTTP/1.0
Connection: Keep-Alive
User-Agent: Mozilla/3.0 (Win95; I)
Host: pc229.west.ora.com
Accept: image/gif, image/x-xbitmap, image/jpeg,
    image/pjpeg, */*
```

---

* *send* in the following output listing is a socket function that sends a stream in a connected socket. In the output, 73 identifies the socket, while 179 is the value returned by the function and represents the total number of bytes sent.

This is a request header. The browser indicates that it wants the server to get the document */HELLO.HTM. Get* is more than a generic description of what the server should do; it indicates the HTTP request type. (For details, see "HTTP Request Types," later in this chapter.) The browser also indicates that it's using version 1.0 of the Hypertext Transfer Protocol.

 Note that a portion of the first line in this HTTP header is actually an artifact of the TCP/IP packet sniffer used in this demonstration and not part of the actual HTTP request sent. The same is true for all HTTP segments in this chapter.

---

2. The server receives* the headers sent by the browser, as shown in the following output produced by our spy program, and processes the request:

```
[21:recv: completed (179)]GET /hello.htm HTTP/1.0
Connection: Keep-Alive
User-Agent: Mozilla/3.0 (Win95; I)
Host: pc229.west.ora.com
Accept: image/gif, image/x-xbitmap, image/jpeg, image/pjpeg, */*
```

3. The server sends the document *HELLO.HTM* to the browser:

```
[21:send:(535)]HTTP/1.0 200 OK
Date: Monday, 30-Sep-98 23:33:00 GMT
Server: WebSite/1.1
Allow-ranges: bytes
Accept-ranges: bytes
Connection: Keep-Alive
Content-type: text/html
Last-modified: Monday, 30-Sep-98 23:30:38 GMT
Content-length: 297

<HTML>
<HEAD><TITLE>Hello, World!</TITLE></HEAD>
<BODY>
<FORM ACTION="/cgi-win/hello.exe" METHOD="POST">
What is your name? <INPUT TYPE="text" NAME="name" SIZE=60><BR>
<INPUT TYPE="submit" VALUE="Submit the form">
<INPUT TYPE="reset" VALUE="Clear all fields">
</FORM>
</BODY> </HTML>
```

Here, WebSite sends a total of 535 bytes to the browser. This consists of a *response header*, followed by a blank line, followed by the HTML document itself. The header fields indicate, among other things, the number of bytes (the Content-length header) and the format (the Content-type header) of the transmitted data. "200 OK" is a status code indicating that the browser's

---

* The *recv* function is used to receive data from a socket. In the output, the initial number, 21, represents the socket used by the server. "Completed (179)" indicates the function's return value, in this case that it completed normally by receiving 179 bytes. Note that this corresponds to the number of bytes sent by the browser.

request was fulfilled. The server also indicates that, like the browser, it's using version 1.0 of HTTP.

4. The browser reads the headers and data sent by the server:

```
[73:recv: posted]
[73:recv: completed (260)]HTTP/1.0 200 OK
Date: Monday, 30-Sep-98 23:33:00 GMT
Server: WebSite/1.1
Allow-ranges: bytes
Accept-ranges: bytes
Connection: Keep-Alive
Content-type: text/html
Last-modified: Monday, 30-Sep-98 23:30:38 GMT
Content-length: 297

<HTML>
<HEAD><TITLE>H
[73:recv: posted]
[73:recv: completed (275)]ello, World!</TITLE></HEAD>
<BODY>
<FORM ACTION="/cgi-win/hello.exe" METHOD="POST">
What is your name? <INPUT TYPE="text" NAME="name" SIZE=60><BR>
<INPUT TYPE="submit" VALUE="Submit the form">
<INPUT TYPE="reset" VALUE="Clear all fields">
</FORM>
</BODY> </HTML>
```

Although two *recv* operations are required to retrieve the header records along with the document, the total number of bytes read in these two operations equals the total number of bytes sent by the server.

5. The browser displays the form asking for the user's name and, when the user fills it out and clicks the Submit button, sends the following to the server:

```
[70:send:(232)]POST /cgi-win/hello.exe HTTP/1.0
Referer: http://pc229.west.ora.com/hello.htm
Connection: Keep-Alive
User-Agent: Mozilla/3.0 (Win95; I)
Host: pc229.west.ora.com
Accept: image/gif, image/x-xbitmap, image/jpeg, image/pjpeg, */*
[70:send:(69)]Content-type: application/x-www-form-urlencoded
Content-length: 14
[70:send:(2)]
[70:send:(16)]name=Jayne+Doe
```

Because the browser is transmitting form data, the HTTP request type is "POST," as the very first header record indicates. Similarly, the Content-length and Content-type records indicate that the browser is transmitting 14 bytes of x-www-form-urlencoded data in the body of the request. This consists of the information input by the user in the form's single data field, the name text box.

6. The server receives the header records and form data transmitted by the browser in the previous step. (Since it's basically identical to the text sent by the browser, we won't duplicate it here.) The URL (*/cgi-win/hello.exe*) causes

the server to launch the CGI application *HELLO.EXE* and to transmit the form's data to it. The CGI application may do some back-end processing, then builds an HTML document on the fly and returns it to the server.

7. The server returns the HTML document to the browser along with the necessary header records, as the following output from WSock32 Spy shows:

```
[18:send:(422)]HTTP/1.0 200 OK
Date: Monday, 30-Sep-98 23:33:10 GMT
Server: WebSite/1.1
Allow-ranges: bytes
Accept-ranges: bytes
Connection: Keep-Alive
Content-type: text/html
Content-length: 231

<HTML><HEAD>
<TITLE>Welcome to this Web Page!</TITLE></HEAD>

<BODY><H1>Welcome to Our Web Server!</H1><p><p>
Hello, Jayne Doe! We're glad that you took
the time out of your busy day to visit us!
<HR></PRE></BODY></HTML>
```

Notice that the server indicates to the browser that it's sending 231 bytes of an HTML document.

8. The browser receives the data stream sent by the server and uses it to render the HTML page.

Hopefully, this gives you a fairly good sense of what's involved in the interchange between browser and server. It's important, though, to take a more in-depth look at some of the points that we've touched on only briefly, as well as to cover some additional features that are not included in this simple example.

HTTP Request Types

The request type is passed by the client to the server to indicate what the server should do with the URL that's also supplied by the browser. Although the HTTP specification details a number of request types, like PUT and DELETE, only two are supported by all servers and in common use: GET and POST. A GET request asks the server to "get" a piece of information, typically a document, and return it to the client. If the request includes any additional information, these are appended as arguments to the URL. A POST request, on the other hand, provides the server with information to be "posted" to the URL; typically, it's used to send the contents of an HTML form to the server, or to provide the server with information that's needed for back-end processing. The information itself is contained in the body of the request.

Most servers cannot handle data received from either the POST or GET methods internally. Normally, POST requests, as well as GET requests that also send data to the server, are handled by accessory programs or DLLs (CGI and ISAPI applications and ISAPI filters). Both POST and GET requests can return any kind of data of any size.

While it may seem when transmitting data to a web server that GET and POST are similar, one rule is hard and fast: *A GET request must never change anything.* Don't write an ASP script that makes changes to a database, for instance, in response to a GET request. The reason for this is discussed in greater detail in the following section, "Form Submission."

GET Versus POST

In the event that you're confused about the difference between these two methods, GET can be used to retrieve any document, POST cannot. On the other hand, both GET and POST can be used to pass data to the object indicated by the URL. When GET is used for this purpose, the data is included in the URL as the argument string; in order to extract this data with Win-CGI, you have to parse the argument string. When POST is used, the data is passed to the server in the body of the request message. So, in cases in which data is sent to the server, GET and POST differ in the method used to transmit that data.

Form Submission

A user enters input into the fields of a form. When the form is submitted, the data contained in each field of the form is transferred to the server, which then passes it to ASP. This data is sent in the format *name=value*, where *name* is the name assigned to the field by the NAME= attribute of the <INPUT> tag, and *value* is the value entered in that field. For example, if the user enters "Archie" in a field prompting for his first name, the browser may send along the string `first_name=Archie`.

If the form is written to use METHOD=GET, the form data is appended to the URL as an argument string. If the form contains many fields or if fields contain long strings of text, the complete URL can become very large and unwieldy. In addition, the limit of the number of characters submitted in a GET—typically about 2000—is much lower than in a POST.

If the form instead uses METHOD=POST, the *name=value* pairs are sent as the *body* of the request instead of being appended to the URL. In addition to the greater ease of handling of POST requests, most servers offer better performance when extracting data from the body of a request than from a URL in the request header.

Always use the POST method with forms that change something or cause any irreversible action (most do). POST is safer and more efficient; GET should never be used to change anything. In developing your ASP scripts, you can decide whether you want to support data passed to your program using the GET method.

HTTP Request and Response

Headers are the most misunderstood part of HTTP, yet understanding their role can make understanding the properties and methods of both the ASP Request and Response objects much easier.

Take a look at any Internet email message. It consists of two parts, the header and the body. The header consists of several lines that describe the body of the message and perhaps the way the message was handled as it was routed to you. The header and body are separated by a blank line. (For more information on header syntax, consult RFC-822.)

An HTTP message (either a request or a response) is structured the same way. The first line is special, but the rest of the lines up to the first blank line are headers just like in a mail message. The header describes the request and its content, if any, or the response and its content.

The request

In an earlier section, "HTTP: A Simple Example," we saw a number of requests from the browser. Here is another example of a simple HTTP request:

```
POST /cgi-win/hello.exe HTTP/1.0
Accept: image/gif, image/jpeg, */*
User-Agent: Mozilla/2.0N (Windows; I; 32Bit)
Content-type: application/x-www-form-urlencoded
Content-length: 14
[mandatory blank line]
name=Jayne+Doe
```

The first line, which is known as the *request-line*, describes the type of request (or *method*)—in this case POST, the URL, and, finally, the version of the HTTP protocol that the client uses. The second line describes the types of documents that the client can accept. The third line is an "extra" header that's not required by HTTP. It gives the name and version of the client software. Following this, as discussed in the section "HTTP: A Simple Example," are two lines describing the information contained in the body of the request.

Everything up to the mandatory blank line is part of the HTTP request header. In addition to the example lines here, there can be other lines in this section. For example, if the browser is sending information contained in a "cookie," that information also will be in the request header.

Below the mandatory blank line is the HTTP request body. In most cases, this section of the request is empty (for example, when the browser is requesting only a static page and is not sending any information). However, when the POST method is used, the information sent to the web server is located in this section of the request.

The response

Here is an example of a simple HTTP response:

```
HTTP/1.0 200 OK
Date: Thursday, 02-Nov-95 08:44:52 GMT
Server: WebSite/1.1
Last-Modified: Wednesday, 01-Nov-95 02:04:33 GMT
Content-Type: text/html
Content-length: 8151
```

Request Object

```
[mandatory blank line]
<HTML><HEAD>
<TITLE>...
```

The first line of the response is also special and is known as the *status-line*. It contains the protocol version the server uses, plus a *status code* and a *reason phrase*. The server uses the status code and reason phrase to inform the browser whether it was able to respond to the browser's request; in this case, it's successfully filled the browser's request for a document. The second line contains the date and time the server handled the request. Third is a header line describing the server software and version. The fourth line indicates the date and time when the requested document was last modified. The last two lines describe the type of data and the number of bytes in the requested document. This is followed by exactly one blank line, then the body of the message, which contains the document data that the server is sending back for the browser to display.

As with the HTTP request, everything above the mandatory blank line is considered part of the HTTP response header. Everything below this line is part of the response body.

This chapter covers the ASP Request object, which you can use to access both the header and the body of the HTTP request. The next chapter discusses the ASP Response object, which you use in manipulating the HTTP response from the web server.

The HTTP Request and the ASP Request Object

As mentioned earlier, the ASP Request object allows you to access both the header and body of the HTTP request sent to the web server by the client's browser. The method of retrieving information from the HTTP request is basically the same for an ASP script as it is for a CGI application. The exceptions come not from the actual request mechanics but from how each type of application is loaded into the web server (CGI versus an ISAPI filter), as described in the first two chapters of this book.

Just as with CGI applications, the client browser can send information to an ASP script in two different manners. First, it can send information by means of an HTML form using the GET method:

```
<HTML>
<HEAD><TITLE>Welcome to the Corp.</TITLE></HEAD>
<BODY>
<FORM ACTION=" http://mycorp.com/secure.asp" METHOD="GET">
First name: <INPUT TYPE="text" NAME="first_name" SIZE=60><BR>
Last name: <INPUT TYPE="text" NAME="last_name" SIZE=60><BR>
<INPUT TYPE="submit" VALUE="Submit the form">
<INPUT TYPE="reset" VALUE="Clear all fields">
</FORM>
</BODY> </HTML>
```

When the client submits a GET request, the information about the request is appended to the end of the request URL as name/value pairs separated by ampersands and preceded by a question mark. Each name corresponds to an element in the form. For example, suppose the user entered Horatia and Thompson into the two fields in the last example and clicked on the Submit button. The submission of the preceding form is, as far as the server is concerned, identical to the following:

```
http://mycorp.com/secure.asp?first_name=horatia&last_name=thompson
```

This is an important point. Following this example, consider the following line of code:

```
http://mycorp.com/secure.asp?first_name=horatia&last_name=thompson
```

If the user were to type this into the address line or click on a link containing the preceding as a URL, the web server would treat that resulting HTTP request exactly as if the information had been sent as part of a form using the GET request. From within your ASP application, you can access this information through the QueryString collection of the Request object. For example:

```
<%
strFirstName = Request.QueryString("first_name")
%>
```

will initialize the *strFirstName* variable to the value sent in the first_name parameter. The QueryString collection is discussed in detail later in this chapter.

Just as with CGI applications, you also can send information to an ASP script using the POST method. In this case, instead of being part of the HTTP request header, the information would be in the body of the request object:

```
<HTML>
<HEAD><TITLE>Welcome to the Corp.</TITLE></HEAD>
<BODY>
<FORM ACTION="http://mycorp.com/secure.asp" METHOD="POST">
First name: <INPUT TYPE="text" NAME="first_name" SIZE=60><BR>
Last name:<INPUT TYPE="text" NAME="last_name" SIZE=60><BR>
<INPUT TYPE="submit" VALUE="Submit the form">
<INPUT TYPE="reset" VALUE="Clear all fields">
</FORM>
</BODY> </HTML>
```

This form's submission would result in an HTTP request similar to the following:

```
POST /secure.asp HTTP/1.0
Accept: image/gif, image/jpeg, */*
User-Agent: Mozilla/2.0N (Windows; I; 32Bit)
Content-type: application/x-www-form-urlencoded
Content-length: 35
[mandatory blank line]
first_name=horatio&last_name=aubrey
```

For your application to manipulate the information sent in that HTTP request, you would have to use the Form collection of the Request object:

```
<%
strFirstName = Request.Form("first_name")
%>
```

This will initialize the *strFirstName* variable to the value sent in the first_name parameter. The Form collection is discussed in detail later in this chapter.

The ASP Request Object

The properties, collections, methods, and events of the ASP Request object are shown in the following box.

Request Object Summary

Properties
> TotalBytes

Collections
> ClientCertificate
> Cookies
> Form
> QueryString
> ServerVariables

Methods
> BinaryRead

Events
> None

Comments/Troubleshooting

In the previous discussion of ASP and the GET and POST methods, we saw that information from a GET is retrieved by using the QueryString collection and that information from a POST is retrieved by using the Form collection. This is true, but there is a simpler way: you do not have to specify a collection. For example, the code:

```
strName = Request("name")
```

returns the value of the "name" key regardless of the collection in which it's located, because IIS searches all collections. When you specify a value in this manner, ASP looks through each Request object collection in the following order:

1. QueryString

2. Form

3. Cookies

4. ClientCertificate

5. ServerVariables

The variable you are initializing will receive the value in the first instance of the name/value pair whose name matches the string requested. For this reason, it is important to realize that if you have the same name/value pair in two or more collections, you will receive the first one found according to the preceding sequence, unless you specify a particular collection.

As with the other collections in the ASP object model, all the collections discussed in this chapter for the Request object support the Item and Key properties, the Count method, and the `For..Each` construct.

Properties Reference

TotalBytes

Var = `Request.TotalBytes`

The TotalBytes property is a read-only value that specifies the total number of bytes posted to the web server by the client in the HTTP request body. This property is important when preparing to read data from the request body using the BinaryRead method of the Request object.

Parameters

Var

> Receives the total number of bytes in the client's HTTP request body when it posts data to the web server. Remember that the TotalBytes property is read-only.

Example

In this example, assume that the user has responded to the following form:

```
<HTML>
<HEAD><TITLE>File Upload Form</TITLE></HEAD>
<BODY>
<FORM ENCTYPE = "multipart/form-data"
ACTION= "http://mycorp.com/secure.asp" METHOD="POST">
Select a file to upload:
<INPUT TYPE="file" NAME="filename"><BR>
<INPUT TYPE="submit" VALUE="Submit the form">
</FORM>
</BODY> </HTML>
```

You can use the TotalBytes property to determine exactly how many bytes of information were sent to the web server in the HTTP request:

```
<%
' The following code retrieves the total number of
' bytes sent in the user's HTTP request. This variable
' is then used to determine how many bytes to retrieve
' using the Request object's BinaryRead method.
Dim lngTotalByteCount
Dim vntRequestData

lngTotalByteCount = Request.TotalBytes

vntRequestData = Request.BinaryRead(lngTotalByteCount)

%>
```

Notes

Most often, you will not need to access data in the HTTP request body at the low level provided by the Request object's BinaryRead method and so will not need to retrieve the value of the TotalBytes property. You will use the Form and QueryString collections for almost all of your request data access.

 In the preceding example, the value of *vntRequestData* represents the *total* bytes sent, not just the byte count of the uploaded file; i.e., all header-related HTTP request information also counts toward this total. To retrieve from the preceding upload only the file contents, you would have to parse out the header information.

Collections Reference

ClientCertificate   Request.ClientCertificate

The ClientCertificate collection of the Request object provides access to the certification fields of the client's digital certificate. Client certificates are sent to the web server when a client's browser supports the Secure Sockets Layer and that browser is connected to a web server also running the Secure Sockets Layer (i.e., the URL starts with *https://* rather than *http://*). For example, if you were using Internet Explorer and were connected to an Internet Information Server web site with SSL running, each request made by your browser would include your client certificate, if you have one. The fields of a client certificate are specified in the International Telecommunications Union (ITU) recommendation X.509.

The ClientCertificate collection, like other ASP collections, has the following properties:

Item

Returns the value of a specific element in the collection. To specify an item, you can use an index number or a key.

Key

Represents the name of a specific element in the ClientCertificate collection. Just as each element's value is represented by the Item property, each element's name is represented by its Key property.

If you do not know the name of a specific key, you can obtain it using its ordinal reference. For example, assume that you want to learn the key name for the third element in the collection and, subsequently, that element's value. You could use the following code:

```
strKeyName = Request.ClientCertificate.Key(3)
strKeyValue = Request.ClientCertificate.Item(strKeyName)
```

If, on the other hand, you know that the third element's key name is "ISSUER," you could simply use the following code to retrieve the value of that element:

```
strKeyValue = Request.ClientCertificate.Item("ISSUER")
```

As with other ASP collections, you can retrieve the value of any field of the Client-Certificate collection through the use of the Item property. Note that, because Item is the default property of the collection, the syntax can be abbreviated so that it does not explicitly show the use of the Item property. For example:

```
strCertIssuer = Request.ClientCertificate("Issuer")
```

is only an abbreviated form of:

```
strCertIssuer = Request.ClientCertificate.Item("Issuer")
```

 For more information on the Item, Key, and Count properties of a collection, see the discussion in the section "Contents Collection" in Chapter 4, *Application Object*.

The available Key values are predefined and are as follows:

Certificate
> A string value that contains the entire binary stream from the certificate content. The content is retrieved in standard ASN.1 (Abstract Syntax Notation One) format, the international standard for representing data types and structures.

Flags
> A set of flags that provide additional information about the client's certificate. These flags are integer values that can be represented by the constants ceCertPresent and ceUnrecognizedIssuer if the VBScript include file *cervbs.inc* is included in your scripts (see Chapter 11, *Preprocessing Directives, Server-Side Includes, and GLOBAL.ASA*, for more on including files). As the constant names suggest, ceCertPresent signifies that a client certificate is present, and ceUnrecognizedIssuer signifies that the client's digital certificate was issued by an unknown certificate authority.

Issuer
> A string that contains several pieces of information about the issuer of the client's digital certificate. If no SubKey parameter (discussed later) is added, using the Issuer key returns a comma-delimited list of all the Issuer subfield values (e.g., C=US, O=VeriSign, GN=Weissinger, etc.).

SerialNumber
> An ASCII representation of the hexadecimal bytes of the client's certification serial number. This value is provided by the issuer. Retrieving the Serial-Number key would provide a number such as 0A-B7-34-23.

Subject
> A list of comma-delimited strings that provide information about the owner of the digital certificate. If no SubKey is provided, the entire comma-delimited list of subfields is retrieved, similar to that described for the Issuer key.

ValidFrom
> The date the certificate becomes valid. This key's value is provided as a date and time. For example, a possible value of the ValidFrom key (in the U.S.) could be 1/29/98 12:01:00 A.M.

ValidUntil

The date the certificate becomes invalid. This key's value is provided as a date and time. For example, a possible value of the ValidUntil key (in the U.S.) could be 1/28/99 11:59:59 P.M.

You can add a "subkey" to some of the Key values to retrieve an individual subfield from either the Issuer or Subject key lists. For example, if you wanted to obtain the country of origin subkey value from the Issuer key list, you would retrieve the value:

```
Request.ClientCertificate("IssuerC")
```

If you wanted to retrieve the locality subkey value from the Subject key list, you would retrieve its value using the syntax:

```
Request.ClientCertificate("SubjectL")
```

 You also can retrieve a value from a specific subkey, including those not listed here, from the Certificate key string value using the sub-key's ASN.1 identifier. An ASN.1 identifier is a list of numbers separated by a period, similar in appearance to an IP address, but not limited to 0 through 255. For example: 3.56.7886.34.

The available subkeys are as follows:

C   The country of origin for the Subject or Issuer.

CN The common name of the Subject key. Note this subkey is not defined for the Issuer key.

GN The given name of the Subject or Issuer.

I   The initials of the Subject or Issuer.

L   The locality of the Subject or Issuer.

O   The organization or company name of the Subject or Issuer.

OU The name of the specific organizational unit within an organization or company for a Subject or Issuer.

S   The state (or province) of the Subject or Issuer.

T   The title of the Subject or Issuer.

Example

```
<%

' The following code retrieves the country of origin
' for the client's certificate issuer.
strCertIssuerCountry = Request.ClientCertificate("IssuerC")

%>

<!-- #include file="cervbs.inc" -->
```

```
<%
' The next example code determines whether the
' issuer is recognized by using the flags key.
If Request.ClientCertificate("Flags") _
    and ceUnrecognizedIssuer Then
%>
    Your identification is in question because your issuer
    is not recognized.
<%
Else
%>
    Welcome to our site.
<%
End If

' Finally, the following code iterates through the
' ClientCertificate collection and writes the key-key
' value pairs to the response buffer.
For Each key In Request.ClientCertificate
    Response.Write "The " & key & " key contains the value "
    Response.Write Request.ClientCertificate(key) & "<BR>"
Next

%>
```

Notes

Before you can retrieve information from a client's digital certificate, you must ensure that the client's web browser uses the SSL3.0/PCT1 protocol in its requests to your site. The simplest way to do this is to attempt to retrieve an element from the ClientCertificate collection.

You also must ensure that you have set up your IIS web server to request client certificates.

If the client sends no digital certificate, any key you attempt to retrieve from the ClientCertificate collection will be empty.

The ITU Recommendation X.509 is just that—a recommendation. It has not been recognized as an official standard. For this reason, various companies' certificates may function slightly differently or may not contain all the fields you are attempting to retrieve. To ensure you are properly identifying your clients, it is wise to do some experimentation with the ClientCertificate collection before relying on it.

Request Object

Cookies

Request.Cookies

Before discussing the Cookies collection, we'll briefly introduce/review the concept of HTTP cookies. This will be only a brief overview. For more information, visit either the Netscape Preliminary Specification at *http://www.netscape.com/ newsref/std/cookie_spec.html*, or visit Cookie Central, a clearinghouse of all cookie-related information. I can specifically recommend *http://www.cookiecentral.com/ unofficial_cookie_faq.htm*.

The problem with a stateless protocol like HTTP is that it forces both the server and client to do a great deal of repetitive work. For example, with a truly stateless protocol, the web server would have to ask you who you are every single time you navigate to a page on the site—even if you navigate to this new page from another page within the same site. Likewise, your interaction would be limited to what you can enter and save on one page of information, because without some way of storing the data from one page, a second page has no way of getting to that data.

Netscape Communications Corp. foresaw this problem early on and devised a method by which small pieces of information could be stored by the web server on the web client's machine. This information would, in turn, be sent to the server each time the client requested a page from the same area from which she received the information. That little bit of information is at the root of Netscape's Persistent Client State Mechanism or "cookies," as they are known. (It's interesting to note that, according to the Netscape preliminary specification, this state object was called a cookie "for no compelling reason.")

Through the use of cookies, web servers can store information on the client machine in a safe, easy-to-retrieve fashion that makes almost all e-commerce possible. Web sites can now keep track of who you are, when you last visited, and what type of books you like, for example.

Cookies are very simple. They are sent to the client using a Set-Cookie HTTP response header in the following format (note that the Set-Cookie header should all be on one line):

```
Set-Cookie: NAME=VALUE; expires=DATE; domain=DOMAIN_NAME;
path=PATH; secure
```

The syntax breaks down as follows:

NAME=VALUE

The name/value pair of the specific cookie the web server wishes saved on the client machine. The value can contain any character but white space, commas, or semicolons. This part of the cookie is mandatory.

expires

Holds a date after which the browser can dispose of the cookie. If no expires attribute is given, this defaults to the end of the current HTTP session. The format of the expires date is the following:

```
Wdy, DD-Mon-YYYY HH:MM:SS GMT
```

Note that only Greenwich mean times are allowed.

domain

Each time the user navigates to a specific URL, the domain attributes of all the cookies on the user's machine are compared against the domain of the URL. If the domain attribute of any cookie on the user's machine matches the "tail" of the URL domain (the last two segments of the full domain name), then that cookie is sent as a Request header (more on this later) to that URL. A domain must have at least two periods in its name to set the domain attribute of a cookie sent to the client. For example, *www.microsoft.com* can send cookies to your machine (and does), but *mydomain.com* cannot. The actual value of the Microsoft-related cookie `domain` attribute would be `Microsoft.com`.

This cookie would thus be sent to any URL ending with *Microsoft.com*, including *www.microsoft.com*, *home.microsoft.com*. Likewise, only pages within this domain can set cookies with this domain attribute. For example, *www.microsoft.com* can send cookies with a domain of *Microsoft.com*, but *www.ora.com* cannot.

If no domain attribute is included in the cookie sent to the client browser, the default is the domain name of the sender of the cookie. This is an optional parameter.

path
:   The subset of URLs within the domain defined by the cookie's `domain` attribute. Its value determines whether the cookie is sent back to the server. If no path attribute is sent, the default is the path of the document the browser is viewing. For example, cookies from *http://www.oreilly.com/newtitles/ upcoming.ASP* without a path attribute set would default to `/newtitles/`. The browser will send cookies from this page only to those pages in this path. The most general path for a domain is "/". This is an optional attribute.

    This discussion of path brings up a sometimes confusing point. Does the browser's machine store one cookie for each page in a path or does it only store a single cookie that is used repeatedly? The answer is that the browser stores a cookie for each individual cookie value. There is no single cookie that contains those cookie values for the current page. Each cookie value has its own entry.

secure
:   When present for a cookie, instructs the browser to send this cookie only to pages within the path specified in the `path` property if the server and browser are communicating over a secure channel (HTTPS, for example).

If the user navigates to a URL for which a cookie is present on the local machine, the browser will send a Request header in the following format:

```
Cookie:Name1=Value1;Name2=Value2;   NameX=ValueX;
```

where:

NameX
:   Is the name of a cookie for that URL.

ValueX
:   Is the value of the corresponding cookie with the name *NameX*. This value must be a string with no spaces, semicolons, or commas.

An example will help to make this clearer. Suppose a client navigates to a URL and his browser receives the following HTTP response headers:

```
Set-Cookie: userid=a.keyton.weissinger; domain=yourbooks.com;
path=/; expires=Thursday, 10-Nov-2000 23:59:59

Set-Cookie: usersel=aspbooks; domain=yourbooks.com;
path=/sales/; expires=Monday, 01-Jan-2010 23:59:59
```

Between now and 10 November 2000 at 11:59 P.M., the first cookie will be sent to the web server any time the client navigates to any page within any domain whose last two segments are *yourbooks.com*. The HTTP request header will resemble the following:

```
Cookie: userid=a.keyton.weissinger
```

Between now and 1 January 2010 at 11:59 P.M., the second cookie will be sent to any page in the *yourbooks.com* domain whose path is */sales/something*. For example, the following cookie request header:

```
Cookie: usersel=aspbooks
```

would be sent to *http://www.yourbooks.com/sales/default.ASP* or to *http://www. yourbooks.com/sales/final/asp*, or even to *http://www.yourbooks.com/sales/ checkout/default.ASP*.

Finally, if both sets of criteria (for both cookies userid and usersel) are met, the following cookie header will be sent by the user browser:

```
Cookie: userid=a.keyton.weissinger; usersel=aspbooks
```

There are several other details about cookies that you should be aware of if you plan to make extensive use of them. See either of the preceding references for more information. With this brief overview concluded, we'll now move on to the Cookies collection of the Request object.

The Cookies collection of the Request object enables your ASP application to retrieve the values of cookies and cookie dictionary items from the client's HTTP request body.

The Cookies collection, like the other ASP collections, has the following properties:

Item

Represents the value of a specific cookie in the collection. To specify a cookie, you can use an index number or a key.

Key

Represents the name of a specific element in the Cookies collection. Just as each element's value is represented by the Item property, each element's name is represented by its Key property.

If you do not know the name of a specific key, you can obtain it using its ordinal reference. For example, assume that you want to learn the key name for the third element in the collection and, subsequently, that element's value. You could use the following code:

```
strKeyName = Request.Cookies.Key(3)
strKeyValue = Request.Cookies.Item(strKeyName)
```

If, on the other hand, you know that the third element's key name is "STATE," you could simply use the following code to retrieve the value of that element:

```
strKeyValue = Request.Cookies.Item("STATE")
```

Count

Represents the number of elements in the collection.

As with other ASP collections, you can retrieve the value of any field of the Cookies collection through the use of the Item property. Note that in the examples and explanations given here, the syntax has been abbreviated so that it does not explicitly show the use of the Item property. For example:

```
strLastSearch = Request.Cookies("LastSearch")
```

is only an abbreviated form of:

```
strLastSearch = Request.Cookies.Item("LastSearch")
```

 For more information on the Item, Key, and Count properties of a collection, see the discussion in the section "Contents Collection" in Chapter 4.

In addition to storing simple values, a cookie in the Cookies collection can represent a cookie dictionary. A dictionary is a construct that is similar to an associative array in that each element of the array is identifiable by its name.

However, it is important to note that although a cookie can contain a cookie dictionary, it cannot contain more complex data types, such as objects.

To determine a specific value within a cookie dictionary, you must use a SubKey. For example, suppose a specific cookie represents the five colors chosen by a user on a web page. The cookie itself is called Colors and the subkeys have the following names: color1, color2, . . . color5. To determine the value residing in color3, you would use code resembling the following:

```
strColor3 = Request.Cookies("Colors")("color3")
```

To determine whether a specific cookie has subkeys, you must use the HasKeys property of that specific cookie, as in the following:

```
blnHasKeys = Request.Cookies("Colors").HasKeys
If blnHasKeys Then
    strColor3 = Request.Cookies("Colors")("color3")
End If
```

Example

```
<%
' The following code iterates through the Cookies collection.
' If a given cookie represents a cookie dictionary, then
' a second, internal for...each construct iterates through
' it retrieving the value of each subkey in the dictionary.
Dim strCookie
Dim strSubKey

Dim str3rdCookieValue
Dim strCompanyCookieValue

For Each strCookie In Request.Cookies
    If Request.Cookies(strCookie).HasKeys Then

        ' The cookie is a dictionary. Iterate through it.
```

```
%>
        The cookie dictionary <%=strCookie%> has the
        following values:
<%

        For Each strSubKey In Request.Cookies(strCookie)
%>
                SubKey: <%= strSubKey %><BR>
                Value:
            <%=Request.Cookies(strCookie)(strSubKey)%><BR>
<%
        Next
    Else
        ' The cookie represents a single value.
%>
        The cookie <%=strCookie%> has the following value:
        <%=Request.Cookies(strCookie)%> <BR>
<%
    End If

Next

    ' The following code retrieves the value of the third cookie
    ' in the Cookies collection.
    str3rdCookieValue = Request.Cookies(3)

    ' The following code retrieves the value of the "company"
    ' cookie in the Cookies collection.
    strCompanyCookieValue = Request.Cookies("Company")

%>
```

Notes

When accessing a cookie that represents a cookie dictionary, if you do not specify a subkey, you will retrieve a string value similar to the following:

```
FirstSubKey=FirstSubKeyValue&SecondSubKey=SecondSubKeyValue
```

Part of the cookie structure on the client's machine is a path representing the web page from which the client received the cookie. An important point about retrieving cookie values comes into play when two cookies with the same name, but different paths, exist. In such a case, attempting to retrieve the cookie will retrieve only the cookie from the deeper directory. For example, if the web page *http://www.MyCompany.com/ContribApp/Contrib1.ASP* has a cookie named UserPref and a second web page with a deeper path, for example, *http://www.MyCompany.com/ContribApp/Addresses/AddrContrib1.ASP*, also has a cookie named UserPref, then attempting to retrieve the UserPref cookie will retrieve only the second UserPref cookie.

If you attempt to retrieve the value of a subkey for a cookie name that does not represent a cookie dictionary, the result will be null. For this reason, it is important to take advantage of the HasKeys property before attempting to retrieve the value of a subkey.

As you know, the HTTP Persistent Client State Mechanism (cookies to most people) is a continuously evolving recommendation. Any cookie draft remains valid for only six months. The current draft, as of this writing, can be found at *ftp://ftp.isi.edu/internet-drafts/draft-ietf-http-state-man-mec-08.txt*.

From this document (or its more recent equivalent), you will learn that the latest draft for the cookies specification goes far beyond that originally proposed by Netscape. Obviously, the current Cookies collection of the Request object supports only some of this specification. It is assumed that as the draft becomes a standard, more aspects of cookies will be retrievable through the Request Cookies collection.

Form

The Form collection allows you to retrieve the information input into an HTML form on the client and sent to the server using the POST method. This information resides in the body of the HTTP request sent by the client.

The Form collection, like the other ASP collections, has the following properties:

Item

Represents the value of a specific element in the collection. To specify an item, you can use an index number or a key. In the case of the Form collection, the index number represents the number of the element on the HTML form. For example, suppose you have the following HTML form:

```
<FORM ACTION = "RecordPrefs.asp" METHOD = POST>
Name: <INPUT TYPE = TEXT NAME = "Name"><BR>
Color Pref: <SELECT NAME = "optColor">
<OPTION VALUE = "red" SELECTED>Red
<OPTION VALUE = "blue" >Blue
<OPTION VALUE = "green" >Green
</SELECT><BR>
Have a Modem? <INPUT TYPE = CHECKBOX NAME = "Modem"><BR>
<INPUT TYPE=submit VALUE=submit>
</FORM>
```

From within RecordPrefs.asp, the first element (element 1) is "Name." The third element is "Modem." Note that the numbering begins with 1 (one).

Key

Represents the name of a specific element in the Form collection. Just as each element's value is represented by the Item property, so each element's name is represented by its Key property.

If you do not know the name of a specific key, you can obtain it using its ordinal reference. For example, assume that you want to learn the key name for the third element in the collection and, subsequently, that element's value. You could use the following code:

```
strKeyName = Request.Form.Key(3)
strKeyValue = Request.Form.Item(strKeyName)
```

If, on the other hand, you know that the third element's key name is "STATE," you could simply use the following code to retrieve the value of that element:

```
strKeyValue = Request.Form.Item("STATE")
```

Note that you cannot always count on the order with which the Form elements are stored. For example, you may have eight items in your submitted form. You have no way of knowing that the first element in your form is the first element of the Form collection. For this reason, you should always use a key string to identify the specific element of the Form collection that you want.

Count

Returns the number of elements in the collection.

As with other ASP collections, you can retrieve the value of any field of the Form collection through the use of the Item property. Note that in the following examples and explanations, the syntax has been abbreviated so that it does not explicitly show the use of the Item property. For example:

```
strFirstName = Request.Form("txtFirstName")
```

is only an abbreviated form of:

```
strFirstName = Request.Form.Item("txtFirstName")
```

 For more information on the Item, Key, and Count properties of a collection, see the discussion in the section "Contents Collection" in Chapter 4.

Example

The examples of the Form collection of the Request object will all use the following HTML form:

```
<HTML>
<HEAD>
<TITLE>User Information</TITLE>
</HEAD>
<BODY>
<CENTER>
<H1>User Information</H1>
Please enter your user information using the form below:
<FORM NAME = "frmInfo" ACTION="UserInfo.ASP"
      METHOD = "POST">
First Name:  <INPUT TYPE="text" NAME = "txtFirstName"><BR>
Last Name:   <INPUT TYPE="text" NAME = "txtLastName"><BR>
Zipcode:     <INPUT TYPE="text" NAME = "txtZipCode"><BR>
Occupation:  <INPUT TYPE="text" NAME = "txtOccupation"><BR>
Please select your connection speed:
<SELECT NAME = "optConnSpeed">
<OPTION VALUE = "28.8" SELECTED>28.8 Modem
<OPTION VALUE = "ISDN" >ISDN
<OPTION VALUE = "T1" >T1
<OPTION VALUE = "T3" >T3
</SELECT><BR>
```

```
Below, select all the peripherals you have:
<INPUT TYPE = "checkbox" NAME = "chkPeriph"
      VALUE = "Joystick">Joystick<BR>
<INPUT TYPE = "checkbox" NAME = "chkPeriph"
      VALUE= "GraphicsAccel">3D Graphics Card<BR>
<INPUT TYPE = "checkbox" NAME = "chkPeriph"
       VALUE = "Printer">Printer<BR>
<BR>
Check here if it's ok to send your information:
<INPUT TYPE = "checkbox" NAME = "chkSellInfo"><BR>

<INPUT TYPE = "Submit" VALUE = "Submit User Info">

</FORM>
</BODY>
</HTML>
```

Once the client clicks on the form's Submit button, the form information is sent to the web server via the HTTP Post method in the body of the HTTP request body.

The following code could be used in *UserInfo.ASP* to determine the values of the specific elements of the form frmInfo in the previous example. It is assumed in the following code that you know before writing it the exact fields in the form that are to be processed.

```
<%

' The following code example demonstrates the use of
' the Form collection of the Request object to retrieve
' the values entered by the client into an HTML form.
Dim strFirstName
Dim strLastName
Dim strZipCode
Dim strOccupation
Dim blnSendInfo
Dim strConnSpeed
Dim intPeriphCount
Dim aryPeripherals()
Dim chkItem

intPeriphCount = 0

' Retrieve the information from the form's text boxes.
strFirstName    = Request.Form("txtFirstName")
strLastName     = Request.Form("txtLastName")
strZipCode      = Request.Form("txtZipCode")
strOccupation   = Request.Form("txtOccupation")

' Retrieve the information from the Sell Information
' checkbox.
blnSendInfo     = Request.Form("chkSellInfo")

' Determine the connection speed from the Connection
' Speed option buttons.
strConnSpeed    = Request.Form("optConnSpeed")
```

```
' Populate an array with the peripherals the user has.
For Each SubKey in Request.Form("chkPeriph")
   ReDim Preserve aryPeripherals(intPeriphCount + 1)
   intPeriphCount = intPeriphCount + 1
   aryPeripherals(intPeriphCount) = _
      Request.Form("chkPeriph")(intPeriphCount)

Next
%>
```

Notes

If you refer to an element without an index and that element contains multiple values, your code will return a comma-delimited string. For example, suppose that instead of using a subkey with the chkPeriph element of the Form collection earlier in this chapter, we included the following line of code:

```
response.write Request.Form("chkPeriph")
```

Assuming we chose all three options (Joystick, GraphicsAccel, and Printer), this line of code would result in the following string:

```
Joystick, GraphicsAccel, Printer
```

Your application also can retrieve unparsed data from the client's HTTP request. To retrieve unparsed data from the HTTP request body, use Request.Form without any parameters. Note that the use of unparsed HTTP request data—specifically binary data—in this manner can be problematic. However, there are several ActiveX controls and Java applets that can be used to retrieve binary data more efficiently.

To submit information from an HTML form to an ASP application, you must set the <FORM> tag's ACTION attribute to the name of the file that will process the HTML form data. This Active Server Page can be in the same virtual directory or can be specified in terms of its virtual directory. You can do this from an HTML page or from another ASP file. However, one of the most powerful uses of this process is the construction of an ASP that calls itself. This is not necessarily faster, but its development is more efficient.

The following example demonstrates a simple ASP that constructs an HTML form whose entered data is processed by the same ASP:

```
<%
' UserInfo2.ASP
' The following code determines whether the HTML form (see
' the bottom portion of the script) has been filled out. If
' it has, then some processing takes place and one HTML output
' is sent back to the client. If not, the HTML form is sent to
' the client.
If Not IsEmpty(Request.Form("txtFirstName")) And _
   Not IsEmpty(Request.Form("txtLastName")) Then

   ' The form has been filled out and the reply is
   ' a brief thank you.
%>
```

```
<HTML>
<HEAD><TITLE>Thank You</TITLE>
</HEAD>
<BODY>
    Thank you, <%= Request.Form("txtFirstName")%> 
<%= Request.Form("txtLastName")%> for your information.
Have a nice day.
    </BODY>
    </HTML>
<%
Else
%>
    <HTML>
    <HEAD><TITLE>Thank You</TITLE>
    </HEAD>
    <BODY>

    <FORM NAME = "frmInfo" ACTION="UserInfo2.ASP"
          METHOD = "POST">
    First Name:  <INPUT TYPE="text" NAME="txtFirstName"><BR>
    Last Name:   <INPUT TYPE="text" NAME="txtLastName"><BR>

    <INPUT TYPE = "Submit" VALUE = "Submit User Info">

    </FORM>
    </BODY>
    </HTML>
<%
End If

%>
```

This script first determines whether the form elements have been filled out by the client. If so, then this script sends a brief "Thank You" to the client and the script ends. If the information was not entered, the form is presented to the user. This technique, though it uses only a rudimentary form here, is very powerful and can significantly help you to modularize your code, a sometimes difficult task in ASP application development.

If your HTML form contains ActiveX controls in addition to (or instead of) standard HTML form elements, you can refer to their values in the same manner. For example, suppose you have the following (simple) HTML form containing a single Microsoft Forms 2.0 textbox:

```
<FORM NAME = "frmInfo" ACTION="UserInfo.ASP"
      METHOD = "POST">
First Name:
<OBJECT NAME = "txtFirstName" WIDTH=211 HEIGHT=20
   CLASSID="CLSID:8BD21D10-EC42-11CE-9E0D-00AA006002F3">
   <PARAM NAME="VariousPropertyBits" VALUE="746604571">
   <PARAM NAME="BackColor" VALUE="16777215">
   <PARAM NAME="MaxLength" VALUE="255">
   <PARAM NAME="Size" VALUE="5574;529">
   <PARAM NAME="Value" VALUE="">
   <PARAM NAME="BorderColor" VALUE="0">
```

```
      <PARAM NAME="FontCharSet" VALUE="0">
      <PARAM NAME="FontPitchAndFamily" VALUE="2">
      <PARAM NAME="FontWeight" VALUE="0">
   </OBJECT>
   <INPUT TYPE = "Submit" VALUE = "Submit User Info">

   </FORM>
```

You could refer to the value entered into the textbox from *UserInfo.ASP* using the following line of code:

```
   strFirstName = Request.Form("txtFirstName")
```

If you have an HTML form containing ActiveX controls whose values are validated using client-side script, make sure that none of your elements (the submission button, for example) have the name Submit. This seems like a small point, but if you overlook it, you will not be able to submit your form! Try it.

Remember that data in the Form collection represents only that data in the HTTP request body. You also can use the HTTP Get method to send data from the client to the server. Using Get results in the information being sent from the client in the HTTP request header. To retrieve this data, you must use the Request object's QueryString collection.

QueryString   Request.QueryString(*element*)[(*key*)|.Count]

The QueryString collection allows you to retrieve the information sent by the client using the HTTP Get method with an HTML form and data appended to the URL when the page is requested. The QueryString collection is less capable than the Form collection, since there is a limit to the amount of data that can be sent in the header of an HTTP request. In my experience, this limit is around 2000 characters. More characters than this, sent as part of the QueryString, will not be processed, although the script still executes.

The QueryString collection, like the other ASP collections, has the following properties:

Item

> Returns the value of a specific element in the collection. To specify an item, you can use an index number or a key. In the case of the QueryString collection, the index number represents the number of the element as it appears in the URL or the number of the element on the HTML form (assuming a GET method is used to send the data). If the POST method is used to submit form data, however, these HTML elements do not exist in the QueryString collection, but rather in the Form collection of the Request object.

Key

> Returns the name of a specific element in the QueryString collection. Just as each element's value is represented by the Item property, each element's name is represented by its Key property.

> If you do not know the name of a specific key, you can obtain it using its ordinal reference. For example, assume that you want to learn the key name

---

for the third element in the collection and, subsequently, that element's value. You could use the following code:

```
strKeyName = Request.QueryString.Key(3)
strKeyValue = Request.QueryString.Item(strKeyName)
```

If, on the other hand, you know that the third element's key name is "STATE," you could simply use the following code to retrieve the value of that element:

```
strKeyValue = Request.QueryString.Item("STATE")
```

Count

The number of elements in the collection.

As with other ASP collections, you can retrieve the value of any field of the QueryString collection through the use of the Item property. Note that in the following examples and explanations, the syntax has been abbreviated so that it does not explicitly show the use of the Item property. For example:

```
strFirstName = Request.QueryString("FirstName")
```

is only an abbreviated form of:

```
strFirstName = Request.QueryString.Item("FirstName")
```

 For more information on the Item, Key, and Count properties of a collection, see the discussion in the section "Contents Collection" in Chapter 4.

Example

```
<%
' This code iterates through the QueryString collection
' and fills an array with the values retrieved.
Dim item
Dim aryQueryValues()
Dim intItemCount

intItemCount = 0

For Each item In Request.QueryString
    ReDim Preserve aryQueryValues(intItemCount + 1)
    aryQueryValues(intItemCount) = _
                Request.QueryString(item)
    intItemCount = intItemCount + 1
Next
%>
```

Notes

Like the elements of the Form collection, elements of the QueryString collection can represent multiple values. For example, suppose your ASP file receives a submission from the following HTML form:

```
<FORM NAME = "frmInfo" ACTION="UserInfo2.ASP"
    METHOD = "GET">
```

```
Below, select all the peripherals you have:
<INPUT TYPE = "checkbox" NAME = "chkPeriph" VALUE =
   "Joystick">Joystick<BR>
<INPUT TYPE = "checkbox" NAME = "chkPeriph" VALUE=
   "GraphicsAccel">3D Graphics Card<BR>
</FORM>
```

Assume the user checks both checkboxes. The resulting information would be interpreted in the ASP exactly as if the ASP had been requested using the following URL:

```
UserInfo2.ASP?chkPeriph=Joystick&chkPeriph=GraphicsAccel
```

To refer to the first element, you could use the following code (note that like other ASP collections, the elements start at 1):

```
strFirstOption = Request.QueryString("chkPeriph")(1)
```

If you do not specify a subkey, as in:

```
strOptions = Request.QueryString("chkPeriph")
```

then *strOptions* would have the following value:

```
Joystick, GraphicsAccel
```

Also like the Form collection, the QueryString collection contains information sent from the client to the web server. This information can be in the form of parameter/value pairs appended to the end of the requested URL in the HTTP request header, appended to the URL in the address field of the browser, or from an HTML form whose action is set to the HTTP Get method.

There are some limitations to the use of the QueryString collection, the most important of which is its limited length. Although this length varies with the amounts of client and web server available memory, you should not count on being able to send more than ~1800 characters from the client to the server using the QueryString collection. This ~1800-character "limit" is counted from the end of the script name being called to the end of the parameter list appended to the requested URL, including the names, not just the values, of the parameters sent.

Like elements of the Form collection, elements of the QueryString collection can contain multiple values. To determine the number of values available for a specific element of the collection, use the Count property of the element in question. The value of the Count property is equal to the number of values contained in the element and is zero (0) if the element is not in the collection.

You can retrieve all the values for a given multiple-value element by leaving off the index parameter for the specific element. The values are returned as a comma-delimited string containing only the values from the element being addressed.

Also like the Form collection, you are able to retrieve unparsed data in the QueryString collection. To retrieve the raw, unparsed QueryString collection data, use the syntax Request.QueryString without any element parameter.

The data in the QueryString collection is also accessible from the ServerVariables collection of the Request object, using the HTTP_QUERYSTRING parameter. This is covered in more depth in the section on the ServerVariables collection.

Finally, note that you must encode several special characters when used in the QueryString:

&   The ampersand is used by ASP to delineate separate parameter/value pairs that have been added to the QueryString collection.

?   The question mark delineates the beginning of the QueryString that is added after the filename extension in the filename requested in the URL from the client.

%   The percentage symbol is used in the encoding of other special characters.

+   The plus sign is recognized in the QueryString as representing a space.

These characters can be encoded automatically using the URLEncode and HTMLEncode methods of the Server object on the server side and custom script on the client side.

ServerVariables   *Var* = Request.ServerVariables(*key*)

The ServerVariables collection contains several predefined environment variables in the context of the client's specific HTTP request of the web server.

The ServerVariables collection, like the other ASP collections, has the following properties:

Item
> The value of a specific element in the collection. To specify an item, you can use an index number or a key.

Key
> Returns the name of a specific element in the ServerVariables collection. Just as each element's value is represented by the Item property, each element's name is represented by its Key property.

> If you do not know the name of a specific key, you can obtain it using its ordinal reference. For example, assume that you want to learn the key name for the third element in the collection and, subsequently, that element's value. You could use the following code:

```
strKeyName = Request.ServerVariables.Key(3)
strKeyValue = Request.ServerVariables.Item(strKeyName)
```

> If, on the other hand, you know that the third element's key name is "QUERY_STRING," you could simply use the following code to retrieve the value of that element:

```
strKeyValue = _
        Request.ServerVariables.Item("QUERY_STRING")
```
> Or, simply:

```
strKeyValue = Request.ServerVariables("QUERY_STRING")
```

Count
> The number of elements in the collection.

As with other ASP collections, you can retrieve the value of any field of the Server-Variables collection through the use of the Item property. Note that in the following examples and explanations (and in nearly all examples from other sources), the syntax has been abbreviated so that it does not explicitly show the use of the Item property. For example:

```
strRemoteAddr = Request.ServerVariables("REMOTE_ADDR")
```

is only an abbreviated form of:

```
strRemoteAddr = Request.ServerVariables.Item("REMOTE_ADDR")
```

 For more information on the Item, Key, and Count properties of a collection, see the discussion in the section "Contents Collection" in Chapter 4.

The possible values for *Key* are in the following list. Although they typically appear in uppercase, *Key* is actually case insensitive. Note that like elements from other ASP collections, the element values from the ServerVariables collection also can be retrieved using an index number. However, it is important to realize that the following list is in alphabetical order, not in the order in which the elements exist in the ServerVariables collection.

ALL_HTTP

One long string containing all the HTTP headers sent by the client's browser. Each of the following elements can be parsed from this element.

ALL_RAW

One long string containing all the HTTP headers in their original state as sent by the client browser. The primary difference between the ALL_RAW and the ALL_HTTP values is that the values of the ALL_HTTP element are all prefixed with HTTP_ and the header name is always capitalized. Each of the following elements can be parsed from this element.

APPL_MD_PATH

Internally, the IIS metabase holds all the settings of the server. It is similar in function to the registry except for the fact that the metabase holds only information about those items added (as snap-ins) into the Microsoft Management Console. This can include Internet Information Server, Index Server, and SQL Server 7.0, among others. The information in the metabase almost exclusively represents installation and configuration information.

The APPL_MD_PATH element of the ServerVariables collection represents the metabase-specific path for the ISAPI DLL. This is the metabase path from which the ISAPI DLL is called, not its physical location on the server. For example, on my Windows 95 machine (running Personal Web Server) the value of this element is the following:

```
/LM/W3SVC/1/ROOT
```

APPL_PHYSICAL_PATH

The physical path of the APPL_MD_PATH element. This value is retrieved from the conversion of APPL_MD_PATH by IIS. For example, on my system this translates to C:\Inetpub\wwwroot\.

AUTH_PASSWORD

If IIS security is set to Basic Authentication, `AUTH_PASSWORD` represents the password entered in the authentication box when the client logs into the web server. If a password is not supplied, its value is a null string.

AUTH_TYPE

The method of authentication set on the web server. This authentication method is used to validate all users requesting scripts on the server protected by Windows NT security.

AUTH_USER

The raw username entered upon authentication of the client by the web server.

CERT_COOKIE

A unique ID for the client's digital certificate. The value for this element can be used as a signature for the entire certificate. This element has a value only for clients using the HTTPS protocol. Note that the ClientCertificate collection contains all client-related digital certificate information. The ClientCertificate collection is easier to use than the HTTP header information. Note also that if the client does not send a digital certificate, these `CERT_` elements still exist in the ServerVariables collection, but they are empty (i.e., they have no value).

CERT_FLAGS

`CERT_FLAGS` represents a two-bit value. Bit #0 is set to 1 if the client certificate is present. Bit #1 is set to 1 if the client certificate's certifying authority is invalid (i.e., the issuer is not found in the list of verified certificate issuers that resides on the web server). Note that these values correspond to the `ceCertPresent` and `ceUnrecognizedIssuer` constants for the Flags element of the ClientCertificate collection.

CERT_ISSUER

The issuer of the client certificate, if one exists. The value of this element is a comma-delimited string that contains the subfields for each of the possible subelements described in the Issuer element section of the ClientCertificate collection explanation earlier in this chapter.

CERT_KEYSIZE

The number of bits used in the Secure Sockets Layer connection key size (for example, 64 or 128).

CERT_SECRETKEYSIZE

The number of bits in the secret server certificate private key (for example, 1024).

CERT_SERIALNUMBER

The value of the client's certificate serial number.

CERT_SERVER_ISSUER

The issuer of the server certificate.

CERT_SERVER_SUBJECT

The subject field of the server certificate. Like the Subject field of the client certificate, this element's value is a comma-delimited string containing the subfields described in the Subject element section of the ClientCertificate collection description.

CERT_SUBJECT

The subject field of the client certificate. This element's value is a comma-delimited string containing the subfields described in the Subject element section of the ClientCertificate collection description.

CONTENT_LENGTH

The total length of the body of the HTTP request body sent by the client. You can use this value to determine the length of the raw HTTP content in the client's HTTP request. This value does not include the length of any data presented through the request header (i.e., information sent with a GET method), only that information in the request body.

CONTENT_TYPE

This is the MIME type of the content sent by the client. When used with HTTP queries that contain attached information (such as HTTP GET, POST, and PUT actions), this can allow you to determine the data type of the client's HTTP request content data. The most common value for this element is application/x-www-form-urlencoded. If you were to include a file element in your HTML form, you would set the ENCTYPE parameter (and thus the CONTENT_TYPE header in your request) to multipart/form-data.

GATEWAY_INTERFACE

The revision of the Common Gateway Interface that is used by the web server. This string value is in the format CGI/*revision* #. For example, if you were connected to an IIS 4.0 web server, the value of this item would be CGI/1.1.

HTTP_[HeaderName]

The value sent in the HTTP header called *headername*. To retrieve the value of any HTTP header not mentioned in this list (including custom headers), you must prefix the header name with HTTP_. Note that if you specify an HTTP_CUSTOM_SELECTION header, IIS will actually look for an HTTP header labeled as Custom-Header by the client in its HTTP request. In other words, when looking for an HTTP header with hyphens in the name in the ServerVariables collection, use underscores instead. Note that attempting to retrieve a nonexistent header returns an empty string, not an error. For example, each of the following:

HTTP_ACCEPT
HTTP_AUTHORIZATION (same as the AUTH_TYPE element)
HTTP_ACCEPT-LANGUAGE
HTTP_CONNECTION
HTTP_HOST
HTTP_REFERER
HTTP_USER-AGENT

requires code resembling the following to receive its value:

```
strUserAgent = _
        Request.ServerVariables("HTTP_USER_AGENT")
```

HTTPS

This element's value is the string "ON" if the client's HTTP request was sent using SSL. It is "OFF" otherwise.

HTTPS_KEYSIZE
>The same as CERT_KEYSIZE described earlier.

HTTPS_SECRETKEYSIZE
>The same as CERT_SECRETKEYSIZE described earlier.

HTTPS_SERVER_ISSUER
>The same as CERT_SERVER_ISSUER described earlier.

HTTPS_SERVER_SUBJECT
>The same as CERT_SERVER_SUBJECT described earlier.

INSTANCE_ID
>The ID of the current IIS instance specified in textual format. If this element evaluates to 1, then the value is a string. The INSTANCE_ID represents the number of the instance of the web server to which this request belongs. This is useful only if there is more than one instance of the web server running on your server. Otherwise, this value is always 1, representing the first (and only) instance of the web server on the machine.

INSTANCE_META_PATH
>The path in the metabase for the instance of IIS to which the client's HTTP request is sent. As discussed in the earlier section on the APPL_MD_PATH element of the ServerVariables collection, the metabase holds information specific to the installation and configuration of your web server. For my machine running Personal Web Server, the value of this element is /LM/W3SVC/1.

LOCAL_ADDR
>The TCP/IP address of the web server that is accepting the client HTTP request. This element of the ServerVariables collection is especially important when your web server resides in a server farm of several machines with distinct IP addresses, all answering requests to the same domain name. If the server is accessed as *localhost*, its value is 127.0.0.1.

LOGON_USER
>The Windows NT user account with which the user has logged onto the system. This is true regardless of the security type you have set for your web server (i.e., anonymous, basic, or Windows NT challenge/response).

PATH_INFO
>The virtual path of the web page from which the client makes its HTTP request. If this information evaluates to a virtual directory, the virtual directory is mapped to a physical directory before it is sent to the CGI filter.

PATH_TRANSLATED
>The virtual-to-physical mapping of the value of the PATH_INFO element of the ServerVariables collection.

QUERY_STRING
>The values sent by the client after the question mark (?) at the end of the HTTP request URL. This element also contains the information sent to the web server using the HTTP GET method. All the information in this element is also available via the QueryString collection (which is easier to utilize, as it does not require parsing).

Request
Object

REMOTE_ADDR

The TCP/IP address of the client.

REMOTE_HOST

The IP address from which the web server receives the client's HTTP request. If the HTTP request does not include this information, the `REMOTE_ADDR` element's value will be set and this value will be empty.

REQUEST_METHOD

The method by which the client made the HTTP request (`GET`, `POST`, `HEAD`, etc.).

SCRIPT_NAME

The entire virtual path to the current script. It does not include the base portion of the URL, which is represented by the URL element of the Server-Variables collection. It is used (largely internally) for self-referencing URLs. This is equivalent to the value of the `PATH_INFO` element.

SERVER_NAME

The web server's TCP/IP address, its DNS or hostname as it would appear in a self-referencing URL.

SERVER_PORT

The server port to which the client's HTTP request is sent. This is typically 80 or 8080 for most web servers.

SERVER_PORT_SECURE

If the HTTP request is being managed by the web server on a secure port, this value evaluates to 1. If the port is not secure, this value is 0.

SERVER_PROTOCOL

The name and version of the protocol used by the web server to handle the client request. For example, if the client is using Microsoft Internet Explorer 4.01 and the web server is IIS 4.0, this value is the string "HTTP/1.1."

SERVER_SOFTWARE

The name and version of the web server software handling the client HTTP request. For example, again using Microsoft IIS 4.0, an example value for this element of the ServerVariables collection is Microsoft-IIS/4.0.

URL

The base URL requested by the client in its HTTP request.

Example

```
<%

' The following code determines the value of the
' LOGON_USER item of the ServerVariables collection. This
' code can be used to determine the identity of the
' client.
Dim strUserName

strUserName = Request.ServerVariables("LOGON_USER")

%>
```

Notes

As the list earlier in this section illustrates, the ServerVariables collection contains many very useful pieces of information regarding the client's HTTP request. Perhaps the most important elements allow you to determine the identity and address of the user. These elements allow you to customize your security efforts.

Also, many of the Request object's other collections' data can be obtained through the ServerVariables collection (usually with more effort, however).

Methods Reference

BinaryRead   *MySafeArray=Request.BinaryRead(ByteCount)*

The BinaryRead method reads a number of bytes directly from the HTTP request body sent by the client as part of an HTTP Post. The data read from an HTTP request using the BinaryRead method is returned into a SafeArray. A *SafeArray* is a special variant array that contains, in addition to its items, the number of dimensions in the array and the upper bounds of the array.

 In actuality, a SafeArray is not an array at all. It's a special type of structure used internally to maintain information held in its array portion. The dimensions and upper bounds values are available only from C/C++ as elements of the structure. You cannot manipulate these values (or even retrieve them) through script.

Parameters

MySafeArray

> The name of a SafeArray used to store the information returned from a BinaryRead.

ByteCount

> The number of bytes read using the BinaryRead method. Typically, this variable's value evaluates to the number of bytes returned using the TotalBytes property of the Request object described previously.

Example

```
<%

' The following code determines the total number of bytes
' sent in the client's HTTP request. It then reads the
' bytes, checks for errors, and if there are none,
' reports to the client that the read was successful.
Dim lngTotalByteCount
Dim vntRequestData

On Error Resume Next

lngTotalByteCount = Request.TotalBytes
```

```
vntRequestData = Request.BinaryRead(lngTotalByteCount)
If Err = 0 Then
    ' For details about the Response object, see Chapter 8.
    ' For now, suffice it to say the following code sends
    ' information to the client.
    Response.Clear
    Response.Write lngTotalByteCount & _
                    " bytes successfully read.<BR>"
    Response.End
End If

%>
```

Notes

If your web application's client piece could control exactly what was sent in the HTTP request body, this method would be invaluable, since it would enable your client to upload information on a byte level (or upload files). However, controlling the information sent in a Post request at byte level is difficult. There are, however, several file-transfer controls available via third parties that allow you to add file-transfer functionality to your application more efficiently and with less difficulty.

It is important to note that if you have previously retrieved information from the Form collection of the Request object, subsequent calls to the BinaryRead method will cause an error. Likewise, if you have previously called the BinaryRead method of the Request object and subsequently attempt to retrieve information from the Form collection, your script will result in an error.

CHAPTER 8

Response Object

Just as the Request object allows you to retrieve and manipulate information sent by the client browser in its HTTP request, the Response object gives you a great deal of control over the HTTP response to the client. This control comes in three broad categories:

- Control over what data and data types are sent to the client in the headers of the HTTP response

- Control over what data and data types are sent to the client in the body of the HTTP response

- Control over when and how that data is sent

Control over the HTTP response headers includes setting cookies on the client machine, setting various preexisting HTTP header values (such as the content type and expiration information for a given page), and, finally, adding your own custom headers to the HTTP response.

You control the HTTP response body directly through the Write and BinaryWrite methods. As you might infer from the names, these methods of the Response object allow you to write information directly to the response body, which will be received by the client just like any other information received in an HTML request response.

Finally, the Response object allows you to control how and when the response is sent to the client. For example, using the properties and methods involved in buffering the response, you can determine whether to send the HTTP response as a single unit to the client or to send the results of the request piecemeal. You can dynamically determine whether the client is still connected to your web site. You can redirect her request as though she requested something else. Finally, you can use the Response object to write entries into the web server log.

Response Object Summary

Properties
  Buffer
  CacheControl
  Charset
  ContentType
  Expires
  ExpiresAbsolute
  IsClientConnected
  PICS
  Status

Collections
  Cookies

Methods
  AddHeader
  AppendToLog
  BinaryWrite
  Clear
  End
  Flush
  Redirect
  Write

Events
  None

Comments/Troubleshooting

As you will see, the many methods of the Response object give you powerful control over what you can send to the client in the headers and body of the HTTP response. However, one of the most valuable uses for the Response object is in debugging your scripts. Although Microsoft's Internet Information Server 4.0 does allow for server-side debugging, these debugging tools—at least currently—are sometimes not quite as functional as you need them to be when working on some piece of have-to-finish code. The Response object allows you to view the current state of your server-side scripts on the fly, as follows.

Assume you want to view the current value for your server-side variable, *strMyValue*, at a certain place in your script. You can insert the following code and view the value anywhere in your script:

```
Response.Clear
Response.Write "The value of strMyValue is " & strMyValue
Response.End
```

Although simple, this code actually does three very important things. First, it clears the buffer (assuming your Buffer property is set to True) that the output of your server scripting has been filling to be sent to the browser. Next, it inserts only a single line of text displaying your variable's value. Finally—and this is very important—it completely ends processing of your server script and sends the contents of the Response object's buffer to the user. No code after Response.End is processed! This can be invaluable for those pieces of code that work up until a certain point but not afterward.

Properties Reference

Buffer

Response.Buffer[=*blnSetting*]

The Buffer property determines whether the content created by your script is delivered to the client browser as a whole or sent immediately to the client browser as each line is created and entered into the HTML stream. If set to **True**, then all scripts on the page are run before the results of that script are sent to the client browser.

The default value for the Buffer property is **False** unless you set ASPBufferingOn in the metabase (through a Windows Scripting Host script or through the Microsoft Management Console for your web site). If set in the metabase, the value there can be overridden using the Buffer property on a page. For example, if you set ASPBufferingOn to **True**, you could later use the Buffer property to override this behavior and force IIS not to buffer the page.

Parameters

blnSetting
> Specifies whether the HTTP response that results from the web server's processing of your script is buffered and then sent to the client or sent to the client as it is created:

True
> Causes the web server to buffer all results of your script until all processing is complete or until the Flush or End method of the Response object is invoked. Note that even if buffering is set to **True**, if you call the End method, the contents of the buffer are sent to the client and all subsequent results from the processing of your script are *not* sent to the client.

False
> Instructs the web server to send information to the client as your script is processed, instead of waiting until all processing is complete. Note that if Buffer is set to **False**, any call to the Clear, End, or Flush methods of the Response object will result in a runtime error.

Example

Consider the following example. Note that we haven't set the Buffer property of the Response object explicitly, so it's **False**:

```
<%@ LANGUAGE="VBScript" %>
<HTML>

<%
CODE THAT RETRIEVES A FIELD VALUE FROM A DATABASE
%>
```

The response is not buffered before it is sent to the requesting browser. For this reason, if the previous database action results in an error, the user will see half a page ending in an error notice. Now examine the second code example:

```
<%@ LANGUAGE="VBScript" %>
<%Response.Buffer = True %>
<HTML>

<%
On Error Resume Next
' CODE THAT RETRIEVES A FIELD VALUE FROM A DATABASE
If Err.Number <> 0 Then
    Response.Clear
    Response.Write "There has been an error. Here is the SQL"
    Response.Write "statement that caused the problem: "
    Response.Write strSQL
    Response.End
End If
%>
```

In this second example, the response is buffered first and completed before it is sent to the requesting browser. For this reason, we have the opportunity to clear the buffer and place a simple error notice in it that provides more information than does the unbuffered example shown earlier. The code here doesn't provide much interaction, but you get the idea.

If the response is not buffered, the client will receive the HTTP response to its request as it is built—even if that building results in errors.

Notes

The first thing to remember is that the Buffer property must be set before the <HTML> tag is generated for the HTTP response. Attempting to set the Buffer property after the <HTML> tag will result in a runtime error.

If your script includes a preprocessing directive setting the language for the page, for example, this directive must be placed *before* you attempt to set the Buffer property's value. If you attempt to set the language for the page after setting the value for the Buffer property, you will experience an error.

If the Buffer property is set to True and your script does not call the Flush method anywhere, then the web server will honor Keep-Alive requests sent by the client. Keep-Alive requests from the browser inform the server that it should maintain a connection between itself and the client. If the client's Keep-Alive request is honored on the server, it is not forced to reestablish the connection each time it makes an HTTP request. It is, in effect, already connected. This saves the client from having to resolve the URL again.

If the Buffer property is set to False or if you use the Flush method somewhere in your script, the server will be forced to create a new connection to the client in response to each request.

When should you buffer your scripts? The answer to this question depends on two things: how long is too long for your clients to wait, and how complex your scripts are.

If your clients are introductory-level users of the Internet, their patience is typically fairly low; these clients need immediate action upon clicking the Submit button in your forms. More experienced users understand more about the back end of Internet applications and are, perhaps, more understanding of lag times in script results.

More important than this is how important it is for you to present the response as a single unit. For scripts that do a great deal of iterative processing, where each loop is directly affected by the loop before, it may be important to present the final result as a single unit. However, if your script consists of several definable sections, each of which is easily capable of being displayed on its own, then buffering may be less important.

One strategy for dealing with the lag times for complex scripts whose results are required in a single unit is to provide a "please wait" page in some form. This interim page informs the user that his request was received and that the script is processing.

For example, suppose the client browser requests an ASP script that retrieves and formats data from a very complex query requiring a long load time (30 seconds, for example). Rather than forcing the client to click on a link and have nothing happen for 30 seconds (in which time the inexperienced web user might very well click on the same link or button repeatedly), you might first display a page like the following:

```
<HTML>
<HEAD><TITLE>Please Wait</TITLE></HEAD>
<BODY LANGUAGE = "VBScript" OnLoad = "WinLoad()">
Your request is being processed, please wait...
<SCRIPT LANGUAGE = "VBScript">
Sub WinLoad()
    Parent.Location.HREF = "/Reports/Longreport.asp"
End Sub
</SCRIPT>
</BODY>
</HTML>
```

The short page will take very little time to load, and when it does, the user will see a "please wait" message until the next script has been processed and the report is ready for viewing, at which time the "please wait" page is unloaded and the report is loaded.

Finally, if you find that most of your scripts require buffering, you might consider setting the metabase ASPBufferingOn (using the App Options Configuration page for your virtual directory; see Appendix D, *Configuration of ASP Applications on IIS*) so that all scripts are buffered by default.

CacheControl   Response.CacheControl[=*ProxyCacheControlSetting*]

The CacheControl allows you to set whether proxy servers serving your pages can cache your page. If your page's content is large and doesn't change often, you might want to allow proxy servers to cache the page and thus serve it faster to requesting client browsers.

Parameters

ProxyCacheControlSetting

Determines whether proxy servers used to access your web site can cache your pages. The default for this property is `Private`, indicating that the proxy servers cannot cache your page. If this value is `Public`, however, proxy servers can cache the page. Note that `Private` and `Public` are string values.

Example

Setting this property is a simple affair, as the following code demonstrates. You may be asking yourself if there is any way to determine if the client is accessing the web page through a proxy server. Although there is, if you know ahead of time of the existence of the possible proxy servers, this is problematic and cumbersome. Furthermore, there is no need to determine this before setting this property. Either the client request is being handled by a proxy server and this property will affect the caching of the page, or this property is completely ignored.

```
<%

' The following code sets the HTTP cache control header so
' that this page can be cached by the proxy servers being
' used to access the page.
Response.CacheControl = "Public"
%>
<HTML>
<%
' Note that the CacheControl property was set BEFORE the
' <HTML> tag was constructed.
%>
```

Notes

Clearly, if the proxy server can cache your page, then the client's access times when accessing the page though a proxy server will be decreased. However, this is less useful if the page changes frequently. Also note that just because you set the value of the CacheControl property to `Public`, the proxy server is not required to cache your page(s). This must be configured on the proxy server.

Setting a value for CacheControl alters the value in the cache control HTTP header sent to the client upon a request.

If you use this property, you must do so before sending any response to the client (i.e., *before* the <HTML> tag is generated for your page). If you attempt to set the value for this (or any other HTTP header) after the <HTML> tag has already been sent to the client, an error will result unless the response is buffered.

Keep in mind that setting this property does not guarantee caching on the proxy server. The proxy server itself must be configured to cache these pages before this property will have any effect.

Charset

The Charset allows you to specify a character set for the HTTP response content. The name of this character set is added to the end of the Content-Type header/value pair in the HTTP response headers.

Parameters

strCharsetName

The *strCharsetName* is a string corresponding to a character set. The default character set is ISO-LATIN-1.

Example

If you do not set the Charset property, the Content-Type HTTP response header looks like the following:

```
content-type:text/html
```

If you set the Charset property, as in the following line of code:

```
<%
Response.Charset("ISO-LATIN-7")
%>
```

the value you use to set the Charset property value (the string "ISO-LATIN-7" in the preceding code) is appended to the end of the Content-Type HTTP response header value:

```
content-type:text/html;charset=ISO-LATIN-7
```

Notes

Although Charset is referred to in both this book and the Microsoft documentation as a property, it is really a method that takes a string argument representing the name of the charset to be added to the end of the Content-Type HTTP response header. For this reason, if you attempt to set the value of the Charset "property" as you would any other Response object property, you will receive an error:

```
<%
' Next line will NOT work:
Response.Charset = "ISO-LATIN-7"
%>
```

If the value you set for the Charset property does not represent a valid character set, this value is ignored by the client's browser, and the default character set is used instead.

Note that you can append the name of only one character set to the end of the Content-Type header/value pair. Each subsequent change of the Charset property's value simply replaces the last setting. For example, the following code:

```
<%
Response.Charset("ISO-LATIN-7")
Response.Charset("ISO-LATIN-3")
%>
```

Response Object

results in the following Content-Type HTTP response header/value pair:

```
content-type:text/html;charset=ISO-LATIN-3
```

Also note that if your content type is exclusively nontext (image data, for example), the character set value is ignored by the browser.

Finally, the default character set for the Apple Macintosh and compatibles is not ISO-LATIN-1, as it is for IBM PCs and compatibles. If you do not set the Charset property, all Macintosh browsers will interpret requested pages to be in the Macintosh character set. Microsoft's Personal Web Server for Macintosh automatically converts the character set of the requested content to ISO-LATIN-1 and will ignore any other Charset property settings you provide in your script.

Like other properties that result in a change to the HTTP response header values, the Charset property must be set before the server sends the <HTML> tag to the client unless the response is buffered.

ContentType   Response.ContentType[=*strContentType*]

The ContentType allows you to set the value for the Content-Type setting in the HTTP response header. This value defines the type of data being sent in the Response body. The client browser uses this information to determine how to interpret downloaded HTTP response content.

Parameters

strContentType
> Represents the content type. This string is in a type/subtype format. The type portion of the value represents the general content category and the subtype represents the specific type of content.

Example

```
<%

' The following code sets the value of the Content-Type
' HTTP response header according to the value of a
' local variable.
If strData = "jpg" Then
    Response.ContentType = "image/JPEG"
Else
    Response.ContentType = "text/plain"
End If

%>
```

Notes

Some of the possible values for ContentType type/subtype pairs are listed in Table 8-1.

Table 8-1: Available Content-Type HTTP Header Values

Type	SubType	Description
Text	Plain, RichText	Textual information
Multipart	Mixed, Alternative, Parallel, Digest	Data in response consists of multiple parts of independent data
Message	Partial, External-body	An encapsulated message
Image	JPEG, GIF	Image data
Audio	Basic	Audio data
Video	MPEG	Video data
Application	ODA, PostScript, Active	Typically uninterpreted binary data or data to be processed by a mail-based application

The number of subtypes is expected to grow significantly over time. The best reference for the available subtypes is the latest MIME RFC (RFC 2231 as of this writing). Many of the new subtypes are expected to come from industry. For example, Microsoft has already added the x-cdf subtype to the application type for its Channel Definition Format.

Like other properties that result in a change to the HTTP response header values, the ContentType property must be set before the server sends the <HTML> tag to the client unless the response is buffered.

As another example of the ContentType property, see the code example for the Response object's BinaryWrite method later in this chapter.

Expires

Response.Expires[=intNumMinutes]

The Expires property specifies the length of time (in minutes) that the client machine will cache the current page. If the user returns to the page within the amount of time set for the Expires property, the user will view the cached version of the page. If the Expires property is not set, content expiration set for the virtual directory (through the Properties page for the virtual directory on the Microsoft Management Console) will be used. Its default is 24 hours.

Parameters

intNumMinutes

The number of minutes you wish the client's browser to cache the current page

Notes

If you wish to prevent the client's browser from caching the page, use a value of 0 for *intNumMinutes*. Doing so will force the client to rerequest the page from the web server every time the client navigates to the page.

If you attempt to set the Expires property more than once in a script, the shortest setting is used. For example, the page that includes the following script will result in the client caching the page for five minutes, even though the last setting of the Expires property is 20 minutes:

```
<%

Response.Expires = 10
Response.Expires = 5
Response.Expires = 20

%>
```

Like other properties that result in a change to the HTTP response header values, the Expires property must be set before the server sends the <HTML> tag to the client unless the response is buffered.

ExpiresAbsolute   Response.ExpiresAbsolute[=[*Date*] [*Time*]]

Specifies a date and time on which the content of the current page will cease being cached on the client machine. If no time is specified when setting the ExpiresAbsolute property, the time is taken to be midnight on the date specified. Before the date specified in the ExpiresAbsolute property, the client will display the cached version of the current page if the user navigates to it.

Parameters

Date

> A calendar date after which the current page will no longer remain cached. The date value you use should be in the standard month/day/year format. However, the value sent in the Response header will conform in format to the RFC 1123 date format.

Time

> Specifies the exact time on *Date* after which the current page will no longer be cached on the user machine. If no date is specified, the client browser will expire the page at midnight of the current day. The web server converts the time you use to GMT before sending this header to the client.

Example

```
<%
' The following code sets the current page's caching on the
' client machine to end at 9 P.M. on 7 May 1998 GMT. NOTE
' the use of the "#" to designate the date and time.
Response.ExpiresAbsolute=#May 7, 1998 21:00:00#
%>
```

Notes

As the example demonstrates, you must use the pound character (#) to designate the date and time used in the ExpiresAbsolute property value.

Like the Expires property, setting this property multiple times results in the current page's caching ending on the earliest date and time specified in the script.

Like other properties that result in a change to the HTTP response header values, the ExpiresAbsolute property must be set before the server sends the <HTML> tag to the client unless the response is buffered.

IsClientConnected

Response.IsClientConnected

A read-only property that evaluates to True if the client is still connected to the web server since the last use of the Response object's Write method and returns False otherwise.

Parameters

None

Example

```
<%
' The following code determines whether the client
' is still connected to the server. If it is still
' connected, then the SessionID (see Chapter 10) will be
' used to retrieve the user information from a database.
If Response.IsClientConnected Then
    strUserName = fn_strGetUserName(Session.SessionId)
End If
%>
```

Notes

The IsClientConnected property gives you the ability to determine whether the client has disconnected. This is very important if the current script is long. If the client is no longer connected, it may be important to discontinue processing a script.

The following example demonstrates checking for the client connection before continuing in a long script. If the client is no longer connected, the easiest way to stop all processing is to use the Response object's End method.

```
<%Response.Buffer = True%>
<HTML>
<HEAD><TITLE>One Long Script</TITLE></HEAD>
<BODY>
<%

' The following code is the first of two segments
' in this script that will take a long time to process:
[SOME LONG CODE]

' Now before performing the second half of this long script,
' check to see if the client is still connected.
If Response.IsClientConnected Then
    [SECOND LONG CODE SEGMENT]
Else
    ' The client is no longer connected, end the script's
    ' processing.
    Response.End
```

```
End If
%>
</BODY></HTML>
```

This property is useful only for those clients using HTTP 1.1. If the browser uses HTTP 1.0, IIS tracks the session using individual HTTP requests and Keep-Alive requests by the client, not a constant connection that is only consistent with the later (1.1+) version of HTTP.

If your ASP file in which you use IsClientConnected is running under IIS 4.0, then the property value is only accurate if the file sends content to the client (i.e., if it is a file containing only server-side code, the resulting value of IsClientConnected is not correct). However, in IIS 5.0, IsClientConnected works regardless of whether or not the current file sends content to the client.

PICS   Response.PICS(*strPICSLabel*)

Adds a PICS (Platform for Internet Content Selection) label to the HTTP response header. This PICS system labels your web content to enable rating services (such as the Recreational Software Advisory Council (RSAC) and SafeSurf, a parents' organization) to rate that content according to various criteria set by content control software such as NetNanny and CyberWatch.

Parameters

strPICSLabel

> A string value that contains the entire contents of the PICS label you wish to add. A PICS label consists of the following parts:

> – The URL of the rating service that produced the label.

> – The set of PICS-defined (and extensible) attribute/value pairs that contains information about the rating of the content itself, such as the date it was assigned and an expiration date for the rating.

> – A set of attribute/value pairs designed by the rating service that represents the rating given the content. For example, the RSAC has four attributes for which they rate software: violence, sexual content, language, and nudity. These four attributes and their corresponding values would appear similar to the following: (V 0 S 1 L 3 N 0).

Example

```
<%
' The following piece of code sets a PICS label for the
' content of this page corresponding to the rating discussed
' earlier.
Dim strPicsLabel

strPicsLabel = _
        "(PICS-1.1 <HTTP://www.rsac.org/ratingsv01.html> "
strPicsLabel = strPicsLabel & "labels on " & Chr(34)
strPicsLabel = strPicsLabel & "2000.07.20T06:00-0000" & _
                Chr(34)
strPicsLabel = strPicsLabel & " until " & Chr(34)
```

```
strPicsLabel = strPicsLabel & "2000.12.31T23:59-0000" & _
               Chr(34)
strPicsLabel = strPicsLabel & "ratings (V 0 S 1 L 3 N 0))"

Response.PICS(strPicsLabel)
%>
```

Notes

The PICS label in the example states that:

- The PICS draft used is 1.1.

- The rating service is RSAC.

- The URL for the rating service is *http://www.rsac.org/ratingsv01.html.*

- The content label is to go into effect at 6 A.M. GMT 7/20/2000.

- The content label expires at 11:59 P.M. GMT on 12/31/2000.

- In the content label, the violence level is 0, the sexual content level is 1, the adult language level is 3, and the nudity level is 0.

The actual PICS label that is added to the HTTP response header is the following:

```
PICS-label:(PICS-1.1 http://www.rsac.org/ratingsv01.html
labels on "1998.03.20T06:00-0000" until
"1999.12.31T023:59-0000" ratings (v 0 s 1 1 3 n 0))
```

If you attempt to add an invalid PICS label to the HTTP header, the client machine will ignore it. Note that each subsequent setting of the PICS property value over-writes the last value. Only the final setting is actually sent to the client machine.

Note also that the dates in the PICS label are in quotation marks. For this reason you must use the Chr(34) character (34 is the ASCII equivalent to the quotation mark). This is easiest to handle by simply typing out the label as it should appear in the final PICS label and then replacing each quotation mark in the line of code with the following:

```
" & Chr(34) & "
```

Like other properties that result in a change to the HTTP response header values, adding a PICS label must be done before the server sends the <HTML> tag to the client unless the response is buffered.

Status   Response.Status(*strStatusDescString*)

Specifies the HTTP status line that is returned to the client machine from the web server.

Parameters

strStatusDescSetting

The *strStatusDescSetting* is a string value containing a three-digit status code that indicates the status of the HTTP request and a short explanation of the status code.

The possible values of the *strStatusDescSetting* parameter are described in the current HTTP specification* and fall into the following high-level categories:

1xx

> The 100 range is set aside for sending information-only response statuses to the client.

2xx

> The 200 range is set aside for sending successful response statuses to the client.

3xx

> The 300 range is set aside for redirection of the client. This status range should be used for requested pages that have been moved temporarily or permanently.

4xx

> The 400 range is set aside for sending notices of client error to the client. For example, you have undoubtedly seen the 404 Not Found error status sent back to your browser when you attempt to navigate to a page that has been moved or that does not exist.

5xx

> The 500 range is set aside for sending notices of server error to the client. For example, attempts to reach pages on a server that is unable to handle the request due to temporary overloading or server maintenance could result in the response status 503 Service Not Available.

Example

```
<%
' The following code sets the Status property of the
' Response object to 404 Not Found. Unless other content is
' generated for the page, the status code will be
' interpreted by itself by the client.
strStatusText = _
    "404 Not Found The Web server cannot find the "
strStatusText = strStatusText & "file or script you asked "
strStatusText = strStatusText & "for. Please check the URL "
strStatusText = strStatusText & "to ensure that the path "
strStatusText = strStatusText & "is correct."
Response.Status = strStatusText
%>
```

Notes

As with setting other Response headers, each subsequent setting of the Status property value resets the last setting.

Like other properties that result in a change to the HTTP response header values, the Status property must be set before the server sends the <HTML> tag to the client unless the response is buffered.

---

* The latest version of the HTTP specification can be found at *http://www.w3c.org/protocols*.

Collections Reference

Cookies

The Cookies collection of the Response object enables your ASP application to use the Set-Cookie HTTP response header to write cookies to the client's machine. If you attempt to set the value of a cookie that does not yet exist, it is created. If it already exists, the new value you set overwrites the old value already written to the client machine.

As with the Cookies collection of the Request object, each cookie in the Cookies collection of the Response object can also represent a cookie dictionary. Recall from Chapter 7, *Request Object*, that a cookie dictionary is a construct that is similar to an associative array in that each element of the array is identifiable by its name. For more information on cookie dictionaries, see the section on the Cookies collection of the Request object in Chapter 7.

The Cookies collection of the Response object, like other ASP collections, has the following properties:

Item

Returns the value of a specific element in the collection. To specify an item, you can use an index number or a key.

Key

Returns the name of a specific element in the Cookies collection. Just as each element's value is represented by the Item property, so each element's name is represented by its Key property.

If you do not know the name of a specific key, you can obtain it using its ordinal reference. For example, assume that you want to learn the key name for the third element in the collection and, subsequently, that element's value. You could use the following code:

```
strKeyName = Response.Cookies.Item(3)
strKeyValue = Response.Cookies.Item(strKeyName)
```

If, on the other hand, you know that the third element's key name is COLOR_PREF, you could simply use the following code to retrieve the value of that element:

```
strKeyValue = Response.Cookies.Item("COLOR_PREF")
```

Count

The Count property of the Cookies collection represents the current number of cookies in the collection.

As with other ASP collections, you can retrieve the value of any field of the Cookies collection through the use of the Item property. However, as in other places in this book, in the following examples, the syntax has been abbreviated so that it does not explicitly show the use of the Item property. For example:

```
Response.Cookies("UserPref") = "Red"
```

is an abbreviated form of:

```
Response.Cookies.Item("UserPref") = "Red"
```

To set the value of a cookie, you would use code similar to the following:

```
Response.Cookies("LastSearch") = _
    "SELECT * FROM Details WHERE Color = 'Red'"
```

 For more information on the Item, Key, and Count properties of a collection, see the discussion in the section "Contents Collection" in Chapter 4, *Application Object.*

The previous code would create the cookie `UserPref` if it doesn't already exist (or overwrite the original value if it does). This cookie would translate into a SET-COOKIE response header being added to the response sent back to the client browser. The client browser would receive this response header and create (or overwrite) a `UserPref` cookie on the user machine.

Each element in the Cookies collection (or subkey, if the cookie is a cookie dictionary) also has the following cookie-specific attributes:

Domain
> Sets the cookie so that the client sends the cookie's value only to pages in the domain set in the Domain property. The Domain property is write-only. For example, suppose we wanted to add the domain "mycorp.com" to the following `LastSearch` cookie. This would cause the client to send this cookie's value to the *mycorp.com* domain when it requests pages from it:
>
> ```
> Response.Cookies("LastSearch").Domain = "mycorp.com"
> ```

Expires
> The date on which the cookie expires and is discarded on the client machine. For example, suppose we want the cookie to expire on January 29, 2000. We could use the following code:
>
> ```
> Response.Cookies("LastSearch").Expires = #1/29/2000#
> ```
>
> If you do not set the Expires property value, the cookie resides on the client machine for the duration of the client's session. The cookie also will reside on the client machine only for the duration of the client's session if the date value you set for the Expires property is earlier than the current date. The Expires property is write-only.

HasKeys
> As previously mentioned, a cookie in the Cookies collection also can represent a cookie dictionary. To determine whether a specific cookie has subkeys, you must use the HasKeys property of that cookie, as in the following:
>
> ```
> blnHasKeys = Response.Cookies("Colors").HasKeys
> If blnHasKeys Then
>     strColor3 = Response.Cookies("Colors")("color3")
> End If
> ```
>
> The HasKeys property is read-only.

Path

The Path property represents the virtual directory on the server to which the cookie will be sent by the client browser when the client browser requests a page from within that virtual path. For example, if we want the client to send this cookie to only those scripts in the */Apps/SearchApps* virtual directory, we'd use the following line of code:

```
Response.Cookies("LastSearch").Path = "/Apps/SearchApps"
```

If the cookie's Path attribute is not set, the path defaults to the path of the current ASP application. The Path property is write-only.

Secure

The Secure property allows you to specify whether the cookie is sent from the client only if the client is using the Secure Sockets Layer. For example, suppose we have stored some sensitive information in a cookie (this is not wise, but there are occasions when you might do so), and you want the user's browser to send this information only if it is using the Secure Sockets Layer. This will significantly decrease the probability that a sensitive cookie could be intercepted. You would use the following simple line of code:

```
Response.Cookies("SensitiveCookie").Secure = True
```

The Secure property takes a Boolean value. The Secure property is write-only.

Example

The following is a more complete example of the use of the Cookies collection of the Response object. It demonstrates many of the items discussed earlier.

```
<HTML>
<HEAD><TITLE>Search Cookie Example</TITLE></HEAD>
<BODY>
<H3>Welcome to the Search Results Options Page.</H3>
You can use the following form to select your search results display
options. These options will be saved on your machine as a set of cookies.
<FORM ACTION="/SaveSearchCookie.asp" METHOD = POST>
First Name:<INPUT TYPE = TEXT NAME = "txtFirstName"><BR>
Last Name:<INPUT TYPE = TEXT NAME = "txtLastName"><BR>
User ID:<INPUT TYPE = TEXT NAME = "txtUserId"><BR>
Check All that Apply:
Show Descriptions:
<INPUT TYPE = CHECKBOX NAME = "chkUserPrefs"VALUE = "Desc">
Show Hit Count (display how many matches found per result):
<INPUT TYPE = CHECKBOX NAME = "chkUserPrefs"VALUE = "Count">
Show Relevance with Graph:
<INPUT TYPE = CHECKBOX NAME = "chkUserPrefs"
VALUE = "Graph">
Use Small Fonts(will show more results per page):
<INPUT TYPE = CHECKBOX NAME = "chkUserPrefs"
VALUE = "Small">
<INPUT TYPE = SUBMIT VALUE = "Save Selections">
</FORM>
</BODY>
</HTML>
```

The following code (*SaveSearchCookie.ASP*) will retrieve the values selected in the previous form and save them to the user's machine as cookies:

```
<%
' The following code retrieves user information from the
' Form collection of the Request object (see Chapter 7) and
' then writes the information to a set of cookies on the
' client machine.
Dim strFirstName
Dim strLastName
Dim strUserId
Dim intCounter
Dim intPrefCounter
Dim strKeyName
Dim arstrUserPrefs()

' Retrieve user information...
strFirstName   = Request.Form("txtFirstName")
strLastName    = Request.Form("txtLastName")
strUserId      = Request.Form("txtUserId")

intPrefCounter = 1

For intCounter = 1 to Request.Form("chkUserPrefs").Count
   ReDim Preserve arstrUserPrefs(intPrefCounter)
   arstrUserPrefs(intPrefCounter - 1) = _
      Request.Form("chkUserPrefs")(intCounter)
   intPrefCounter = intPrefCounter + 1
Next

' Write the user information to the client machine.
' Save all the information in cookies, but set the
' Expires property only for the UserId. We'll want
' that to remain on the client machine after the session
' is complete.
Response.Cookies("UserFirstName") = strFirstName
Response.Cookies("UserLastName") = strLastName

For intCounter = 1 to intPrefCounter - 1
   strKeyName = "Pref" & CStr(intCounter)
   Response.Cookies("UserPrefs")(strKeyName) = _
      arstrUserPrefs(intCounter - 1)
Next

' Note in the first line below, that when no property
' is specified, the value of the cookie is set.
Response.Cookies("UserId") = strUserId
Response.Cookies("UserId").Expires = #December 31, 1999#
Response.Cookies("UserId").Domain = "www.customsearch.com"
Response.Cookies("UserId").Path = "/usersearch/"
Response.Cookies("UserId").Secure = True
%>
```

Notes

In the example, the UserFirstName cookie is sent to the client machine. For this example, let's assume the value of the *strFirstName* variable is the string "David." The actual HTTP response header sent to the client machine is:

```
Set-Cookie:USERFIRSTNAME=david
```

Also for this example, assume the three values sent are 800 (for client browser width), 8 (for color depth in bits), and English (for English language preference). The actual HTTP response header sent to the client is the following:

```
Set-Cookie:USERPREFS=PREF1=800&PREF2=8&PREF3=english
```

If the string value sent for a value of a cookie contains spaces, those spaces are replaced with plus signs (+) in the HTTP response header.

If you sent a subsequent cookie value to the `UserPrefs` cookie on the client machine without specifying a *SubKey*, as in the following:

```
Response.Cookies("UserPrefs") = "german"
```

the two values for `PREF1` and `PREF2` will be overwritten and the Count property for the `UserPrefs` cookie will return 1.

Alternatively, if you send a subsequent cookie value and specify a *SubKey* to a client machine where the cookie has a value but no keys, the value already in place on the client machine is overwritten.

If, while you are generating values for the Cookies collection of the Response object, you need to determine if there are already subkeys defined for a given cookie, you can evaluate the HasKeys property of the cookie. If the cookie has subkeys defined, the HasKeys property evaluates to **True**.

Like other properties that result in a change to the HTTP response header values, the Cookies collection values must be set before the server sends the <HTML> tag to the client unless the response is buffered.

Methods Reference

AddHeader   Response.AddHeader *strName*, *strValue*

Allows you to add your own HTTP response header with a corresponding value. If you add an HTTP header with the same name as a previously added header, the second header will be sent in addition to the first; adding the second header does not overwrite the value of the first header with the same name. Also, once the header has been added to the HTTP response, it cannot be removed.

If the client sends the web server an HTTP header other than those listed in the section on the ServerVariables collection in Chapter 7, you can use *HTTP_ HeaderName* to retrieve it. For example, if the client sends the HTTP header:

```
ClientCustomHeader:CustomHeaderValue
```

then you could retrieve the value for this element using the following syntax:

```
<%
Request.ServerVariables("HTTP_ClientCustomHeader")
%>
```

This is an advanced method and should not be used without careful planning. If another method of the Response object will meet your needs, use it instead of using the AddHeader method.

Parameters

strName

The name of the HTML header you wish to add to the response header

strValue

The initial value of the new header you are adding to the response header

Example

```
<%
' The following code adds the CUSTOM-ERROR HTML header to
' the HTTP response headers.
Response.AddHeader "CUSTOM-ERROR", "Your browser is not IE."
%>
```

Notes

Like the other methods and properties of the Response object that alter the HTTP response headers, you must call the AddHeader method before sending the <HTML> tag to the client. If you have previously set the Buffer property value of the Response object to **True**, you can use AddHeader unless you have previously called the Flush method. If you call AddHeader after sending the <HTML> tag to the client or calling the Flush method, your call to AddHeader will result in a runtime error.

You should not use underscores in your custom headers. Doing so will increase your chances of ambiguity with headers already present. Use hyphens to separate multiple words instead. Also, note that to retrieve the value of a custom header with hyphens, you replace them with underscores when retrieving the values of your custom headers.

AppendToLog   Response.AppendToLog *strLogEntry*

Adds a string to the web server log entry for the current client request. You can only add up to 80 characters at a time, but you are able to call the AppendToLog method multiple times.

Logging web site activity

IIS allows you to log user activity into a text file* or into an ODBC-compliant database. This logging is separate from Windows NT logging, and the records in the

---

* The log files for IIS are found in *winnt\system32\LogFiles\W3svc1\ex[date].log*. Each entry into the (IIS default) log contains time, caller IP, caller method (GET/POST), uri-stem (no server path), and resulting status.

IIS log cannot be viewed using the Windows NT Event Viewer tool. To view the IIS log files, you must open them as you would any other ASCII text file, import them into a spreadsheet or database program, or, if you've been logging to an ODBC database, view them through queries to that database.

Specifically, you can log the following aspects of users' visits to your web site, among other things:

- Date/time of user visit

- Requested pages

- IP address of user

- Length of time connected to server

Using this information and information your application adds to this log through Response.AppendToLog, you can plan future development for your site, plan security, and plan for new servers if the load warrants it.

Parameters

strLogEntry

The string you want added to the current client request's entry in the web server. This string can be up to 80 characters in length. Note that the string you append to the web server log entry cannot contain commas, since the fields in the IIS web log entries are comma delimited.

Example

```
<%
' Assume you have constructed one string containing all that
' you'd like logged to the web's server. This string is
' declared as strOrigLogContent. The following Do...While
' loop code will loop through your content and log it to the
' web server 79 characters at a time.
Do While Len(strOrigLogContent) > 0
    If Len(strOrigLogContent) >= 79 Then
        strLogString = Left(strOrigLogContent, 79)
    Else
        strLogString = strOrigLogContent
    End If

    ' Log the content.
    Response.AppendToLog strLogString

    If Len(strOrigLogContent) > Len(strLogString) Then
        strOrigLogContent = _
            Right(strOrigLogContent, _
            Len(strOrigLogContent) - Len(strLogString))
    Else
        strOrigLogContent = ""
    End If
Loop
%>
```

Notes

Before you are able to append information to the web server log in IIS, you must enable the URL Query option of the Extended Logging Properties sheet for the web site whose activity the log files are being used to record.

This method can be an invaluable time saver in maintaining detailed information about actions on your web site. If you have a unique identifier for each user that is stored in the log file with the entry (which contains an IP address, possibly a Windows NT account name, and the date and time of the visit), you can quickly determine who was visiting the site at the time of an unexpected error on your site. This method cannot be relied on for security, since you cannot be 100% certain of the user's identity, but it can help.

BinaryWrite   Request.BinaryWrite *arbyteData*

Writes information directly to the response content without any character conversion. If your application involves writing binary data to the client, you must use this method to ensure that data you send is not converted to character data from the original binary.

Parameters

arbyteData
    An array of bytes you wish to write to the response content

Example

The following example code is lengthy for the simple call to BinaryWrite, but it demonstrates a very useful concept, especially if you are forced to deal with binary data from a database.

```
<%

' The following code retrieves a binary object
' (in this case a JPG image) and writes it to the
' client using BinaryWrite. (For more information
' on ActiveX Data Objects usage, see Chapter 12.)

' Create an ADO connection object.
Set adoCon = Server.CreateObject("ADODB.Connection")

' Use the Open method of the Connection object
' to open an ODBC connection with the database
' represented by the DSN ImageDatabase.
adoCon.Open "ImageDatabase"

' Use the Execute method of the ADO Connection object
' to retrieve the binary data field from the database.
Set adoRecImgData = adoCon.Execute _
    ("SELECT ImageData FROM Images WHERE ImageId = 1234")

' Create a Field object by setting one equal to a
' specific field in the recordset created previously.
```

```
Set adoFldImage = adoRecImgData("ImageData")

' Use the ActualSize property of Field object to retrieve
' the size of the data contained in the Field object. After
' this line you will know how many bytes of data reside in
' the Field object.
lngFieldDataLength = adoFldImage.ActualSize

' Use the BinaryWrite method to write 4K bytes of binary
' data at a time. So, first we need to determine how many
' 4K blocks the data in the Field object represents.
lngBlockCount = lngFieldDataLength / 4096

' Now let's get how many bytes are left over after removing
' lngBlockCount number of bytes.
lngRemainingData = lngFieldDataLength Mod 4096

' We now must set the HTTP content type Response header
' so that the browser will recognize the data being sent
' as being JPEG image data.
Response.ContentType = "image/JPEG"

' Loop through and write the first lngBlockCount number
' of binary blocks of data.
For intCounter = 1 to lngBlockCount
    Response.BinaryWrite adoFldImage.GetChunk(4096)
Next

' Now write the last remainder of the binary data.
Response.BinaryWrite adoFldImage.GetChunk(lngRemainingData)

' Close the recordset.
adoRecImgData.Close
%>
```

Notes

At first, the BinaryWrite method seems to be of limited use, until you have binary data stored in a database that must be sent to the client; then, BinaryWrite is invaluable. As the code sample demonstrates, one example of this is the display of image data that is stored and retrieved from a DBMS capable of storing binary data.

I have used this method to display JPEG images stored in a Microsoft SQL Server database (using code similar to the preceding), and it works quite well. Because you are sending the HTTP response containing only the image data (not a link request to the image), it may even be faster than sending images to the client upon a straight client request, assuming your database access is suitably fast.

Clear   Response.Clear

Empties the current contents of the Response buffer. It does so without sending any of the buffered response to the client.

Parameters

None

Example

```
<% Response.Buffer = True%>
<HTML>
<HEAD><TITLE>Response Clear Method Example</TITLE></HEAD>
<BODY>
<%
On Error Resume Next

[CODE TO DO SOME CALCULATIONS]
lngFormulaElement1 = 47
lngFormulaElement2 = lngFormulaElement1 - 47
lngFormulaElement3 = 23

' This next line results in a division-by-zero error
' (Error Number 11).
lngNewCalcTotal = lngFormulaElement3 / lngFormulaElement2

' This next line will still be processed because we used
' ON ERROR RESUME NEXT.
If Err <> 0 Then
    ' The following code clears the Response buffer, writes
    ' an error message, and ends the response, forcing IIS to
    ' send the response to the client. Note that the Buffer
    ' property has to be set to True for the following code
    ' to work properly.
    Response.Clear
    Response.Write "Your request resulted in the error: " & _
        Err.Description
    Response.Write " Error Number: " & Err.Number
    Response.Write "<BR>Call your web admin at 555-HELP for "
    Response.Write "more information."
    Response.End
End If
%>
. . . [additional code]
```

Notes

The Clear method of the Response object does not clear any HTTP headers, only the content. As noted in the example, the Buffer property of the Response object must be set to **True** or the use of this method will result in a runtime error.

One of the most important uses for the Clear method is to clear the buffer and send to the client browser something else instead, often error information, as is the case with the example.

For errors to be caught and error information to be sent to the client in this fashion, not only must the Buffer property be set to **True**, but also you must use the following line of code to ensure that your error trap will be processed:

```
On Error Resume Next
```

End

Ends all storage of information in the response buffer and sends the current contents of the buffer immediately to the client. Any code present after the call to the End method is not processed. Any memory set aside by the script up until the call to End (such as database objects previously used in the script) is released.

Parameters

None

Example

See the previous example for the Clear method.

Notes

If the Buffer property is set to **True**, calling the End method will flush the Response buffer exactly as if you had called the Flush method (see the next section). However, unlike calling the Flush method, no code after the call to End is processed by the web server.

Flush

Immediately sends all data currently in the response buffer to the client. Unless the Buffer property of the Response object is set to **True**, this method will result in a runtime error. This method allows you to send various portions of the response to the client at your discretion.

Parameters

None

Example

```
<% Response.Buffer = True%>
<HTML>
<HEAD><TITLE>Response Flush Method Example</TITLE></HEAD>
<BODY>
<%
' Suppose for this example that this first part of the
' script retrieves some information from a database and
' that retrieval takes a long time, say 30 seconds.
' (Don't worry about the details of the ActiveX Data Object
' calls. They are covered later in the book and serve only
' as an example here of something that might take a long time.)
Set adoCon = Server.CreateObject("ADODB.Connection")
adoCon.Open MyDatabase
Set adoRec = adoCon.Execute([BIG SQL STATEMENT])

' Rather than continue to the second part of the script, in
' which a second slow SQL statement (say another 15 seconds)
' executes, first we'll use the Flush method to force the
' first part of the script results to the client. This way,
' the user can be looking at the results of the first query
```

```
' while waiting for the second.
Response.Flush

' [Second LONG SQL statement.]
Set adoRec2 = adoCon.Execute([BIG SQL STATEMENT])
%>
</BODY></HTML>
```

Notes

Using the buffering capacity of the Response object, you are able to send the response to the client in parts. For example, suppose you are presenting a description of your worldwide organization followed by a list of offices derived from information in a database. The organization description is straight text, and thus it takes very little time to prepare and send it to the client. The second part takes more time. You could use the Flush method of the Response object to send the organizational description to the client first and then send the list when it is complete. Without this approach, the user can get the impression that the page is slow to download.

One caution, however: if you use the Flush method on an Active Server Page, the server will ignore Keep-Alive requests sent by the client for that page. This will force a new connection to be made for each piece of information sent to the client.

Redirect   Response.Redirect *strURL*

Redirects the client's request to another URL.

Parameters

strURL

The Universal Resource Locator string for the new location to which you wish to redirect the client

Example

```
<%
' The following code determines whether the client has
' security clearance for a certain page. If not, it
' is redirected to another URL.
[...Code to determine user's clearance for the current page...]

If Not(strUserSecurity = "ADMIN" or strUserSecurity = "SUPERADMIN") Then
    Response.Redirect "/security/noclearance.asp?usrid=09563"
End If
%>
```

Notes

The *strURL* value you use when calling the Redirect method can be an exact URL with DNS or a virtual directory and filename. It also can be the name of a file that resides in the same folder as the requested page.

If your script has written any content to the HTTP response body, that content is ignored by the script once the call to the Redirect method is executed.

Calling the Redirect method is conceptually the same as setting the Status property to "302 Object Moved" and sending the user to a new location using the Location HTTP header.

Note that upon redirection, some older (HTTP 1.0) client browsers will mistakenly change POST requests to GET requests when the new URL is called. This is an important consideration when the client's POSTed information contains more data than the GET method can handle. It is assumed that new browsers supporting the HTTP 1.1 protocol have fixed this problem.

If your ASP file is running under IIS 5.0, you should consider using the Server method Execute or Transfer. Neither of these methods involve the costly trip to the client and back to the server that Redirect requires.

Write

Response.Write vntData

Writes information directly to the HTTP response body.

Parameters

vntData

    The information to be inserted into the HTML text stream that will be received by the client browser. This includes text, HTML tags, client-side script, and so on. The data variables in the ASP script itself are of the data type variant. The value cannot contain the %> character sequence; the web server will interpret it as the end of your active server script. If your script requires this character sequence, use the escape sequence %\> instead.

Example

```
<%
strDirCommand = "Dir /w"

' The following code writes an entire HTML table to the HTTP
' response body.
Response.Write "<TABLE>"
Response.Write "<TR>"
Response.Write "<TD WIDTH = 50%\>"
Response.Write "Command"
Response.Write "</TD>"
Response.Write "<TD WIDTH = 50%\>"
Response.Write "Description"
Response.Write "</TD>"
Response.Write "</TR>"
Response.Write "<TR>"
Response.Write "<TD WIDTH = 50%\>"
Response.Write Chr(34) & strDirCommand & Chr(34)
Response.Write "</TD>"
Response.Write "<TD WIDTH = 50%\>"
Response.Write "This allows you to see a list of the "
Response.Write "files in <BR> your current folder."
```

```
Response.Write "</TD>"
Response.Write "</TR>"
Response.Write "</TABLE>"
%>
```

Notes

As demonstrated in the example program, you can use the Write method to write HTML and client-side script to the response body that the client browser will interpret as plain HTML.

To send a carriage return/line feed or a quotation mark, use the *Chr* function, as demonstrated the following code:

```
' Note:  Chr(34) is a quotation mark. Chr(13) & Chr(10) is
' the equivalent of a carriage return, followed by a
' linefeed.
Response.Write "Hamlet said, " & Chr(34) & _
    "To be, or not to be." & Chr(34) & Chr(13) & Chr(10)
```

Finally, you can use the Write method to send the value of a server-side script to the client browser. This method is sometimes cleaner in your code than going back and forth between server-side code and client code using the <%=...%> notation. For example, the following code displays the value of the *strHighestPrice* data value using both the <%=...%> and the Response.Write methods:

```
<%
Response.Write "The highest price is " & strHighestPrice
Response.Write ".<BR>"

' The same line as the preceding using the other format:
%>
The highest price is <%=strhighestPrice%>.<BR>
```

CHAPTER 9

Server Object

The Server object provides several miscellaneous functions that you can use in your Active Server Page applications. Although most of its methods are esoteric and seldom used, three methods, CreateObject, Execute, and Transfer, and the Server object's single property, ScriptTimeout, are invaluable. You will use these in many of your scripts.

The Server object, as its name implies, represents the web server itself, and much of the functionality it provides is simply functionality the web server itself uses in the normal processing of client requests and server responses.

Server Object Summary

Properties
    ScriptTimeout

Collections
    None

Methods
    CreateObject
    Execute
    GetLastError
    HTMLEncode
    MapPath
    Transfer
    URLEncode

Events
    None

Comments/Troubleshooting

Use of the Server object's property and methods is straightforward. Typically, if you are using the Server object's functionality with the correct syntax, you will experience the expected outcome. If you experience errors, it typically indicates a problem with IIS itself either in its configuration or in its installation.

Properties Reference

ScriptTimeout   Server.ScriptTimeout [= *lngNumSeconds*]

Specifies the maximum amount of time the web server will continue processing your script. If you do not set a value for this property, the default value is 90 seconds.

Parameters

lngNumSeconds
> The number of seconds you want the web server to continue processing your script before it times out, sending the client an ASP error.

Example

```
<%

' The following code sets the amount of time before the
' script times out to 100 seconds. If the script takes
' more time than 100 seconds, the script will time out and
' a timeout error will be sent to the client.
Server.ScriptTimeout = 100

%>
```

Notes

The number used in setting the ScriptTimeout property's value must be greater than or equal to that set in the AspScriptTimeout property in the IIS metabase or the setting will be ignored. For example, the default setting of AspScriptTimeout in the IIS metabase is 90 seconds. If you use the ScriptTimeout property to decrease this time to 10 seconds without first changing the setting in the metabase, the script will still time out after 90 seconds.

You should consider decreasing the AspScriptTimeout property in the IIS metabase. 90 seconds is a long time to wait for processing a web request. Show me a user who is willing to wait for a minute and a half, and I'll show you a user who has fallen asleep. However, if your application requires a longer timeout setting, consider using an interim "Please wait . . ." page whose OnLoad event will in turn call the longer script or ASP page. This will give the user some notice that her wait will be a long one.

This technique is demonstrated in the following code. Assume that you must call the *InfoSearch.ASP* script, and you know that it takes a single parameter, *strSrchItem*, and that it takes up to two minutes to complete its tasks. Instead of calling *InfoSearch.ASP* immediately, you could call the following page instead:

```
<HTML>
<HEAD><TITLE>Search Wait</TITLE></HEAD>
<BODY LANGUAGE="VBScript" OnLoad = "PageLoad()">
Please wait, your request is being processed...
<SCRIPT LANGUAGE="VBScript">
Sub PageLoad()
Parent.Location.HREF = _
"InfoSearch.ASP?<%=Request.ServerVariables("QUERY_STRING")%>"
End Sub
</SCRIPT>
</BODY>
</HTML>
```

As you can see, when this script loads, it calls the page with the long script, sending the original query string (retrieved from the ServerVariables collection of the Request object; see Chapter 7, *Request Object*, for more details). This gives the user immediate feedback without forcing him to sit watching a blank screen waiting for a script to complete processing.

Methods Reference

CreateObject   Set *objMyObject* = Server.CreateObject(*strProgId*)

Instantiates an object on the server. Once instantiated, this object's properties and methods can be used just as you can use the properties and methods of the built-in objects that come with ASP. The DLLs from which these objects are instantiated must be installed and registered on the web server machine separately from your installation of IIS.

Parameters

objMyObject

The name of a variable that will contain a reference to the object you are instantiating.

strProgId

The programmatic ID for the class from which you would like to instantiate an object. The format for the *strProgId* parameter is:

`[LibraryName.]Component[.Version]`

This value is found in the registry and represents how the component's DLL is registered there. Although it sometimes contains the DLL name, it often does not. For example, the DLL from which you instantiate the Ad Rotator object is *adrot.dll*. However, its ProgID is MSWC.AdRotator.1, as defined by the default value of the following registry key:

`HKEY_CLASSES_ROOT\CLSID\{1621F7C0-60AC-11CF-9427-444553540000}\ProgID`

As you will note, this is the ProgID for the registered DLL and contains version information in addition to its registered name. Sometimes, however, you may have several different versions of the same DLL registered on your machine. In this case, you can use the default value of the `VersionIndependentProgID` registry key to instantiate the most recent version of the DLL. In our example (the ad rotator), the version-independent ProgID is `MSWC.AdRotator`.

Example

```
<%

' The following code uses the CreateObject method of
' the Server object to instantiate an Ad Rotator object
' on the server.
Dim objAdRotator

Set objAdRotator = Server.CreateObject("MSWC.AdRotator")

%>
```

Notes

When a client browser requests an ASP script containing objects, ASP instantiates the objects (thus triggering their default constructor functions, if they exist) and then immediately—before any script is processed—calls the OnStartPage method of every object on the page that has a defined OnStartPage event handler. The OnStartPage method allows the object to use the ObjectContext object to retrieve pointers to the built-in ASP objects. The details behind the ObjectContext object and the OnStartPage methods of server components is beyond the scope of this book. For more information on this, see Shelley Powers' book, *Developing ASP Components*, published by O'Reilly & Associates.

Using the CreateObject method creates a server-side object with page-level scope, unless CreateObject is called in the Application_OnStart or Session_OnStart events, in which case the object will be instantiated with application- or session-level scope, respectively. Objects with page-level scope are destroyed and the memory they occupy is released at the end of the page.

To create an object with application scope, you must call the CreateObject method in the Application_OnStart event (see Chapter 4, *Application Object*, for more details) or use the <OBJECT> tag in the *GLOBAL.ASA* file and set the SCOPE parameter to Application. (For more details on the *GLOBAL.ASA* file, see Chapter 11, *Preprocessing Directives, Server-Side Includes, and GLOBAL.ASA*.)

Likewise, to create an object with session scope, you must call the CreateObject method in the Session_OnStart event (see Chapter 10, *Session Object*, for more details) or use the <OBJECT> tag in the *GLOBAL.ASA* file and set the SCOPE parameter to Session. Also, you can use a Session variable to hold the object instantiated using CreateObject, as in the following example:

```
Set Session("objMyAdRot") = _
    Server.CreateObject("MSWC.AdRotator")
```

Objects with application-level scope are not destroyed until the Application_ OnEnd event is fired. Session-scoped objects are similarly destroyed at the end of a user's session or when the Abandon method of the Session object is called; see Chapter 10 for more details.

Once an object is instantiated, it can be destroyed by setting its value to the keyword Nothing, as in the following example code:

```
Set objMyAdRot = Nothing
```

You also can simply replace the value of the object variable to release the memory being used for the original object:

```
Set objMyAdRot = strSomeOtherValue
```

You cannot use CreateObject to create an instance of one of the built-in objects. For example the following code will generate a runtime error:

```
Set objMySession = Server.CreateObject("Session") ' WRONG
```

Execute   Server.Execute (*strPath*)

The Execute method allows you to call and execute an ASP script from within another ASP script. When the called script has finished executing, control returns to the ASP page that issued the Server.Execute method call. Using the Execute method, you can break complex applications down into modular, reusable components that can be called when needed. The Execute method is new to ASP 3.0/IIS 5.0.

Parameters

strPath

> The absolute or relative path to the ASP script you wish to execute. Only scripts within the current application's application space can be executed using this method.

Example

In this example, the second script, which displays a text advertisement, is called (using the Execute method) by the first script only if the current user has not entered the "No Ad" club.

```
**** BEGIN ExecuteExamplePage.ASP ********
<HTML>
 HEAD
<TITLE>
Execute Example Form
</TITLE>
</HEAD>
<BODY>
<%
' This script executes an advertisement if the current
' user is not a member of the "No advertisement" club.

' Dimension Local variables.
Dim blnNoAdClub

' Test Session variable.
Session("blnNoAdClub") = False

' Set variables.
blnNoAdClub = Session("blnNoAdClub")
```

```
' If the user belongs in the "No Ad" club don't show an ad.
If Not(blnNoAdClub) Then
    Server.Execute ("DisplayAdvertisement.asp")
End If
%>
```

FROM HERE DOWN IS ALL CONTENT FROM ExecuteExampleForm.asp

This page may or may not have an advertisement line at the top.

```
</BODY>
</HTML>
**** END ExecuteExamplePage.ASP ********

**** BEGIN DisplayAdvertisement.ASP ********
<%
Dim intSal
Dim strPos
Dim strAdString

' Test Session variable.
Session("intSal") = 4
Session("strPos") = "vp"

intSal = Session("intSal")
strPos = Session("strPos")

' Initialize first part of ad banner text.
strAdString = "Click here to request a credit card"

' Add credit limit phrase to ad.
Select Case intSal
    Case 0 ' From $10K to $20K in salary.
        strAdString = strAdString & " with a limit of up to $5000"
    Case 1 ' From $20K+ to $40K in salary.
        strAdString = strAdString & " with a limit of up to $10000"
    Case 2 ' From $40K+ to $60K in salary.
        strAdString = strAdString & " with a limit of up to $20000"
    Case 3 ' From $60K+ to $80K in salary.
        strAdString = strAdString & " with a limit of up to $50000"
    Case 4 ' From $80K+ in salary.
        strAdString = strAdString & " with a limit of up to $100000"
    Case Else ' Assume lowest salary range.
        strAdString = strAdString & " with no limit"
End Select

' Add exclusivity phrase if necessary.
If UCase(strPos) = "VP" Then
    strAdString = strAdString & " just for executives!"
Else
    strAdString = strAdString & "!"
End If

' Display advertisement text string.
```

```
Response.Write "<FONT SIZE=""5"" COLOR = ""red"">" & strAdString & "</
FONT><BR><BR>"

%>
**** END DisplayAdvertisement.ASP ********
```

Notes

The Execute method provides ASP developers an excellent opportunity to break up their applications into manageable, reusable components of code that can be called only when necessary. In the past, an ASP developer was forced to either programmatically redirect the execution of a page to another page (a costly exercise in execution speed, since it required that a header be sent to the browser to redirect the browser's request) or include another file using the #INCLUDE pre-processor directive. Neither alternative was very useful. As previously mentioned, the Redirect method of the Server object (see later in this chapter) calls for another server-to-client-server round of calls for a page that was slow. The #INCLUDE directive forces the ASP ISAPI filter to retrieve the included file from the file system, insert it into the current script, and interpret all the included code even if it is never used by the including script.

The Execute method, on the other hand, allows you to execute other scripts programmatically only when the logic in the calling script requires it. That is, the Execute method allows you to dynamically include scripts.

Note that just as with other scripts, scripts called through the Execute method can add or modify HTTP headers included in the response. However, just as with standalone scripts, if the called script adds or modifies any HTTP headers after any response is sent, an error will be generated.

As you might expect, the variable scope for each script (calling script and called script) is distinct. For example, in the following code, you have a variable called strName in both scripts.

```
CALLING SCRIPT
<%
Dim strName
strName = "Com"
Server.Execute("CalledScript.asp")
%>

CalledScript.asp
<%
Dim strName
Response.Write strName
%>
```

In the preceding example, *strName* is declared in both scripts. However, it is not initialized in the second script. In this example, Response.Write would result in nothing being written to the Response, as the value of *strName* in the called script is undefined.

When an ASP page calls Server.Execute to branch to another ASP page, all of the former's built-in ASP objects are passed to the called script. For example, any values in the Request object's Form collection are available to the ASP page invoked by the call to the Server object's Execute method.

Note that according to the Microsoft documentation, the Execute method will allow you to add a QueryString parameter to the end of the called URL. However, as of the writing of this addition of this book (March 2000), adding a QueryString to a URL will generate an error. According to Microsoft Technical Support, this is a known bug in IIS 5.0 and a fix is in development.

Finally, if you call a script using the Execute method from within a script that you have set to transactional and the called script causes the transaction to be aborted, the OnTransactionAbort event on the called page will be called first and then, after the called script has completed execution, the OnTransactionAbort event on the calling page is executed. For example, suppose the following script, *CallingScript. ASP*, calls the *CalledScript.ASP* script further.

```
CALLINGSCRIPT.ASP
<%@ TRANSACTION=Required%>
<%
Server.Execute "CalledScript.asp?strName=bob"
Sub OnTransactionAbort()
    'Clean up code for CallingScript.asp.
End Sub

Sub OnTransactionCommit()
    Commit code for CalledScript.asp.
End Sub


CALLEDSCRIPT.ASP
<%@ TRANSACTION=Required%>
<%
.
.
.
'Processing code....
.
.
.
OnTransactionAbort()
    'Clean up code for CalledScript.asp.
End Sub

OnTransactionCommit()
    Commit code for CalledScript.asp.
End Sub
```

If in *CalledScript.ASP* script, an error occurs that forces the transaction to abort, then the OnTransactionAbort event code for *CalledScript.ASP* would be executed and then the OnTransactionAbort event code for *CallingScript.ASP* would be executed.

GetLastError   Set *objASPErr* = Server.GetLastError ()

The GetLastError method of the Server object allows you to display information about any error that occurs in your script. The GetLastError method returns a

---

single ASPError object (see Chapter 5, *ASPError Object*). You can use the returned ASPError object to display or programmatically respond to error information. The GetLastError method is new to ASP 3.0/IIS 5.0

Parameters

`objASPErr`

The name of the ASPError object returned by the GetLastError method.

Example

```
<%
' Instantiate an ASPError object using the GetLastError method of the
' Server object.
Set objASPError = Server.GetLastError
%>
     .
     .
     .
HTML Display Etc.
<%
' Use the properties of the ASPError object (returned by the GetLastError
' object) to display information about the error.

' *** FOR MORE INFORMATION, SEE THE ASPERROR OBJECT CHAPTER.

Response.Write Server.HTMLEncode(objASPError.Category)
If objASPError.ASPCode > "" Then
    Response.Write Server.HTMLEncode(", " & objASPError.ASPCode)
End If
Response.Write Server.HTMLEncode(" (0x" & Hex(objASPError.Number) & ")" )
& "<br>"
If objASPError.ASPDescription > "" Then
    Response.Write Server.HTMLEncode(objASPError.ASPDescription) & "<br>"
ElseIf (objASPError.Description > "") Then
    Response.Write Server.HTMLEncode(objASPError.Description) & "<br>"
End if
     .
     .
     .
```

Notes

In this code example (derived from the default *500-100.ASP* script that comes with IIS 5.0), the script begins by instantiating an ASPError object using the GetLast-Error method. It then displays information about the last error by using the properties of the ASPError object. For more information on the properties of the ASPError object, see Chapter 5.

It is important to note that you cannot use the GetLastError method in the script in which the error occurs. For example, the following code will not work as you might expect it to:

```
<%
On Error Resume Next
Session("MyVar"3333) = "keyton"
```

```
Set objError = Server.GetLastError()
Response.Write objError.ASPCode
%>
```

You might expect that, because you had used the On Error Resume Next statement, you could then react to errors later in the script by using the GetLastError
method. Unfortunately, this is not the case. IIS 5.0 responds instantly to errors and
redirects the client using the Server.Transfer method ("behind the scenes") to an
error-handling page. By default, this error page is *iisHelp/Common/500-100.ASP*.
It is in this page that you can customize error handling using the GetLastError
method.

For more information on the *500-100.ASP* error-handling page and on error-
handling in your scripts in general, see Chapter 5.

The GetLastError method works for preprocessing errors, script compilation errors,
and run-time errors.

It is important to note that the GetLastError method will only return error information successfully if no content has been sent to the client. If content has already
been sent to the client, the GetLastError method itself causes an error. For this
reason, if you have scripts within which you feel that you will need to handle
various errors, it is a good idea to set the Buffer property of the Response object
to True (See Chapter 8, *Response Object*):

```
Response.Buffer = True
```

For more information on the GetLastError method and the ASPError object it
returns, see Chapter 5.

HTMLEncode   Server.HTMLEncode (*strHTMLString*)

If you ever need to display the actual HTML code involved in an HTML page or
ASP script, you must use the HTMLEncode method of the Server object. The
HTMLEncode method of the Server object allows you to encode the HTML string
so that, when it is displayed in the browser, the browser does not simply interpret
the HTML as instructions for text layout.

Parameters

strHTMLString
    The string whose HTML code you wish to encode for display on the client
    machine.

Example

```
<%

' The following code encodes these HTML tags so that they can
' be displayed without interpretation on the client browser:
' <TABLE><TR><TD></TD></TR></TABLE>
Dim strOldHTML
Dim strNeutralCode

strOldHTML = "<TABLE><TR><TD>"
strNeutralCode = Server.HTMLEncode(strOldHTML)
```

```
' The variable strNeutralCode now holds the following code:
' &lt;TABLE&gt;&lt;TR&gt;&lt;TD&gt;
' but will be displayed on the client's machine as
' <TABLE><TR><TD>
' and the &lt;TABLE&gt;&lt;TR&gt;&lt;TD&gt; will be
' seen only if you view the source code on the client.
Response.Write strNeutralCode

%>
```

Notes

The HTMLEncode method is a straightforward method that is simple to use. It makes it possible to display the source code of your HTML page or to demonstrate the use of various HTML tags in a web page. It is also invaluable for displaying the output of database queries.

MapPath   Server.MapPath(*strPath*)

The MapPath method allows you to determine the physical path on the server, given a virtual or relative path.

Parameters

strPath

A complete virtual path or a path relative to the path of the current script's home directory on the server. The method determines how to interpret the string depending on if it starts with either a slash (/) or a backslash (\). If the *strPath* parameter begins with either of these characters, the string is assumed to be a complete virtual path. Otherwise, the physical path returned is the path relative to the current script's physical directory on the web server.

Example

```
<%

' The following line of code determines the physical path
' of the current script for later use.
strSearchPath = _
    Server.MapPath("/searchscripts/start/searchstart.asp")

' This following code then uses the strSearchPath string to
' determine the file attributes for the current file for
' display in the client-side HTML.
Set fs = Server.CreateObject("Scripting.FileSystemObject")
Set f = fs.GetFile(strSearchPath)
datFileLastModified = f.DateLastModified
%>
<HTML>
<HEAD><TITLE>MapPath Example</TITLE></HEAD>
<BODY>
The current script was last modified <%=datFileLastModified%>.
</BODY>
</HTML>
```

Notes

There are two important facts to remember when using the MapPath method. The first is that it does not support the standard MS-DOS relative directory notation ("." and ".."). For this reason, the following line of code will result in a runtime error:

```
strSearchPath = Server.MapPath("../start/searchstart.asp")
```

Second, the MapPath method does not check to ensure whether a given physical directory exists. For this reason, this method is useful in determining the physical path for a new file to be created by the web server in response to a line of script code.

Finally, to determine the physical path of the current file, you can use the `PATH_INFO` element of the Request object's ServerVariables collection (for more details, see Chapter 7). For example, assume the current script is *searchstart.ASP* and it is located in the */searchscripts/start/* virtual directory. The following line of code would set the value of ***strSearchPath*** to *D:\apps\searchscripts\start\searchstart.ASP*:

```
strSearchPath = _
    Server.MapPath(Request.ServerVariables("PATH_INFO"))
```

Transfer   Server.Transfer (*strPath*)

The Transfer method allows the developer to redirect execution from one script to another script without an HTTP response being sent to the client. All information from the first script, including values in the Request and other objects, is available in full to the second script. Unlike Server.Execute, Server.Transfer does not return control to the script that called the Transfer method when the called ASP page has Finished executing. The method is new to ASP 3.0/IIS 5.0.

Parameters

strPath
> The relative or absolute path to the second script to which execution will be redirected.

Example

```
******** BEGIN Transfer Example: First Script ********

<%
' Transfer Example: First Script

' First Script calls Second Script, which uses Transfer
' to redirect execution to Third Script.
%>
<HTML>
<HEAD>
<TITLE>
Server.Transfer Example
</TITLE>
</HEAD>
<BODY>
```

```
<FORM ACTION="TransferExample_Process1.asp?qsvalue=hannah1" METHOD="post">
First Name: <INPUT TYPE="text" NAME="txtFName" VALUE=""><BR>
Last Name: <INPUT TYPE="text" NAME="txtLName" VALUE=""><BR>
Address: <INPUT TYPE="text" NAME="txtAddress" VALUE=""><BR>
City: <INPUT TYPE="text" NAME="txtCity" VALUE=""> 
State: <INPUT TYPE="text" NAME="txtState" VALUE=""><BR>
Zipcode: <INPUT TYPE="text" NAME="txtZipcode" VALUE=""><BR>
<INPUT TYPE="submit" VALUE="Submit">
</FORM>
</BODY>
</HTML>
******** END Transfer Example: First Script ********




******** BEGIN Transfer Example: Second Script ********
<%
Application("strExample1") = "ApplicationStringValue"
Session("strExample2") = "SessionStringValue"
Server.Transfer "TransferExample_Process2.asp"
Application("strExample1") = "NEWApplicationStringValue"
Session("strExample2") = "NEWSessionStringValue"
%>
******** END Transfer Example: Second Script ********




******** Begin Transfer Example: Third Script ********
<%
' Transfer Example: Third Page

' First Page calls Second Page, which uses Transfer
' to redirect execution to Third Page.
%>
<HTML>
<HEAD>
<TITLE>
Server.Transfer Example
</TITLE>
</HEAD>
<BODY>
<%
Response.Write "First Name: " & Request.Form("txtFName") & "<BR>"
Response.Write "Last Name: " & Request.Form("txtLName") & "<BR>"
Response.Write "Address: " & Request.Form("txtAddress") & "<BR>"
Response.Write "City: " & Request.Form("txtCity") & "<BR>"
Response.Write "State: " & Request.Form("txtState") & "<BR>"
Response.Write "Zipcode: " & Request.Form("txtZipcode") & "<BR><BR>"

Response.Write "Application Variable: " & Application("strExample1") & "<BR>"
Response.Write "Session Variable: " & Session("strExample2") & "<BR>"

%>
```

```
</BODY>
</HTML>
******** END Transfer Example: Third Script ********
```

Notes

If you use this code, create the three scripts, and test them in a browser, you will see something similar to the following as a final result:

```
First Name: keyton
Last Name: weissinger
Address: 123 Main Street
City: Somewhereville
State: Alabama
Zipcode: 30087

Application Variable: ApplicationStringValue
Session Variable: SessionStringValue
```

Note that the Application and Session variables are not updated by the code in the block after the call to the Transfer method.

As demonstrated in the example, when you call the Transfer method, all information available to the first script from the built-in ASP objects is also available to the second script. Note, however, that this is not the case for script-level variables. If you declare and initialize a variable in the first script, it is not available in the second script.

Also, if there are any variables with Application- or Session-level scope, the second script also has access to these—even if the second script is in another application space.

It is important to note two things about the Transfer method. The first is that, as you might expect, an error will be raised if you attempt to use the Transfer method after some response has already been sent to the client, so set the Buffer property of the Response object to **True** to avoid this problem, if appropriate.

The second thing to note about the Transfer method is that no further script after the call to Transfer method is executed. For example, in the following example, the third and fourth lines of code will be completely ignored:

```
Session("intMyVar") = 1
Server.Transfer "SomeOtherScript.asp"
Session("intMyVar") = 2
Session("intMyOtherVar") = 3
```

After the execution of the preceding block of code, the Session variable, *intMyVar* will still have the value of 1 and the *intMyOtherVar* variable will still be undefined unless defined elsewhere before the execution of this block of code.

URLEncode   Server.URLEncode (*strURL*)

Encodes a string that can then be sent over the address line as a query string.

Parameters

strURL

> The string value you want to encode to send over the address line as a query string.

Example

```
<%

' The following encodes the URL
' http://www.myserver.com/apps/search.asp
Dim strOldURL
Dim strNewURL

strOldURL = "http://www.myserver.com/apps/search.asp"
strNewURL = Server.URLEncode(strOldURL)

' This encoding results in the following string value being
' placed in the strNewURL variable:
' http%3A%2F%2Fwww%2Emyserver%2Ecom%2Fapps%2Fsearch%2Easp

' This new string value could be used in a query string to
' represent a "next script," as demonstrated here:

%>
<HTML>
<HEAD><TITLE>URLEncode Example</TITLE></HEAD>
<BODY>
<FORM ACTION="/apps/CalcAndRedirect.asp?newURL=<%=strNewURL%>" METHOD =
POST>
<INPUT TYPE = TEXT NAME = "First Value">
<INPUT TYPE = TEXT NAME = "Second Value">
<INPUT TYPE = SUBMIT NAME = "Calculate Results">
</FORM>
</BODY>
</HTML>
```

Notes

The URLEncode method, like the HTMLEncode method, is straightforward and easy to use. It is imperative that you use the URLEncode method any time you are forced to send information over the address line instead of posting information using the POST method. If you do not encode your information and place it into the QueryString collection (through the GET method), its interpretation is unpredictable, depending on the data sent.

If you send information in the query string (i.e., from visible frame to visible frame), but not over the address line, this encoding is done for you.

CHAPTER 10

Session Object

One of the greatest challenges you face in constructing a full-featured web application is keeping track of user-specific information while a user navigates your site without asking her to identify herself at every request from the server. Among other pieces of information that you need to maintain are a user's identification, a user's security clearance if applicable, and, in more advanced applications, user preferences that allow you to customize your web site's look and feel in response to selections made by the user. The primary problem with maintaining user-specific information is limitations in the currently standard HTTP 1.0 protocol.

Although HTTP 1.0 does provide a mechanism for persistent connections that allows you to maintain user identification and user-specific data, its utility is limited. Without getting into the technical details, the Hypertext Transfer Protocol 1.0 allows client browsers to send Keep-Alive messages to proxy servers. These messages basically tell the proxy server to maintain an open connection with the requesting client. However, these connection requests are often unrecognized by the proxy server. This problem in the proxy server results in a hung connection between the proxy server and the requested web server. In a nutshell, maintaining connections with web servers is prone to error and thus is unreliable in HTTP 1.0, still by far the protocol most commonly used by client browsers.

Microsoft Internet Information Server's (and other web servers') solution to this problem is to use the HTTP Persistent Client State Mechanism—better known as cookies—to identify the user. IIS handles this mechanism through the use of the Session built-in object.

The Session object represents the current user's session on the web server. It is user specific, and its properties and methods allow you to manipulate the information on the server that is specific to that user for the duration of that user's connection. This duration is defined as the time from the client's first request of a page within your web application until 20 minutes (20 minutes is a default value that can be changed—see "Timeout," later in this chapter) after the user's last request to the web server.

A user session can be initiated in one of three ways:

- A user not already connected to the server requests an Active Server Page that resides in an application containing a *GLOBAL.ASA* file with code for the Session_OnStart event.

- A user requests an Active Server Page whose script stores information in any session-scoped variable.

- A user requests an Active Server Page in an application whose *GLOBAL.ASA* file instantiates an object using the <OBJECT> tag with the SCOPE parameter set to Session.

Note that a user session is specific to a given application on your web site. In fact, it is possible to maintain session information for more than one application at a time if one application is rooted in a virtual directory that resides under the virtual directory designating another application.

The web server identifies each user with a unique SessionID value. This SessionID variable is assigned to each user at the beginning of his session on the web server and is stored in memory on the web server. The SessionID is stored on the client by writing a cookie containing the SessionID to the user's machine. This cookie is sent to the server each time the user makes a request. To identify the user, the server retrieves the cookie and matches it up with a SessionID held in memory.

In addition to the SessionID variable, you can store other information specific to individual users. You can initialize (or change) any session-level variable anywhere in any Active Server Pages script. To ensure that a session-level variable is initialized to a specific value, you can script code in the Session_OnStart event procedure in the *GLOBAL.ASA* file. This event procedure is fired when the user's session starts. The *GLOBAL.ASA* file (see Chapter 11, *Preprocessing Directives, Server-Side Includes, and GLOBAL.ASA*) is a special file that you can code specific to each ASP application. This file's code is processed when the user session begins.

As discussed earlier, the Session object is very important in maintaining information about individual users. You also can use the Session object to handle some of the special issues that are specific to non-English-speaking clients requesting information from your web site.

Comments/Troubleshooting

One of the most important things that you need to keep in mind when using the Session object is its scope. Any information you store with session-level scope is in scope for the duration of the user's session in a given application. This is a fine point. For example, assume your code deals with a session-level variable that was defined in the context of the Search application on your web site. This application's virtual directory, */search*, reflects the following physical directory:

```
D:\www\apps\search
```

The current script, *SearchStart.ASP*, resides in this directory. Assume that you have initialized a session-level variable, **strSearchPref**, in this script. Now the user moves to another application script, *ContribMain.ASP*, that resides in a separate

---

Session Object Summary

Properties
    CodePage
    LCID
    SessionID
    Timeout

Collections
    Contents
    StaticObjects

Methods
    Abandon
    Contents.Remove
    Contents.RemoveAll

Events
    Session_OnEnd
    Session_OnStart

---

application whose virtual directory, */contrib*, reflects the following physical directory:

```
D:\www\apps\contrib
```

If this user does not return to a script in the virtual directory encompassing the Search application within 20 minutes (or whatever the session duration is set to), the *strSearchPref* session-level variable value is reset. This is an important source of errors in complex web applications. A user session's session-level variables expire when the session ends, even if the time spent away from the application was spent in applications on the same web site.

One way to avoid this problem is to nest applications. For example, you can place the */contrib* virtual directory underneath the search directory, as reflected in the following path:

```
D:\www\apps\search\contrib
```

Using this configuration, all requests to the contribution application's virtual path, */contrib*, remain in the context of the search application.

I've noted that you can change the default length of time after which a user session ends. Why would you want to do this? There are two possible reasons. The first is that you want to save the user's session information for longer than 20 minutes. For example, you may know beforehand that a user will leave your site for more than 20 minutes and then return. The second possibility is that you want to terminate the user's session information sooner. For example, say you know your users do not stay connected to your site for very long and you want to minimize the impact on server memory consumption that saving session information in memory consumes. See "Timeout," later in this chapter, for how to set this information differently from the default.

All of this session-level information storage is based on the use of cookies sent to the client and then sent back to the server. What if the user has cookies turned off or is using an older browser that does not support the use of cookies? Well, if you are using Windows NT or Basic Authentication, you can identify the user from the LOGON_USER element of the Request object's ServerVariables collection. From this information, you can retrieve user-specific data from a database or text files on the server. If you are not using Windows NT or Basic Authentication, you will likely not be able to identify the user. In the past, you could use a user's IP address as an identifier, but with dynamically generated IP addresses using DHCP and firewalls, the IP address should be considered useless for the purpose of user identification.

Properties Reference

CodePage   Session.CodePage (= *intCodePageValue*)

Specifies or retrieves the code page that will be used by the web server to display dynamic content in the current script. A code page is a character set containing all the alphanumeric characters and punctuation used by a specific locale.

Parameters

intCodePageValue

An unsigned integer corresponding to a specific character set installed on the server. Setting the CodePage property will cause the system to display content using that character set. The following table lists only a few of the possible valid values for this parameter:

CodePage Value	Language
932	Japanese Kanji
950	Chinese
1252	American English (and most European languages)

Example

```
<%

' In the following code, assume that the original code
' page setting is 1252 for American English. The
' example demonstrates the use of the CodePage property
' of the Session object to temporarily set the character
' set to Chinese so the text sent to the browser uses the
' Chinese character set:
Dim uintOrigCodePage
Dim uintChineseCodePage

uintChineseCodePage = 950
uintOrigCodePage = Session.CodePage

Session.CodePage = uintChineseCodePage
%>
```

```
'  +-----------------------------------------------------------+
'  | This text is sent to the client browser using the         |
'  | Chinese character set.                                     |
'  +-----------------------------------------------------------+
<%

'  Remember to reset your CodePage property if you don't want
'  the rest of of the text created and placed into the HTML
'  stream to be displayed using the new character set.
Session.CodePage = uintOrigCodePage

%>
```

Notes

Remember that, by default, Active Server Pages uses whatever character set you set for the script page using the CODEPAGE directive (see Chapter 11). Setting the CodePage property overrides this only for text sent to the browser. Script text is still communicated between ASP and your script or your script and ActiveX components using the same character set declared using the CODEPAGE directive.

LCID   Session.LCID (= *intLCID*)

The locale represents a user preference for how certain information is formatted. For example, some locales have dates formatted in the Month/Day/Year format. This is the standard U.S. locale. Each locale is identified by that locale's unique LCID, or locale ID. This code is defined in the operating system.

You can set the locale identifier for your script's content using the LCID property of the Session object. The LCID property represents the valid locale identifier that will be used to display dynamic content to the web browser.

Parameters

intLCID
    A valid 32-bit locale identifier.

Example

```
<%

'  The following code demonstrates the use of the LCID property
'  to temporarily set the locale identifier to Standard French.

Dim intOrigLCID
Dim intFrenchLCID

intFrenchLCID = 1036
intOrigLCID = Session.LCID

Session.LCID = intFrenchLCID
%>
```

```
' +-----------------------------------------------------------+
' | This text sent to the client browser will be formatted    |
' | according to the rules set by the locale identifier for   |
' | Standard French. For example, dates would be formatted    |
' | using the Day/Month/Year format, instead of the U.S.      |
' | standard Month/Day/Year.                                  |
' +-----------------------------------------------------------+
<%

    ' The next line resets the LCID property:
    Session.LCID = intOrigLCID

%>
```

Notes

Similar to the CodePage property in syntax, the LCID property allows you to set the formatting rules for times and dates, and it also sets rules for alphabetizing strings.

If you use the ASP LCID directive, you are setting the locale identifier for the script's environment on the server. The Session.LCID property uses this value as a default. If you wish to send string or date/time information to the client using different formatting rules, you must set the LCID property of the Session object. However, doing so has no impact on how the strings and date/time values are formatted internally to the script.

SessionID
Session.SessionID

A read-only value that uniquely identifies each current user's session. This value is of data type Long and is stored as a cookie on the client machine. During a user's session, the user's browser sends this cookie to the web server as a means of identifying the user.

Parameters

None

Example

```
<%

    ' The following code retrieves the current SessionID for
    ' a given user:

    Dim lngUserSessionId

    lngUserSessionId = Session.SessionID

%>
```

Notes

The SessionID property is generated the first time a user requests a page from the web server. The web server creates a value for the SessionID property using a complex algorithm and then stores this value in the form of a cookie on the user's machine. Subsequently, each time the user requests a page from the web server, this cookie is sent to the server in the HTTP request header. The server is then able to identify the user according to her SessionID. The cookie is reinitialized only when the client restarts her browser or when the webmaster restarts the web server.

Note that the SessionID cookie lasts on the client browser and is sent to (and recognized by) the web server until one of the two machines (client or web server) is restarted. This time period has nothing to do with the Timeout property of the Session object. For example, assume a user's session ends or is abandoned by using the Abandon method of the Session object. Then the user (without having restarted her browser) revisits the site. Assuming also that the web server has not been restarted since the end of the last session, the web server will start a new session for the user but will use the same SessionID, which is again sent to the web server as part of the HTTP request.

This last point is important and is worth noting. *Only* if both the client browser and the web server applications have not been restarted can you assume a SessionID uniquely identifies a user. Do not use this value as a primary key, for example, as it is reset anytime either browser or server is stopped and restarted.

Remember also that a browser that does not support cookies or that has cookies turned off will not send the SessionID as part of the HTTP request header. In this case, you must rely on some other method to identify users. You also can prevent the web application from using cookies by using the `EnableSessionState` preprocessor directive (for more details, see Chapter 11).

To maintain information without using cookies, you could either append information from each request onto the QueryString or post the identifying information from a hidden form element on your page.

Timeout   `Session.Timeout (= ` *`intMinutes`* `)`

The length of time in minutes the web server will maintain a user's session information without requesting or refreshing a page. This value is set to 20 minutes by default.

Parameters

intMinutes

    The number of minutes for which the web server will maintain session information

Example

```
<%

    ' The following code resets the Timeout property of the
    ' Session object from its default of 20 minutes to 5
    ' minutes.

    Session.Timeout = 5

%>
```

Notes

The Timeout property is straightforward in use. You can set this property's value as high as you like, but note that the value for the Timeout property directly affects the memory consumption on the web server that each user session requires.

Consider setting this number lower (as in the example) when your site's users visit for only brief periods. If, however, each page is visited for a longer period of time (for example, one page may provide a client-side scripted calculator), you may want to consider increasing this value.

Note that, unlike most properties of the Session object, this property affects *all* user sessions, not just the current session. If you set the value of the Timeout property of the Session object to 120 minutes, *every* user's session information will remain in memory on the web server until 120 minutes after he last requests or refreshes a page.

Collections Reference

Contents Collection   `Session.Contents(Key)`

Contains all of the variables and objects added with session-level scope through script (i.e., *not* through the use of the `<OBJECT>` tag).

The Contents collection of the Session object, like other ASP collections, has the following properties:

Item

Retrieves the value of a specific member of the Contents collection. You specify which member using a string key (whose value is obtainable using the index through the Key property, described later in this section) or using an index number. For example, if you wish to initialize an element in the Contents collection with a value of Pi, you might use a line of code similar to the following:

```
Session.Contents.Item("Pi") = 3.14
```

In the preceding line of code, the desired element in the collection is specified using the key value "Pi." Thus initialized, you can then retrieve the value of this element of the Contents collection using the following line of code:

```
dblMyVar = Session.Contents.Item("Pi")
```

For reasons that will become clear in a moment, let's assume that this is the first element added to the Contents collection.

You could also retrieve the value of an element in the Contents collection using its index in the collection rather than a key, as demonstrated in the following line of code:

```
dblMyVar = Session.Contents.Item(1)
```

Note that you use a 1 (one), not a 0 (zero), to represent the first element in the Contents collection. This is a subtle point, since using a zero in this line of code will result in the variable *dblMyVar* being initialized with an undefined value. Unfortunately, this will not result in an error. It will result only in an improperly initialized variable:

```
dblMyVar = Session.Contents.Item(0) ' WRONG.
```

Item is the default property of the Contents collection and the Contents collection is the default collection of the Application object. This means that each of the following three lines of code is interpreted in exactly the same manner in your application:

```
Session.Contents.Item("Pi") = 3.14
Session.Contents("Pi") = 3.14
Session("Pi") = 3.14
```

Correspondingly, you would assume that the following three lines of code are also equivalent:

```
Session.Contents.Item(1) = 3.14159
Session.Contents(1) = 3.14159
Session(1) = 3.14159
```

However, this is only the case if the first element in the Contents collection has previously been defined using a key. Although not mentioned in the documentation that accompanies ASP, to use either of the preceding first two lines of code, the element must have been previously defined using a key. For example, assume you decide to add a second element to the Contents collection. You cannot initialize this element using either of the following lines of code:

```
Session.Contents.Item(2) = 3.14159     ' WRONG.
Session.Contents(2) = 3.14159          ' WRONG.
```

Unfortunately, even this exception has an exception. You *can* use the following code to initialize a second variable:

```
Session(2) = 3.14159
```

When you consider these inconsistencies, it becomes quickly apparent that it is always safest to use a key rather than an index when referencing the value of a specific element in the Contents collection.

Also, it is important to use a key when referring to a specific member of the Contents collection because that member's index may change. For example, suppose you have the following code in your application:

```
Session("strFirstName") = "Arthur"
Session("strMiddleName") = "Keyton"
Session("strLastName") = "Weissinger"
```

Assuming these variables are the first three added to the Contents collection, you could later refer to each using its index:

```
strFirst = Session(1)
strMiddle = Session(2)
strLast = Session(3)
```

However, if you use the Remove method, which completely removes a variable from the collection (see later in this chapter), to remove the *strMiddleName* variable, the index numbers will change:

```
Session.Contents.Remove("strMiddleName")

strFirst = Session(1)        ' Initializes to "Arthur"
strMiddle = Session(2)       ' Initializes to "Weissinger"
strLast = Session(3)         ' Initializes to Undefined.
```

Key

Represents the name of a specific element in the Contents collection. Remember from earlier that each element's value is represented by the Item property. Similarly, each element's name is represented by its Key property.

If you do not know the name of a specific key, you can obtain it using its ordinal reference. For example, assume that you want to learn the key name for the third element in the collection and, subsequently, retrieve that element's value. You could use the following code:

```
strKeyName = Session.Contents.Key(3)
strKeyValue = Session.Contents.Item(strKeyName)
```

Count

Returns the current number of elements in the collection.

As with other ASP collections, you can retrieve the value of any field of the Contents collection through the use of the Item property. However, as in other places in this book, in the following examples, the syntax has been abbreviated so that it does not explicitly show the use of the Item property. For example:

```
strSecurityCode = Session("UserSecurityCode")
```

is an abbreviated form of:

```
strSecurityCode = Session.Contents.Item("UserSecurityCode")
```

 For more information on the Item, Key, and Count properties of a collection, see the discussion in the section "Contents Collection" in Chapter 4, *Application Object.*

Until ASP 3.0, items stored to the Contents collection remained in memory until the user session ended. ASP 3.0, on the other hand, adds two methods that allow members of the collection to be removed.

Remove   Session.Contents.Remove(*Key* | *Index*)

Removes a specific member from the Contents collection. An addition in IIS 5.0, the Remove method allows you to remove from memory a specific variable from the Session's Contents collection without removing all the others.

The Remove method is an important addition to the Contents collection because it allows for better memory control and cleanup. It allows you to remove from memory some of your collection's elements without abandoning the user's session. As discussed under the Item property of the Contents collection, it is very important to use a string key instead of an index when calling the Remove method. An element's index may change over the life of the application, and your call to Remove may lead to unpredictable results.

Parameters

Key

> A string variable that specifies the name of the specific member of the Contents collection to be removed.

Index

> An integer variable that specifies the index of the specific member of the Contents collection to be removed.

Example

The following script removes two members of the Contents collection:

```
<%
' This script assumes you have been "carrying around" various form
' variables for an online membership request form. The user has filled
' out the form, she has a username and is now a member. Now you would
' like to remove her form data which you stored in Session variables
' because it was convenient and the form's security had to be relatively
' high.
strFirstName = Session("strFirstName")
strLastName  = Session("strLastName")



   .
   .
   .
Session.Contents.Remove("strFirstName")
Session.Contents.Remove("strLastName")
   .
   .
   .
%>
```

RemoveAll   Session.Contents.RemoveAll

Removes all members from the Contents collection. An addition in IIS 5.0, the RemoveAll method allows you to remove from memory all Session-scoped variables without abandoning the Session.

Like the Remove method, the RemoveAll method is an important addition to the Contents collection because it allows for better memory control and cleanup. It allows you to remove all Session-scoped variables without abandoning the session itself.

Parameters

None

Examples

The following script removes all members of the Contents collection:

```
<%
' This script assumes you have been "carrying around" various form
' variables for an online membership request form. The user has
```

```
' filled out the form, she has a username
' and is now a member. Now you would like to remove her form data which
' you stored in Session variables because it was convenient and the
' form's security had to be relatively high.
' strFirstName = Session("strFirstName")
' strLastName  = Session("strLastName")

  .
  .
  .
Session.Contents.RemoveAll
  .
  .
  .
%>
```

The following script is the first of two ASP scripts that the user will visit (the first redirects the user's browser to the second). In this first script, the user's session-level variables are created (*SessionVar1*, *SessionVar2*, and *SessionVar3*).

```
<HTML>
<HEAD><TITLE>Session Contents Example Page1</TITLE></HEAD>
<BODY>
<%
Dim strVar1
Dim strVar2
Dim strVar3

strVar1 = "Session Variable 1"
strVar2 = "Session Variable 2"
strVar3 = "Session Variable 3"

' Each of the next three varieties of syntax
' are equivalent.
Session.Content.Item("SessionVar1") = strVar1
Session.Content("SessionVar2") = strVar2
Session("SessionVar3") = strVar3

Response.Redirect SessionPage2.asp
%>
</BODY>
</HTML>
```

In this second script, we'll take a look at the current elements in the Contents collection of the Session object.

```
<HTML>
<HEAD><TITLE>Session Contents Example Page2</TITLE></HEAD>
<BODY>
<%
Dim intContentsCount
Dim strAppStatus
Dim strKey
Dim intCounter
Dim objMyComponent
```

```
Dim arystrNames()


intContentsCount = Session.Contents.Count
strAppStatus = "Open"
%>
There are <%= intContentsCount %> items in the
Session's Contents collection. <BR>
<%
For Each strKey in Session.Contents
%>
    The next item in Session's Contents collection<BR>
    has <%= strKey %> as its key and
    <%= Session.Contents(strKey) %>
    as its value.<BR>
<%
Next

' Set the AppStatus item in the Contents collection.
' If this Session variable has been created before this,
' this line resets its value. If it has not been
' created, this line creates it.
strAppStatus = "Page2...InProcess..."
Session("AppStatus") = strAppStatus

%>
The first three elements of the Session's Contents
collection are as follows: <BR>
<%
' Retrieve the first three elements of the Contents
' collection.
For intCounter = 1 to 3
%>
    <%= Session.Contents(intCounter) %> <BR>
<%
Next
%>
A second trip through the first three items.
<%
' This could just as accurately have been written
' like this:
For intCounter = 1 to 3
%>
    <%= Session.Contents.Item(intCounter) %> <BR>
<%
Next

' Add an object to the Contents collection, then use that
' object's PrintDoc method through the Contents collection.
' (NOTE: For more on the Server object, see Chapter 9.)

'************************************************************
' If you try this script on your own, it will raise an error
' because of the lack of the Server component.
'************************************************************
```

```
Set objMyComponent = Server.CreateObject("MyComp.clsSpecial")
Session ("objRef") = objMyComponent

' Call the object's method through the Contents collection.
Session ("objRef").PrintDoc
%>
</BODY>
</HTML>
```

Notes

If you add an object variable to the Session object's Contents collection, you can access that object's methods and properties through the Contents syntax. For example, the following code creates an instance of the MyServerComp object and then refers to its LastUpdated property:

```
Dim datLastUpdatet
Set Session.Contents(objSessionMyObj) = _
    Server.CreateObject("MyCompanyDLL.MyServerComp")
datLastUpdated = Session.Contents(objSessionMyObj).LastUpdated
```

When adding an array to the Contents collection, add the entire array. When changing an element of the array, retrieve a copy of the array, change the element, and then add the array as a whole to the Contents collection again. The following example demonstrates this point:

```
<% Response.Buffer = True%>
<HTML>
<HEAD><TITLE>Session Array Example</TITLE></HEAD>
<BODY>
<%
' Create an array variable and add it to the
' Contents collection.
ReDim arystrNames(3)

arystrNames(0) = "Chris"
arystrNames(1) = "Julie"
arystrNames(2) = "Vlad"
arystrNames(3) = "Kelly"

Session.Contents("arystrUserNames") = arystrNames
%>
The second name in the User Names array is <BR>
<%= Session("arystrUserNames")(1) %>
<%

' Change an element of the array being held in the
' Contents collection. Use a different (new) array
' to temporarily hold the contents. Creating a new
' array is the safest way to work with Session
' arrays because most of the time you cannot be
' guaranteed how many elements are contained
' in a Session array created in another script.
arystrNames2 = Session("arystrUserNames")
arystrNames2(1) = "Mark"
```

```
Session("arystrUserNames") = arystrNames2
' The second name is now Mark.
%>
<BR><BR>Now, the second name in the User Names array is <BR>
<%= Session("arystrUserNames")(1) %><BR>
<BR><BR><BR><BR><BR>
NOTE: The first element of the Contents collection is still
1, not 0 -- even though the first element of the array in element 1
("arystrUserNames") is 0:<BR><BR>
<%= Session.Contents(1)(0)%> <BR>
</BODY></HTML>
```

Objects created in the *GLOBAL.ASA* file are not actually instantiated on the server until the first time a property or method of that object is called.

If you intend to use a given object in a transaction using the ObjectContext object, do not give that object application or session scope. An object used in a transaction is destroyed at the end of the transaction, and any subsequent reference to its properties or calls to its methods will result in an error.

You will notice that the Contents (and StaticObjects) collection for the Session object is very similar to the Contents collection of the Application object.

Although the Contents collection is the default collection of the Session object, there is one unusual behavior that differentiates it from the Contents collection of the Application object: You cannot retrieve an item directly from the Session object, because your implicit references to the Contents collection (the Session object's default collection) and the Item method (the collection's default value) cannot be resolved successfully.

Suppose you have the following code:

```
<HTML>
<HEAD><TITLE>Strange Behaviour</TITLE></HEAD>
<BODY>
<%
Session.Contents.Item("Item1") = "SessionVar1"
Session.Contents.Item("Item2") = "SessionVar2"
Session.Contents.Item("Item3") = "SessionVar3"
%>
. . . [additional code]
```

Because the Contents collection is the default collection of the Session object, you can refer to Item2 using the following line of code:

```
strNewVar = Session("Item2")
```

However, unlike the Contents collection of the Application object, you cannot refer to the same element using the following line of code. This line of code will either be ignored or will raise an error, depending on the variable you are trying to retrieve:

```
strNewVar = Session(2)
```

However:

```
strNewVar = Session.Contents.Item(2)
```

or:

```
strNewVar = Session.Contents(2)
```

work just fine.

I was unable to find this behavior documented anywhere, but I found it to be consistent on IIS and Personal Web Server.

StaticObjects Collection

Session.StaticObjects(*Key*)

Contains all of the objects with session-level scope that are added to the application through the use of the <OBJECT> tag. You can use the StaticObjects collection to retrieve properties of a specific object in the collection. You also can use the StaticObjects collection to use a specific method of a given object in the collection.

The StaticObjects collection of the Session object, like other ASP collections, has the following properties:

Item

Represents the value of a specific element in the collection. To specify an item, you can use an index number or a key.

Key

Represents the name of a specific element in the collection. For example:

```
strFirstObjName = _
    Session.StaticObjects.Key(1)
```

retrieves the name of the first element in the StaticObjects collection of the Session object.

Use the value of the Key property to retrieve the value of an element by name. For example, suppose the first element's name is *objMyObject*. The code:

```
strKey = Session.StaticObjects.Key(1)
Session.StaticObjects.Item(strKey).Printer = "Epson 540"
```

then sets the value of the Printer property of the *objMyObject* element in the StaticObjects collection of the Session object.

Count

Returns the current number of elements in the collection.

As with other ASP collections, you can retrieve the value of any field of the StaticObjects collection through the use of the Item property. However, as in other places in this book, in the following examples, the syntax has been abbreviated so that it does not explicitly show the use of the Item property. For example:

```
strPrinterName = Session.StaticObjects("objMyObj").Printer
```

is an abbreviated form of:

```
strPrinterName = Session.StaticObjects.Item("objMyObj").Printer
```

For more information on the Item, Key, and Count properties of a collection, see the discussion in the section "Contents Collection" in Chapter 4.

Example

```
' <<<<<<<<<<<<<<< FROM GLOBAL.ASA >>>>>>>>>>>>>>>>>
' This code resides in the GLOBAL.ASA file at the
' root of the current application. The following
' <OBJECT> tag is only processed once for the current
' application.
' See Chapter 11 for more details on the GLOBAL.ASA file.

<OBJECT RUNAT=Server
SCOPE=Session
ID=AppInfo1
PROGID="MSWC.MyInfo">
</OBJECT>

<OBJECT RUNAT=Server
SCOPE=Session
ID=AppInfo2
PROGID="MSWC.MyInfo">
</OBJECT>

' <<<<<<<<<<<<<<<<<<<<<<<<<<<>>>>>>>>>>>>>>>>>>>>>>>>>>


<%
' The following code initializes the AppInfo1 component.
' This initialization code can reside anywhere.
AppInfo1.PersonalName = "Gertrude Stein"
AppInfo1.PersonalAddress = "233 Main Street"

AppInfo2.PersonalName = "David Davidson"
AppInfo2.PersonalAddress = "19A West Avenue"

' The following code uses the StaticObjects collection
' of the Session object to retrieve the value
' of the PersonalName property of both AppInfo1 and AppInfo2.
For Each objInfo In Session.StaticObjects
%>
    The personal name is <BR>
    <%= Session.StaticObjects(objInfo).PersonalName%>
<%
Next
%>

There are <%= Session.StaticObjects.Count %> items
in the Session's StaticObjects collection.
```

Notes

The Session object's StaticObjects collection allows you to access any given object instantiated with session scope through the use of an `<OBJECT>` tag. Objects instantiated using Server.CreateObject are not accessible through this collection.

The StaticObjects example in the IIS 5.0 documentation by Microsoft suggests that if you iterate through this collection, you will be able to reference each object's properties. This is somewhat misleading, as it suggests that the collection actually represents all the properties of the objects rather than the objects themselves. If you want to access the properties or methods of objects in the StaticObjects collection, you must use the dot operator outside of the parentheses around the Key, followed by the property or method name, as demonstrated here:

```
<%= Session.StaticObjects(objInfo).PersonalName%>
```

This line of code works because `Session.StaticObjects(objInfo)` returns a reference to the *objInfo* object.

Objects created in the *GLOBAL.ASA* file are not actually instantiated on the server until the first time a property or method of that object is called. For this reason, the StaticObjects collection cannot be used to access these objects' properties and methods until some other code in your application has caused them to be instantiated on the server.

If you intend to use a given object in a transaction using the ObjectContext object, do not give that object application or session scope. Objects used in transactions are destroyed at the end of the transaction and any subsequent reference to their properties or calls to their methods will result in an error.

Methods Reference

Abandon   Session.Abandon

Releases the memory used by the web server to maintain information about a given user session. It does not, however, affect the session information of other users. If the Abandon method is not explicitly called, the web server will maintain all session information until the session times out.

Parameters

None

Example

The following script allows the user to click on a link that will redirect his browser to a page that will clear his session variables:

```
<HTML>
<HEAD><TITLE>Session Abandom Example Page1</TITLE></HEAD>
<BODY>
Click <A HREF = "/SessionAbandonPage2.asp">here</A> to reset your user
preferences.
</BODY>
</HTML>
```

The following script actually clears the session variables:

```
<HTML>
<HEAD><TITLE>Session Abandom Example Page2</TITLE></HEAD>
<BODY>
<%

' The following code abandons the current user session.
' Note that the actual information stored for the current
' user session is not released by the server until the
' end of the current Active Server Pages.

Session.Abandon

%>
Your user preferences have now been reset.
</BODY>
</HTML>
```

Notes

If you make heavy use of the Session object's Contents collection, the Abandon method can come in very handy. Suppose, for example, that you have many different user preferences saved as session variables and, as in the example, you want to remove them all and allow the user to select all new ones. Without the Abandon method, you would have to remove each variable from the Contents collection by hand—a slow and laborious prospect if you have several variables. The Abandon method allows you to remove them all in one line of code.

The Abandon method is actually processed by the web server after the rest of the current page's script is processed. After the current page's processing is complete, however, any page request by the user initiates a new session on the web server.

In the following example, the session variable *intUserAge* is available to your script until the end of the page. The Abandon method does not remove the variable from memory until the end of the page:

```
Session("intUserAge") = 23
Session.Abandon
[...More Code...]
' The current line successfully retrieves the value of
' intUserAge.
intAgeCategory = CInt(Session("intUserAge") / 10)
[...End of Script. Session information is removed from web memory now...]
```

Events Reference

Session_OnEnd   Session_OnEnd

Triggered when the user's session times out or when your scripts call the Abandon method of the Session object.

The OnEnd event procedure, if it exists, resides in the *GLOBAL.ASA* file for the application that contains the requested page.

Parameters

None

Example

```
<SCRIPT LANGUAGE = "VBScript" RUNAT = Server>

Sub Session_OnEnd

    ' If the user has a search results recordset open, close
    ' it:
    If IsObject(adoRSResults) Then
        Set adoRSResults = Nothing
    End If

End Sub

</SCRIPT>
```

Notes

In the code for the OnEnd event procedure, you have access only to the Application, Server, and Session objects. Most important, you have no access to the Response object or Request object, and, for this reason, you cannot redirect the client or send cookies to (or receive cookies from) the client machine.

One of the possible uses of the OnEnd event is to write information concerning the user to a log file or other text file on the server for later use. If you intend to do this, there are several important points you must remember. First, before you can save any information, that information must be saved to a session variable because, as mentioned earlier, you do not have access to the Request object, which is the most common source of user information. The following code demonstrates one possible method of storing a session-level variable:

```
<SCRIPT LANGUAGE = "VBScript" RUNAT = Server>

Sub Session_OnEnd

    ' Assume that SessionVar1 contains some user-preference
    ' information.

    ' It is not important that you understand exactly what is
    ' happening in the following code (you can learn more about
    ' File objects in Chapter 19). Just suffice it to say
    ' that these lines of code write the value of the
    ' SessionVar1 Session variable to the text file
    ' UserPref.txt.
    Set fs = Server.CreateObject("Scripting.FileSystemObject")
    Set f = fs.GetFile("d:\UserPref.txt")
    Set ts = f.OpenAsTextStream(ForAppending,_
                        TristateUseDefault)
    ts.Write Session(SessionVar1)
    ts.Close
```

```
' Note that more often than not, if you want to save this
' information to the server at the end of a user's session,
' it may very well be more efficient to store it to a
' database than to a text file. However, the general
' principal (of storing Session variable information in
' the OnEnd event) is similar.

End Sub

</SCRIPT>
```

Note that you cannot use the AppendToLog method of the Response object, because the Response object is unavailable. In addition, if you intend to write directly to the web server's hard drive, you must know the physical path of the file to which you want to write. This is because, although you do have access to the Server object, you cannot use its MapPath method in the OnEnd event (for more information about the MapPath method, see "MapPath" in Chapter 9, *Server Object*).

Session_OnStart

Triggered any time a user who does not already have a session instantiated on the web server requests any page from the server. The code in the OnStart event of the Session object, if it exists, is processed before any code on the requested page.

The OnStart event procedure, if it exists, resides in the *GLOBAL.ASA* file for the application that contains the requested page.

Parameters

None

Example

```
<SCRIPT LANGUAGE = "VBScript" RUNAT = Server>

Sub Session_OnStart

    Dim strSiteStartPage
    Dim strCurrentPage
    Dim timUserStartTime
    Dim strUserIPAddress
    Dim strUserLogon

    ' Use the OnStart event to initialize session-level
    ' variables that your scripts can use throughout the
    ' the duration of the user's session.
    Session("timUserStartTime") = Now()
    Session("strUserIPAddress") = _
            Request.ServerVariables("REMOTE_ADDR")

    ' Use the OnStart event to redirect the client if
    ' she attempts to enter the site from somewhere
    ' other than the site's home page.
```

```
strCurrentPage = Request.ServerVariables("SCRIPT_NAME")
strSiteStartPage = "/apps/home/startpage.asp"

If StrComp(strCurrentPage, strSiteStartPage, 1) Then
    Response.Redirect(strSiteStartPage)
End If

' You can also use the OnStart event of the Session
' object to assess user security access from the very
' beginning of the user's session. Note this code requires
' use of either the Basic authentication or Windows
' NT Challenge Response access control on the web server.
strUserLogon = Request.ServerVariables("LOGON_USER")
[...Code to Determine Security Level...]
```

```
End Sub
```

```
</SCRIPT>
```

Notes

If the client's browser does not support cookies or if the user has manually turned cookies off, the Session_OnStart event is processed *every* time the user requests a page from the site. No session is started or maintained.

Like the OnEnd event, one of the possible uses of the OnStart event is to write information concerning the user to a log file or other text file on the server for later use. If you intend to do this, note that you cannot use the AppendToLog method of the Response object, and if you intend to write directly to the web server's hard drive, you must know the physical path of the file to which you want to write. This is because, although you do have access to the Server object, just as in the OnEnd event of the Session object, you cannot use the MapPath method of the Server object in the Session_OnStart event.

CHAPTER 11

Preprocessing Directives, Server-Side Includes, and GLOBAL.ASA

This chapter provides a catch-all description of several features of Active Server Pages applications that do not neatly fit into groups defined on the basis of the ASP object model:

- *Preprocessing directives*, the method by which you instruct the web server to perform certain functions *before* processing the script in the Active Server Pages

- Server-Side Includes, which allow you to easily include commonly used code into your scripts; this allows you to write reusable code that need only be stored and maintained in one centralized location

- The *GLOBAL.ASA* file

Preprocessing Directives

Active Server Pages provides *preprocessing directives* similar to the compiler directives in C and similar languages. Like these precompilation directives, ASP directives instruct the web server to perform a function before the script is completed and sent to the client. The web server performs the other directives before interpreting the script itself. ASP directives, with the exception of `<%= expression %>`, must appear on the first line of a script and cannot be included using a Server-Side Included file. The format for these directives (with the aforementioned exception of the `<%= expression %>` directive) is the following:

```
<%@ DIRECTIVE=Value%>
```

where `DIRECTIVE` is one of the ASP directives listed in this section and `Value` is a valid value for the directive. Note that you must include a space between the @ character and the directive. Also note that the preprocessing directive must be placed within `<%...%>` delimiters.

The valid ASP preprocessing directives are listed as follows and are explained in depth later in this chapter:

CODEPAGE
ENABLESESSIONSTATE
LANGUAGE
LCID
TRANSACTION

Preprocessing Directives: Comments/Troubleshooting

The space between the @ character and the directive and the requirement that directives be placed on the first line of a script are syntactically the most important features of an ASP directive. The failure to include the space or to include directives on the first line of a script are the most common errors when using directives.

You may ask yourself how you can have more than one directive in a script if directives, with the exception of `<%= expression %>`, must be placed on the first line of a script. To include more than one directive, use the following syntax:

```
<%@ DIRECTIVE1=Value DIRECTIVE2=Value %>
```

You must include at least one space between each directive. Also, you must *not* place spaces around the equal signs (=).

Preprocessing Directives Reference

CODEPAGE   `<%@CODEPAGE=uintCodePage%>`

Sets the character set (or code page) to be used to interpret the script on the server. Different languages and locales use unique code pages. This directive provides similar functionality for the interpretation of scripts on the server as the CodePage property of the Session object provides for client-side interpretation of the HTML sent to the client. However, it is important to note that the CODEPAGE preprocessing directive dictates how the script itself is interpreted, whereas the CodePage property of the Session object dictates how the resulting HTML is processed.

Parameters

`uintCodePage`
> An unsigned integer value corresponding to a valid code page for the web server running the ASP script

Example

```
<%@ CODEPAGE=932%>

' This code sets the code page to OEM 932, which is
' used for Japanese Kanji.
```

Notes

You can have both the CODEPAGE directive and the CodePage property for the Session object in the same script. This results in the server-side script being interpreted using the unsigned integer set for the CODEPAGE directive and the client information being interpreted using the code page set of the CodePage property of the Session object.

ENABLESESSIONSTATE

`<%@ ENABLESESSIONSTATE=True|False%>`

Turns the storage of user-specific session information on (**True**) or off (**False**). This value is **True** by default.

Parameters

None

Example

```
<%@ ENABLESESSIONSTATE=False%>

' This code prevents the web server from storing
' user session information.
```

Notes

You also can enable session-state storage using the registry, but this directive allows significantly more flexibility (and on a script-by-script basis). If you have used a registry setting to control session-state information, then using this directive overrides that setting.

Setting this directive to **False** prevents you from storing any information in session-scoped variables or objects. This forces you to rely on other methods of maintaining information about each user, if you need to. However, it does provide some benefits:

- It does not rely on your clients' browsers using cookies.

- It increases the speed with which your server scripting is processed by the web server.

LANGUAGE

`<%@ LANGUAGE=ScriptingEngine%>`

Sets the default scripting engine the web server will use to process the script in your ASP. This is set to VBScript by default.

Parameters

`ScriptingEngine`

A valid scripting engine recognized by Internet Information Server. The valid scripting engines include VBScript, JScript, PerlScript, Python, and REXX.

Example

```
<%@ LANGUAGE="JScript"%>

' This code sets the language for the current page to
' JScript, Microsoft's interpretation of the JavaScript
' scripting language. All script on this page will be
' interpreted using the JScript DLL.
```

Notes

Setting the LANGUAGE directive does not prevent you from using other scripting engines on your script page. It only sets the default scripting engine for interpretation of script on the current page. The following example shows how you can set the default scripting engine for the page to JScript and still use VBScript for a specific procedure:

```
<%@ LANGUAGE="JScript"%>
<SCRIPT LANGUAGE="VBScript" RUNAT="Server">
Sub ShowReport()
    ' This script will be interpreted using the VBScript
    ' scripting engine.
End Sub
</SCRIPT>
```

Furthermore, setting the LANGUAGE directive value has no effect on the scripting engine used on the client side. Even if you set the LANGUAGE of the server-side script to PerlScript,* for example, you can still set the LANGUAGE attribute of the client-side <SCRIPT> tag to JScript, as in the following example:

```
<%@ LANGUAGE="PerlScript"%>

<%
' All server-side script is interpreted using the PerlScript
' scripting engine.
%>

HTML here...
<SCRIPT LANGUAGE="JScript">
Sub btnReport_onClick
    ' This script will be interpreted using the JScript
    ' scripting engine.
End Sub
</SCRIPT>
```

LCID   `<%@ LCID=dwordLCID%>`

Sets a valid locale identifier for a given script. This directive specifies various formats (such as dates and times) to use for data on the server side.

Parameters

dwordLCID
    A DWORD (32-bit unsigned) value that represents a valid locale ID.

Example

```
<%@ LCID=1036%>

' This code sets the locale ID for the server-side
' script to that for French.
```

---

* Note that only the VBScript and JScript scripting engines are included with IIS. All other scripting engines must be obtained and installed separately.

Notes

Just as setting the `CODEPAGE` directive has no effect on the CodePage property of the Session object and what character set is used on the client side, setting the `LCID` directive has no effect on the LCID used on the client side. However, it is important to note that the LCID preprocessing directive dictates how the script itself is interpreted, whereas the LCID property of the Session object dictates how the resulting HTML is processed.

TRANSACTION   `<%@ TRANSACTION=strValue%>`

Instructs the web server to treat the entire script as a single transaction. If you set the script as requiring a transaction, the web server uses Microsoft Transaction Server to ensure that the entire script is processed as a single unit (or transaction) or not at all. Currently, only database manipulation is available in transactions.

Parameters

`strValue`

> The possible values for the `strValue` parameter are as follows:

> `Required`
>> Instructs the web server that the current script requires a transaction

> `Requires_New`
>> Instructs the web server that the current script requires a new transaction

> `Supported`
>> Instructs the web server *not* to start a transaction

> `Not_Supported`
>> Instructs the web server *not* to start a transaction

Example

```
<%@ TRANSACTION=Required%>

' This code instructs the web server to start a new
' transaction for the current script.
```

Notes

Note that the value for the `TRANSACTION` directive is not a string. For this reason, you must use an underscore for those values that contain a space (`Requires_New` and `Not_Supported`). As discussed in Chapter 6, *ObjectContext Object*, only a single script can be encapsulated in a transaction. You must ensure that the `TRANSACTION` directive is the first line in a transactional script. Otherwise, it will result in an error. Finally, you cannot encapsulate the *GLOBAL.ASA* code in a transaction.

If an error occurs in a script encapsulated in a transaction, Microsoft Transaction Server will roll back any actions that support transactions. Currently, only database actions support transactions. For example, not all disk activity is supported by MTS-based transactions and must be rolled back manually.

Server-Side Includes

Similar to preprocessing directives, Server-Side Includes allow you to include various values (for instance, the last modified date of a file) or a complete file in your script. The following are the Server-Side Include directives supported by IIS:

#config
> Configures the format for error messages, dates, and file sizes as they are returned to the client browser

#echo
> Inserts the value of an environment variable (equivalent to the various elements of the Request object's ServerVariables collection) into a client's HTML page

#exec
> Inserts the results of a command-line shell command or application

#flastmod
> Inserts the last modified date/time for the current page

#fsize
> Inserts the file size of the current file

#include
> Includes the contents of another file into the current file

All directives are allowed in HTML. Only the #include directive, however, is allowed in both HTML and ASP pages. The #include directive is the only one detailed here.

Server-Side Includes: Comments/Troubleshooting

Including files is an excellent method for writing reusable code. We use it often for code we use in almost every script, such as establishing a connection to a database or closing the connection once your code has no more need of it. Your Server-Side Include files need not end with any specific file extension, but Microsoft suggests the *.INC* file extension as a way of maintaining easily manageable sets of ASP scripts and include files for your projects. Remember that your Server-Side Include files cannot include other files, nor can they contain preprocessing directives described earlier in this chapter.

#include

```
<!-- #include PathType = "strFileName" -->
```

The #include Server-Side Include allows you to insert the contents of a given file into the HTML content or ASP script. You must surround the #include Server-Side Include statement in an HMTL comment. Otherwise, the text of the Server-Side Include will be displayed as straight text.

Parameters

PathType
> The type of path specified in the *strFileName* parameter. The possible values for *PathType* are described in the following table:

PathType Value	Description
File	Treats the value of the *strFileName* parameter as a relative path from the current directory
Virtual	Treats the value of the *strFileName* parameter as a full virtual path

strFileName

The *strFileName* parameter represents the name of the file whose contents you want inserted into the HTML content.

Introduced with IIS 5.0, there is a second way to include a file. You can use the <SCRIPT> tag combined with the SRC attrribute using the following format:

```
<SCRIPT LANGUAGE = "VBScript" RUNAT=SERVER SRC="strFileName">
</SCRIPT>
```

In the preceding code, the *strFileName* parameter is the same as that used with the INCLUDE directive and can be an absolute or relative path.

Example 1

The following script contains only a simple "back to top" line of code and a horizontal line with a graphic.

```
<!-ReturnTop.INC -->
<CENTER>
<HR>
Click <A HREF = #top>here</A> to go back to the top of the page.<BR>
<IMG SRC = "/Images/CorpLogo.GIF"></CENTER><BR>
```

We could now include this file anywhere we needed a return to the top of a page:

```
<HTML>
<HEAD><TITLE>Include Example</TITLE></HEAD>
<BODY>
<%
[CODE TO RETRIEVE GLOSSARY TERMS FROM SQL SERVER DATABASE]
' Filter the recordset to include only the A's.
adoRecGlossary.Filter = "UPPER(SUBSTRING(GlossTerm, 1)) = 'A'"

' Iterate through the items in the filtered recordset.
Do While Not adoRecGlossary.EOF
%>
    Term: <%=adoRecGlossary("GlossTerm")%><BR>
    Definition: <%=adoRecGlossary("GlossDef")%><BR>
<%
    adoRecGlossary.MoveNext
Loop

' Next include the link to top file:
%>
<!-- #include virtual = "/Includes/ReturnTop.INC" -->

<%
' Repeat for the next letter...
```

```
... [additional code]
%>
</BODY>
</HTML>
```

Example 2

The following script contains ASP code that will be included in a file using the
<SCRIPT> tag combined with the SRC method:

```
' ReturnTop2.INC
Response.Write "<CENTER>"
Response.Write "<HR>"
Response.Write "Click <A HREF = #top>here</A> to go back to the top of
the page.<BR>"
Response.Write "<IMG SRC = ""/Images/CorpLogo.GIF""></CENTER><BR>"
```

We could now include this file anywhere we needed a return to the top of a page:

```
<HTML>
<HEAD>
<TITLE>Include Example 2</TITLE>
</HEAD>
This page will now include a file...<BR>
<SCRIPT LANGUAGE="VBScript" RUNAT-"SERVER" SRC="ReturnTop2.INC">
</SCRIPT>
    .
    .
    .
```

Notes

Using the INCLUDE directive, you can include files containing HTML or ASP code
or a combination of the two. Using the SCRIPT tag method to include a file (as in
the preceding example) the file you include must contain only ASP code.

The examples demonstrate how using include files can reduce the amount of
redundant work you are required to do, but these examples are very simple.
Suppose, as another example, that you have an include file containing the DSN of
your database, the username, and the password. You could use that include file all
over your site. It would then be a very simple matter to change username and
password: you'd just change it in the include file.

If you use the #include Server-Side Include to incorporate the contents of an
ASP, you must use the <%...%> pair around any script. Otherwise, the contents of
the file are treated as regular HTML code.

One use for this Server-Side Include is to localize the portions of your script that
are used often, such as database access information. This also allows you to
change usernames and passwords quickly and efficiently. If you choose to use the
#include Server-Side Include in this manner, ensure that whatever file you
include is secured properly.

You can include files within files that are, in turn, included in other files. You can
also include the contents of a given file multiple times in the same script. One
example of this is in a simple error-handling script. For example, consider the
following file:

```
<%
If Err.Number <> 0 Then
%>
<HTML>
<HEAD><TITLE>Error Notice</TITLE></HEAD>
<BODY>
There has been an error in your script (<%=Request.
ServerVariables("SCRIPT_NAME")%>.<BR>
Please contact customer service at 1-800-555-HELP and tell
them that you've experienced an error in (<%=Request.
ServerVariables("SCRIPT_NAME")%> and that the parameters sent to the
script were the following:<BR>
(<%=Request.ServerVariables("QUERY_STRING")%>.<BR><BR>
We apologize for the inconvenience.
</BODY>
</HTML>
<%
End If
%>
```

This file (named *ERROR.INC* in this example) could then be included into your
script anywhere you think an error might arise. For example, in the following
code, *ERROR.INC* is included after the ADO connection is established and after the
recordset object is created (note that for this form of error trapping to work, the
Buffer property of the Response object must be set to True):

```
<%Response.Buffer = True%>
<HTML>
<HEAD><TITLE>Database Info Page</TITLE></HEAD>
<BODY>
<%
Set adoCon = Server.CreateObject("ADODB.Connection")
AdoCon.Open "MyDatabase"
%>
<!-- #include virtual = "/Accessory/ERROR.INC" -->
<%
Set adoRec = adoCon.Execute ("SELECT * FROM TopSales")
%>
<!-- #include virtual = "/Accessory/ERROR.INC" -->
<%
. . . [additional code]
%>
</BODY>
```

In this script, if an error is raised when opening the database connection or when
creating the recordset, the user will see the contents of the *ERROR.INC* file,
containing a standard error notice and a help line phone number.

When you include a file, make sure that the included file does not include the
current file. This will result in a service-stopping error on the web server, requiring
that you stop and restart the web service.

You must also remember that Server-Side Includes are processed before any script
code. For this reason, you cannot dynamically determine which file to include. For
example, the following script will result in a runtime error:

```
<%
Dim strFileName
strFileName = "/Apps/CustomConstants.INC"
%>
<!-- #include file="<%=strFileName%>"-->
```

Finally, Server-Side Includes must be placed outside script delimiters (<%...%>), <SCRIPT></SCRIPT> tags, and <OBJECT></OBJECT> tags. For example, the following code will result in a runtime error (there is no closing %> delimiter):

```
<%
Dim strLastName
strLastName = "Weissinger"

<!-- #include file="/Apps/CustomConstants.INC"-->
```

The following code will also fail:

```
<SCRIPT LANGUAGE="VBScript">
Sub btnHello_Click()
    Dim strLastName
     strLastName = "Weissinger"

    <!-- #include file="/Apps/CustomConstants.INC"-->

End Sub
</SCRIPT>
```

This is the only Server-Side Include that you can use in both HTML and ASP files. If you use the #include Server-Side Include in a file, that file's extension must be one of those mapped to *SSINC.DLL*, the dynamic link library that interprets Server-Side Includes.

GLOBAL.ASA

The *GLOBAL.ASA* file is where you declare objects, variables, and event handlers (for the OnStart and OnEnd event procedures for the Application and Session objects, specifically) that have session or application scope. There can be only one *GLOBAL.ASA* file per virtual directory or ASP application. For example, suppose you have a Search ASP application made up of all the scripts in the */Search* virtual directory. You can have only one *GLOBAL.ASA* file in the virtual directory, and it must be in the root of the directory (*/Search*). A second *GLOBAL.ASA* file anywhere else in any subdirectory of */Search* will be ignored by *ASP.DLL*.

The *GLOBAL.ASA* file can contain no displayable content; any such content is ignored by *ASP.DLL*. Any script that is not encased in a <SCRIPT> tag results in an error, as does the instantiation of a server component that does not support session- or application-level scope. Finally, this file must be named *GLOBAL.ASA* and cannot reside anywhere other than in the root of the virtual directory that makes up the ASP application. Like other scripts, you can use any supported scripting language in the *GLOBAL.ASA* file, and you can group event procedures that use the same language within a common set of <SCRIPT>...</SCRIPT> tags.

The *GLOBAL.ASA* file section of this chapter covers the following topics:

- Application object events and application scope
- Session object events and session scope
- Type library declarations

GLOBAL.ASA: Comments/Troubleshooting

When you make changes to the *GLOBAL.ASA* file for an application, the web server completes all current requests for the given application before recompiling the *GLOBAL.ASA* file. According to Microsoft, once the current requests are processed, the file is recompiled, and any new sessions started in the current application trigger the processing of the *GLOBAL.ASA* file code. During this re-compilation, the server ignores all new requests for scripts within the application. Unfortunately, the reality is that this does not work at all with Personal Web Server, IIS 3.0, and IIS 4.0. You are forced to reboot the machine before the new *GLOBAL.ASA* is processed!

Note that any sessions that remain current during this time are unaffected by your changes to *GLOBAL.ASA*. Once the web server has recompiled the *GLOBAL.ASA* file, all active sessions are deleted and the Session_OnEnd and Application_OnEnd event procedures in the (new) *GLOBAL.ASA* file are called. The users must make a new request in the web application for new sessions to begin. All new sessions will start with processing of the new *GLOBAL.ASA* file.

An important consideration for developing your own *GLOBAL.ASA* files is that changing any code included in the file through the use of a Server-Side Include does not result in the recompilation of the *GLOBAL.ASA* file by the web server. You must actually resave the *GLOBAL.ASA* file (even if it hasn't changed!) to trigger its recompilation.

You can have procedures and functions in your *GLOBAL.ASA* file. However, these procedures can be called only by the Session_OnStart, Session_OnEnd, Application_OnStart, and Application_OnEnd event procedures (all of which can reside only in the *GLOBAL.ASA* file). If you wish to use these functions/proce-dures in other files in your application, you should consider using a Server-Side Include file containing the script you wish called.

Finally, like all other scripts in your web application, you must be careful to secure your *GLOBAL.ASA* file using Windows NT security. Otherwise, clients can access this file. Considering that the *GLOBAL.ASA* often contains security-related code for your application, this caveat is very important.

GLOBAL.ASA Reference

Application Object Events and Application Scope

```
<SCRIPT LANGUAGE=strLangEngine RUNAT = SERVER>
Sub Application_OnStart
     Event procedure code...
End Sub
```

```
Sub Application_OnEnd
        Event procedure code...
End Sub
</SCRIPT>
```

In the *GLOBAL.ASA* file, you can include event procedure code for the two events of the Application object: OnStart and OnEnd. These two events are triggered when the first client requests a page within your application and at the end of the last user's session in your application, respectively. These events are covered in detail in Chapter 4, *Application Object*. In this chapter we will reiterate some of the topics covered there and how those topics relate to the *GLOBAL.ASA* file and its use.

To review the information covered in the Application Object chapter, an ASP application is made up of all the files in a virtual directory and all the files in subfolders under that virtual directory. When a variable or object has application scope, it holds the same value(s) for every current user of the application, and any user can change the value(s) of an application-scoped variable or object. Such a change affects the value as viewed by *any* user thereafter.

Parameters

strLangEngine

A string whose value represents the name of a valid server-side scripting engine. This engine is VBScript by default on IIS web servers, but you can use JScript, PerlScript, Python, REXX, or any other scripting engine that supports the IIS scripting context.

Example

```
[Excerpt from GLOBAL.ASA]

<OBJECT RUNAT=Server
SCOPE=Application
ID=AppInfo1
PROGID="MSWC.MyInfo">
</OBJECT>

<SCRIPT LANGUAGE = "VBScript" RUNAT="Server">
Sub Application_OnStart

    Dim objCounters
    Dim gdatAppStartDate

    ' The following object variable will hold a Counters
    ' component.
    Set objCounters = Server.CreateObject("MSWC.Counters")

    ' The following application-level variable will
    ' hold the start date of the application.
    gdatAppStartDate = Date()

End Sub

Sub Application_OnEnd
```

```
' The following code destroys the application-scoped
' Counters component.
Set objCounters = Nothing

' The following clears the application-level variable.
gdatAppStartDate = ""

' NOTE: This code is not strictly necessary in this
' instance as this object and variable will be released
' from memory by the web server itself when the application
' ends. This example simply demonstrates how these event
' procedures work. For suggestions for the Application
' object's use, see the following and Chapter 4.

End Sub

</SCRIPT>
```

Notes

There are several points to remember about the *GLOBAL.ASA* file in general and the Application event procedures, specifically. The first is that there is no reason that you must have a *GLOBAL.ASA* file. Your ASP application will function completely normally without it. In fact, the lack of a *GLOBAL.ASA* file will increase the speed of access for the first requested page in your ASP application, since running the *GLOBAL.ASA* and then running your requested script will always be slower than running only the requested script.

Next, if you do have a *GLOBAL.ASA* file, there is no real need for you to code your own Application_OnEnd event procedure, since the web server itself will release the memory used for application-scoped objects and variables at the end of the application. If, however, you wish to save information (in a database, for example) specific to a particular application's run time, you could code for this in the Application_OnEnd event procedure. For example, you could create an application-level page counter variable and record its value to a text file at the end of an application for use the next time the application's files are requested and the application is restarted. (Note that there are better ways of performing this operation.)

For further notes on the event procedures of the Application object, see Chapter 4.

Session Object Events and Session Scope

```
<SCRIPT LANGUAGE=strLangEngine RUNAT = SERVER>
Sub Session_OnStart
     Event procedure code...
End Sub

Sub Session_OnEnd
     Event procedure code...
End Sub
</SCRIPT>
```

In the *GLOBAL.ASA* file, you can include event procedure code for the two events of the Session object: OnStart and OnEnd. These two events are triggered when a client requests a page within your application for the first time and at the end of the user's session (20 minutes after the user's last request, by default), respectively. These events are covered in detail in Chapter 10, *Session Object*. In this chapter, we will reiterate some of the topics covered there and how those topics relate to the *GLOBAL.ASA* file and its use.

Parameters

strLangEngine

A string whose value represents the name of a valid server-side scripting engine. This engine is VBScript by default on IIS web servers, but you can use JScript, PerlScript, Python, REXX, or any other scripting engine that supports the IIS scripting context.

Example

```
[Excerpt from GLOBAL.ASA]

<OBJECT RUNAT=Server
SCOPE=Session
ID=Tool1
PROGID="MSWC.Tools">
</OBJECT>

<SCRIPT LANGUAGE = "VBScript" RUNAT="Server">
Sub Session_OnStart

    Dim strLogonUser
    Dim StrUserSecurity

    ' The following session-level variables will hold
    ' the user's logon name and security clearance.
    strLogonUser = Request.ServerVariables("USER_LOGON")
    strUserSecurity = "PUBLIC"

End Sub

Sub Session_OnEnd

    ' The following code destroys the session-scoped
    ' Tools component.
    Set Tool1 = Nothing

    ' The following clears the session-level variables.
    strLogonUser = ""
    strUserSecurity = ""

    ' NOTE: This code is not strictly necessary in this
    ' instance as this object and variable will be released
    ' from memory by the web server itself when the session
    ' ends. This example simply demonstrates how these event
```

```
' procedures work. For suggestions for the Application
' object's use, see later in this chapter and Chapter 10.

End Sub

</SCRIPT>
```

Notes

For notes on the Session event procedures, see Chapter 10.

Type Library Declarations

```
<!-- METADATA TYPE="TypeLibrary"
FILE="FileName"
UUID="TypeLibraryUUID"
VERSION="MajorVersionNumber.MinorVersionNumber"
LCID="LocaleID"
-->
```

Type libraries are accessory files that contain information about the properties and methods of COM objects. These files describe any constants used by the object and the data types of acceptable property values. A type library enables your application to more accurately report errors in your use of the object to which the type library corresponds. It also allows you to use constants defined in the object's DLL. This can significantly lower the complexity of an object's code and increase the readability and reuse of your code without forcing you to create and use Server-Side Includes that can be difficult to maintain for all of your objects.

As you know, you can instantiate application-scoped and session-scoped objects in the *GLOBAL.ASA* file. If any of these objects have a corresponding type library, you can declare its use in the application's *GLOBAL.ASA* file.

Parameters

FileName

> The full physical (not virtual) path and filename of the type library file for the object in question. If you include both a *FileName* and a *TypeLibraryUUID* parameter to the **TypeLibrary** declaration, the web server will identify the type library using the filename. You must include either a *FileName* or a *TypeLibraryUUID*.

TypeLibraryUUID

> The universally unique identification number of the type library. This is different from the UUID for the COM object and is defined in the registry as a subkey of **HKEY_CLASSES_ROOT\TypeLib**. If you include both a *FileName* and a *TypeLibraryUUID* parameter to the **TypeLibrary** declaration, the web server will identify the type library using the filename. You must include either a *FileName* or a *TypeLibraryUUID*.

MajorVersionNumber

> The major version number of the type library. If this optional parameter is supplied and the web server cannot find the file with the correct major

---

version number, the web server will raise an error. If you include a *MajorVersionNumber*, you must also include a *MinorVersionNumber* parameter.

MinorVersionNumber
> The minor version number of the type library. If this optional parameter is supplied and the web server cannot find the file with the correct minor version number, the web server will raise an error. If you include a *MinorVersionNumber*, you must also include a *MajorVersionNumber* parameter.

LocaleID
> Each type library can support different locales. The *LocaleID* parameter represents the locale to use for this type library. If this locale is not found in the type library, the web server will raise an error. Like the VERSION parameter of the TypeLibrary declaration, this parameter is optional.

Example

```
[Excerpt from GLOBAL.ASA]

<!-- METADATA TYPE="TypeLibrary"
FILE="Report.LIB"
VERSION="1.5"
LCID="1306"
-->
```

Notes

This code declares the use of Version 1.5 of the Report COM object's type library. The LCID used is that for French. If Version 1.5 of this COM object's type library is not found or the LCID 1306 (for French) is not supported by the type library, the code will result in an error.

When you use a type library from within an ASP application, you are actually using a wrapper-encapsulated version of the type library. IIS creates this wrapper for your type library in the background.

For coding style, Microsoft suggests that you include your type library declarations near the top of the *GLOBAL.ASA* file. However, I've seen no effect from placing it in other places in the file. Also, you are not required to place the TypeLibrary declaration outside of the <SCRIPT> tags.

One problem with using type libraries from multiple COM objects in one ASP application (especially if the COM objects were written by different developers) is the redundancy of constants within the object. You can avoid this redundancy by referring to any constant using the name of the COM object itself as a prefix for the constant name. For example, the adStoredProcedure constant of the ADODB type library can be referred to as ADODB.adStoredProcedure.

Finally, the web server can return one of the errors listed in the following table if you incorrectly declare your type library:

Error Code	Description
ASP 0222	An invalid type library declaration.
ASP 0223	Type library does not exist. For example, if the type library listed in the METADATA tag does not exist, you will receive this error.
ASP 0224	The type library you declared cannot be loaded for some unknown reason, even though it was successfully found.
ASP 0225	The web server is unable, for whatever reason, to create a wrapper for the type library you declared in the METADATA tag.

PART III

Installable Component Reference

The following chapters cover the installable components that come with IIS 4.0:

CHAPTER 12

ActiveX Data Objects 2.6

One of the most popular reasons for constructing an ASP application is to enable people on an intranet or the Internet to manipulate data remotely. To allow for data manipulation throughout the enterprise, Microsoft introduced their Universal Data Access. The goal of Universal Data Access, as its name implies, is to allow tool- and language-independent access to data regardless of its location in the enterprise. From relational databases to email message stores, Microsoft hopes to allow developers access without special implementation-specific language or tools requirements.

Microsoft's Universal Data Access strategy is embodied in the Microsoft Data Access Components SDK. The current version (version 2.6 as of this writing) contains the following pieces:

ActiveX Data Objects (ADO) (covered in this chapter)
A set of components that allow programmatic access to data through an OLE DB provider.

OLE DB (not covered in this chapter)
A set of low-level programming interfaces that expose data using the Component Object Model (COM). Programming data access through OLE DB interfaces provides DBMS functionality appropriate to the data store.

Open Database Connectivity (ODBC) (not covered in this chapter)
ODBC is a C programming language interface for access to data from a variety of DBMSes. The ODBC interface allows for maximum interoperability at the expense of DBMS-specific access methods that allow for more flexible or efficient programmability.

As previously mentioned, this chapter will focus exclusively on ActiveX Data Objects and specifically on accessing ADO through Active Server Pages.

As of the writing of this edition of this book, ActiveX Data Objects are currently in version 2.6. It encompasses the following components:

ADO

> The components that you will use most often in your ASP applications, ADO enables your client applications to manipulate data through an OLE DB provider. Figure 12-1 illustrates this.

RDS

> Recently included as part of ADO, Remote Data Services allow you to move data from the server to the client, manipulate that data, and return updates to the server in one round trip.

ADOX

> An extension to ADO, ActiveX Data Objects Extensions for Data Definition Language (DDL) and Security, ADOX includes objects that allow for the programmatic creation and manipulation of schemas and access to security.

ADO MD

> ActiveX Data Objects (Multidimensional) are a further extension of ADO that enables access to multidimensional data.

In this book, I will focus exclusively on the most commonly used components of ADO, and not on RDS, ADOX, or ADO MD.

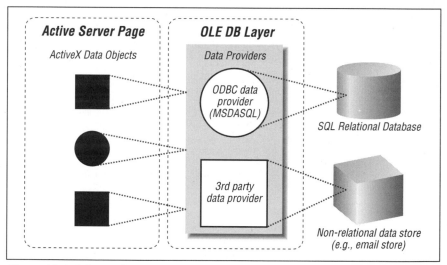

Figure 12-1: Relationship among Active Data Objects, OLE DB, and the underlying data stores

ActiveX Data Objects is a COM interface (specifically a dual-interface COM wrapper) for OLE DB. It provides a method of manipulating data that is fast, simpler than traditional CGI data access, more powerful than the Internet Database Connector, and small in terms of memory and disk size required. The following is a list of some of the features of ADO:

•   ADO is a free-threaded object library, allowing you to easily use it in a multiuser client server environment such as a web application.

- You can create objects in the ADO hierarchy independently. Unlike more familiar data access methods, like Data Access Objects (DAO) and Remote Data Objects (RDO), in which you have to traverse the hierarchy to instantiate objects in the tree, ADO allows you to create objects independently of each other. You can create a standalone Recordset, for instance, whereas with DAO or RDO, you have to create other objects before you can instantiate a Recordset object. This allows you to improve your applications' performance by instantiating only those objects that you need.

- Using ADO, you can cache data locally and then update the underlying database in a batch fashion. This significantly decreases the overhead of going back and forth to the database as often as you have to with DAO or RDO.

- You can use several different cursor types. In fact, ADO allows you to use custom cursor types on a provider-by-provider basis. For example, if a given data provider (say Oracle) allows you to use a specific cursor type that is not allowed by other ODBC databases, you can still use this cursor type from within your ADO application.

- You can limit the number of rows returned to you from a query or table. This is *very* important in web applications, when the amount of data returned to the client has a direct impact on the speed with which it is received by that client.

- You can return multiple recordsets using a single query. Once instantiated, you can then iterate through the recordsets just as you would iterate through fields in a single recordset. This is also very important for performance optimization and speed considerations.

Although the ActiveX Data Objects provide all of the preceding functionality, it is imperative that you know the underlying data provider's ability to meet these functionality requirements.

In an attempt to ease the manipulation of data from nonrelational data sources, Microsoft has recently (with ADO 2.5) introduced two new objects: the Record object and the Stream object. Specifically, the Record and Stream objects were introduced to allow for the manipulation of data from email messages and files in a directory. The Record object can represent a row in a Recordset object, but it can also represent a file or directory from the file system or a folder or message in an email system. The Stream object allows developers to read, write, and manage the binary stream of bytes that comprise the file/directory or message/folder.

Also introduced with ADO 2.5 was the ability to use Uniform Resource Locators (URLs) to specify connection strings and/or command text to designate data sources and file/directory locations. You can use URLs with Connection, Recordset, Record, and Stream objects.

While ActiveX Data Objects is a very powerful set of objects that allow you to create very powerful applications, full coverage of its features would require a book to itself. For this reason, this chapter lists the various properties and methods of ADO objects and details only those that will allow you the most common functionality.

Accessory Files/Required DLL Files

msado15.dll

This is the dynamic link library for the ADO COM objects. You must install this on the web server (using the latest executable setup file from Microsoft) before you can instantiate or use any of the ADO objects.

adovbs.inc

This file contains VBScript declarations for all the constants used by the Active Data Objects library. You can include this file in your script using the `#include` directive and refer to any of these ADO constants. (There are other includes for use with non-VB languages: *adoint.h* and *adoid.h* for C/C++ programming, and *adojavas.inc* for Java programming.)

Instantiating Active Data Objects

To create an object variable containing an instance of an Active Data object, use the CreateObject method of the Server object. The syntax for the CreateObject method is:

```
Set objMyObject = Server.CreateObject(strProgId)
```

where the parameters are as follows:

objMyObject

The name of the object variable created using the CreateObject method of the Server object.

strProgId

The programmatic identifier (ProgId) of the component you are trying to instantiate. Table 12-1 lists the available Active Data Objects and their corresponding ProgIds.

Table 12-1: Active Data Objects

Active Data Object	ProgId
Command	`ADODB.Command`
Connection	`ADODB.Connection`
Error	`ADODB.Error`
Field	`ADODB.Field`
Parameter	`ADODB.Parameter`
Property	`ADODB.Property`
Record	`ADODB.Record`
Recordset	`ADODB.Recordset`
Stream	`ADODB.Stream`

Example

```
<%

' This code uses the Server object's CreateObject
' method to instantiate an ADO Connection object and
```

```
' a Recordset object. For more details about the Open
' method and the ActiveConnection property in the
' example, see the "Connection Object" section later in this chapter.

Dim adoCon
Dim adoRec

Set adoCon = Server.CreateObject("ADODB.Connection")
Set adoRec = Server.CreateObject("ADODB.Recordset")

' Open the database connection to my database.
adoCon.Open "MyDatabase"

' Set the Connection object to which the Recordset
' object is attached to adoCon.
adoRec.ActiveConnection = adoCon

%>
```

For more details on the use of the CreateObject method, see its entry in Chapter 9, *Server Object.*

Comments/Troubleshooting

There are several small "gotchas" that I've learned the hard way when using ADO with ASP. I detail these later in this chapter when discussing the particular properties or methods that caused the problems. The only comment I have on ADO is this: When you begin to write your ASP database application, take some time to delve deeper into ADO. There are several more advanced topics in ADO that I do not cover here.

Once you find out how to use ADO to perform the functions you want, take time to look at your specific data provider and at what parts of ADO are supported. Does it support all the cursor types that you need? Does ADO support all the functionality you need? Are there properties of ADO that you cannot use because your data provider does not provide them, or, more likely, does your data provider provide functionality that ADO does not support?

The answers to these questions and the research that goes into to finding them can save you a great deal of time during development. This may seem self-evident, but it is extremely important—especially when deciding whether to use ADO. Though ADO has improved a great deal since its release, it is still young. Although Microsoft has poised OLE DB and its automation wrapper, ADO, to take the data access spotlight, it has only recently released ADO. As a result, ADO still has some maturing to do.

One final note: Microsoft has recently released for public download an unsupported HTML Table component that will allow you to display the contents of an ADO recordset in an HTML table simply and easily. This component was just released as this book was nearing its last stages of development, so it is not covered here. Download it from *http://www.microsoft.com/windows/downloads/ default.ASP* and experiment on your own.

Object Model

Figure 12-2 shows a diagram of the ADO object hierarchy. Following it is a brief description of each of the nine objects that make up ADO. For each object, I list and very briefly describe all of the properties, collections, and methods (ADO objects do not respond to any events). As stated before, this is meant only as an overview. However, for several of the more commonly used properties, collections, and methods, I have added some more in-depth coverage in this chapter's Properties Reference, Collections Reference, and Methods Reference.

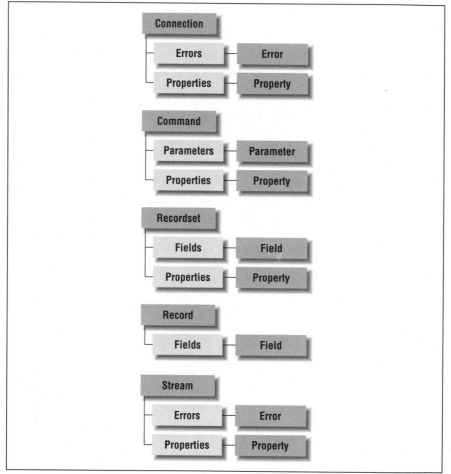

Figure 12-2: The ADO object model

Command Object

The Command object allows you to manipulate database commands. Although you can execute a command string on a Connection object or as part of opening a Recordset object, the Command object allows you more flexibility. Chief among its extended functionalities is the ability to add, remove, and define query parameters using the Command object's Parameters collection. You can define the text of a database command, such as a SQL statement, using the CommandText property of the Command object. Table 12-2 lists the Command object's properties, Table 12-3 lists its Collection object, and Table 12-4 lists its methods.

Table 12-2: Command Object Properties

Property	Description
ActiveConnection[a]	The name of the Connection object to which the Command object belongs.
CommandText[a]	A string containing the text of the command you wish to execute against the database. It can be a query, SQL statement, the name of a stored procedure, or some other database manipulation command.
CommandTimeout[a]	A Long representing the number of seconds ADO should wait for the results of a Command object's execution before raising an error. The default value is 30 seconds.
CommandType[a]	The type of command that is executed using the Command object.
Name	A string representing the name of the Command object.
Prepared	A Boolean value that, if `True`, indicates the underlying data provider is instructed to store a compiled version of the command before executing it.
State	An integer value indicating whether the Command object is open (`adStateOpen` from *ADOVBS.INC*) or closed (`adStateClosed`).

[a] These items are discussed in more detail later in this chapter.

Table 12-3: Command Object Collections

Collection	Description
Parameters	All the instantiated Parameter objects that, in turn, contain the parameters for the current Command object.
Properties	The data provider-specific properties for the Command object. If the data provider does not support any custom properties, this collection is empty.

Table 12-4: Command Object Methods

Method	Description
Cancel	Cancels the execution of a pending Execute or Open method call. Example: `Command.Cancel`
CreateParameter	Creates a new Parameter object for the Command object's Parameters collection. Syntax: Set `Parameter` = `Command`.`CreateParameter([Name], [Type], [Direction], [Size], [Value])`

Table 12-4: Command Object Methods (continued)

Method	Description
Execute[a]	Executes the command contained in the Command object's CommandText property. Syntax: Set *Recordset = Command.* Execute([RecordsAffected], [Parameters], [Options])

[a] Indicates more detail can be found later in this chapter.

Connection Object

The Connection object represents a single connection to the underlying data provider. As such, the Connection object maintains information about that data provider. In the context of a web application, it represents one connection from the web server to a database server. As with the other ActiveX Data Objects, your ability to use any of the Connection object's methods or properties is directly dependent on the underlying data provider's support for the feature. Tables 12-5, 12-6, 12-7, and 12-8 list the Connection object's properties, collection objects, methods, and events respectively.

Table 12-5: Connection Object Properties

Property	Description
Attributes	The value of the Attributes property of the Connection object represents the characteristics for the object. Use the Attributes property to set whether the Connection object performs retaining commits or retaining aborts. This Long value is read/write.
CommandTimeout[a]	The number of seconds the Connection should wait for the result of a call to the Execute method before raising an error. The default value is 30 seconds.
ConnectionString[a]	A string containing the information for the current connection. This string contains the definition of the Provider, Data Source, User Id, Password, File Name (for a provider-specific file), Remote Provider, and remote Server.
ConnectionTimeout[a]	The number in seconds to wait while attempting to make a connection using the ConnectionString before raising an error. The default value is 15 seconds.
CursorLocation	Indicates where the cursor for the current connection should be created: on the client (**adUseClient** from *ADOVBS.INC*) or on the server (**adUseServer**, the default).
DefaultDatabase	The default database. If no database is explicitly stated in the execution string, this database is used. If only one database is being used, this database is the default database.

Table 12-5: Connection Object Properties (continued)

Property	Description
IsolationLevel	The isolation level óf the connection, which determines what happens to the underlying records of a database when a transaction is committed or aborted.
Mode	The level of permissions for the connection itself allowed by the provider. For example, you can use the Mode property to instruct the provider to not accept any other connections until after your connection is closed.
Provider	The name of the data provider used for the connection. The default for this string value is MSADSQL (Microsoft OLE DB Provider for ODBC).
State	An integer value representing whether the Connection object is open (adStateOpen from *ADOVBS.INC*) or closed (adStateClosed).
Version	The current version of ADO.

a These items are discussed in more detail later in this chapter.

Table 12-6: Connection Object Collections

Collection	Description
Errorsa	All the current Error objects generated by errors from the last execution on the data provider. If there have been no errors, this collection is empty.
Properties	The data-provider-specific properties for the Connection object. If the data provider does not support any custom properties, this collection is empty.

a These items are discussed in more detail later in this chapter.

Table 12-7: Connection Object Methods

Method	Description
BeginTrans	Begins a transaction in the underlying data provider. None of the changes made during the transaction are recorded until you explicitly commit the transaction. Syntax: *Connection*.BeginTrans
Cancel	Cancels execution of a pending (asynchronous) Execute or Open method call. Syntax: *Connection*.Cancel
Closea	Closes the current connection. You must close a Connection object's connection to one data provider before opening a connection to another data provider. Syntax: *Connection*.Close
CommitTrans	Commits a transaction in the underlying data provider. None of the changes made during the transaction are recorded until you explicitly commit the transaction. Syntax: *Connection*.CommitTrans

Table 12-7: Connection Object Methods (continued)

Method	Description
Execute[a]	Executes a query, stored procedure, or other SQL statement sent as a parameter to this method. Syntax: `Set Recordset = Connection.Execute(CommandText, [RecordsAffected], [Options])`
Open[a]	Explicitly opens a connection to a data provider. Syntax: `Connection.Open [ConnectionString], [UserID], [Password], [Options]`
OpenSchema	Obtains information on the database structure from the data provider. Syntax: `Set Recordset = Connection.OpenSchema(QueryType, [Criteria], [SchemaID])`
RollbackTrans	Aborts a transaction in the underlying data provider. All of the changes that have taken place since the beginning of the transaction will be committed, and all previously made data changes will revert to their previous values. Syntax: `Connection.RollbackTrans`

a These items are discussed in more detail later in this chapter.

Table 12-8: Connection Object Events

Name	Description
BeginTransComplete	This event is fired when a BeginTrans method call completes execution.
CommitTransComplete	This event is fired when a CommitTrans method call completes execution.
ConnectComplete	This event is fired when a Connection object is successfully instantiated.
Disconnect	This event is fired when a Connection object is set to nothing and the connection is disconnected.
ExecuteComplete	This event is fired after a call to the Execute method of a Command object.
InfoMessage	This event is a notice that a Connection object event has fired and the underlying data provider has raised additional information for use by your application.
RollbackTransComplete	This event is fired when a RollbackTrans method call has completed execution.
WillConnect	This event is fired upon the initiation of the connection object, but before the connection is established.
WillExecute	This event is fired before the successful execution of a command against the database through the current Connection object.

Error Object

An Error object can contain the details of a data provider error. These provider errors can result from incorrect use of ADO syntax, or from lack of support for a particular property or method by the underlying data provider. It is important to realize that the Error object represents the details of an error from the provider, and not from ADO. ADO errors are caught by the web server at execution time as runtime errors.

Provider errors are specific to a particular Connection object. When an error occurs with the data provider, one or more errors are raised by that provider and added to the Connection object's Errors collection, which is cleared each time a new operation causes an error to be returned from the data provider.

From the Error object, you can retrieve the name, number, and description of each error caused by the invalid operation. In addition, you can retrieve Help information and information about the state of the data provider from the Error object. Table 12-9 lists the Error object's properties; it has no collection objects or methods.

Table 12-9: Error Object Properties

Property	Description
Description[a]	The descriptive string associated with a given error. This descriptive string can be set by ADO or by the data provider.
HelpContextID	The value of a Help file's context ID, if the accompanying HelpFile property indicates that there is a Windows help file associated with an Error object.
HelpFile	A string that evaluates to the path and filename of a Windows Help file if one exists for the Error object.
NativeError	The error code raised by the native data provider. This is a Long value.
Number[a]	A Long that represents the error number for the Error object. If no error has occurred, the Number property evaluates to 0.
Source	A string that represents the name of the object or application that caused the ADO error.
SQLState	A five-character error code that the provider returns when an operation involving the processing of a SQL statement raises an error. The values of these error codes are documented in the current ANSI SQL standard.

[a] These items are discussed in more detail later in this chapter.

Field Object

Each recordset you create is made up of a collection of Field objects. A Field object represents the data from a specific column in the query or table called from the data provider by the ADO application. All the data in a given field in the recordset has the same data type. The Value property of the Field object represents the actual field value for that field in the current record.

The Field object allows you to view or change the data in a field of a record in your recordset. Tables 12-10, 12-11, and 12-12 list its properties, collections, and methods, respectively.

Table 12-10: Field Object Properties

Property	Description[a]
ActualSize	A long that represents the size of the field's value in number of characters. Some data providers allow the user to set this property to reserve space for BLOB data. However, most often this is a read-only property.
Attributes	Allows you to retrieve several different characteristics of the Field object, such as whether the data for a field is retrieved with the rest of the record or only when you specifically use the field, whether you can change the value of the field, etc. This is a read-only property.
DefinedSize	The size of the Field object. This is different from the ActualSize property. The value of the ActualSize property could indicate that the length of the value in a Field object is one character, but the value of the DefinedSize property could be larger. You can use DefinedSize to determine if a value you want to input into a new record's field is larger than the size of the field.
Name[a]	The field's name from the database table or query. It is read-only.
NumericScale	The number of decimal places to which numeric values will be resolved. The data type of this property is Byte.
OriginalValue	The actual value of the field before any changes were made. This property value allows you to programmatically revert the field's value.
Precision	The number of significant digits to which numeric values will be resolved. The data type of this property is Byte.
Status	The Status property indicates whether a Field object has been added to the Fields collection. Its value is cached until a call to the Update method.
ype	An integer that represents the data type of the field's contents. For the Field object, this is a read-only property.
UnderlyingValue	Read-only property indicating current value of the current field in the database for the current row.
Value	The value assigned to the current Field object.

[a] These items are discussed in more detail later in this chapter.

Table 12-11: Field Object Collection

Collection	Description
Properties	Contains the data provider-specific properties for the Field object. If the data provider does not support any custom properties, this collection is empty.

Table 12-12: Field Object Methods

Method	Description
AppendChunk	Appends a large amount of text or a binary object to a Field object. Syntax: *Field*.AppendChunk Data
GetChunk	Retrieves a large amount of text or a binary object from a Field object. Syntax: *Variable* = *Field*.GetChunk(Size)

Parameter Object

A Parameter object holds the values of specific parameters for a parameterized Command object. In other words, if a given SQL statement or other command takes a given set of parameters that change each time you execute the command, a Parameter object can be used to hold those parameters' values.

Each instantiated Command Object has a Parameters collection to which you can add parameters.

In addition to holding parameters of a straight SQL statement, a Parameter object can also represent the in/out or return values of a stored procedure.

Table 12-13: Parameter Object Properties

Property	Description
Attributes	Sets or determines whether a given parameter will accept various data, such as signed values, null values, or long values.
Direction	Reflects whether the parameter represents an input parameter, an output parameter, or both.
Name	The name of the parameter, if it has one.
NumericScale	The number of decimal places to which numeric values will be resolved. The data type of this property is Byte.
Precision	The number of significant digits to which numeric values will be resolved. The data type of this property is Byte.
Size	A Long representing the maximum number of bytes or characters valid for the Parameter object.
Type	An integer that represents the data type of the parameter's contents. For the Parameter object, this is a read/write property.
Value	The actual value of the contents of the parameter.

Table 12-14: Parameter Object Collections

Collection	Description
Properties	Contains the data-provider-specific properties for the Field object. If the data provider does not support any custom properties, this collection is empty.

Table 12-15: Parameter Object Methods

Method	Description
AppendChunk	Appends a large amount of text or a binary object to a Parameter object. Syntax: `Parameter.AppendChunk Data`

Property Object

A Property object represents a custom or unique property that is specific to ADO objects instantiated using a specific data provider. For example, if a Recordset object was instantiated using records from an Oracle database, that recordset may have special properties not supported by "typical" ADO. You would retrieve/set the values for these properties using an ADO Property object. This advanced feature of ADO allows you to take full command of your underlying data provider.

Each Command, Connection, Field, and Recordset object you instantiate maintains its own Properties collection. This way, you have access to custom properties of your data provider for all three object types. Table 12-16 lists the Property object's properties.

Table 12-16: Property Object Properties

Property	Description
Attributes	Allows you to determine whether a given property is supported, required, or optional, and whether the Property is read-only or read/write.
Name	The underlying name assigned by the data provider's name to a given property that's being manipulated through the use of a Property object.
Type	An integer that represents the data type of the property's contents. For the Property object, this is a read-only property.
Value	The actual value of the property.

Record Object

The Record object represents a row in a Recordset or a file or directory in a file system or web site. The Record object has a Fields collection that allows you to view the individual Field objects that make up the Record. Tables 12-17, 12-18, and 12-19 list the Record object's properties, collections, and methods, respectively.

Table 12-17: Record Object Properties

Property	Description
ActiveConnection	Indicates the specific Connection object to which the current Record's Recordset object belongs.
Mode	Indicates the available permissions for modifying the data in the current Record object.
ParentURL	Indicates the absolute URL of the parent record in the underlying data source for the current Record object. This is a read-only property.

Table 12-17: Record Object Properties (continued)

Property	Description
RecordType	Indicates the type of the record: simple record, structured document, or collection. This is a read-only property.
Source	Indicates what the current Record represents: a URL or a reference to an open Recordset object.
State	Indicates whether the current Record object is open or closed. If the current Record is open, State also indicates the state of any currently executing asynchronous actions. This is a read-only property.

Table 12-18: Record Object Collections

Collection	Description
Fields	Collection containing all the Field objects associated with the current Record object. This is a read-only property.
Properties	Collection containing all the Property objects associated with the current Record object. This is a read-only property.

Table 12-19: Record Object Methods

Method	Description
Cancel	Cancels any asynchronous actions currently executing against the Record object. Syntax: *Record*.Cancel
Close	Closes the open Record. Syntax: *Record*.Close
CopyRecord	Copies the current Record object. Can also be used to copy a file or a directory from one location to another. Syntax: Variable = *Record*.CopyRecord([Source], [Destination], [UserName], [Password], [Options], [Async])
DeleteRecord	Deletes the object the Record object represents (or a file or directory). Syntax: *Record*.DeleteRecord [Source], [Async]
GetChildren	Returns a Recordset object containing the files and folders from the directory represented by the current Record object. Syntax: Set *Recordset* = *Record*.GetChildren()
MoveRecord	Moves the object underlying the Record object from one location to another. Syntax: Variable = *Record*.MoveRecord([Source], [Destination], [UserName], [Password], [Options], [Async])
Open	Opens or creates a new, blank file or directory or opens an existing one. Syntax: *Record*.Open [Source], [ActiveConnection], [Mode], [CreateOptions], [Options], [UserName], [Password]

Recordset

A Recordset object represents the records returned from a query (or table) and a cursor into those records. When instantiating a Recordset object, you can automatically create a connection to the underlying data provider on opening the recordset. However, if you use an already open Connection object for your recordset, you can significantly reduce your memory consumption overhead, since each Connection object can maintain multiple recordsets. However, if you open a recordset without using an already open Connection object, that connection can support only that single recordset. You can read more about this feature in the section on the Open method of the Recordset object. Tables 12-20, 12-21, and 12-22 list the Recordset object's properties, collections, and methods, respectively.

Table 12-20: Recordset Object Properties

Property	Description
AbsolutePage	Allows you to determine the exact page of records in which the current record resides. Each recordset is broken up by the data provider and ADO into pages of PageSize number of records, with the last page possibly containing fewer records. This is a read-only value of type Long.
AbsolutePosition[a]	The ordinal number of the current record in the recordset. This is a read/write value of type Long.
ActiveCommand	Read-only property containing the name of the Command object that was used to create the current Recordset object.
ActiveConnection[a]	The currently open Connection object to which the recordset is affiliated.
BOF[a]	Indicates whether the current record pointer is pointing to the beginning of the recordset (i.e., the beginning of file), which is one position earlier in the recordset than the first record. If you use the MovePrevious method to move one position before the first record in the recordset, the BOF property will evaluate to **True**. This is a Boolean read-only value.
Bookmark	Allows you to retrieve a unique identification number for the current record in the Recordset. If you set this property to a valid Bookmark for another record, the current record pointer will be moved to the record identified by the value you set.
CacheSize	The number of records cached locally in memory. The default of this Long value is 1. If you change this value in code, be aware that the value of the CacheSize property must be greater than one, and that the value you set has a direct relationship on performance. Forcing the server to cache more than one record locally increases memory consumption per user and decreases performance.
CursorLocation	Indicates to the web server where the cursor for the current recordset should be created: on the client (adUseClient from *ADOVBS.INC*) or on the server (adUseServer, the default).

Table 12-20: Recordset Object Properties (continued)

Property	Description
CursorType[a]	The type of cursor ADO creates to the underlying data provider. This is an integer whose value is read-only if the Recordset object is already opened, but read/write if it is closed. The default value for this property is `adOpenForwardOnly`.
DataMember	Specifies the name of the Data member to obtain from the object referenced by the DataSource property. This is a write-only property.
DataSource	Specifies an object containing data that will be represented as a Recordset object. This is a write-only property.
EditMode	The current editing state for the current record. The value of this property indicates whether there is an edit in progress, whether a record has been edited but not saved, or whether a new record is to be added to the recordset.
EOF[a]	Indicates whether the current record pointer is pointing to the end of the recordset (i.e., end of file), which is one position after the actual last record in the recordset. If you use the Recordset object's MoveNext method to move one position after the last record, the EOF property will evaluate to `True`. This is a Boolean read-only value.
Filter[a]	Allows you to selectively filter out records from being visible in a Recordset.
Index	The name of the Index currently being used in the data represented by the Recordset object.
LockType	Reflects the current locking scheme placed on the records during editing. For example, `Read-Only`, `Pessimistic`, `Optimistic`, or `BatchOptimistic`.
MarshalOptions	Sets or retrieves a setting that determines how records are marshaled between the client and server. Marshaling involves packaging and sending groups of records from the client to the server. This property determines whether only those records that have been modified or whether all records are marshaled back to the server.
MaxRecords[a]	Sets or retrieves the maximum number of records returned in a recordset by a specific query. This is a Long value with a default of 0, meaning that there is no maximum.
PageCount	Determines how many pages of records were returned by the data provider into a specific Recordset object. If the data provider does not support this property, or if the page count is for some other reason undeterminable, the value of this integer is −1.
PageSize	The total number of records that make up one page of records. This Long value is −1 if the data provider does not support the PageSize property or if the page size is undeterminable.

ActiveX Data Objects 2.6

Table 12-20: Recordset Object Properties (continued)

Property	Description
RecordCount[a]	For Recordset objects that support approximate positioning or bookmarks, the RecordCount property represents the exact number of records returned into the Recordset object. If this property is unsupported by the underlying data provider, or is for some other reason undeterminable, its value is –1.
Sort	Specifies the name of one or more fields in the records in the Recordset object upon which the data will be sorted. This property also reflects the direction in which the composite records will be sorted along the named fields.
Source[a]	The source string from which the records were returned from the data provider. The value of the property could be a SQL string, a stored procedure, the name of a Command object, or a table name.
State	An integer value representing whether the Recordset object is open (**adStateOpen** from *ADOVBS.INC*) or closed (**adStateClosed**).
Status	The status of the current record in relation to a batch update or other bulk manipulation of the data.
StayInSync	A Boolean value that reflects whether the parent row in a hierarchical Recordset object should change upon a change in the underlying child records. This is a read-only property.

[a] These items are discussed in more detail later in this chapter.

Table 12-21: Recordset Object Collections

Collection	Description
Fields	Contains each Field object, corresponding to each column of data in the recordset.
Properties	Contains the data provider-specific properties for the Recordset object. If the data provider does not support any custom properties, this collection is empty.

Table 12-22: Recordset Object Methods

Method	Description[a]
AddNew[a]	Adds a new record to the recordset and to the underlying data if the recordset is updateable. Syntax: *Recordset*.**AddNew** [FieldList], [Values]
Cancel	Cancels the execution of a pending, asynchronous Open operation. Syntax: *Recordset*.**Cancel**
CancelBatch	Cancels all pending updates if a recordset is in batch update mode. Syntax: *Recordset*.**CancelBatch** [AffectRecords]

Table 12-22: Recordset Object Methods (continued)

Method	Description[a]
CancelUpdate	Cancels updates to the current record. Syntax: `Recordset.CancelUpdate`
Clone[a]	Creates a duplicate of the current recordset. Syntax: `Set Recordset = Recordset.Clone([LockType])`
Close[a]	Closes the current recordset. Syntax: `Recordset.Close`
CompareBook- marks	Determines the equality of two bookmarks created for a single Recordset object. Syntax: `intResult = Recordset.` `CompareBookmarks(Bookmark1, Bookmark2)`
Delete[a]	Deletes the current record or a group of records from the recordset and the underlying data (if the cursor type of the recordset supports updating). Syntax: `Recordset.Delete AffectRecords`
Find	Searches the records making up the current Recordset object for records matching the supplied search criteria. Syntax: `Recordset.Find Criteria, [SkipRows],` `[SearchDirection], [Start]`
GetRows[a]	Retrieves multiple records from a recordset into an array. Syntax: `aryResult = Recordset.GetRows([Rows],` `[Start], [Fields])`

GetString	Retrieves a recordset as a string.
	Syntax: `Set vntResult = Recordset.`
	`GetString(StringFormat, [NumRows],`
	`[ColumnDelimiter], [RowDelimiter], [NullExpr])`

Move[a]	Moves the current record pointer a certain number of positions forward or backward from the current record. To use this method, the recordset must support both forward *and* backward movement. Syntax: `Recordset.Move NumRecords, [Start]`
MoveFirst[a]	Moves the record pointer to the first record in the recordset. Syntax: `Recordset.MoveFirst`
MoveLast[a]	Moves the record pointer to the last record of the recordset. Syntax: `Recordset.MoveLast`
MoveNext[a]	Moves the record pointer forward one position. Syntax: `Recordset.MoveNext`
MovePrevious[a]	Moves the current record pointer back one position. Syntax: `Recordset.MovePrevious`
NextRecordset[a]	You can create a Recordset object using multiple commands. The NextRecordset method allows you to navigate from one command's resulting recordset to another command's resulting recordset. Syntax: `Set Recordset = Recordset.` `NextRecordset([RecordsAffected])`

·*Table 12-22: Recordset Object Methods (continued)*

Method	Description[a]
Open[a]	Opens a recordset. Syntax: *Recordset*.Open [Source], [ActiveConnection], [CursorType], [LockType], [Options]
Requery[a]	Repopulates the current recordset by rerunning the command that generated it. Syntax: *Recordset*.Requery [Options]
Resync[a]	Refreshes the data in the current recordset without rerunning the query. Syntax: *Recordset*.Resync [AffectRecords], [ResyncValues]
Save	Saves the current Recordset object to a file. Syntax: *Recordset*.Save [Destination], [PersistFormat]
Seek	Searches the current Index in the recordset to locate a specific value. Syntax: *Recordset*.Seek KeyValues, SeekOption
Supports[a]	Determines whether a specific data provider supports a given functionality. Syntax: blnResult = *Recordset*.Supports(CursorOptions)
Update[a]	Saves your changes to the current record into the database. Syntax: *Recordset*.Update [Fields], [Values]
UpdateBatch	Saves all changes in the current batch to the database. Syntax: *Recordset*.UpdateBatch [AffectRecords]

[a] indicates more detail can be found later in this chapter.

Stream Object

The Stream object represents a stream of text or data. It allows you to persist a set of records or data in memory. Although typically used with OLE DB data providers and semi-structured data, it can also be used for simple data from a Recordset object by specifying a valid Stream object in the Recordset's Destination property. By setting the Destination property to a valid Stream object, all data in the Recordset is then stored in the Stream object and can be manipulated, copied, or saved to a file. This method of saving data allows more flexibility than the Recordset object's Save method. Tables 12-23 and 12-24 list the Stream object's properties and methods, respectively.

Table 12-23: Stream Object Properties

Property	Description
Charset	Identifies which character set is used by the Stream.
EOS	Evaluates to True if the current character or byte is the end of the Stream. This is a read-only property.

Table 12-23: Stream Object Properties (continued)

Property	Description
LineSeparator	Indicates what character or character sequence should be evaluated as the end of a line. The default is carriage-return + linefeed (vbCrLf).
Mode	Indicates the permissions available for changing data in a Connection object.
Position	Specifies the current byte or character position in the current Stream object.
Size	Indicates the length in bytes of the current Stream. This is a read-only property.
State	Indicates whether the current Stream is open or closed. If the current Stream is open, this property also indicates the state of any asynchronous actions being executed on the Stream. This is a read-only property.
Type	Indicates whether the contents of the current Stream are data (byte) or character (text) based.

Table 12-24: Stream Object Methods

Method	Description
Cancel	Terminates the execution of a pending, asynchronous Open command. Syntax: *Stream*.Cancel
Close	Closes the current stream. Syntax: *Stream*.Close
CopyTo	Copies bytes or characters from one Stream object to another. Syntax: *Stream*.CopyTo DestStream, [CharNumber]
Flush	Flushes all contents from the current data stream to the underlying Stream object. Syntax: *Stream*.Flush
LoadFromFile	Loads a Stream from a file. Syntax: *Stream*.LoadFromFile FileName
Open	Opens a Stream object from a URL or an existing Record object. If no URL or Record is specified a blank Stream object is created. Syntax: *Stream*.Open [Source], [Mode], [Options], [UserName], [Password]
Read	Reads a specified number of bytes from the Stream. Syntax: Set vntResult = *Stream*.Read([NumBytes])
ReadText	Reads a specified number of characters from a text Stream. Syntax: Set vntResult = *Stream*.ReadText([NumChars])
SaveToFile	Saves the current Stream to a file. Syntax: *Stream*.SaveToFile FileName, [Options]
SetEOS	Sets the current byte or character position as the end of the Stream. Syntax: *Stream*.SetEOS

Table 12-24: Stream Object Methods (continued)

Method	Description
SkipLine	Skips a line when reading characters from a text Stream. Syntax: `Stream.SkipLine`
Write	Writes byte data to a Stream. Syntax: `Stream.Write Buffer`
WriteText	Writes character data to a Stream. Syntax: `Stream.WriteText Data, [Options]`

Properties Reference

AbsolutePosition (Recordset Object)

`rsObj.AbsolutePosition (= lngRecordPosition)`

Returns or sets the current record based on its ordinal position in the recordset. This is a read/write value of type Long.

Parameters

`rsObj`

> A reference to a Recordset object

`lngRecordPosition`

> The position of the current record or the new position to which you wish to move the record pointer

Example

The following example demonstrates the use of the AbsolutePosition property. The use of AbsolutePosition is in bold to distinguish it in this example. The other parts of the script will be used to demonstrate other parts of ADO. Also, in the following example, you will notice that I am careful not to specify my data provider. The reason for this is that only some data providers support the AbsolutePosition property; for example, SQL Server does not.

```
<%@ LANGUAGE="VBSCRIPT" %>
<%response.buffer = true%>

<HTML>
<HEAD>
<TITLE>ADO Examples</TITLE>
</HEAD>
<BODY>
<%
' Include ADOVBS.INC so we can use the ADO constants.
%>
<!-- #include virtual = "/MySSIncludes/adovbs.inc" -->
<%
' Instantiate an ADO Connection object.
Set objDBConn = Server.CreateObject("ADODB.Connection")

' Construct the connection string for the Connection object
```

```
strConn = _
    "driver={MyDBType};;uid=sa;pwd=;database=SalesDB"

' Using the connection string, open the connection.
objDBConn.Open strConn

' Instantiate an ADO Recordset object.
Set rsHighSales = _
    Server.CreateObject("ADODB.Recordset")

' Set the CursorType property of the recordset, so we
' can navigate within the recordset.
rsHighSales.CursorType = adOpenDynamic

' Set our CursorLocation to locate the cursor on the
' client side so we can use the AbsolutePosition
' property.
rsHighSales.CursorLocation = adUseClient

' Construct the SQL to be used to open the recordset.
strSQL = _
    "SELECT Buyer, Price FROM Sales WHERE Price > 70000"

' Open the recordset.
rsHighSales.Open strSQL, objDBConn

' Move to current record pointer to the third record
' in the recordset.
rsHighSales.AbsolutePosition = 3

' Display the Buyer and Price field values for the
' third record in the recordset.
%>

Third Buyer: <%=rsHighSales("Buyer")%><BR>
Third Price: <%=rsHighSales("Price")%><BR>

<%
' Release the memory consumed by objects.
Set rsHighSales = Nothing
Set objDBConn = Nothing
%>
</BODY>
</HTML>
```

Notes

You can use AbsolutePosition to retrieve or set the position of the current record pointer within the recordset. This number is one-based, meaning that if you wish to set the current record pointer to point to the first record in the recordset, you would set its value to 1.

As with other properties of the Recordset object, the validity of the AbsolutePosition property depends on whether the underlying data provider supports the property. Also, you can only use the AbsolutePosition property of the Recordset object if the cursor type for the recordset supports backward movement in the cursor.

If you attempt to retrieve the position of the current record pointer, you may receive one of the following constant values, depending on the state of the current record pointer:

adPosUnknown
> Either the recordset is empty, the current position is unknown, or the underlying data provider does not support this property.

adPosBOF
> The current record is one before the first record in the recordset.

adPosEOF
> The current record is one after the last record in the recordset.

Note that when you set a value for the AbsolutePosition property—even if the new current record is already in the cache—the cache is reloaded. The number of records loaded into the cache is determined by the CacheSize property.

Finally, if you want to uniquely identify a given record, use the Bookmark property, rather than the AbsolutePosition value, because this value can change.

ActiveConnection (Command, Recordset Objects)

Obj.ActiveConnection (= *strConnectionName*)

Indicates an open Connection object to which a Recordset or Command object belongs.

Parameters

Obj
> A reference to a Command or Recordset object

strConnectionName
> The name of a valid, open Connection object

Example

This example demonstrates how you set the ActiveConnection property of a Recordset object. To set the ActiveConnection property of a Command object, you would use exactly the same technique.

```
<%@ LANGUAGE="VBSCRIPT" %>
<% Response.Buffer = True %>
<HTML>
<HEAD>
<TITLE>ADO Examples</TITLE>
</HEAD>
<BODY>
<%
' Include ADOVBS.INC so we can use the ADO constants.
%>
<!-- #include virtual = "/MySSIncludes/adovbs.inc" -->
```

```
<%
' Instantiate an ADO Connection object.
Set objDBConn = Server.CreateObject("ADODB.Connection")

' Construct the connection string for the Connection object.
strConn = _
    "driver={SQL Server};;uid=sa;pwd=;database=SalesDB"

' Using the connection string, open the connection.
objDBConn.Open strConn

' Instantiate an ADO Recordset object.
Set rsHighSales = _
                Server.CreateObject("ADODB.Recordset")

' Set the ActiveConnection property of the recordset.
rsHighSales.ActiveConnection = objDBConn

' Construct the SQL to be used to open the recordset.
strSQL = _
    "SELECT Buyer, Price FROM Sales WHERE Price > 70000"

' Open the recordset. Note the lack of a connection
' object specification.
rsHighSales.Open strSQL

%>

First Buyer: <%=rsHighSales("Buyer")%><BR>
First Price: <%=rsHighSales("Price")%><BR>

<%
' Release the memory consumed by objects.
Set rsHighSales = Nothing
Set objDBConn = Nothing
%>
</BODY>
</HTML>
```

Notes

You can set or retrieve the name of any valid (open) connection object by using the ActiveConnection property. If the Connection object is not yet open when you attempt to set the property, an error occurs. If you attempt to call the Execute method of a Command object or the Open method of a Recordset object without first setting the ActiveConnection property to the name of a valid, open Connection object, ADO will raise a runtime error. The only exception to this is if you use the ActiveConnection argument of the Recordset object's Open method; in this case, the ActiveConnection property will be set for you to the name of the Connection object specified in the Open method call.

If you set the ActiveConnection property to Nothing, you will disconnect the Command or Recordset object from the open Connection object. If you do this with a Recordset object that is open, an error will occur.

Also, if a Command object has parameters whose values are provided by the data provider, and you set the ActiveConnection property of this Command object to Nothing or to another Connection object, these values will be cleared. If you set the values of the Parameter objects, resetting the ActiveConnection property has no effect on your parameters' values.

BOF (Recordset Object)   rsObj.BOF

If the value of the BOF property of a Recordset object is True, the current record pointer is positioned one record before the first record in the recordset. This is a read-only property. You can use the BOF property in conjunction with the EOF property to ensure that your recordset contains records and that you have not navigated beyond the boundaries of the recordset.

Parameters

rsObj

> A reference to a Recordset object

Example

The following example demonstrates the use of BOF to determine whether the opened recordset contains any records. Note that EOF is also True if there are no records in the recordset. We could just as easily have used the EOF property in this case as BOF.

```
<%@ LANGUAGE="VBSCRIPT" %>
<% Response.Buffer = True %>
<HTML>
<HEAD>
<TITLE>ADO Examples</TITLE>
</HEAD>
<BODY>
<%
' Include ADOVBS.INC so we can use the ADO constants.
%>
<!-- #include virtual = "/MySSIncludes/adovbs.inc" -->
<%
' Instantiate an ADO Connection object.
Set objDBConn = Server.CreateObject("ADODB.Connection")

' Construct the connection string for the Connection object.
strConn = _
    "driver={SQL Server};;uid=sa;pwd=;database=SalesDB"

' Using the connection string, open the connection.
objDBConn.Open strConn

' Instantiate an ADO Recordset object.
Set rsHighSales = _
    Server.CreateObject("ADODB.Recordset")

' Set the ActiveConnection property of the recordset.
rsHighSales.ActiveConnection = objDBConn
```

```
' Construct the SQL to be used to open the recordset.
strSQL = _
    "SELECT Buyer, Price FROM Sales WHERE Price > 70000"

' Open the recordset. Note the lack of a connection
' object specification.
rsHighSales.Open strSQL

' Use the BOF property to determine whether
' there are records in the recordset.
If Not rsHighSales.BOF Then
    ' There are records. Use the EOF property to loop
    ' through all the records in the recordset and
    ' display them to the screen.
    Do While Not rsHighSales.EOF
%>
    Buyer: <%=rsHighSales("Buyer")%><BR>
    Price: <%=rsHighSales("Price")%><BR>
<%
    rsHighSales.MoveNext
    Loop
Else
    ' There are no records. Tell the user.
%>
    There are no high sales.
<%
End If

' Release the memory consumed by objects.
Set rsHighSales = Nothing
Set objDBConn = Nothing
%>
</BODY>
</HTML>
```

Notes

The BOF property's value is True if there are no records in the recordset, or if you have navigated to the position before the first record in the recordset. If there are no records in the recordset, the value of both the BOF and EOF properties are True. This is the only occasion in which this is true. Obviously, a True value of the BOF property indicates that some navigational methods (in particular, Move-Previous and Move using a negative argument) of the Recordset object are not allowed.

CommandText (Command Object)

$$objCmd.\texttt{CommandText} \ (= strCommandText)$$

A string value that represents the actual command you wish to run against the database. The default value for this property is an empty string (""). This command can be a SQL statement or the name of a stored procedure.

Parameters

ocjCmd

    A reference to a Command object

strCommandText

    A string containing the command you wish to run against the database

Example

The following example demonstrates how to use the CommandText property to invoke a stored procedure with two parameters.

```
<%@ LANGUAGE="VBSCRIPT" %>
<% Response.Buffer = True %>
<HTML>
<HEAD>
<TITLE>ADO Examples</TITLE>
</HEAD>
<BODY>
<%
' Include ADOVBS.INC so we can use the ADO constants.
%>
<!-- #include virtual = "/bc_SSIncludes/adovbs.inc" -->
<%
' Instantiate an ADO Connection object.
Set objDBConn = Server.CreateObject("ADODB.Connection")

' Construct the connection string for the Connection object.
strConn = _
    "driver={MyDBType};;uid=sa;pwd=;database=SalesDB"

' Using the connection string, open the connection.
objDBConn.Open strConn

' Create a stored procedure command object
Set objSPCmd = Server.CreateObject("ADODB.Command")

' Set active connection equal to current Connection object.
Set objSPCmd.ActiveConnection = objDBConn

' Set command object type to stored procedure.
objSPCmd.CommandType = adCmdStoredProc

' Set the parameter values.
lngHighPrice = 70000
datFirstDate = "03/02/98"

' Set stored procedure command text. The parameters
' indicate the minimum price that must be paid to
' qualify a sale as a "high sale" and the date after
' which we want to collect sales into our recordset.
strCommandString = "GetHighSales (" & lngHighPrice & _
                    "," & datFirstDate & ")"
objSPCmd.CommandText = strCommandString
```

```
' Open the recordset using the results from the Command object.
rsHighSales = objSPCmd.Execute

%>

First Buyer: <%=rsHighSales("Buyer")%><BR>
First Price: <%=rsHighSales("Price")%><BR>

<%
' Release the memory consumed by objects.
Set rsHighSales = Nothing
Set objSPCmd    = Nothing
Set objDBConn   = Nothing
%>
</BODY>
</HTML>
```

Notes

If you use a SQL command for the CommandText property of a Command object, you must ensure that the SQL syntax is that expected by the underlying data provider. ADO will not translate from one "dialect" of SQL to another.

Depending on the type of command (set using the CommandType property), ADO may alter the actual string sent to the data provider. For example, suppose you set the CommandText of a stored procedure-type Command object to the following:

```
objSPCmd.CommandText = "GetHighSales (70000)"
```

ADO will actually send the following string to the data provider as the command:

```
{ call GetHighSales (70000) }
```

Notice that the braces and the `call` keyword are added.

CommandTimeout (Command, Connection Objects)
Obj.CommandTimeout (= *lngNumSeconds*)

Sets the maximum amount of time (in seconds) that ADO will wait for the results of a command to execute before raising an error. The default for this Long value is 30 seconds.

Parameters

Obj
> A reference to a Command or Connection object

lngNumSeconds
> The number of seconds ADO will wait for the results of a command before raising an error

Example

The following example demonstrates how to use the CommandTimeout property to increase the amount of time ADO will wait for the results of a stored procedure call before raising an error.

```
<%@ LANGUAGE="VBSCRIPT" %>
<% Response.Buffer = True %>
<HTML>
<HEAD>
<TITLE>ADO Examples</TITLE>
</HEAD>
<BODY>
<%
' Include ADOVBS.INC so we can use the ADO constants.
%>
<!-- #include virtual = "/bc_SSIncludes/adovbs.inc" -->
<%
' Instantiate an ADO Connection object.
Set objDBConn = Server.CreateObject("ADODB.Connection")

' Construct the connection string for the Connection object.
strConn = _
    "driver={MyDBType};;uid=sa;pwd=;database=SalesDB"

' Using the connection string, open the connection.
objDBConn.Open strConn

' Create stored procedure command object.
Set objSPCmd = Server.CreateObject("ADODB.Command")

' Set the active connection equal to the current
' Connection object.
Set objSPCmd.ActiveConnection = objDBConn

' Set the Command object type to stored procedure.
objSPCmd.CommandType = adCmdStoredProc

' Set the parameter values.
lngHighPrice = 70000
datFirstDate ='03/02/98'

' Set stored procedure command text. The parameters
' indicate the minimum price that must be paid to
' qualify a sale as a "high sale" and the date after
' which we want to collect sales into our recordset.
strCommandString = "GetHighSales (" & lngHighPrice & _
                    "," & datFirstDate & ")"
objSPCmd.CommandText = strCommandString

' Set the Command object's CommandTimeout property so
' that ADO will wait 60 seconds for the results of the
' comand before raising an error.
objDBCmd.CommandTimeout = 60

' Open the recordset using the results from the Command object.
Set rsHighSales = objSPCmd.Execute

%>
```

```
First Buyer: <%=rsHighSales("Buyer")%><BR>
First Price: <%=rsHighSales("Price")%><BR>

<%
' Release the memory consumed by objects.
Set rsHighSales = Nothing
Set objSPCmd    = Nothing
Set objDBConn   = Nothing
%>
</BODY>
</HTML>
```

Notes

If you create and open a Connection object and set its CommandTimeout property and then use its name to set the ActiveConnection property of a previously instantiated Command object, the Command object does *not* inherit the CommandTimeout property value of the Connection object.

If you set this property's value to 0, the command will wait indefinitely for the results to be returned.

It is imperative to remember the current setting of the Server object's ScriptTimeout property. (The default of the ScriptTimeout property of the Server object is 90 seconds.) For example, suppose the ScriptTimeout is set to 30 seconds and the CommandTimeout for the Command object on an active server page is set to 45 seconds. You may not be able to view the outcome of the command's execution—regardless of whether or not the command is executed successfully by the data provider.

CommandType (Command Object)

```
                         objCmd.CommandType (= intCommandType)
```

Sets or determines the type of command being executed using the Command object. The different types of command include text, stored procedure, and table. The default is Unknown. If you attempt to call the Execute method of a Command object without setting the CommandType property's value, an error will occur for any type of command other than straight text.

Parameters

objCmd
> A reference to a Command object

intCommandType
> The type of command. It can be represented by any of the following constants:

adCmdUnspecified (-1)
> This indicates that the CommandType property has not yet been specified.

adCmdText (1)

The command is a text command, such as a simple SQL statement; CommandText is evaluated as a textual definition of a command.

adCmdTable (2)

The Command object represents a table; CommandText is evaluated as the name of a table.

adCmdStoredProc (4)

The Command object represents a stored procedure; CommandText is evaluated as the name of a stored procedure in the underlying data provider.

adCmdUnknown (8)

The Command object type is unknown; this is the default value.

adCmdFile (256)

The Command object represents a file in which is stored a persistent Recordset object.

adCmdTableDirect (512)

The Command object represents a table from which all columns are retrieved.

Example

This example demonstrates how to use the CommandType property of the Command object to instruct ADO to treat the CommandText property's value as the name of a stored procedure.

```
<%@ LANGUAGE="VBSCRIPT" %>
<% Response.Buffer = True %>
<HTML>
<HEAD>
<TITLE>ADO Examples</TITLE>
</HEAD>
<BODY>
<%
' Include ADOVBS.INC so we can use the ADO constants.
%>
<!-- #include virtual = "/bc_SSIncludes/adovbs.inc" -->
<%
' Instantiate an ADO Connection object.
Set objDBConn = Server.CreateObject("ADODB.Connection")

' Construct the connection string for the Connection object.
strConn = "driver={MyDBType};;uid=sa;pwd=;database=SalesDB"

' Using the connection string, open the connection.
objDBConn.Open strConn

' Create a stored procedure Command object.
Set objSPCmd = Server.CreateObject("ADODB.Command")

' Set the active connection equal to the current
' Connection object.
```

```
Set objSPCmd.ActiveConnection = objDBConn

' Set the Command object type to stored procedure.
objSPCmd.CommandType = adCmdStoredProc

' Set the parameter values.
lngHighPrice = 70000
datFirstDate ='03/02/98'

' Set the stored procedure command text. The parameters
' indicate the minimum price that must be paid to
' qualify a sale as a "high sale" and the date after
' which we want to collect sales into our recordset.
strCommandString = "GetHighSales (" & lngHighPrice & _
                   "," & datFirstDate & ")"
objSPCmd.CommandText = strCommandString

' Set the Command object's CommandTimeout property so
' that ADO will wait 60 seconds for the results of the
' command before raising an error.
objDBCmd.CommandTimeout = 60

' Open the recordset using the results from the Command object.
Set rsHighSales = objSPCmd.Execute

%>

First Buyer: <%=rsHighSales("Buyer")%><BR>
First Price: <%=rsHighSales("Price")%><BR>

<%
' Release the memory consumed by objects.
Set rsHighSales = Nothing
Set objSPCmd   = Nothing
Set objDBConn   = Nothing
%>
</BODY>
</HTML>
```

Notes

Setting the value of the CommandType property optimizes the command's performance. You do not have to set the CommandType property, however. If you do not know at design time the type of command that will be used in the CommandText property, you can leave the value for this property at its default of adCmdUnknown. In this case, however, you will experience decreased performance because ADO is forced to take the value of the CommandText property and query the underlying data provider to determine how to execute the command.

If you set the CommandType property incorrectly (to something other than adCmdUnknown) and attempt to call the object's Execute method, ADO will raise a runtime error.

ConnectionString (Connection Object)

objConn.ConnectionString (= *strConnectionString*)

Specifies or retrieves the information used to establish an open connection to an underlying data provider.

Parameters

strConnectionString

> A string value made up of the following elements (in order) broken up by semicolons.

Provider=

> The name of the underlying OLE DB data provider for the connection.

Data Source=

> The name of a data source for the underlying data provider. For example, for SQL Server or Access, this represents a registered ODBC data source name.

User ID=

> The username to use when establishing the connection.

Password=

> The password to use when establishing the connection.

File Name=

> The name of a data provider-specific file. This could, for example, represent a text file containing preset connection information. Using a File Name element in your ConnectionString loads the provider into memory. For this reason, you cannot have both a Provider and a File Name element in your ConnectionString property value.

Remote Provider=

> (For use with Remote Date Services only.) The name of the data provider to use on the server when opening a client-side connection.

Remote Server=

> (For use with Remote Date Services only.) The path name of the remote server to use when opening a client-side connection.

URL=

> An absolute URL identifying a resource such as a file or a directory.

Example

```
<%@ LANGUAGE="VBSCRIPT" %>
<% Response.Buffer = True %>
<HTML>
<HEAD>
<TITLE>ADO Examples</TITLE>
</HEAD>
<BODY>
<%
' Include ADOVBS.INC so we can use the ADO constants.
%>
<!-- #include virtual = "/bc_SSIncludes/adovbs.inc" -->
```

```
<%
' Instantiate an ADO Connection object.
Set objDBConn = Server.CreateObject("ADODB.Connection")

' Build the connection string for the Connection object.
strConn = _
    "Provider={SQL Server};Data Source=SalesDB;User ID=sa;Password=;"

' Using the ConnectionTimeout property increases the
' amount of time ADO will wait while establishing a
' connection to the data provider before it raises
' an error.
objDBConn.ConnectionTimeout = 60

' Using the connection string, open the connection.
objDBConn.Open strConn
.
.
.
```

Notes

ADO only recognizes the first seven elements of a ConnectionString property value. However, you can provide as many as you like. If you provide more than seven, the extra elements are passed directly through to the data provider without any intervening actions taken by ADO.

The underlying data provider may alter the contents of the ConnectionString property value when the connection is established.

If you use the *ConnectionString* parameter of the Connection object's Open method and also set a value for the ConnectionString property before calling the Open method, the value passed to the Open method is the value that the ConnectionString property eventually receives.

ConnectionTimeout (Connection Object)

*objConn.*ConnectionTimeout (= *lngNumSeconds*)

Sets or retrieves the number of seconds ADO will wait while attempting to establish a connection before raising an error. The default value for this property is 15 seconds.

Parameters

lngNumSeconds
A long that represents the number of seconds ADO will wait while attempting to establish a connection to the underlying data provider.

Example

For an example of the ConnectionTimeout property, see the code example for the ConnectionString property.

Notes

You can instruct ADO to wait indefinitely for the connection to the underlying data provider to be established by setting the value of the ConnectionTimeout property to 0.

Note, however, that it is imperative to remember the current setting of the Server object's ScriptTimeout property. (The default of the ScriptTimeout property is 90 seconds.) For example, suppose the ScriptTimeout is set to 30 seconds and the ConnectionTimeout for the Connection object on an active server page is set to 45 seconds. You may not be able to see the result of attempting to establish a connection to the underlying data provider regardless of success or failure.

CursorType (Recordset Object)

`rsObj`.CursorType (= *intCursorType*)

The CursorType property of the Recordset object allows you to specify or retrieve the type of cursor used to create the recordset.

Parameters

intCursorType

> An integer value representing the type of cursor to use for the Recordset object. It can be any of the following constants:

> adOpenForwardOnly

>> This is the default. A forward-only cursor, as its name implies, only allows movement forward from the current record. Otherwise this cursor type is identical to the static cursor. There is one exception to this, however: some data providers will allow you to call the MoveFirst method to move the current record pointer back to the first record in the database. This is the fastest cursor type.

> adOpenKeyset

>> In a keyset cursor, you cannot see new records added by other users, and you cannot access records that have been deleted by other users. You can, however, see the changes to records in your recordset made by other users. All types of movement are possible in a keyset cursor recordset.

> adOpenDynamic

>> Dynamic cursors are the most flexible (and slowest) of the four types. In a dynamic cursor, additions, changes, and deletions are all visible in your recordset. All types of movement are possible in a dynamic cursor recordset.

> adOpenStatic

>> Static cursors provide a static snapshot of the records in your recordset. This is useful for generating reports, but the records in the recordset are not updateable. Additions, changes, and deletions made by other users are not visible in your recordset.

Example

```
<%@ LANGUAGE="VBSCRIPT" %>
<%response.buffer = true%>

<HTML>
<HEAD>
<TITLE>ADO Examples</TITLE>
</HEAD>
<BODY>
<%
' Include ADOVBS.INC so we can use the ADO constants.
%>
<!-- #include virtual = "/MySSIncludes/adovbs.inc" -->
<%
' Instantiate an ADO Connection object.
Set objDBConn = Server.CreateObject("ADODB.Connection")

' Construct the connection string for the Connection object.
strConn = _
    "driver={MyDBType};;uid=sa;pwd=;database=SalesDB"

' Using the connection string, open the connection.
objDBConn.Open strConn

' Instantiate an ADO Recordset object.
Set rsHighSales = _
    Server.CreateObject("ADODB.Recordset")

' Set the CursorType property of the recordset, so we
' can navigate within the recordset.
rsHighSales.CursorType = adOpenDynamic

' Set our CursorLocation to locate the cursor on the
' client side so we can use the AbsolutePosition
' property.
rsHighSales.CursorLocation = adUseClient

' Construct the SQL to be used to open the recordset.
strSQL = _
    "SELECT Buyer, Price FROM Sales WHERE Price > 70000"

' Open the recordset.
rsHighSales.Open strSQL, objDBConn

' Move to current record pointer to the third record
' in the recordset.
rsHighSales.AbsolutePosition = 3

' Display the Buyer and Price field values for the
' third record in the recordset.
%>
```

```
Third Buyer: <%=rsHighSales("Buyer")%><BR>
Third Price: <%=rsHighSales("Price")%><BR>

<%
' Release the memory consumed by objects.
Set rsHighSales = Nothing
Set objDBConn = Nothing
%>
</BODY>
</HTML>
```

Notes

The CursorType property of the Recordset object is read-only if the recordset is already open, but read/write otherwise.

If you attempt to set the CursorType property to a value not supported by your underlying data provider, the data provider may return a cursor of a different type than you set. However, if this happens, the CursorType property value reflects this change. Then, once the recordset is closed, the CursorType property value reverts to the value you set. You can use the Supports method of the Recordset object to determine which cursors are supported by a given data provider, according to Table 12-25.

Table 12-25: Determining Cursor Support with the Supports Method

CursorType Value	The Supports Method Must Return True for these ADO Constants
adOpenForwardOnly	None.
adOpenKeyset	adBookmark, adHoldRecords, adMovePrevious, adResync
adOpenDynamic	adMovePrevious
adOpenStatic	adBookmark, adHoldRecords, adMovePrevious, adResync

What happens if one of the tests on the right fail for your selected cursor type? Suppose you attempt to set the CursorType to one of the cursor type constants on the left, but one or more of the Supports method calls on the right returns False. The result is unpredictable, but most often the underlying data provider will simply change the cursor type when you attempt to open the recordset.

Description (Error Object)   objError.Description

A read-only string that provides textual information describing the error that the underlying data provider raised in response to incorrect syntax or lack of support. Description is a property of each Error object in the Connection object's Errors collection. It is *not* the same as the Description property of the ASP Err object.

Parameters

None

Example

The following example demonstrates the use of the Description property of the Error object. Notice that for this example to work properly, the Response object's Buffer property must be set to True because we use the Response's Clear and End methods.

```
<%@ LANGUAGE="VBSCRIPT" %>
<%Response.Buffer = True%>

<HTML>
<HEAD>
<TITLE>ADO Examples</TITLE>
</HEAD>
<BODY>
<%
' Include ADOVBS.INC so we can use the ADO constants.
%>
<!-- #include virtual = "/MySSIncludes/adovbs.inc" -->
<%
' Instantiate an ADO Connection object.
Set objDBConn = Server.CreateObject("ADODB.Connection")

' Construct the connection string for the Connection object.
strConn = _
    "driver={MyDBType};;uid=sa;pwd=;database=SalesDB"

' Using the connection string, open the connection.
objDBConn.Open strConn

' Check if attempting to open a connection to the
' provider resulted in ADO adding Error objects to the
' Connection's Errors collection.
If objDBConn.Errors.Count > 0 Then
    ' An error occurred and ADO added an Error object to
    ' the Connection's Errors collection. Clear the
    ' Response buffer and alert the user of the error.
    Response.Clear
    Response.Write _
        "One or more errors have occurred.<BR>"
    For intCounter = 0 to objDBConn.Errors.Count - 1
        Response.Write "The " & intCounter & " error's "
        Response.Write "error number is " & _
            objDBConn.Errors(intCounter).Number & ".<BR>"
        Response.Write "The description for this "
        Response.Write "error is <BR>" & _
        objDBConn.Errors(intCounter).Description & ".<BR>"
    Next
    Response.End
End If
    .
    .
    .
```

Notes

Each time an error occurs in the data provider, ADO adds an Error object to the Errors collection of the Connection object corresponding to that data provider. The provider is responsible for generating and sending the actual error text to ADO, but ADO can modify it before setting the description that it adds to the Connection object's Errors collection.

Note that if you have code in your scripts to react programmatically to errors in the Connection object's Errors collection, you may want to consider moving this error handling to the *500-100.ASP* (or customized equivalent) error page, if you are using IIS 5.0 or higher. For more information on use of the *500-100.ASP* error handling page used by IIS 5.0, see Chapter 5, *ASPError Object*.

EOF (Recordset Object)   rsObj.EOF

If the value of a Recordset object's EOF property is **True**, the current record pointer is positioned one record after the last record in the recordset. This is a read-only property. You can use the EOF property in conjunction with the BOF property to ensure that your recordset contains records and that you have not navigated beyond the boundaries of the recordset. Note that the value of EOF is also **True** if there are no records in the recordset.

Parameters

None

Example

The following example demonstrates the use of EOF to iterate through a set of records. Assuming that there are records in the recordset, we know that EOF will be true once we have iterated through all the records and the record pointer is pointing at the position after the last record in the recordset.

```
<%@ LANGUAGE="VBSCRIPT" %>
<% Response.Buffer = True %>
<HTML>
<HEAD>
<TITLE>ADO Examples</TITLE>
</HEAD>
<BODY>
<%
' Include ADOVBS.INC so we can use the ADO constants.
%>
<!-- #include virtual = "/MySSIncludes/adovbs.inc" -->
<%
' Instantiate an ADO Connection object.
Set objDBConn = Server.CreateObject("ADODB.Connection")

' Construct the connection string for the Connection object.
strConn = _
    "driver={SQL Server};;uid=sa;pwd=;database=SalesDB"
```

```
' Using the connection string, open the connection.
objDBConn.Open strConn

' Instantiate an ADO Recordset object.
Set rsHighSales = _
    Server.CreateObject("ADODB.Recordset")

' Set the ActiveConnection property of the recordset.
rsHighSales.ActiveConnection = objDBConn

' Construct the SQL to be used to open the recordset.
strSQL = _
    "SELECT Buyer, Price FROM Sales WHERE Price > 70000"

' Open the recordset. Note the lack of a connection
' object specification.
rsHighSales.Open strSQL

' Use the BOF property to determine whether
' there are records in the recordset
If Not rsHighSales.BOF Then
    ' There are records. Use the EOF property to loop
    ' through all the records in the recordset and
    ' display them to the screen.
    Do While Not rsHighSales.EOF
%>
    Buyer: <%=rsHighSales("Buyer")%><BR>
    Price: <%=rsHighSales("Price")%><BR>
<%
    rsHighSales.MoveNext
    Loop
Else
    ' There are no records. Tell the user.
%>
    There are no high sales.
<%
End If

' Release the memory consumed by objects.
Set rsHighSales = Nothing
Set objDBConn = Nothing
%>
</BODY>
</HTML>
```

Notes

The EOF property's value is True in the following instances:

- There are no records in the recordset. In this case, the value of both the BOF and EOF properties are True. This is the only occasion on which this is true.
- You have navigated to the position after the last record in the recordset.

Obviously, the value of the EOF property indicates that some navigational methods of the Recordset object (MoveNext, and Move using a positive argument) are not allowed.

Filter (Command, Recordset Objects)

rsObj.Filter (= vntFilterCriteria)

The Filter property of the Recordset object allows you to view a subset of records contained in the recordset. This subset could match a more exact set of criteria than the criteria used to create the original recordset. When you are finished using the subset of records, you can restore the view of the recordset back to its original state of displaying all the records. Using a filter does not remove records from the recordset but only makes them unviewable. For this reason, restoring the recordset to its original state does not require requerying the database.

Parameters

vntFilterCriteria

Controls what records will appear in the filtered view of your recordset. This variant value can contain any one of the following filtering types:

Criteria text string

Criteria strings are basically equivalent to SQL WHERE clauses without the WHERE keyword. For example, suppose your recordset (*adoRec*) was constructed using the following SQL statement:

SELECT SalesPrice, Cost, Buyer FROM Sales

You could then apply a filter to this recordset to show only those sales whose sales prices were above $1000 by using the following line of code:

adoRec.Filter = "SalesPrice > 1000"

Bookmark Array

You can set the Filter property to the name of an array of bookmarks that point to records in the recordset. These bookmarks are retrieved using the Bookmark property of the Recordset object for a specific record.

ADO Filter Constant

These ADO Filter constants provide special filtering criteria not easily obtained otherwise: The adFilterNone constant restores the recordset view to allow viewing of all the records in the recordset. The adFilterPendingRecords constant retrieves only those records that have been changed but not yet updated on the server. The adFilterAffectedRecords constant retrieves only those records affected by the Recordset object's Delete, Resync, UpdateBatch, or CancelBatch methods. The adFilterFetchedRecords constant retrieves all the records in the current cache, i.e., all those records retrieved from the last command on the database. The **adFilterConflictedRecords** constant retrieves the records that your application failed to update in the last batch update.

Example

The following example demonstrates the use of the Filter property. The important sections are in bold. Assume that the first recordset (before applying the Filter property) consists of the following records, in the following order:

Buyer	Price
Chris	70000
Toby	80000
Simon	90345
Dave	100000
Mark	78658
Josh	89000

```
<%@ LANGUAGE="VBSCRIPT" %>
<%response.buffer = true%>

<HTML>
<HEAD>
<TITLE>ADO Examples</TITLE>
</HEAD>
<BODY>
<%
' Include ADOVBS.INC so we can use the ADO constants.
%>
<!-- #include virtual = "/MySSIncludes/adovbs.inc" -->
<%
' Instantiate an ADO Connection object.
Set objDBConn = Server.CreateObject("ADODB.Connection")

' Construct the connection string for the Connection object.
strConn = _
    "driver={MyDBType};;uid=sa;pwd=;database=SalesDB"

' Using the connection string, open the connection.
objDBConn.Open strConn

' Instantiate an ADO Recordset object.
Set rsHighSales = _
    Server.CreateObject("ADODB.Recordset")

' Construct the SQL to be used to open the recordset.
strSQL = _
    "SELECT Buyer, Price FROM Sales WHERE Price > 70000"

' Open the recordset.
rsHighSales.Open strSQL, objDBConn

' Display the Buyer and Price field values for the
' current (first) record in the new Recordset BEFORE
' applying the filter. The first buyer will be Chris
```

```
' and the first price will be 70000. There are also six
' viewable records at this point.
%>


Current (first) Buyer: <%=rsHighSales("Buyer")%><BR>
Current (first) Price: <%=rsHighSales("Price")%><BR>


<%


' Now apply a criteria string to the Filter property to
' filter out some of the records.
rsHighSales.Filter = "Price > 80000"


' Again, display the Buyer and Price field values for
' the current (first) record in the new recordset. The
' first buyer will NOW be Simon and the first price
' will be 90345. Now only three records are viewable.
%>


Current (first) Buyer: <%=rsHighSales("Buyer")%><BR>
Current (first) Price: <%=rsHighSales("Price")%><BR>


<%


' Release the memory consumed by objects.
Set rsHighSales = Nothing
Set objDBConn = Nothing
%>
</BODY>
</HTML>
```

Notes

The Filter property allows you to easily filter out the records that you don't need from a large recordset without having to requery the database. Once you have finished with the records that appear in the filtered view of the recordset, you can restore the view of all of the records without requerying the database. Once you have created your filtered recordset, the set of filtered records becomes the current cursor. This is a very convenient way to narrow a set of records without creating a new query and executing it against the database. However, it is important to recognize that although the Filter property is convenient, it will never be faster than simply honing the query that you send to the data provider.

If records in the underlying database have been affected since you populated your recordset (e.g., if a record has been deleted from the underlying table), information will be added to the Errors collection. However, this will only result in warnings unless every record in the filtered recordset results in an error.

When you set the Filter property, the current record pointer moves to the first record in the subset of records that meet the requirements in the Filter string. If you reset the recordset, the current record pointer goes back to the first record in the recordset that meets the criteria in the original command that makes up the recordset.

In addition to being able to reset the recordset using the ADO `adFilterNone` constant, you can also achieve the same result by setting the Filter property value to an empty string.

MaxRecords (Recordset Object)

```
rsObj.MaxRecords (= lngNumRecords)
```

Specifies the maximum number of records returned from a command. If set to zero (0), this property indicates that the data provider should return all records that meet the criteria in the command. This is the default.

Parameters

lngNumRecords

A Long value that represents the maximum number of records you want returned from your command against the database.

Example

The following example sets the MaxRecords property so that it returns only four records.

```
<%@ LANGUAGE="VBSCRIPT" %>
<% Response.Buffer = True %>
<HTML>
<HEAD>
<TITLE>ADO Examples</TITLE>
</HEAD>
<BODY>
<%
' Include ADOVBS.INC so we can use the ADO constants.
%>
<!-- #include virtual = "/MySSIncludes/adovbs.inc" -->
<%
' Instantiate an ADO Connection object.
Set objDBConn = Server.CreateObject("ADODB.Connection")

' Construct the connection string for the Connection object.
strConn = _
    "driver={SQL Server};;uid=sa;pwd=;database=SalesDB"

' Using the connection string, open the connection.
objDBConn.Open strConn

' Instantiate an ADO Recordset object.
Set rsHighSales = _
    Server.CreateObject("ADODB.Recordset")

' Set the ActiveConnection property of the recordset.
rsHighSales.ActiveConnection = objDBConn

' Construct the SQL to be used to open the recordset.
strSQL = _
    "SELECT Buyer, Price FROM Sales WHERE Price > 70000"
```

```
' Set the maximum number of records the data provider
' can return into your recordset to four records.
rsHighSales.MaxRecords = 4

' Open the recordset. Note the lack of a connection
' object specification.
rsHighSales.Open strSQL

' Use the BOF property to determine whether
' there are records in the recordset.
If Not rsHighSales.BOF Then
%>
    Buyer: <%=rsHighSales("Buyer")%><BR>
    Price: <%=rsHighSales("Price")%><BR>
<%
Else
   ' There are no records. Tell the user.
%>
    There are no high sales.
<%
End If

' Release the memory consumed by objects.
Set rsHighSales = Nothing
Set objDBConn = Nothing
%>
</BODY>
</HTML>
```

Notes

The MaxRecords property is read/write if the Recordset object is closed, but read-only if it is open. This is functionally equivalent to the SET ROWS command in ANSI SQL.

Name (Command, Field, Parameter, Property Objects)

Obj.Name (= *strObjName*)

Each Command, Field, Parameter, and Property object has a Name property, which is a string value that identifies that object. The value for the Name property does *not* have to be unique within a collection. Note, however, that if two objects in a collection have the same name, you must use its ordinal position rather than just its name to ensure you retrieve the correct one. For example, suppose you have a recordset with two field objects both with the name "SalesPerson." The first SalesPerson field is the first in the collection and the second is the fifth. The following line of code will always retrieve the value in the first column only:

```
strEmployee = rsSales("SalesPerson")
```

To retrieve the value of the second SalesPerson field, you must use its ordinal reference:

```
strSecondEmployee = rsSales.Fields(5).Value
```

Parameters

strObjName

A string value that represents the name of the object.

Example

The following example demonstrates the use of the Name property to retrieve the names of the first and second Field objects in the Fields collection of the *rsHighSales* Recordset object.

```
<%@ LANGUAGE="VBSCRIPT" %>
<% Response.Buffer = True %>
<HTML>
<HEAD>
<TITLE>ADO Examples</TITLE>
</HEAD>
<BODY>
<%
' Include ADOVBS.INC so we can use the ADO constants.
%>
<!-- #include virtual = "/MySSIncludes/adovbs.inc" -->
<%
' Instantiate an ADO Connection object.
Set objDBConn = Server.CreateObject("ADODB.Connection")

' Construct the connection string for the Connection object.
strConn = _
    "driver={SQL Server};;uid=sa;pwd=;database=SalesDB"

' Using the connection string, open the connection.
objDBConn.Open strConn

' Instantiate an ADO Recordset object.
Set rsHighSales = _
    Server.CreateObject("ADODB.Recordset")

' Set the ActiveConnection property of the recordset.
rsHighSales.ActiveConnection = objDBConn

' Construct the SQL to be used to open the recordset.
strSQL = _
    "SELECT Buyer, Price FROM Sales WHERE Price > 70000"

' Open the recordset. Note the lack of a connection
' object specification.
rsHighSales.Open strSQL

' Use the BOF property to determine whether
' there are records in the recordset.
If Not rsHighSales.BOF Then
    ' There are records. Use the EOF property to loop
    ' through all the records in the recordset and
    ' display them to the screen.
    Do While Not rsHighSales.EOF
```

```
%>
    <%=rsHighSales.Fields(0).Name%>:
        <%=rsHighSales("Buyer")%><BR>
    <%=rsHighSales.Fields(1).Name %>:
        <%=rsHighSales("Price")%><BR>
<%
        rsHighSales.MoveNext
    Loop
Else
    ' There are no records. Tell the user.
%>
    There are no high sales.
<%
End If

' Release the memory consumed by objects.
Set rsHighSales = Nothing
Set objDBConn = Nothing
%>
</BODY>
</HTML>
```

Notes

You can retrieve or set the name of a Command, Field, Parameter, or Property object. However, there are some exceptions. First, if a Parameter object has already been added to a Command object's Parameters collection, you cannot set its Name property. Also, if a Field object is part of the Fields collection of an open Recordset object, you cannot set its name.

Number (Error Object) *objError*.Number

A read-only string that provides the error code number that the underlying data provider raised in response to incorrect syntax or lack of support. This Number property is a property of each Error object in the Connection object's Errors collection. It is *not* the same as the Number property of the ASPError or the VBA Error objects.

Parameters

None

Example

The following example demonstrates the use of the Number property of the Error object. Notice that for this example to work properly, the Buffer property of the Response object must be set to **True** because we use the Response object's Clear and End methods.

```
<%@ LANGUAGE="VBSCRIPT" %>
<%Response.Buffer = True%>

<HTML>
<HEAD>
<TITLE>ADO Examples</TITLE>
```

```
</HEAD>
<BODY>
<%
' Include ADOVBS.INC so we can use the ADO constants.
%>
<!-- #include virtual = "/MySSIncludes/adovbs.inc" -->
<%
' Instantiate an ADO Connection object.
Set objDBConn = Server.CreateObject("ADODB.Connection")

' Construct the connection string for the Connection object.
strConn = _
    "driver={MyDBType};;uid=sa;pwd=;database=SalesDB"

' Using the connection string, open the connection.
objDBConn.Open strConn

' Check to see if attempting to open a connection to
' the provider resulted in ADO adding Error objects to
' the Connection's Errors collection.
If objDBConn.Errors.Count > 0 Then
    ' An error occurred and ADO added an Error object to
    ' the Connection's Errors collection. Clear the
    ' Response buffer and alert the user of the error.
    Response.Clear
    Response.Write _
        "One or more errors has occurred.<BR>"
    For intCounter = 0 to objDBConn.Errors.Count
        Response.Write "The " & intCounter & " error's "
        Response.Write "error number is " & _
            ojDBConn.Errors(intCounter).Number & ".<BR>"
        Response.Write "The description for this "
        Response.Write "error is <BR>" & _
            ojDBConn.Errors(intCounter).Description & ".<BR>"
    Next
    Response.End
End If
    .
    .
    .
```

Notes

Each time an error occurs in the data provider, ADO adds an Error object to the
Errors collection of the Connection object corresponding to that data provider. The
provider is responsible for generating and sending the actual error text to ADO.
The value of the Number property is unique for each error.

Note that if you have code in your scripts that reacts programmatically to errors in
the Connection object's Errors collection, you may want to consider moving this
error handling to the *500-100.ASP* (or customized equivalent) error page if you
are using IIS 5.0 or higher. For more information on use of the *500-100.ASP* error
handling page used by IIS 5.0, see Chapter 5.

RecordCount (Recordset Object)   rsObj.RecordCount

Provides you with the current number of records in the Recordset object (or the number of records in the Recordset object that meet the criteria in the Filter property, if one is supplied). If ADO cannot ascertain the total number of records, the value of this property is –1. The Recordset object must be open before you can retrieve a value for this property. Also, the Recordset object must be of a cursor type that supports movement (forward and backward) or it must be fully populated before the value for the RecordCount property is accurate.

Parameters

None

Example

```
<%@ LANGUAGE="VBSCRIPT" %>
<% Response.Buffer = True %>
<HTML>
<HEAD>
<TITLE>ADO Examples</TITLE>
</HEAD>
<BODY>
<%
' Include ADOVBS.INC so we can use the ADO constants.
%>
<!-- #include virtual = "/MySSIncludes/adovbs.inc" -->
<%
' Instantiate an ADO Connection object.
Set objDBConn = Server.CreateObject("ADODB.Connection")

' Construct the connection string for the Connection object.
strConn = _
    "driver={SQL Server};;uid=sa;pwd=;database=SalesDB"

' Using the connection string, open the connection.
objDBConn.Open strConn

' Instantiate an ADO Recordset object.
Set rsHighSales = _
    Server.CreateObject("ADODB.Recordset")

' Set the ActiveConnection property of the recordset.
rsHighSales.ActiveConnection = objDBConn

' Set the recordset's cursor type to adOpenStatic so
' that the recordset supports the RecordCount property.
rsHighSales.CursorType = adOpenStatic

' Construct the SQL to be used to open the recordset.
strSQL = _
    "SELECT Buyer, Price FROM Sales WHERE Price > 70000"

' Open the recordset. Note the lack of a connection
```

```
' object specification.
rsHighSales.Open strSQL

' Use the BOF property to determine whether
' there are records in the recordset.
If Not rsHighSales.BOF Then
    ' There are records. Use the EOF property to loop
    ' through all the records in the recordset and
    ' display them to the screen.

    ' If the record count can be determined, display it
    ' to the user. Otherwise, let him/her know that the
    ' count cannot be determined.
    If Not (rsHighSales.RecordCount = -1) Then
%>
        There are <%=rsHighSales.RecordCount%> records.
<%
    Else
%>
        ADO cannot determine the number of records in
        your recordset.
<%
    End If
Else
    ' There are no records. Tell the user.
%>
    There are no high sales.
<%
End If

' Release the memory consumed by objects.
Set rsHighSales = Nothing
Set objDBConn = Nothing
%>
</BODY>
</HTML>
```

Notes

You can determine whether your recordset supports the RecordCount property by using the Recordset object's Supports method with the adApproxPosition or adBookmark arguments, as demonstrated in the following code:

```
blnApproxPos = rsExample.Supports(adApproxPosition)
blnBookmark = rsExample.Supports(adBookmark)
```

These calls to the Supports method allow you to determine if the Recordset object supports approximate positioning or bookmarking, respectively. If the value of *blnApproxPos* or *blnBookmark* is True, then RecordCount immediately reflects the actual number of records in the recordset.

If the recordset does not support approximate positioning, an attempt to retrieve the value of the RecordCount property will represent a possible drain on resources, since your code will be forced to traverse the recordset and populate it before RecordCount represents a valid count of rows in the recordset.

Source (Error Object)   *objError*.Source

A string value that represents the name of the application or object that caused
ADO or the underlying data provider to add an Error object to the Errors collection of the Connection object.

Parameters

None

Example

```
<%@ LANGUAGE="VBSCRIPT" %>
<%Response.Buffer = True%>

<HTML>
<HEAD>
<TITLE>ADO Examples</TITLE>
</HEAD>
<BODY>
<%
' Include ADOVBS.INC so we can use the ADO constants.
%>
<!-- #include virtual = "/MySSIncludes/adovbs.inc" -->
<%
' Instantiate an ADO Connection object.
Set objDBConn = Server.CreateObject("ADODB.Connection")

' Construct the connection string for the Connection object.
strConn = _
    "driver={MyDBType};;uid=sa;pwd=;database=SalesDB"

' Using the connection string, open the connection.
objDBConn.Open strConn

' Check to see if attempting to open a connection to
' the provider resulted in ADO adding Error objects to
' the Connection's Errors collection.
If objDBConn.Errors.Count > 0 Then
    ' An error occurred and ADO added an Error object to
    ' the Connection's Errors collection. Clear the
    ' Response buffer and alert the user of the error.
    Response.Clear
    Response.Write _
        "One or more errors have occurred.<BR>"
    For intCounter = 0 to objDBConn.Errors.Count
        Response.Write "The " & intCounter & " error's "
        Response.Write "error number is " & _
            ojDBConn.Errors(intCounter).Number & ".<BR>"
        Response.Write "The description for this "
        Response.Write "error is <BR>" & _
            ojDBConn.Errors(intCounter).Description & _
            ".<BR>"
        Response.Write "The object or application that "
```

```
            Response.Write "caused this error to be raised "
            Response.Write " is " & _
                ojDBConn.Errors(intCounter).Source & ".<BR>"
        Next
        Response.End
    End If
    .
    .
    .
```

Notes

The Error object's Source property allows you to programmatically determine which object or application caused the data provider to raise an error. The value of this string property can be an application name, a class name, or a ProgID for a class. For errors in ADODB, the value of this property will be the following:

ADODB.*strObjName*

where ***strObjName*** represents the name of the instantiated ADODB object that caused the error. This is a read-only property.

Note that if you have code in your scripts that reacts programmatically to errors in the Connection object's Errors collection, you may want to consider moving this error handling to the *500-100.ASP* (or customized equivalent) error page, if you are using IIS 5.0 or higher. For more information on use of the *500-100.ASP* error handling page used by IIS 5.0, see Chapter 5.

Source (Recordset Object)   rsObj.Source (= *strSource*)

A string value that represents the source for the records in the recordset. This can be the name of a stored procedure or a Command object, a table name, or a SQL statement.

Parameters

strSource
> A string value that can hold the name of a stored procedure or a Command object, the name of a table in the database, or a simple SQL statement.

Example

In this example, we set the Source property to a simple SQL statement.

```
<%@ LANGUAGE="VBSCRIPT" %>
<% Response.Buffer = True %>
<HTML>
<HEAD>
<TITLE>ADO Examples</TITLE>
</HEAD>
<BODY>
<%
' Include ADOVBS.INC so we can use the ADO constants.
%>
<!-- #include virtual = "/MySSIncludes/adovbs.inc" -->
<%
```

```
' Instantiate an ADO Connection object.
Set objDBConn = Server.CreateObject("ADODB.Connection")

' Construct the connection string for the Connection object.
strConn = _
    "driver={SQL Server};;uid=sa;pwd=;database=SalesDB"

' Using the connection string, open the connection.
objDBConn.Open strConn

' Instantiate an ADO Recordset object.
Set rsHighSales = _
    Server.CreateObject("ADODB.Recordset")

' Set the ActiveConnection property of the recordset.
rsHighSales.ActiveConnection = objDBConn

' If you set the Source property of the Recordset
' object, you do not need to specify a source string
' when you call the Recordset object's Open method.
rsHighSales.Source = _
    "SELECT Buyer, Price FROM Sales WHERE Price > 70000"

' Open the recordset. Note the lack of a connection
' object specification.
rsHighSales.Open
    .
    .
    .
```

Notes

The Source property is read/write if the recordset is closed, but read-only other-wise. If you set the value of the Source property to the name of a Command object, the ActiveConnection property of the Recordset will inherit the value of the ActiveConnection property of the Command object—even if you have already set the ActiveConnection property of the Recordset object. Also, if you set the value of the Source property to the name of a Command object, retrieving the value of the recordset's Source property will return the value of the Command's CommandText property, not the name of the Command object.

Even if you set the Source property, you can still optimize the call to the Open method by setting values for the *Options* parameter of the Recordset.Open method.

If the value of your Source property is a simple SQL statement, as it is in the preceding example, it doesn't matter whether you set the Source property and then call the Open method or pass the SQL statement as an argument to the Open method.

Collections Reference

Errors Collection

Each Connection object has its own Errors collection. ADO adds Error objects to this collection each time the underlying data provider for that Connection object raises an error because of incorrect syntax or lack of support.

Parameters

None

Example

For examples, see the details for the Description, Number, and Source (Error object) properties earlier in this chapter.

Notes

ADO clears the Errors collection of the affected Connection object each time a new error occurs. It does *not* simply add another Error object to those already in the Errors collection. These added Error objects represent a data provider error, *not* an ADO or ASP error. For this reason, even if ADO adds an Error object to a Connection object's Errors collection, that error does not trigger a runtime error (which could be caught by a script's On Error trap) unless there is *also* a corresponding ADO error.

Every Error object currently in the Errors collection of a given Connection object represents error information raised by the data provider for a single error-causing operation on the data.

Note that if you have code in your scripts that reacts programmatically to errors in the Connection object's Errors collection, you may want to consider moving this error handling to the *500-100.ASP* (or customized equivalent) error page, if you are using IIS 5.0 or higher. For more information on use of the *500-100.ASP* error handling page used by IIS 5.0, see Chapter 5.

Methods Reference

AddNew (Recordset Object)
rsObj.AddNew FieldName(s), FieldValue(s)

Creates and initializes a new record in the underlying database. To determine whether the underlying data provider supports this functionality, call the Supports method of the Recordset with the ADO adAddNew constant as an argument. If the resulting value is True, then you can use AddNew.

Parameters

FieldName(s)

> The name of a single field in the new record, or the name of an array containing the names of multiple fields in the new record. If FieldName(s) is the name of a field name array, you must also pass the name of a value

ActiveX Data
Objects 2.6

AddNew (Recordset Object)   241

array, and the number of elements for both arrays must be the same or an error occurs.

FieldValue(s)

The value of a single field in the new record or the name of an array containing the values of multiple fields in the new record. If *FieldValue(s)* is a value array, *FieldName(s)* must be the name of a field name array, and the number of elements for both arrays must be the same or an error occurs.

Example

The following example demonstrates the use of the AddNew method both without and with arguments.

```
<%@ LANGUAGE="VBSCRIPT" %>
<% Response.Buffer = True %>
<HTML>
<HEAD>
<TITLE>ADO Examples</TITLE>
</HEAD>
<BODY>
<%
' Include ADOVBS.INC so we can use the ADO constants.
%>
<!-- #include virtual = "/MySSIncludes/adovbs.inc" -->
<%
Dim astrFieldNames()
Dim astrFieldValues()

' Instantiate an ADO Connection object.
Set objDBConn = Server.CreateObject("ADODB.Connection")

' Construct the connection string for the Connection object.
strConn = _
    "driver={SQL Server};;uid=sa;pwd=;database=SalesDB"

' Using the connection string, open the connection.
objDBConn.Open strConn

' Instantiate an ADO Recordset object.
Set rsSales = Server.CreateObject("ADODB.Recordset")

' Set the the type of cursor we will use.
rsSales.CursorType = adOpenKeyset

' Set the Lock type for the records so that only
' when we update a record is that record locked by ADO.
rsSales.LockType = adLockOptimistic

' Open the Sales table.
rsSales.Open "Sales", objDBConn, , , adCmdTable

' Add a new record using no argument. Note use of the "!" notation.
rsSales.AddNew
rsSales!Buyer = "Josh"
```

```
rsSales!Price = 23478
rsSales.Update

' Add a new record using a field name array and a field
' value array.
ReDim Preserve astrFieldNames(2)

astrFieldNames(0) = "Buyer"
astrFieldNames(1) = "Price"
astrFieldValues(0) = "Mara"
astrFieldValues(1) = 143578

rsSales.AddNew astrFieldNames, astrFieldValues

' No call to the Update method required for this one.

' Release the memory consumed by objects.
Set rsSales = Nothing
Set objDBConn = Nothing
%>
</BODY>
</HTML>
```

Notes

Recordset objects have two distinct update modes: *immediate mode*, meaning that the data provider writes your changes to the database immediately after you call the Update method; and *batch update mode*, where the data provider caches multiple records' changes as you make them and call the Update method, but updates the database only after you call the UpdateBatch method.

If the recordset is in immediate update mode, calling AddNew with no arguments sets the EditMode property of the Recordset object to adEditAdd. Once you call the Update method, the data provider writes your changes to the database and resets the EditMode property to adEditNone. However, if you include one or more field name/field value pairs as arguments, the data provider writes the changes to the database immediately without altering the value of the EditMode property.

If the Recordset object is in batch update mode, however, calling AddNew works exactly as it does when you are in immediate update mode, with one significant exception. Your changes are cached until you call the UpdateBatch method, regardless of whether or not you include field/value pairs with your call to AddNew.

Note that, once a record is added to the database, that record becomes the current record unless the Recordset object you are using does not support bookmarks. If this is the case, you may not be able to access the new record without requerying the database.

Finally, note the use of the ! shorthand in the preceding code. If you wish to specify the value of a specific field in a record, and that record contains no space characters, then the following shorthand can be used:

Recordset!FieldName

where *Recordset* is the name of the Recordset object and *FieldName* is the name of the specific Field to be updated or referenced.

Clone (Recordset Object)   Set *rsObj2* = *rsObj1*.Clone(*LockType*)

Creates an exact duplicate of a recordset and places that recordset into a second Recordset object variable.

Parameters

rsObj1
   The Recordset object you wish to copy.

rsObj2
   The new Recordset object into which you will place the copy of the Recordset object represented by the *rsObj1* parameter.

LockType
   Optional. The LockType parameter specifies the lock type of the original Recordset object being cloned. The possible values are **adLockUnspecified** (lock type of clone will be the same as that of the original, whatever type that is) or **adLockReadOnly** (the original Recordset is read-only).

Example

The following example demonstrates the use of the Clone method of the Recordset object and the fact that the same bookmark values can be used in clones as in the originals to point to the same records.

```
<%@ LANGUAGE="VBSCRIPT" %>
<% Response.Buffer = True %>
<HTML>
<HEAD>
<TITLE>ADO Examples</TITLE>
</HEAD>
<BODY>
<%
' Include ADOVBS.INC so we can use the ADO constants.
%>
<!-- #include virtual = "/MySSIncludes/adovbs.inc" -->
<%
Dim astrFieldNames()
Dim astrFieldValues()

' Instantiate an ADO Connection object.
Set objDBConn = Server.CreateObject("ADODB.Connection")

' Construct the connection string for the Connection object.
strConn = _
    "driver={SQL Server};;uid=sa;pwd=;database=SalesDB"

' Using the connection string, open the connection.
objDBConn.Open strConn

' Instantiate two ADO Recordset objects.
```

```
Set rsSales         = _
    Server.CreateObject("ADODB.Recordset")
Set rsSalesClone    = _
    Server.CreateObject("ADODB.Recordset")

' Open the Sales table.
rsSales.Open "Sales", objDBConn, , , adCmdTable

' Create a bookmark in the original recordset.
rsSales.MoveNext

' The current record now points to the second record in the
' Sales table.
lngOrigBookmark = rsSales.Bookmark

' Clone the original recordset.
Set rsSalesClone = rsSales.Clone()

' The current record pointer in rsSalesClone now points to
' the first record in the Sales table.

' Set the Bookmark property of the clone.
rsSalesClone.Bookmark = lngBookmark

' The current record pointer in rsSalesClone now points to
' the second record in the Sales table.
    .
    .
    .

' Release the memory consumed by objects.
Set rsSales = Nothing
Set objDBConn = Nothing
%>
</BODY>
</HTML>
```

Notes

The Clone method of the Recordset object allows you to create multiple copies of the same recordset without having to query the database more than once. However, it is important to realize that these copies are simply pointers to the same original, not separate Recordset objects. This in effect allows you to maintain more than one current record in the same recordset. The Clone method of creating a new Recordset object is significantly faster than using the Open (or similar) method of creating a Recordset object.

Note that the current record pointer in the new copy of your Recordset object points at the first record in the recordset, and its position has no relationship to the position of the record pointer in the first (copied) Recordset object. Also, closing the original (or any clone) has no effect on the other cloned copies.

If you make any changes to any clone Recordset, all of its clones can see those changes. However, if you call the Requery method for any Recordset, its clones will no longer be in sync with that Recordset, because requerying resets the object to point to a new Recordset object. However, the original is still in existence as long as even one clone still points to it. For this reason the clones still represent the pre-Requery version of the recordset.

A bookmark in a Recordset represents the same record in a clone of that database. Also, if a particular Recordset object does not support bookmarking, it cannot be cloned.

Close (Connection Object, Recordset Object)   *Obj*.Close

Connection.Close closes the connection to the underlying data provider; Recordset.Close closes a recordset. Both versions of the Close method release system resources used to hold the object variables, but do not remove the object from memory. The same object can be opened later without being instantiated again using the Server object's CreateObject method.

Parameters

Obj
> The name of the Connection or Recordset you wish to close.

Example

```
<%@ LANGUAGE="VBSCRIPT" %>
<% Response.Buffer = True %>
<HTML>
<HEAD>
<TITLE>ADO Examples</TITLE>
</HEAD>
<BODY>
<%
' Include ADOVBS.INC so we can use the ADO constants.
%>
<!-- #include virtual = "/MySSIncludes/adovbs.inc" -->
<%
Dim astrFieldNames()
Dim astrFieldValues()

' Instantiate an ADO Connection object.
Set objDBConn = Server.CreateObject("ADODB.Connection")

' Construct the connection string for the Connection object.
strConn = _
    "driver={SQL Server};;uid=sa;pwd=;database=SalesDB"

' Using the connection string, open the connection.
objDBConn.Open strConn

' Instantiate an ADO Recordset object.
Set rsSales       = _
    Server.CreateObject("ADODB.Recordset")
```

```
' Open the Sales table.
rsSales.Open "Sales", objDBConn, , , adCmdTable

' Close the Recordset and Connection - in that order!
rsSales.Close
objDBConn.Close

' The objects still reside in memory here.
' To release the memory consumed by objects, we must
' set the object variables to the keyword Nothing.
Set rsSales = Nothing
Set objDBConn = Nothing
%>
</BODY>
</HTML>
```

Notes

If you close a Connection object, all of the Recordset objects that have that Connection object as the value of their ActiveConnection property are also closed. If you close a Connection object that has Command objects associated with it, the Command objects will stay open but their ActiveConnection will be reset to Nothing. Also, if the Command object had a Parameters collection containing Parameter objects with values provided by the underlying data provider, these parameter values are cleared.

You can open closed Connection objects. You can also reopen closed Recordset objects as long as they still have a valid ActiveConnection object or you supply one before (or while) attempting to reopen them.

If there are any transactions taking place in any of the Recordsets associated with a Connection object when you close it, you will receive an error. If the EditMode property of the Recordset object is anything other than adEditNone, then those changes that you have already made are disregarded and not stored to the database.

As stated in the entry for the Clone method, closing a Recordset object has no effect on any of its clones.

Delete (Parameter Object, Recordset Object)

`rsObj.Delete Record(s)ToBeDeleted`

 Only the Delete method of the Recordset object is covered here.

The Delete method of the Recordset object allows you to delete either the current record or a group of records. To delete a group of records, you must use the Filter property to define the group of records before deleting them.

Parameters

Record(s)ToBeDeleted

An integer constant that defines whether you want to delete only the current record or all records meeting the criteria set forth in the Recordset.Filter property. The possible values for this parameter are:

adAffectAll

If the Filter property of the Recordset object is not set, then the call to the Delete method affects all records. Otherwise, Delete affects only those records visible after application of the Filter.

adAffectAllChapters

All records are deleted, regardless of the presence of a value in the Filter property.

adAffectCurrent

Only the current record is deleted. This is the default.

adAffectGroup

Removes all the records from the database that meet the criteria in the Filter property. Once deleted, you can set the Filter property to adFilterAffectedRecords to view those records affected by the call to the Delete method.

Example

The following example demonstrates the use of the Delete method to delete a group of records that match the criteria in the Recordset object's current Filter property.

```
<%@ LANGUAGE="VBSCRIPT" %>
<% Response.Buffer = True %>
<HTML>
<HEAD>
<TITLE>ADO Examples</TITLE>
</HEAD>
<BODY>
<%
' Include ADOVBS.INC so we can use the ADO constants.
%>
<!-- #include virtual = "/MySSIncludes/adovbs.inc" -->
<%
Dim astrFieldNames()
Dim astrFieldValues()

' Instantiate an ADO Connection object.
Set objDBConn = Server.CreateObject("ADODB.Connection")

' Construct the connection string for the Connection object.
strConn = _
    "driver={SQL Server};;uid=sa;pwd=;database=SalesDB"

' Using the connection string, open the connection.
objDBConn.Open strConn
```

```
' Instantiate an ADO Recordset object.
Set rsSales      = _
   Server.CreateObject("ADODB.Recordset")

' Open the Sales table.
rsSales.Open "Sales", objDBConn, , , adCmdTable

' Set the filter property of the recordset to collect
' all the records you wish to delete.
rsSales.Filter = "Price < 20000"

' Delete the records that meet the Filter criteria.
rsSales.Delete adAffectGroup

' Restore the recordset from its filtered state. This
' will set the current record pointer to the first
' valid record in the recordset, avoiding the error
' that would result when you attempt to ascertain the
' value of the current record when the current record
' has been deleted.
rsSales.Filter = adFilterNone

' Close the Recordset and Connection - in that order!
rsSales.Close
objDBConn.Close

' The objects still reside in memory here.
' To release the memory consumed by objects, we must
' set the object variables to the keyword Nothing.
Set rsSales = Nothing
Set objDBConn = Nothing
%>
</BODY>
</HTML>
```

Notes

If you are in immediate update mode (see the description of update modes in the entry for the AddNew method), calling the Delete method immediately removes the affected record or records from the database. If you are in batch update mode, the affected record or records are marked for deletion but are removed from the database only when you call the UpdateBatch method.

If the Recordset object (or underlying data provider) does not support deletion of records, calling the Delete method results in an error. If you attempt to delete a record that has been deleted or otherwise locked by another user, the data provider raises a warning and ADO adds an Error object to the active connection's Errors collection. Only if all the records you attempted to delete were locked does execution stop.

If you attempt to retrieve the values of fields in records you have deleted, an error will occur. This is important to remember when you realize that if you delete a record, that record remains the current record until after you move from the record using one of the navigational methods.

ActiveX Data Objects 2.6

Finally, if you call the Delete method from within a transaction and you roll back that transaction, the records you attempted to delete are restored regardless of the current update mode.

Execute (Command Object)

```
Set rsObj = cmdObj.Execute(RecordsAffected, _Parameters, Options)
```
(if the call to Execute returns records)

```
cmdObj.Execute(RecordsAffected, Parameters, Options)
```
(if the call to Execute does not return records)

Executes a query, SQL statement, or stored procedure. If it results in the creation of a recordset, that recordset can be immediately assigned to a Recordset object variable.

Parameters

rsObj

A Recordset object that you want initialized and set equal to the collection of records returned by the call to the Execute method.

cmdObj

The name of the Command object whose Execute method you are calling.

RecordsAffected

An optional Long variable that, when the method returns, indicates how many records were affected by the call.

Parameters

An array of variants containing parameters for the command to be executed. You should not put output parameters here, since they will not be returned properly.

Options

The Options parameter can be used to specify the type of command being executed or the Execute options desired.

The ADO constant values for the command type are the same as those for the Command.CommandType property:

adCmdUnspecified (-1)

This indicates that the CommandType property has not yet been specified.

adCmdText (1)

The command is a text command, such as a simple SQL statement; CommandText is evaluated as a textual definition of a command.

adCmdTable (2)

The Command object represents a table; CommandText is evaluated as the name of a table.

adCmdStoredProc (4)

The Command object represents a stored procedure; CommandText is evaluated as the name of a stored procedure in the underlying data provider.

adCmdUnknown (8)

The Command object type is unknown; this is the default value.

adCmdFile (256)

The Command object represents a file in which a persistent Recordset object is stored.

adCmdTableDirect (512)

The Command object represents a table from which all columns are retrieved.

Execute Options

adAsyncExecute (0x10)

Execution should occur asynchronously.

adAsyncFetch (0x20)

Specifies that if there are rows remaining to be retrieved after the first set of records are retrieved (the number of which is equal to the setting for CacheSize), those remaining rows should be retrieved asynchronously.

adAsyncFetchNonBlocking (0x40)

Specifies that the records should be retrieved asynchronously but that the thread used by the system to retrieve the records should not block other threads.

adAsyncExecuteNoRecords (0x80)

Specifies that no records should be returned (for example, if the Command object is being used to update a record). In this case, if there are any records returned they are ignored by the system.

adOptionUnspecified (-1)

To specify no execution options, you can optionally use the adOptionUnspecified constant.

Example

```
<%@ LANGUAGE="VBSCRIPT" %>
<% Response.Buffer = True %>
<HTML>
<HEAD>
<TITLE>ADO Examples</TITLE>
</HEAD>
<BODY>
<%
' Include ADOVBS.INC so we can use the ADO constants.
%>
<!-- #include virtual = "/bc_SSIncludes/adovbs.inc" -->
<%
' Instantiate an ADO Connection object.
Set objDBConn = Server.CreateObject("ADODB.Connection")
```

```
' Construct the connection string for the Connection object.
strConn = _
    "driver={MyDBType};;uid=sa;pwd=;database=SalesDB"

' Using the connection string, open the connection.
objDBConn.Open strConn

' Create stored procedure command object.
Set objSPCmd = Server.CreateObject("ADODB.Command")

' Set the active connection equal to the current
' connection object
Set objSPCmd.ActiveConnection = objDBConn

' Set stored procedure command text. In this example
' UpdateHighSales is a stored procedure that retrieves
' information from some other table and then updates the
' Sales table.
strCommandString = "UpdateHighSales"
objSPCmd.CommandText = strCommandString

' Initialize a Long variable to contain the number of
' affected records when the stored procedure is
' executed.
lngAffectedRecords = 0

' Open the recordset using the results from the Command object.
objSPCmd.Execute lngAffectedRecords, , adCmdStoredProc

' Display on the client the number of records updated.
. %>

There were <%= lngAffectedRecords%> records affected by your call to the
Execute method.

<%
 .
 .
 .
```

Notes

Calling the Execute method returns a Recordset object. Only if there are rows
returned, however, is that Recordset open. You can also use the Execute method
of the Command object to execute a SQL statement and simply disregard the
recordset created. For example, the following line demonstrates this idea using an
UPDATE query:

```
cmdObj.Execute _
    "UPDATE Sales SET Price = 50000 WHERE User ='Henry'"
```

The *Parameters* parameter allows you to specify, if you so desire, values for
some of the command query's parameters. You have two options. You can
provide no parameters in the call to Execute, in which case the command uses the
Parameters collection for the values of the parameters; or you can send in any

number of parameter values with the call to Execute and, thus, override the values set in the Parameters collection. For example, suppose your command takes three parameters for which you have created three Parameter objects. If you use the following call to the Execute method:

```
avntParams = Array(strVal1, strVal2)
cmdObj.Execute lngRecordsAffected, avntParams, _
            adStoredProc
```

the first and second Parameter object values are overridden in the call to the Execute method, but the third parameter takes the value of the third Parameter object in the Command object's Parameters collection.

Execute (Connection Object)

```
Set rsObj = connObj.Execute(CommandText,_
                _RecordsAffected, Options)
```
(if the call to Execute returns records)

```
connObj.Execute(CommandText, RecordsAffected, Options)
```
(if the call to Execute does not return records)

Executes a query, SQL statement, or stored procedure. If it results in the creation of a recordset, that recordset can be immediately assigned to a Recordset object variable.

Parameters

rsObj

A Recordset object that you want initialized and set equal to the collection of records returned by the call to the Execute method.

connObj

The name of the Connection object whose Execute method you are calling.

CommandText

A string value representing a SQL statement, table name, stored procedure, or data provider-specific command.

RecordsAffected

An optional Long variable that, when the method returns, indicates how many records were affected by the call.

Options

See Options parameter of the Execute (Command Object) method earlier in this chapter.

Example

The following example demonstrates how you might use the Execute method of a Connection object to create a read-only, forward-only recordset from the Sales table.

```
<%@ LANGUAGE="VBSCRIPT" %>
<% Response.Buffer = True %>
<HTML>
```

```
<HEAD>
<TITLE>ADO Examples</TITLE>
</HEAD>
<BODY>.
<%
' Include ADOVBS.INC so we can use the ADO constants.
%>
<!-- #include virtual = "/bc_SSIncludes/adovbs.inc" -->
<%
' Instantiate an ADO Connection object.
Set objDBConn = Server.CreateObject("ADODB.Connection")

' Construct the connection string for the Connection object.
strConn = _
    "driver={MyDBType};;uid=sa;pwd=;database=SalesDB"

' Using the connection string, open the connection.
objDBConn.Open strConn

' Create a command text string.
strCommandText = _
    "SELECT * FROM Sales WHERE Price > 70000"

' Create a read-only, forward-only recordset using the
' Execute method of the connection object. Note that we
' have no AffectedRecords parameter.
Set rsSales = objDBConn.Execute strCommandText, , _
    adCmdText
    .
    .
    .
```

Notes

Calling the Execute method of a Connection object returns a Recordset object. Only if there are rows returned, however, is that Recordset open. Just as with the Command object, you can also use the Execute method of the Connection object to execute a SQL statement and simply disregard the recordset created. For example, the following line demonstrates this idea using an UPDATE query:

```
conObj.Execute _
    "UPDATE Sales SET Price = 50000 WHERE User ='Henry'"
```

If your call to the Execute method of the Connection object returns a Recordset, that recordset is always read-only and forward-only. If you need a more flexible Recordset object, you must use the Recordset object's Open method.

Move (Recordset Object)

rsObj.Move lngNumRecords, vntStartBookmark

Moves the current record pointer forward or backward a given number of records, starting at either the current record or from an optional bookmarked record.

Parameters

lngNumRecords

The number of records from the current (or bookmarked) record that you wish to move the current record pointer. This can be a negative number to move backward in the recordset.

vntStartBookmark

A string or variant value that represents the bookmark for a given record. In addition to a string or variant value, you can also use one of the following ADO constants for this optional parameter:

adBookmarkCurrent

Starts at the current record. This is the default value for this parameter.

adBookmarkFirst

Starts at the first record in the current recordset.

adBookmarkLast

Starts at the last record in the current recordset.

Example

The following example demonstrates how to use the Move method to move the record pointer to a position five records after the current record.

```
<%@ LANGUAGE="VBSCRIPT" %>
<% Response.Buffer = True %>
<HTML>
<HEAD>
<TITLE>ADO Examples</TITLE>
</HEAD>
<BODY>
<%
' Include ADOVBS.INC so we can use the ADO constants.
%>
<!-- #include virtual = "/bc_SSIncludes/adovbs.inc" -->
<%
' Instantiate an ADO Connection object.
Set objDBConn = Server.CreateObject("ADODB.Connection")

' Construct the connection string for the Connection object.
strConn = _
    "driver={MyDBType};;uid=sa;pwd=;database=SalesDB"

' Using the connection string, open the connection.
objDBConn.Open strConn

' Create a command text string.
strCommandText = _
    "SELECT * FROM Sales WHERE Price > 70000"

' Create a read-only, forward-only recordset using the
' Execute method of the connection object. Note that we
' have no AffectedRecords parameter.
Set rsSales = objDBConn.Execute strCommandText, , _
              adCmdText
```

```
' Move to a record five after the current record. Then
' check to see if you are at the end of the recordset.
' If you are, move back to the starting record.
vntBookmark = rsSales.Bookmark
rsSales.Move 5, adBookmarkCurrent
If rsSales.EOF Then
    rsSales.Bookmark = vntBookmark
End If
  .
  .
  .
```

Notes

If you attempt to move to a record position before the first record in the recordset, the record pointer is set to one position before the first record and the BOF property of the Recordset object is set to True. If you attempt to move before this position, an error occurs.* A similar situation arises from moving past the end of the recordset.

If you attempt to call the Move method on an empty recordset, an error is raised.

If you include a value for the *vntStartBookmark* parameter, the movement of the current record pointer starts from the records represented by the *vntStartBookmark* value. If you do not include this parameter, the movement starts from the current record.

If you are also using the Recordset object's CacheSize property to set the number of records cached and you attempt to move outside the currently cached set of records, ADO will retrieve another set of records. The size of the retrieved group is dictated by the value of the CacheSize property. ADO will also set the current record pointer to the first record in the newly cached set of records.

If the Recordset object's CursorType is adOpenForwardOnly, you can still move backward in it. The only restriction on this movement is that you cannot move outside of the currently cached group of records or an error will occur. So if you are able to cache the entire recordset, you could move backward as much as you want within a forward-only recordset.

MoveFirst, MoveLast, MoveNext, MovePrevious (Recordset Object)   rsObj.{MoveFirst | MoveLast | MoveNext | MovePrevious}

Moves the record pointer to the first record of the recordset, to the last record of the recordset, forward one position, or backward one position, respectively.

Parameters

None

---

* Note that the error you receive when trying to use any of the Move methods to move to a nonexistent record ("No current record.") could be considered a bit cryptic.

Example

The following example demonstrates how to use the MoveNext method to move the current record pointer to a position five records after the current record. You use the other navigational methods in exactly this same manner. (Note that this is not the most efficient manner to move the current record five positions forward.)

```
<%@ LANGUAGE="VBSCRIPT" %>
<% Response.Buffer = True %>
<HTML>
<HEAD>
<TITLE>ADO Examples</TITLE>
</HEAD>
<BODY>
<%
' Include ADOVBS.INC so we can use the ADO constants.
%>
<!-- #include virtual = "/bc_SSIncludes/adovbs.inc" -->
<%
' Instantiate an ADO Connection object.
Set objDBConn = Server.CreateObject("ADODB.Connection")

' Construct the connection string for the Connection object.
strConn = _
    "driver={MyDBType};;uid=sa;pwd=;database=SalesDB"

' Using the connection string, open the connection.
objDBConn.Open strConn

' Create a command text string.
strCommandText = _
    "SELECT * FROM Sales WHERE Price > 70000"

' Create a read-only, forward-only recordset using the
' Execute method of the connection object. Note that we
' have no AffectedRecords parameter.
Set rsSales = objDBConn.Execute strCommandText, , _
              adCmdText .

' Move to a record five after the current record, using
' the MoveNext method. Then check to see if you are at
' the end of the recordset. If you are, move back to
' the starting record.
vntBookmark = rsSales.Bookmark
rsSales.MoveNext

If rsSales.EOF Then
    rsSales.Bookmark = vntBookmark
End If
.
.
.
```

Notes

To use the MoveLast method, your Recordset object must support bookmarks.

If you call the MoveNext method and the record pointer is pointing to the last record in the database, then the record pointer is moved to one position after the last record, and the EOF property is set to **True**. If you call MoveNext again from this record position, a runtime error is raised.

Likewise, if you call the MovePrevious method and the record pointer is pointing to the first record in the database, then the record pointer is moved to one position before the first record, and the BOF property is set to **True**. If you call MovePrevious again from this record position, a runtime error is raised.

NextRecordset (Command Object, Recordset Object)

Set *rsObj2* = *rsObj1*.NextRecordset(*lngRecordsAffected*)

Clears the current recordset and retrieves the next recordset. This retrieval occurs by iterating through a series of commands sent in with the call to the Recordset.Open method.

Parameters

rsObj2

The Recordset object variable to which you assign the recordset returned from the NextRecordset method.

rsObj1

The current Recordset object. This Recordset can be the same Recordset as that represented by *rsObj2*. If this is the case, the current recordset is cleared. Otherwise, you will have two Recordset objects after the method call: one that represents the current Recordset, and one that represents the Recordset returned from the command.

lngRecordsAffected

The number of records cleared if *rsObj1* = *rsObj2*.

Example

```
<%@ LANGUAGE="VBSCRIPT" %>
<% Response.Buffer = True %>
<HTML>
<HEAD>
<TITLE>ADO Examples</TITLE>
</HEAD>
<BODY>
<%
' Include ADOVBS.INC so we can use the ADO constants.
%>
<!-- #include virtual = "/bc_SSIncludes/adovbs.inc" -->
<%
' Instantiate an ADO Connection object.
Set objDBConn = Server.CreateObject("ADODB.Connection")

' Construct the connection string for the Connection object.
```

```
strConn = _
    "driver={MyDBType};;uid=sa;pwd=;database=SalesDB"

' Using the connection string, open the connection.
objDBConn.Open strConn

' Create a command text string.
strCommandText = _
    "SELECT * FROM Sales WHERE Price > 70000; "
strCommandText = strCommandText & _
    "SELECT * FROM Sales WHERE Buyer LIKE'Chris'; "

' Create a read-only, forward-only recordset using the
' Execute method of the connection object. Note that we
' have no AffectedRecords parameter.
Set rsSales = objDBConn.Execute strCommandText, , _
              adCmdText

' Manipulate recordset containing records from the
' Sales table where Price > 70000.
[CODE HERE]

' Now retrieve the next object into the same
' Recordset object for use later in the script.
rsSales = rsSales.NextRecordset()
    .
    .
    .
```

Notes

You can use the NextRecordset method any time you have a compound command statement in your call to the Open method of the Recordset object (or the Execute method of the Command or Connection object), or a stored procedure that you call returns more than one result set. If you include a compound command statement in your call to the Open method of the Recordset object or the Execute method of the Command or Connection objects such as the following:

```
"SELECT * FROM Sales WHERE Price = 80000; SELECT * FROM Sales WHERE Buyer
='Chris'"
```

ADO only returns the results from the first query, exactly as if you had sent only

```
"SELECT * FROM Sales WHERE Price = 80000."
```

To retrieve the records from the second SELECT statement, you use the NextRecordset method.

If any of your commands could return a row set but actually return no rows, the returned Recordset object is an empty recordset, and its BOF property is True. If any of your commands do not return rows, then if it is successful, it will return a closed Recordset.

If you attempt to call the NextRecordset method of a Recordset object that has an edit pending, you must first call the Update or CancelUpdate method or an error will result.

Open (Connection Object)

> connObj.Open strConnectionString, strUserId, _strPassword

Opens a connection to the data provider.

Parameters

strConnectionString

An optional string containing information about the connection to be made. For more details on what is valid for the *strConnectionString* parameter, see the description of the Connection object's ConnectionString property.

strUserId

A string value that represents the name of the user that will be sent to the data source. This is an optional parameter unless the *strPassword* parameter is used.

strPassword

A string value that represents the password to be used in verifying the user identification sent in the *strUserId* parameter. This is an optional parameter.

Example

The following example demonstrates the construction of a *strConnectionString* parameter and the subsequent call to the Connection object's Open method.

```
<%@ LANGUAGE="VBSCRIPT" %>
<% Response.Buffer = True %>
<HTML>
<HEAD>
<TITLE>ADO Examples</TITLE>
</HEAD>
<BODY>
<%
' Include ADOVBS.INC so we can use the ADO constants.
%>
<!-- #include virtual = "/bc_SSIncludes/adovbs.inc" -->
<%
' Instantiate an ADO Connection object.
Set objDBConn = Server.CreateObject("ADODB.Connection")

' Construct the connection string for the Connection
' object. For more detail on what each element of this
' string represents, see the section of this chapter
' that covers the ConnectionString property.
strConn = _
    "driver={SQL Server};;uid=sa;pwd=;database=SalesDB"

' Using the connection string, open the connection.
objDBConn.Open strConn

' You can now use this Connection object to execute
' commands against the underlying data source.
.
.
.
```

Notes

Before you can create a recordset or issue commands against a data source using the Recordset or Command objects, you must first create a valid, open connection to the data source. The details governing the establishment of this connection (such as the data source and its location) are located in the ConnectionString property of the Connection object you are attempting to open.

You can either send the *strConnectionString* parameter in your call to the Open method or you can set the ConnectionString property before calling the Open method. However, be aware that if you do both, the values in the *strConnectionString* parameter will be used and the ConnectionString property value will change to the value of the parameter when the Connection object becomes open.

As discussed in the ConnectionString property section, you can send user and password information in the ConnectionString property or in the *strConnectionString* parameter. If you use the *strConnectionString* parameter and also include the *strUserId* and *strPassword* parameters, the result is undefined. This may cause an error when opening a connection to some data sources.

To close the Connection object, you use the Connection object's Close method. If you want to free the memory resources held by storing that Connection object (open or closed), you must set the Connection object variable equal to the keyword Nothing.

Open (Recordset Object)　　　　　　　　rsObj.Open vntSource, _
vntActiveConnection, _lngCursorType, lngLockType, lngOptions

Opens a cursor into a data source.

Parameters

vntSource
> A Command object name, SQL statement, table name, or stored procedure name.

vntActiveConnection
> A variant value holding the name of a Connection object or a string containing valid ConnectionString text.

lngCursorType
> The type of cursor you would like to create. If you attempt to create a cursor type not supported by the underlying data source, an error may occur. The valid values for the *lngCursorType* parameter are the following:

adOpenForwardOnly
>> This is the default. This parameter only allows movement forward from the current record. Otherwise this cursor type is identical to the static cursor. There is one exception to this, however. Some data providers will allow you to call the MoveFirst method to move the current record pointer back to the first record in the recordset. This is the fastest cursor type.

---

adOpenKeyset

In a keyset cursor, you cannot see new records added by other users and you cannot access records that have been deleted by other users. You can, however, see the changes to records in your recordset made by other users. All types of movement are possible in a keyset cursor recordset.

adOpenDynamic

Dynamic cursors are the most flexible (and slowest) of the four types. In a dynamic cursor, additions, changes, and deletions are all visible in your recordset. All types of movement are possible in a dynamic cursor recordset.

adOpenStatic

Static cursors provide a static snapshot of the records in your recordset. This is useful for generating reports, but the records in the recordset are not updateable. Additions, changes, and deletions made by other users are not visible in your recordset.

adOpenUnspecified

No cursor type specified.

lngLockType

Determines the type of locking or concurrency that your Recordset will have. The underlying data source must support this locking mechanism. The valid ADO constants for this parameter are as follows:

adLockReadOnly

Default. The records in the cursor are read-only.

adLockPessimistic

The records are locked pessimistically record-by-record. The data provider locks the record upon editing it to insure that changes are saved appropriately.

adLockOptimistic

The records are locked record-by-record only when you attempt to save your changes to the database.

adLockBatchOptimistic

This constant is the same as **adLockOptimistic**, but for batch updates.

adLockUnspecified

No lock type specified.

lngOptions

See Options parameter of the Execute (Command Object) method earlier in this chapter.

Example

```
<%@ LANGUAGE="VBSCRIPT" %>
<% Response.Buffer = True %>
<HTML>
<HEAD>
<TITLE>ADO Examples</TITLE>
</HEAD>
```

```
<BODY>
<%
' Include ADOVBS.INC so we can use the ADO constants.
%>
<!-- #include virtual = "/bc_SSIncludes/adovbs.inc" -->
<%
' Instantiate an ADO Connection object.
Set objDBConn = Server.CreateObject("ADODB.Connection")

' Construct the connection string for the Connection
' object. For more detail on what each element of this
' string represents, see the section of this chapter
' that covers the ConnectionString property.
strConn = _
    "driver={SQL Server};;uid=sa;pwd=;database=SalesDB"

' Using the connection string, open the connection.
objDBConn.Open strConn

' Instantiate a Recordset object.
Set rsSales = Server.CreateObject("ADODB.Recordset")

' Set the ActiveConnection property and initialize the
' string that will be used as the Source parameter.
rsSales.ActiveConnection = objDBConn
strSource = _
    "SELECT COUNT(*) FROM Sales WHERE Price > 23000"

' Open the Recordset...
rsSales.open strSource, , adOpenDynamic, _
               adLockOptimistic, adCmdText
  .
  .
  .
```

Notes

You can either sent the *vntActiveConnection* parameter in your call to the Open method or you can set the ActiveConnection property before calling the Open method. However, be aware that if you do both, the values in the *vntActiveConnection* argument will be used and the ActiveConnection property value will change to the value of the argument when the Recordset object becomes open.

The *vntSource*, *lngCursorType*, and *lngLockType* parameters can also be set using the Source, CursorType, and LockType properties, respectively. However, these properties are read-only after the Recordset is open. Any attempt to change them and reopen the Recordset results in a runtime error.

If you use the name of a Command object for the *vntSource* argument, the ActiveConnection is read-only regardless of whether or not the Recordset is open. The ActiveConnection of the Recordset inherits the ActiveConnection property value of the Command object.

If you do not use *lngOptions* to specify how the data provider should evaluate the *vntSource* parameter, ADO will have to query the data source. This results in a decrease in performance.

To close the Recordset object, you use its Close method. If you want to free the memory resources being held by storing that Recordset object (open or closed), you must set the Recordset object variable equal to the keyword `Nothing`.

Requery (Recordset Object) *rsObj*.Requery Options

Re-executes the original query you ran to retrieve the records in the Recordset object. This refreshes the contents of the recordset.

Parameters

Options

The Options parameter is a bitmask that can be used to specify the Execute options desired.

adAsyncExecute (0x10)

Execution should occur asynchronously.

adAsyncFetch (0x20)

Specifies that if there are rows remaining to be retrieved after the first set of records are retrieved (the number of which is equal to the setting for CacheSize), those remaining rows should be retrieved asynchronously.

adAsyncFetchNonBlocking (0x40)

Specifies that the records should be retrieved asynchronously but that the thread used by the system to retrieve the records should not block other threads.

adAsyncExecuteNoRecords (0x80)

Specifies that no records should be returned (for example, if the Command object is being used to update a record). In this case, if there are any records returned they are ignored by the system.

adOptionUnspecified (-1)

To specify no execution options, you can optionally use the adOptionUnspecified constant.

Example

```
<%@ LANGUAGE="VBSCRIPT" %>
<% Response.Buffer = True %>
<HTML>
<HEAD>
<TITLE>ADO Examples</TITLE>
</HEAD>
<BODY>
<%
' Include ADOVBS.INC so we can use the ADO constants.
%>
<!-- #include virtual = "/bc_SSIncludes/adovbs.inc" -->
<%
' Instantiate an ADO Connection object.
```

```
Set objDBConn = Server.CreateObject("ADODB.Connection")

' Construct the connection string for the Connection object.
strConn = _
    "driver={MyDBType};;uid=sa;pwd=;database=SalesDB"

' Using the connection string, open the connection.
objDBConn.Open strConn

' Create a command text string.
strCommandText = _
    "SELECT * FROM Sales WHERE Price > 70000"

' Create a read-only, forward-only recordset using the
' Execute method of the connection object. Note that we
' have no AffectedRecords parameter.
Set rsSales = objDBConn.Execute strCommandText, , _
                adCmdText

' Assume several changes (by other users) are taking
' place to the underlying records for this Recordset
' object. Now you want to renew this set of records to
' reflect these changes. To do so, call the Requery
' method:
rsSales.Requery

' The rsSales recordset now contains all the changes
' made by other users.
    .
    .
    .
```

Notes

Calling the Requery method is functionally equivalent to closing and re-opening the Recordset object. If you attempt to call the Requery method while editing the current record or adding a new record, an error will result. You must first call the Update or CancelUpdate method.

While a given Recordset is open, several of its cursor properties (for example, CursorType and/or LockType) are read-only. For this reason, if you want to change any of these property values, you must explicitly close the Recordset object. Calling the Requery method only refreshes the Recordset object. It cannot be used to change any of these read-only properties while the Recordset is open.

Furthermore, it is important to note that any bookmarks stored in variables are no longer guaranteed to point to the right (or any) record after the call to Requery.

Resync (Recordset Object)

rsObj.Resync *AffectRecords, ResyncValues*

Refreshes the field values for all the records already in your recordset. It does not show you the records added since first opening the database.

Parameters

AffectRecords

Determines which records in the current Recordset object will be affected by the Resync method call. This parameter is an optional ADO constant that evaluates to one of the following:

adAffectCurrent

Refreshes only the field values in the current record. This is the default value.

adAffectGroup

Refreshes only the field values in the records that match the criteria set in the Recordset object's current Filter property.

adAffectAll

Refreshes the field values in all the records in the current Recordset object.

ResyncValues

Optional. Specifies whether the underlying values should be overwritten:

adResyncAllValues

Default. Resyncs all data. Any pending updates are overwritten.

adResyncUnderlyingValues

Does not overwrite any pending updates.

Example

```
<%@ LANGUAGE="VBSCRIPT" %>
<% Response.Buffer = True %>
<HTML>
<HEAD>
<TITLE>ADO Examples</TITLE>
</HEAD>
<BODY>
<%
' Include ADOVBS.INC so we can use the ADO constants.
%>
<!-- #include virtual = "/bc_SSIncludes/adovbs.inc" -->
<%
' Instantiate an ADO Connection object.
Set objDBConn = Server.CreateObject("ADODB.Connection")

' Construct the connection string for the Connection object.
strConn = _
    "driver={MyDBType};;uid=sa;pwd=;database=SalesDB"

' Using the connection string, open the connection.
objDBConn.Open strConn

' Create a command text string.
strCommandText = _
    "SELECT * FROM Sales WHERE Price > 70000"

' Create a read-only, forward-only recordset using the
```

```
' Execute method of the connection object. Note that we
' have no AffectedRecords parameter.
Set rsSales = objDBConn.Execute strCommandText, , _
          adCmdText

' Assume several changes (by other users) are taking
' place to the underlying records for this Recordset
' object. Now you want to renew this set of records to
' reflect these changes. BUT, you do not care about
' seeing new records - only changes to the records
' currently in the Recordset object. To do so, call the
' Resync method.
rsSales.Resync

' The rsSales recordset now contains all the changes
' made to the records in the current recordset. New
' records do not appear.
.
.
.
```

Notes

Unlike calling the Requery method, calling the Resync method does not result in the query being executed again. The Resync method only synchronizes those records indicated by the *AffectArguments* argument with the data for those records in the underlying database. It does not show new records.

If you attempt to Resync a record that has been deleted from the underlying database by another user, ADO raises a runtime error. If, however, you attempt to synchronize a group of records containing at least one record that still exists in the underlying database, no runtime error occurs. Instead, ADO writes warning information sent by the data provider to an Error object that's included in the active Connection object's Errors collection.

Supports (Recordset Object)

$$blnSupported = rsObj.\text{Supports}(lngCursorOptions)$$

Tests the support for one or more features. This method returns a Boolean value indicating whether the indicated features are or are not supported for the current Recordset object.

Parameters

blnSupported

A Boolean variable that will hold the result of the call to the Supports method.

rsObj

The name of the Recordset object whose functionality you are testing.

lngCursorOptions

One or more of the following constants. If you want to determine whether more than one of the following options is supported, add each object in the call to the Supports method (see the following example).

adAddNew
Determines whether the Recordset supports adding new records.

adApproxPosition
Determines whether the Recordset supports reading and setting the AbsolutePosition and AbsolutePage properties.

adBookmark
Determines whether the Recordset supports the bookmark property to uniquely identify records.

adDelete
Determines whether the Recordset supports deleting records.

adFind
Determines whether the Recordset supports the Find method.

adHoldRecords
Determines whether the Recordset supports retrieving more records without committing pending changes to the currently held records.

adIndex
Determines whether the Recordset supports the Index property.

adMovePrevious
Determines whether the Recordset supports moving the current record pointer backward in the recordset.

adNotify
Determines whether the underlying data source supports notifications that also indicate whether the Recordset events are supported.

adResync
Determines whether the Recordset supports updating the current cursor with the Resync method.

adSeek
Determines whether the Recordset supports the Seek method.

adUpdate
Determines whether the Recordset supports the Update method to save changes to the database.

adUpdateBatch
Determines whether the Recordset supports the UpdateBatch method for batch updating of multiple records.

Example

```
<%@ LANGUAGE="VBSCRIPT" %>
<% Response.Buffer = True %>
<HTML>
<HEAD>
<TITLE>ADO Examples</TITLE>
</HEAD>
<BODY>
<%
' Include ADOVBS.INC so we can use the ADO constants.
%>
```

```
<!-- #include virtual = "/bc_SSIncludes/adovbs.inc" -->
<%
' Instantiate an ADO Connection object.
Set objDBConn = Server.CreateObject("ADODB.Connection")

' Construct the connection string for the Connection object.
strConn = _
    "driver={MyDBType};;uid=sa;pwd=;database=SalesDB"

' Using the connection string, open the connection.
objDBConn.Open strConn

' Create a command text string.
strCommandText = _
    "SELECT * FROM Sales WHERE Price > 70000"

' Create a read-only, forward-only recordset using the
' Execute method of the connection object. Note that we
' have no AffectedRecords parameter.
Set rsSales = objDBConn.Execute strCommandText, , _
               adCmdText

' Assume several changes (by other users) are taking
' place to the underlying records for this Recordset
' object. Now you want to renew this set of records to
' reflect these changes. BUT, you do not care about
' seeing new records - only changes to the records
' currently in the recordset. To do so, call the Resync
' method. However, we only want to attempt the Resync
' if the current recordset supports it. So we must use
' the Supports method.
If rsSales.Supports(adResync) Then
    ' Resync method is supported, so call it.
    rsSales.Resync
End If

' Assuming the recordset supports the Resync method,
' the rsSales recordset now contains all the changes
' made to the records in the current recordset. New
' records do not appear.
.
.
.
```

Notes

Often you will need to dynamically determine the capabilities of cursors on the current data provider. The Supports method of the Recordset object allows you to do just that.

Note, however, that just because a given call to the Supports method returns **True** does not mean that the functionality tested is available all the time. It is still imperative to trap errors raised in response to lack of cursor functionality—even if you call the Supports method every time you attempt to use that functionality.

As previously stated, you can use multiple options when using the Supports method, as the following demonstrates:

```
blnSupportsMultiple = rsExample.Supports(adResync Or _
                             adUpdate)
```

A value of True in the preceding example indicates that the recordset supports both the Resync and Update methods.

Update (Command Object, Recordset Object)

rsObj.Update FieldName(s), FieldValue(s)

Saves changes to the underlying data provider.

Parameters

FieldName(s)

The name of a single field in the record to be updated or the name of an array containing the names of multiple fields in the record to be updated. If *FieldName(s)* is the name of a field name array, *FieldValue(s)* must be the name of a value array, and the number of elements for both arrays must be the same or an error occurs.

FieldValue(s)

The value of a single field in the record to be updated, or the name of an array containing the values of multiple fields in the record to be updated. If *FieldValue(s)* is the name of a value array, *FieldName(s)* must be the name of a field name array, and the number of elements for both arrays must be the same or an error occurs.

Example

The following code example demonstrates a call to the Update method to save changes to the current record to the database.

```
<%@ LANGUAGE="VBSCRIPT" %>
<% Response.Buffer = True %>
<HTML>
<HEAD>
<TITLE>ADO Examples</TITLE>
</HEAD>
<BODY>
<%
' Include ADOVBS.INC so we can use the ADO constants.
%>
<!-- #include virtual = "/bc_SSIncludes/adovbs.inc" -->
<%
' Dimension local array variables.
Dim avntFieldNames()
Dim avntFieldValues()

' Instantiate an ADO Connection object.
Set objDBConn = Server.CreateObject("ADODB.Connection")

' Construct the connection string for the Connection object.
```

```
strConn = _
    "driver={MyDBType};;uid=sa;pwd=;database=SalesDB"

' Using the connection string, open the connection.
objDBConn.Open strConn

' Create a command text string.
strCommandText = _
    "SELECT * FROM Sales WHERE Price > 70000"

' Create a read-only, forward-only recordset using the
' Execute method of the connection object. Note that we
' have no AffectedRecords parameter.
Set rsSales = objDBConn.Execute strCommandText, , _
                adCmdText

' Change the Buyer and Price field values for the first
' record and update the underlying data.
rsSales!Buyer = "Kelly"
rsSales!Price = 45000
rsSales!Update

' Now, change the Buyer and Price field values for the
' second record and update the underlying data - using
' one line of code. Note the next code updates the SAME
' records again - not the next record in the recordset.
ReDim Preserve avntFieldNames(2)
ReDim Preserve avntFieldValues(2)

avntFieldNames = Array("Buyer", "Price")
avntFieldValues = Array("Jeff", 23489)
rsSales!Update avntFieldNames, avntFieldValues
    .
    .
    .
```

Notes

You must use the Recordset object's Update method to write your changes to records in the current Recordset object to the database, with two important exceptions. The first occurs when you call the AddNew method of the Recordset object and include a field/value pair of values or arrays. The second exception is when you are attempting to update a group of records, in which case you must call the UpdateBatch method.

You can also update a record or group of records with one statement, by including arguments in your call to the Update method. To update a single field's value, you must supply a field name and a corresponding field value in your call to Update. To update all records matching the criteria in the current Filter property, you must include the names of an array of field names and an array of corresponding field values. If the number of field names in this first array does not match the number of field values in the second array, an error occurs.

If you move from one record to another while you are in the middle of adding a new record or editing the current record, ADO will automatically call the Update method for you before moving the current record pointer. Also, if you are adding or editing a record and you call the UpdateBatch method, ADO will automatically call the Update method for the current record before executing the UpdateBatch method call.

CHAPTER 13

Ad Rotator Component

The Internet, though begun in an attempt to efficiently share information, is quickly evolving into a powerful avenue for business. One result of this evolution is the rapidly growing tendency for web sites to incorporate advertising into their content pages.

Unfortunately, these ads must be changed often to maintain efficacy, since clients quickly bore of advertising. The manner by which a webmaster changed the advertisements on her site used to involve a time-consuming three-step process. This process involved modifying the content, uploading the file to the server, and changing the links, if necessary, every time an old ad was to be saved and a new one displayed. Though several CGI applications became available to make this process simpler, none of them were less clunky than the original method.

With the advent of the Ad Rotator component, the process by which ads are displayed has become much simpler. This component allows content providers to rapidly change ads without relying on webmasters to change links repeatedly or maintain obtuse naming conventions of ad files for storage until the next time the same ad is used.

The Ad Rotator component allows you to change the advertisements on your web site in an automated fashion using a schedule file that you create. This schedule file contains a list of advertisements, their details (URL, text, etc.), and a weight factor that instructs the web server how often to display that particular ad. Each time a page containing a call to the Ad Rotator component's GetAdvertisement method is called, the schedule file is referenced by the web server to determine which ad to display. The ad itself is made up of a text description (for clients who have graphics turned off), a URI of the graphic for the ad, if one is available, and the percentage of time that the ad should be displayed relative to the other ads listed in the schedule file.

The Ad Rotator component also allows you to easily maintain a record of the number of times users have selected a given advertisement.

Ad Rotator Summary

Properties
    Border
    Clickable
    TargetFrame

Collections
    None

Methods
    GetAdvertisement

Events
    None

Accessory Files/Required DLL Files

Adrot.dll

The dynamic link library for the Ad Rotator component. It must be registered on the web server before it can be instantiated in your web applications. To register the Ad Rotator component on your web server, perform the following steps:

1. Click on the Start button on the taskbar.

2. Select Run from the Start menu.

3. Type in the following line (assuming your WinNT or Windows directory is on your C drive):

   Windows NT: `C:\WinNT\System32\winnt32\inetserv\Regsvr32.exe Adrot.dll`
   Windows 95/98: `C:\Windows\System\Regsvr32.exe Adrot.dll`

Redirection File

The Ad Rotator redirection file is an optional accessory file that allows you to trap clicks on an ad included on a page. It is an Active Server Page that you create to act as a middle script between the script containing the ad and the ad's URL. Each time a user clicks on an ad, the ad's URL is sent to this redirection file. Within this redirection file, you could easily add the name of the ad and other details such as the user's IP address to the web server log or a database or record it some other way.

However, the true power of this redirection file lies in your ability to add a script to this file to save more useful information than simply the number of times the ad was selected. To name just a few obvious examples, you could determine the contents of previously created session variables to get more details on the user: what scripts does he look at, what IP address is he coming from, and what software is he using. Frequently overlooked, this redirection file gives you the opportunity to track the details of your users and, thus, customize your site to its users.

The following is an example of some code from a redirection file:

```
<%
' Dimension local variables
Dim strUserName
Dim strRemoteAddress
Dim strURL
Dim strBrowserType

strUserName = Session("UserName")
strRemoteAddress = Request.ServerVariables("REMOTE_ADDR")
strURL = Request.QueryString("url")
strBrowserType = Session("UserBrowser")

[YOU COULD WRITE THE INFORMATION TO A TEXT FILE OR DATABASE HERE]

Response.Redirect strURL

%>
```

Rotator Schedule File

The rotator schedule file is a custom text file that you create. You can call it anything you wish. In it, you specify the details for the advertisements to be displayed on your site. You can specify the sizes of the advertisements, the URLs of images to be used for your ads, and the percentage of time each ad should be selected and displayed when the Ad Rotator object's GetAdvertisement method is called.

There are two sections in the rotator schedule file. The two sections are separated by a single line containing only an asterisk (*). The first section contains the following information that applies to all the advertisements listed in the file:

- The redirection file to use when an ad is clicked. This file's code will be executed before the user's browser is sent to the ad's URL. As described earlier, the redirection file allows for details of the user to be recorded before sending his browser to the ad URL. One good reason to use a redirection file is so that you can include a default URL that will take the user to a default page if no ad URL is included in the rotator schedule file. For example, your site may have a single HTML file that contains a brief description of all its advertisers. You could use the URL of this page as a default URL in the redirection file.

- The size of the border line for each advertisement.

- The width of the advertisement in pixels.

- The height of the advertisement in pixels.

Each of these elements is optional. If you do not have any of them, the first line will contain an asterisk, there will be no redirection script called, there will be no border, and the advertisement graphics will be the size specified in their individual graphics files.

The second section contains information specific to each ad. This section contains the following information for each advertisement, with each item on its own line:

- The pathname and filename of the graphics image to use for the advertisement.

- The URL of the advertiser's home page. This is designed to allow the user to navigate to the advertiser's home page by clicking on the ad. If the URL is not present and the user clicks on the ad, an error results, unless you use a redirection file that contains a default URL.

- The text for the advertisement.

- The relative weight of the advertisement. For example, suppose a schedule file detailed four ads with weights of 3, 4, 1, and 2. Upon a call to the Ad Rotator's GetAdvertisement method, the web server would retrieve the first ad 30% of the time, the second ad 40% of the time, the third ad 10% of the time, and the last ad 20% of the time.

All of these elements are optional. If you omit one, however, you must insert a hyphen (-) on the line where you would put a value. See the following example:

```
[REDIRECT /Apps/MyRedirectScript.ASP]
[WIDTH 300]
[HEIGHT  50]
[BORDER 3]
*
http://www.ora.com/images/ora.gif
http://www.ora.com
Check out the excellent books at O'Reilly!
20
http://www.BikeCityAthens.com/Graphics/BikeOfTheWeek.gif
http://www.BikeCityAthens.com
-
60
http://www.WidgetWare.com/Images/TodaysWidget.gif
-
-
20
```

In this example, we can ascertain the following:

- The first section sets the redirection URL, the size to 50×300, and the border to three pixels.

- There are three advertisements detailed in the file. These will be displayed 20%, 60%, and 20% of the time, respectively.

- The second ad has no text associated with it. If the client has graphics turned off, she will see nothing.

- The third ad has no home URL. If the user clicks on this ad, an error will be raised if the redirection file has no default URL.

- Finally, like the second ad, the third ad has no text associated with it.

Instantiating the Ad Rotator

To create an object variable containing an instance of the Ad Rotator, use the Server.CreateObject method. The syntax for the CreateObject method is as follows:

```
Set objMyObject = Server.CreateObject(strProgId)
```

where:

- The *objMyObject* parameter represents the name of a variable that will contain a reference to the Ad Rotator component.

- The *strProgId* parameter is the programmatic identifier (ProgId) of the Ad Rotator:

```
MSWC.AdRotator
```

Example

```
<%
' The following code uses the Server object's
' CreateObject method to instantiate an Ad Rotator
' object on the server.
Dim objAdRotator

Set objAdRotator = Server.CreateObject("MSWC.AdRotator")

%>
```

For more details on the use of the CreateObject method, see its entry in Chapter 9, *Server Object*.

Comments/Troubleshooting

The Ad Rotator component is very straightforward and can be a real time saver. Aside from making sure your rotator schedule file is set up correctly, there's little to using the Ad Rotator.

If you don't want the user to be able to click on the ad (for instance, if it is an informational ad only, not meant to lead to an URL), set the Clickable property of the component to **False**, rather than handling it with the URL or in the redirection file. This property's value is **True** by default.

The only problems I've experienced with the use of this component stemmed from incorrect syntax in the schedule file or from the Ad Rotator DLL (*adrot.dll*) not having been registered on the web server. The component is, however, automatically registered when you install IIS, so you have to explicitly remove it for it not to work.

Finally, it can be beneficial to instantiate an AdRotator object at the session level. You also can create an ad object at the application level, but doing so gives you less flexibility on a person-by-person basis.

Figure 13-1 illustrates how the Ad Rotator works.

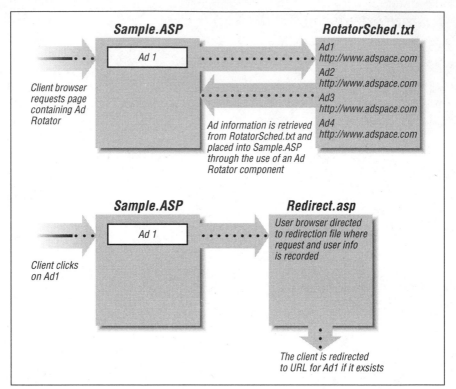

Figure 13-1: The Ad Rotator component, rotator schedule file, and redirection file

Properties Reference

Border   `objAdRot.Border = intSize`

Sets the thickness (in pixels) of the line around your advertisement graphic.

Parameters

`intSize`

The thickness of the ad graphic's border in absolute number of pixels

Example

```
<%
    ' The following code creates an Ad Rotator object and sets
    ' border thickness to two pixels. When displayed, the ad
    ' graphic will be surrounded by a two-pixel border, regardless
    ' of the setting for the border width in the schedule file.

    Dim objAdRot

    objAdRot = Server.CreateObject("MSWC.AdRotator")
```

```
objAdRot.Border = 2

%>
```

Notes

The default border thickness is whatever is set by the [BORDER] value in the Ad Rotator schedule file. If you set a value for the Border property, it will override that set in the schedule file.

In addition to the preceding example, see the full example at the end of this chapter.

Clickable   *objAdRot*.Clickable = *blnClickable*

Sets or returns whether the ad graphic represents a clickable image that will redirect the client to a URL for the ad's home page.

Parameters

blnClickable

A Boolean value that determines whether the ad graphic, when clicked, will transport the user to the homepage of the ad. The default value is **True**.

Example

```
<%

' The following code creates an Ad Rotator object and
' sets its Clickable property to False. This makes the
' ad a standalone image that is not clickable by the
' client.

Dim objAdRot

Set objAdRot = Server.CreateObject("MSWC.AdRotator")
objAdRot.Clickable = False

%>
```

Notes

If the Clickable property is set to **True**, you must have a URL set for this ad in the rotator schedule file or you must use a redirection file with a default URL. If the Clickable property is set to **False** for the component, the ad's URL in the rotator schedule file will be ignored.

In addition to this example, see the full example at the end of this chapter.

TargetFrame   *objAdRot*.TargetFrame = *strFrameName*

Specifies the name of the frame into which the link represented by a clickable ad graphic will be loaded. It is functionally equivalent to setting the Target property of an anchor tag in HTML.

Parameters

strFrameName

> A string value that represents the name of the frame into which you want the linked page loaded. You can this parameter to _BLANK, _CHILD, _NEW, _PARENT, _SELF, or _TOP. These settings have exactly the same effect as setting the TARGET property of an anchor tag.

Example

```
<%

' The following code demonstrates the creation of an
' Ad Rotator object and the subsequent setting of its
' TargetFrame property to _TOP. Assuming the ad graphic
' resides in a frame, this setting will cause the link
' to be loaded into the top frame.

Dim objAdRot

objAdRot = Server.CreateObject("MSWC.AdRotator")
objAdRot.TargetFrame = "_TOP"

%>
```

Notes

Just as when you set the TARGET property of an anchor tag, if you set the value of the TargetFrame property to a nonexistent frame, the ad link will be loaded into a new window, as if you'd set the TARGET property to _self.

In addition to this example, see the full example at the end of this chapter.

Methods Reference

GetAdvertisement ⠀⠀objAdRot.GetAdvertisement(*strAdScheduleFile*)

Retrieves the pertinent information for the next advertisement from the Ad Rotator schedule file.

From this file, GetAdvertisement retrieves general information about the ad (size, default border size, etc.). The call to the GetAdvertisement method also retrieves information about the specific ad that is selected (according to weights) from the schedule file.

For more information about the Ad Rotator schedule file and about the relative weights for the various ads in it, see the discussion on the Ad Rotator schedule file earlier in this chapter.

Once the GetAdvertisement method has retrieved this information, the Ad Rotator object creates the HTML for the ad that is sent to the client.

Parameters

strAdScheduleFile

A string value that represents the full virtual path or the path relative to the current virtual directory for the ad schedule file. For example, suppose the current virtual path is */search* and this can be resolved to the physical path *c:\inetpub\apps\search*. If you specify the *strAdScheduleFile* parameter as */search/AdSched.txt*, the Ad Rotator object will look for *c:\inetpub\apps\ search\AdSched.txt*.

Example

```
<%

' The following code instantiates the Ad Rotator
'object, then retrieves and displays an ad from
'the AdRotSched.txt file.

Dim objAdRot

Set objAdRot = Server.CreateObject("MSWC.AdRotator")

' Display the ad in the HTML sent to the client. Note that
' the following line of code inserts the value returned
' by the call to GetAdvertisement into the HTML stream.
%>
<%= objAdRot.GetAdvertisement("/sched/AdRotSched.txt")%>
```

Notes

Note that you must use a full virtual path or a filename by itself; in the latter case, the Ad Rotator object will attempt to find the file in the current virtual directory.

In addition to the previous example, see the following full example.

Ad Rotator Example

The following code demonstrates a complete Ad Rotator example to illustrate the overall mechanism of the Ad Rotator and its accessory files.

The first file, *SampleHome.ASP*, is the originally requested page containing the ad component. After the ad component retrieves it from the rotator schedule, this page also contains the ad.

```
<%
' +-----------------------------------+
' | SAMPLEHOME.ASP                    |
' +-----------------------------------+
%>
<HTML>
<HEAD><TITLE>Ad Rotator Sample</TITLE></HEAD>
<BODY BGCOLOR = #ffffcc>
<%
' Dimension local variables.
Dim adrotSample
```

```
Dim strAdRotSchedFile
Dim strAdString

Set adrotSample = Server.CreateObject("MSWC.AdRotator")
' Set the ad to have no border.
adrotSample.Border = 0

' Set the ad so that its corresponding URL is loaded
' into a second, blank browser window.
adrotSample.TargetFrame = "_blank"

' No need to set the Clickable property to True. It is
' the default. If we wanted to temporarily change this
' page's ad so that it was informational only, we
' could uncomment the next line.
'adrotSample.Clickable = False

' Retrieve the ad graphic html code (in this case it
' will be "/ads/graphics/FootTown.gif" with a URL of
' "http://www.foottownusa.com/info/introshoes.html."
' (See the sample rotator schedule file for more
' details on this ad.)
strAdRotSchedFile = "/ads/rotshed.txt"
strAdString = adrotSample.GetAdvertisement(strAdRotSchedFile)
%>
<HR>
<%= strAdString%>
<HR>
Welcome to the shoes outlet page. Please visit our sponsors above!
</BODY>
</HTML>
```

When called by the client browser, the previous code will retrieve its current ad information from the following rotator schedule file (*rotshed.txt*). Note that the BORDER entry will be overridden by the Border property setting in the previous code (adrotSample.Border = 0):

```
REDIRECT /Ads/AdRecord.asp
WIDTH 300
HEIGHT 40
BORDER 1
*
/ads/graphics/FootTown.gif
http://www.foottownusa.com/info/introshoes.html
Visit Shoe Town, your one stop shop for your footwear needs!
90
/ads/graphics/RunShoe.gif
http://www.runshoerun.com/running.html
Click here to see the best running shoe company around!
5
/ads/graphics/WalkingShoe.gif
http://www.walkingshoesUSA.com
The Walking Shoes company provides for your every walking need.
5
```

These ads have relative weights of 90% 5%, and 5%, respectively. When retrieving ad information, the script will have a 90% chance of retrieving the first entry and a 5% chance for each of the others. In our example, we'll assume the first sample is retrieved.

The following code (*SampleHome.html*) shows the actual HTML code that is sent to the client:

```
<HTML>
<HEAD><TITLE>Ad Rotator Sample</TITLE></HEAD>
<BODY BGCOLOR = #ffffcc>
<HR>
<A HREF = "/Ads/AdRecord.asp?url=http://www.foottownusa.com/info/
introshoes.html&image=/ads/graphics/FootTown.gif" TARGET = "_blank">
<IMG SRC = "/ads/graphics/FootTown.gif" ALT = "Visit Shoe Town, your one
stop shop for all your footwear needs!" WIDTH = 300 HEIGHT = 40 BORDER =
0>
</A>
<HR>
Welcome to the shoes outlet page. Please visit our sponsors above!
</BODY>
</HTML>
```

Note in the ad hyperlink that the following items were all retrieved from the rotator schedule file:

- The HREF of the redirection file
- The URL of the ad
- The URL of the ad graphic
- The alternate text of the hyperlink
- The width of the ad graphic
- The height of the ad graphic

However, the Border property was set in code:

```
adrotSample.Border = 0
```

The following redirection file records assorted information about the client who clicked on the ad and redirects the client's browser to the ad URL:

```
<%
' +----------------------------------+
' | AdRecord.asp                     |
' +----------------------------------+

' Dimension local variables.
Dim strAdURL
Dim strAdImg
Dim strUserName
Dim strUserIP

' Initialize variables.
strAdURL = Request.QueryString("url")
strAdImg = Request.QueryString("image")
```

```
strUserName = Request.ServerVariables("logon_user")
strUserIP = Request.ServerVariables("REMOTE_ADDR")

' Record the user information in the web server log file.
Response.AppendToLog "Ad Hit URL: " & strAdURL
Response.AppendToLog "Ad Hit Img: " & strAdImg
Response.AppendToLog "Ad Hit Usr: " & strUserName
Response.AppendToLog "Ad Hit IP: " & strUserIP

' Redirect to the ad URL if there is one.
' If there is not, redirect to a general advertisers
' description page.
If strAdURL <> "" Then
    Response.Redirect strAdURL
Else
    Response.Redirect "/ads/AdvertDesc.asp"
End If

%>
```

This code retrieves information about the ad on which the user clicked and then about the user herself (logon name and IP address). This information is then written to the web server log file for later analysis. Finally, the user is redirected to either the URL of the selected ad, if it exists, or to a default ad description page.

CHAPTER 14

Browser Capabilities Component

One of the challenges of constructing a useful web site today is determining what your users' browsers can and cannot interpret in the form of content. Generally, if you know the browser the current user is using, you know its base capabilities. For example, you know that if the user is using Netscape Navigator, then he must have an ActiveX plug-in to use ActiveX controls. However, what if the client is using a less well-known browser? Can you be sure the browser even supports cookies?

In an attempt to help with this problem, Microsoft introduced the Browser Capabilities component. You use the Browser Capabilities component to create a BrowserType object. When you create a BrowserType object, the web server retrieves the HTTP_USER_AGENT header sent by the client. Using this information, the BrowserType object compares the information from this header to entries in a special file (*BrowsCap.ini*). If a match for the current client's browser is found, the BrowserType object determines all the properties for the specific browser. Your scripts can then reference the properties of the BrowserType object to determine the capabilities of the user's browser. The following steps summarize this process:

1. The browser requests a page from the web server. That page contains an instantiated BrowserType object. The browser sends an HTTP_USER_AGENT request header. For example:

   ```
   Mozilla/4.0 (compatible; MSIE 5.0; Windows 98)
   ```

2. The BrowserType object looks this value up in *BrowsCap.ini*, retrieves a list of capabilities for that browser, and loads them as properties of the Browser-Type object itself.

3. The code can then use the properties of the BrowserType object to dynamically determine the user's browser's capabilities.

If the BrowserType object does not find a match for the information from the client's HTTP_USER_AGENT header, all the properties of the BrowserType object have the string value UNKNOWN.

Because browser capabilities change rapidly, Microsoft built into this control the ability to add properties and new browser types by simply altering the accompanying *.INI* file. You can even customize this file to reflect properties that may apply only to your web site.

With the introduction of ASP 3.0, the Browser Capabilities component has been improved to allow your scripts to determine the features of a client's browser with far more exactness. It's one thing to know that your client is using Netscape 4.0. It's another to know that your client's resolution is 1024×768 and that his color depth is 16M colors. The new Browser Capabilities component allows for this and many other details to be uploaded to the server through the use of cookies. However, the simple creation of this client information cookie is only possible for users of Microsoft IE 5.0 or later. This new feature is described at the end of the chapter.

Browser Capabilities Summary

Properties
    PropertyName (Customizable)

Collections
    None

Methods
    None

Events
    None

Accessory Files/Required DLL Files

BrowsCap.dll

The dynamic link library containing the Browser Capabilities component. It must be registered on the web server before it can be instantiated in your web applications.

BrowsCap.ini

The *BrowsCap.ini* file includes the HTTP_USER_AGENT header definitions and the properties for the browsers defined by those headers. For more information about the HTTP headers sent by the client, see the latest specification for the HTTP protocol. You can add to the *BrowsCap.ini* file as many property definitions as you wish. You also can define default values for each property definition.

Your *BrowsCap.ini* file must reside in the same physical directory as *BrowsCap.dll*. This is the \ *WinNT\System32\inetsrv* directory by default for Internet Information Server 5.0.

The format of the *BrowsCap.ini* file must match the following:

```
[; comments]
[UserAgentHTTPHeader]
[Parent = strBrowserDefinition]
[strProperty1 = vntValue1]
. . . [additional code]
[strPropertyN = vntValueN]

; Default Browser Settings
[strDefaultProperty1 = vntDefaultValue1]
. . . [additional code]
[strDefaultPropertyN = vntDefaultValueN]
```

The elements in the previous code break down as follows:

comments

You can add comments to the *BrowsCap.ini* file at any place in the file by starting the comment line with a semicolon. These comments are ignored by the BrowserType object.

UserAgentHTTPHeader

There is one *UserAgentHTTPHeader* sent by the client for each browser type defined in the file. For each browser type thus defined, there is a series of property name/value pairs for that browser. Each *UserAgentHTTPHeader* entry in the *BrowsCap.ini* file must be unique.

If you have several browser types that have the same property/value pairs but slightly different HTTP headers, you can simplify your *BrowsCap.ini* file by using wildcard characters. An asterisk (*) replaces zero or more characters, while a question mark (?) replaces a single character. For example, the *UserAgentHTTPHeader* entry:

```
[Mozilla/4.0 (compatible; MSIE 5.0;* Windows 98) ]
```

is functionally equivalent to all of the following:

```
[Mozilla/4.0 (compatible; MSIE 5.0; Windows 98) ]
[Mozilla/4.0 (compatible; MSIE 5.0; AK; Windows 98) ]
[Mozilla/4.0 (compatible; MSIE 5.0; AOL; Windows 98) ]
```

However, it is important to note that the BrowserType object will first try to match the HTTP header string exactly before it attempts to match the entries that use wildcards. This is important, because if you have both:

```
[Mozilla/4.0 (compatible; MSIE 5.0; AOL; Windows 98)]
```

and:

```
[Mozilla/4.0 (compatible; MSIE 5.0;* Windows 98)]
```

in the same *BrowsCap.ini* file and your user has the AOL version of Internet Explorer 5.0, the first *BrowsCap.ini* entry will always used. If you add items to the wildcard entry, then these entries will be ignored.

Also, if an HTTP header string matches more than one item in the *BrowsCap. ini* file, the properties for the first matching entry are used for the Browser-Type object.

strBrowserDefinition

An optional entry that specifies a parent browser for the current browser. This way, the current BrowserType object will inherit all the properties of the parent browser's entry in the *BrowsCap.ini* file. This makes the definitions of newer versions of browsers in the *BrowsCap.ini* file easier, since they usually support all the functionality of the parent browser. However, it is important to note that if the newer version does not support some property of the parent browser, you can explicitly set the property value for the newer browser, and it will overwrite the inherited version of that same property.

StrProperty(#)=vntValue(#)

A specific property and its value for a particular browser type. *strProperty* is a property name, such as "ActiveXControls," and the *vntValue* parameter represents the value for that particular property. The *vntValue* parameter value is a string by default. If the value represents an integer, it will be prefixed by a pound sign (#). If the value represents a Boolean, the value will be either **True** or **False**. The *strProperty#* name cannot contain spaces.

Each browser definition in the *BrowsCap.ini* file can contain as many or as few property/value pairs as you need. For example, if your site only needs to know if the client's machine supports cookies, the *BrowsCap.ini* file could contain only the single property definition

```
Cookies=True
```

You can also create your own special properties. For example, suppose your company has a specialized version of Internet Explorer:

```
[Mozilla/4.0 (compatible; MSIE 5.0; MyCompany; Windows 98)]
```

This specialized version of IE has been customized so that the user cannot right-click on images and save them. We'll call this feature NoPicSave. You could add the following to your *BrowsCap.ini* file:

```
[Mozilla/4.0 (compatible; MSIE 5.0; MyCompany; Windows 98)]
parent=IE 5.0
NoPicSave=TRUE
```

This code tells the BrowserType object that in addition to all the properties found in the entry for IE 5.0, this customized version of the browser also has the NoPicSave capability. Your code could then look for this entry and show certain (perhaps sensitive) images to only those users with this feature.

Table 14-1 lists some possible property names and their definitions.

Table 14-1: Some Common Custom Properties

Property	Description
Beta	Whether the browser is a beta version
Browser	The name of the browser
Cookies	Whether the browser supports the use of cookies
Frames	Whether the browser supports the use of frames
JavaApplets	Whether the browser supports the use of Java applets
JavaScript	Whether the browser supports the use of JavaScript

Table 14-1: Some Common Custom Properties (continued)

Property	Description
Platform	The platform on which the client is running the browser
Tables	Whether the browser supports the use of HTML tables
VbScript	Whether the browser supports the use of VBScript
Version	The browser's version number

strDefaultProperty# / *vntDefaultValue#*

The [Default Browser Capability Settings] section of the *BrowsCap.ini* file contains property/value pairs for all those properties for which you want to assume a default value. The *vntDefaultValue* parameter value is either a Boolean (indicating whether a specific property is supported) or an integer. If it is an integer, the value is prefixed with a pound sign. The *strDefaultProperty* name cannot contain spaces.

The following is a (greatly abbreviated) *BrowsCap.ini* file:

```
[Microsoft Pocket Internet Explorer/0.6]
browser=PIE
Version=1.0
majorver=1
minorver-0
frames-FALSE
tables=TRUE
cookies=FALSE
backgroundsounds=TRUE
vbscript=FALSE
javascript=FALSE
javaapplets=FALSE
ActiveXControls=FALSE
Win16=False
beta=False
AK=False
SK=False
AOL=False
platform=WinCE

[Netscape 4.00]
browser=Netscape
version=4.00
majorver=4
minorver=00
frames=TRUE
tables=TRUE
cookies=TRUE
backgroundsounds=FALSE
vbscript=FALSE
javascript=TRUE
javaapplets=TRUE
ActiveXControls=FALSE
beta=True
```

```
[Default Browser Capability Settings]
browser=Default
Version=0.0
majorver=#0
minorver=#0
frames=False
tables=True
cookies=False
backgroundsounds=False
vbscript=False
javascript=False
javaapplets=False
activexcontrols=False
AK=False
SK=False
AOL=False
beta=False
Win16=False
Crawler=False
CDF=False
AuthenticodeUpdate=
```

This example file demonstrates all of the features of a *BrowsCap.ini* file. The browser types described by this file are limited to two. A typical *BrowsCap.ini* file could be as large as 30K in size.

Instantiating the Browser Capabilities Component

To create an instance of the Browser Capabilities object, use the Server object's CreateObject method. The syntax for the CreateObject method is as follows:

```
Set objMyObject = Server.CreateObject(strProgId)
```

where:

- The *objMyObject* parameter represents the name of a Browser Capabilities object.

- The *strProgId* parameter represents the programmatic ID (ProgID) for the Browser Capabilities component:

```
MSWC.BrowserType
```

Example

```
<%

' The following code uses the Server object's
' CreateObject method to instantiate a Browser
' Capabilities object on the server.
Dim objBrowsType

Set objBrowsType = Server.CreateObject("MSWC.BrowserType")

%>
```

For more details on the use of the CreateObject method, see its entry in Chapter 9, *Server Object.*

Comments/Troubleshooting

The Browser Capabilities component is fairly easy to use. The most important issue with its use is to include the most up-to-date version of the *BrowsCap.ini* file. The latest copy of the *BrowsCap.ini* file is available from cyScape, a Microsoft Certified Solution Provider (*http://www.cyscape.com/browscap/*). On this web site, cyScape also touts its own product, BrowserHawk, which is a highly advanced replacement for the Browser Capabilities component.

Note, however, that you are not limited to the properties in the *BrowsCap.ini* file from cyScape. You can add you own custom properties and refer to them just as you would to one of the standard properties.

Finally, as noted previously, the new ability of the Browser Capabilities component to retrieve data from a cookie has been added to the Browser Capabilities function. Unfortunately the automatic generation of this information requires that the client browser supports *behaviors*. Currently, behaviors, a way to utilize new behavior in the context of a web page on the fly, are supported only by Microsoft Internet Explorer 5.0. Without the use of behaviors, you would have to query the user to obtain the information to make this cookie, which is unacceptable to most web users. As such, you will likely not use this new feature of the Browser Capabilities component in conjunction with a client not using MSIE 5.0. See the end of this chapter for more information about this new feature of the Browser Capabilities component.

Properties Reference

PropertyName (Customizable) `objBrowsType.strPropertyName`

Determines the value of a given property of a BrowserType object. Note that these properties represent values from the *BrowsCap.ini* file and are read-only. "Customizable" means, as mentioned earlier, that you can add your own property names to the *BrowsCap.ini* file.

Parameters

`strPropertyName`
> The name of a standard or custom property in the *BrowsCap.ini* file. This string value cannot contain spaces. If you attempt to retrieve the value of a property that does not exist in the *BrowsCap.ini* file, the resulting value is the string `Unknown`.

Example

```
<HTML>
<HEAD>
<TITLE>
Browser Capabilities
```

```
</TITLE>
</HEAD>
<BODY>
<%


' The following code example instantiates a BrowserType object and shows
' the user whether the browser supports various functions. Assume that
' the BrowsCap.ini file being used by the BrowserType object is the
' example file shown previously and that the user is using Netscape
' Navigator 4.0.

Dim objBrowsType

Set objBrowsType = Server.CreateObject("MSWC.BrowserType")

' The following properties will all evaluate to True
' and will result in the phrase
'        "Support for property: TRUE":
%>
Support for frames: <%=objBrowsType.frames%><BR>
Support for tables: <%=objBrowsType.tables%><BR>
Support for cookies: <%=objBrowsType.cookies%><BR>
<%
' However, the value of the following property will be
' the string "Unknown" resulting in the phrase
'              '"Support for VRML: Unknown"
' because the vrml property is not defined in the preceding
' BrowsCap.ini file.
%>
Support for VRML: <%=objBrowsType.vrml%><BR>

</BODY>
</HTML>
```

Retrieving Browser Information from Cookies

As discussed previously, the Browser Capabilities component can now retrieve client browser capability information from a cookie accompanying the HTTP request sent by the client. Although you can compile this cookie and send it from the client with the HTTP request any way you like, the most seamless and automatic way is by the use of behaviors.

Here's how it works. First we need to create the cookie. You can accomplish this with something resembling the following code snippet:

```
function window.onload ()
{
    // Note the bdyCCaps is the value for the ID parameter of the BODY tag.
    // The clientCaps behaviour is provided with IE5.
    bdyCCaps.style.behavior = "url(#default#clientCaps)";

    // Determine width and height and add it to the cookie string.
    strCookieString   =  "width= " + bdyCCaps.width;
    strCookieString  +=  "&height= " + bdyCCaps.height;
```

```
// Determine the color depth for the client machine and
// add it to the cookie string.
strCookieString += "&colorDepth= " + bdyCCaps.colorDepth;

// Determine whether the client has cookies enabled and
// add it to the cookie string.
strCookieString += "&cookies= " + bdyCCaps.cookieEnabled;

// Add the cookie string to the Browser Cap cookie to be sent
// to the server.
document.cookie = "BrowsCap= " + strCookieString;
}
```

For more information on the use of behaviors and their importance, see the Microsoft web site. For now, you only need to know that the following properties are available in the clientCaps behavior in IE5:

availHeight
> The height available to web pages in pixels. This allows you to compensate for the amount of screen real estate used by the client browser's navigation bar settings, etc.

availWidth
> The width available to web pages in pixels. This allows you to compensate for the amount of screen real estate used by the client browser's navigation bar settings, etc.

bufferDepth
> The number of bits per pixel used for color in the off-screen buffer (in memory).

colorDepth
> The number of bits per pixel used for color in the destination device or buffer.

connectionType
> The type of connection between the client and the web server.

cookieEnabled
> Whether or not the client has cookies enabled.

cpuClass
> String reflecting the class of the CPU (x86 or Alpha, for example).

height
> Total vertical resolution of the screen.

javaEnabled
> Whether or not the Microsoft Java Virtual Machine is enabled.

platform
> The operating system the client's machine is running (Win16, Win32, WinCE, etc.).

systemLanguage
> Default language setting for the client machine.

userLanguage
> Current user language.

width
> Total horizontal resolution of the screen.

The preceding code will enable you to retrieve the data from the client, but we need a way to obtain this information automatically and "behind the scenes." There are several ways to do this, but the way suggested in Microsoft's documentation is perhaps the most straightforward. Use the METADATA tag to include a file containing the preceding code in the HEAD tag of the page to which your user has navigated. This will force the client's browser to execute this other, "hidden," page before she sees the originally selected script. Here is the "hidden" page in its entirety:

```
<HTML>
<HEAD>
<TITLE>Browser Capabilities Example</TITLE>
<SCRIPT language="JavaScript">
function window.onload ()
{
    // Note the bdyCCaps is the value for the ID parameter of the BODY tag.
    // The clientCaps behaviour is provided with IE5.
    bdyCCaps.style.behavior = "url(#default#clientCaps)";

    // Determine width and height and add it to the cookie string.
    strCookieString   =  "width= " + bdyCCaps.width;
    strCookieString  +=  "&height= " + bdyCCaps.height;

    // Determine the color depth for the client machine and
    // add it to the cookie string.
    strCookieString  +=  "&colorDepth= " + bdyCCaps.colorDepth;

    // Determine whether the client has cookies enabled and
    // add it to the cookie string.
    strCookieString  +=  "&cookies= " + bdyCCaps.cookieEnabled;

    // Add the cookie string to the Browser Cap cookie to be sent
    // to the server.
    document.cookie = "BrowsCap= " + strCookieString;
}
</SCRIPT>
</HEAD>
<BODY ID="bdyCCaps">
</BODY>
</HTML>
```

As you can see, this page does not display anything to the client. However, when it is viewed by the client, it creates and sends a cookie to the server. To get the client browser to perform this function with the least amount of visibility to the client, you will want to force the client machine to send a cookie to the client. Here is a complete example (assume the previous script is called *GetCaps.htm*):

```
<!--METADATA TYPE="Cookie" NAME="BrowsCap" SRC="GetCaps.htm"-->
<HTML>
```

```
<BODY>
<%
' Reading the page above will cause the
' client's machine to send a cookie. The
' Browser Capabilities component can then
' read the setting on the client machine
' from the cookie sent to the server.

' Instantiate a Browser Capabilities object.
Set objBrowsCap = Server.CreateObject("MSWC.BrowserType")

' Display to the client the values sent
' to the server.
Response.write("Width: " + objBrowsCap.width + "<BR>")
Response.write("Height: " + objBrowsCap.height + "<BR>")
Response.write("Color Depth: " + objBrowsCap.colorDepth + "<BR>")
Response.write("Cookies Enabled: " + CStr(objBrowsCap.cookies) + "<BR>")
%>
</BODY>
</HTML>
```

As you can see, the sending of the cookie to the server is automatic. The client never sees that his browser has set up a cookie describing his settings and sent it to the server. From that point forward, you can save the client information or not, as you see fit. The data can then be used for on-the-fly customization of your site's content in response to your client's customization settings.

CHAPTER 15

Collaboration Data Objects
for Windows NT Server

The ability for the server to send messages to clients and vice versa is an increasingly important aspect of many web sites. Using messaging back and forth between web server and client, you can alert the webmaster of issues with the site or send webmasters suggestions and comments. More important than either of those, however, is the ability to send notices and reminders to your users, turning infrequent visitors into subscribers.

"Subscribers" are the most important facets of any web site. With a list of people (or even a count of those people) who have subscribed to your web site (to be notified of updates or changes, for example), you have a concrete, quantifiable estimate of your site's average users.

In the past, such messaging required that the client machine activate a mail program and send the webmaster email. The webmaster would receive this email and, in turn, add the sender to her site's mailing list. As technology for web sites evolved, webmasters were able to send and receive mail from within server-only applications (through web forms, for example), and separate email functionality was not required. The web applications used mail behind the scenes. Such web applications were usually CGI applications and were written in lower-level languages. These applications are simple and work well. However, for the work that goes into writing them, they sometimes lack flexibility. With the advent of Collaboration Data Objects for NTS (formerly known as Active Messaging), you now have a COM interface to a powerful set of objects that makes adding messaging functionality to your ASP application simple.

Collaboration Data Objects for Windows NT Server (CDONTS) is a collection of COM objects that work with Windows NT, IIS, and SMTP (or Microsoft Exchange) to enable your applications to easily send and receive electronic mail. It does not require Microsoft Exchange (or another mail server) but can use it if it exists on the same server on which the application is running. Without a mail server, CDONTS works with SMTP to route all messaging to a mail server on the network or Internet.

296

Like most messaging subsystems, CDONTS receives messages from an Inbox and writes messages to an Outbox. These mail bins exist in different places, depending on the server component with which CDONTS is working. If SMTP is being used, the Inbox and Outbox are actually mapped directly to file system files on the web server. In this instance, CDONTS sends all messages immediately through SMTP, and the Outbox is empty. Likewise, any incoming messages are removed from the Inbox and placed into the file system directly.

You may have heard of CDO before IIS. It is called CDO for Exchange, and its object library is almost exactly the same as that of CDO for NTS. The only difference in functionality is that CDONTS uses the Session object's LogonSMTP method to log on, whereas CDO for Exchange uses the Logon method. The only other difference is the presence of the NewMail object in the CDO for NTS library. This object has no counterpart in CDO for Exchange.

A full explanation of Collaboration Data Objects for NTS, like one for ActiveX Data Objects, would require an entire book to itself. In the interest of space in this book, I will provide only a brief overview of the majority of features of CDONTS, since most ASP applications will not use the bulk of the functionality supported by CDONTS. Instead, I will cover in depth all the properties and methods of the NewMail object. This addition to the CDO library makes it possible to send mail—including attachments—from any ASP application script to any email address using just a few lines of code.

Accessory Files/Required DLL Files

Cdonts.DLL

The dynamic link library and type library for the CDO for NTS COM objects. You must install this on the web server (using the latest executable setup file from Microsoft) before you can instantiate or use any of the CDO objects. It is installed by default when you install IIS 4.0. Microsoft Exchange does not have to be installed before installing CDO. However, SMTP (or Exchange) must be installed before you can successfully send and receive messages.

Instantiating Collaboration Data Objects

To create an instance of a Collaboration Data Object, use the Server.CreateObject method. Its syntax is as follows:

```
Set objMyObject = Server.CreateObject(strProgId)
```

where:

- *objMyObject* represents the name of the collaboration data object variable you are instantiating.

- *strProgId* represents the programmatic ID (ProgID) for the specific Collaboration Data Object you are instantiating. The possible values for this parameter can be found in Table 15-1.

Table 15-1: Values for Collaboration Data Objects

Collaboration Data Object	ProgID
AddressEntry	CDONTS.AddressEntry
Attachment	CDONTS.Attachment
Folder	CDONTS.Folder
Message	CDONTS.Message
NewMail	CDONTS.NewMail
Recipient	CDONTS.Recipients
Session	CDONTS.Session

Example

```
<%

' The following code uses the CreateObject method to
' instantiate a NewMail object on the server.
Dim objNewMail

Set objNewMail = Server.CreateObject("CDONTS.NewMail")

%>
```

For more details on the use of the CreateObject method, see its entry in Chapter 9, *Server Object.*

To use the CDO constants listed in this chapter, you must declare the CDO type library. The following code demonstrates this:

```
[Excerpt from GLOBAL.ASA]

<!-- METADATA TYPE="TypeLibrary"
FILE="CDONTS.DLL"
VERSION="1.2"
-->
```

Examples in this chapter assume you have declared the type library beforehand.

 In this chapter, any CDO constant is followed by the constant's value in parentheses.

Comments/Troubleshooting

The only aspect of the properties and methods of the CDO that I might suggest you pay particular attention to is the use of the various Delete methods. The Delete method for nearly every object that has one allows you to delete the current object. This is intuitive for objects. However, you might expect that the Delete method of a collection would allow you to remove a specific item from the collection, whereas in fact it removes all the members of the collection!

Sending email messages from within your ASP application is simple, especially using the NewMail object. However, one thing that I've taken for granted is the architecture that exists between your web server, your mail server, and the Internet. Unfortunately, this can be quite complex and the source of almost all the errors you will experience trying to message-enable your ASP applications.

If you have CDONTS set up properly on the server, the calls to any of its methods and properties will work flawlessly, in my experience. Place your web server on the other side of a firewall from your mail server or place a proxy server anywhere along the path and you will likely run into issues.

The most important thing to remember when constructing the architecture for messaging from ASP applications on your web server is to ensure that you have the SMTP ports on the firewall set to allow traffic from the web server to reach your mail server. Proxy settings must be addressed on a case-by-case basis. These issues aren't difficult to resolve, just time consuming, especially in larger companies where the web development group is totally different (physically and politically) from the architecture security group that handles the organization's firewalls and proxy servers.

The CDO Object Model

Figure 15-1 shows the 10 objects and collections that make up the CDO object hierarchy. This section lists and very briefly describes all of the properties, collections, and methods (CDO objects do not respond to any events) of each object in the model. As stated before, this is meant only as an overview.

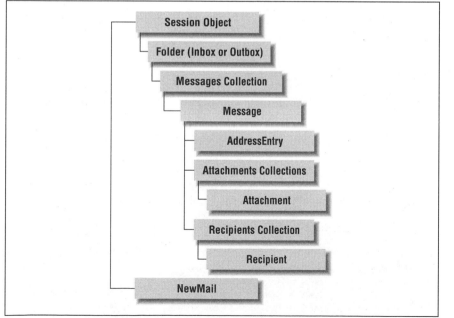

Figure 15-1: The CDO object model

For the properties and methods of the NewMail object in the object model, see the in-depth coverage that follows this overview.

Common Properties

All the objects in the CDONTS object model—except the NewMail object—share four common properties: Application, Class, Parent, and Session. These properties are all read-only. If you ascertain the value of the Application or Session properties from one CDO object, their values will be the same for any other object in the object model.

As you can see from the object model in Figure 15-1, the Session object is the highest object in the hierarchy. As such, it has no Parent or Session property values. These properties always have a value of Nothing for any Session object.

The NewMail object has none of these common properties. Any attempt to retrieve the value of any of the properties listed in Table 15-2 for a NewMail object results in a runtime error.

Table 15-2: Common Properties of CDO Objects

Property	Description
Application	Always contains the string value "Collaboration Data Objects for NTS Version 1.2." It represents the name of the application using the current session.
Class	An integer value representing the type of CDO object: cdoAddressEntry (8) = AddressEntry cdoAttachment (5) = Attachment cdoAttachments (18) =Attachments Collection cdoFolder (2) = Folder cdoMsg (3) = Message cdoMessages (16) = Messages Collection cdoRecipient (4) = Recipient cdoRecipients (17) = Recipients Collection cdoSession (0) = Session
Parent	The immediate parent object of the current object in the CDO object model. This is the parent according to the object model, not the logical parent. For example, the Parent property of an Attachment object is the Attachments collection, not a Message object, even though you add email attachments to an email message. The value for this property for the Session object is Nothing. This property holds an object pointer and is not simply a string containing the name of the parent object. The following is a list of the objects in the CDO object library and their immediate parents according to the hierarchy. Note that the parent of the Session object is Nothing: — AddressEntry: Message — Attachment: Attachments Collection — Attachments Collection: Message — Folder: Session — Message: Messages Collection — Messages Collection: Folder — Recipient: Recipients Collection — Recipients Collection: Message — Session: Nothing

Table 15-2: Common Properties of CDO Objects (continued)

Property	Description
Session	The Session property represents the session within which the current CDO object has been instantiated. If you attempt to retrieve the value of the Session property of a Session object, you will retrieve the Session object itself.

AddressEntry Object

Parent object: Message object.

An object reference is obtained through the Sender Property of a Message object.

Represents information about the sender of a specific Message object, including the sender's email address, name, and email address type. You can obtain a reference to the AddressEntry object only from the Message object's Sender property. The properties of the AddressEntry object are shown in Table 15-3; the properties are all read-only.

Table 15-3: AddressEntry Object Properties

Property	Description
Address	A string value representing the information required to send email to the person or process represented by the current AddressEntry object.
Name	A string value representing the alias or display name for the person represented by the current AddressEntry object.
Type	A string value that identifies the sender's messaging service. For the current version of CDO for NTS, the Type property always holds the string "SMTP."

Attachment Object

Parent object: Attachments collection.

A new object reference is returned from the Add method of the Attachments Collection.

A file or message that is attached to the current Message object. If the current Message object is still in the Inbox, the properties of the Attachment object are all read-only. If, however, the Message object is being prepared for delivery, these properties are all read/write. Remember that CDO for NTS does not control how (or if) the Attachment is displayed in the final Message object. This is controlled by the mail client being used. Table 15-4 and Table 15-5 list the properties and methods of the Attachment object, respectively.

Collaboration Data Objects

Table 15-4: Attachment Object Properties

Property	Description
ContentBase	The Content-Base header of a MIME message attachment. For example, if all the relative URLs in your MIME message are valid only for *http://www.mycorp.com*, then the ContentBase value should be *http://www.mycorp.com/.* Once the ContentBase is set, the relative URLs in the message have meaning. For example, suppose you have a MIME email message containing an image with the SRC property set to */images/myimg.jpg*. The ContentBase lets the mail client know that this means *http://www.mycorp. com/images/myimg.jpg*.
ContentID	The Content-ID header of a MIME message attachment. This is read-only for messages coming in. CDO does not generate Content-ID headers for outgoing messages and attachments. For more information on Content-ID headers, see RFC 2111.
ContentLocation	The Content-Location header of a MIME message attachment.
Name	The name of the Attachment in the current Message object. This is the default property for Attachment objects.
Source	A string value that represents the physical location on the sender's machine of the contents of the attachment. The attachment contents will be added to the Message object from the location listed here.
Type	The type of attachment. The possible values of the Type property are `cdoFileData (1)` (the attachment is the contents of a file) or `cdoEmbeddedMessage (4)` (the attachment is an embedded message).

Table 15-5: Attachment Object Methods

Method	Description
Delete	Removes the current Attachment object from the Attachments collection
ReadFromFile	Reads the contents of a file into an Attachment object
WriteToFile	Writes the contents of an Attachment object to the file system

Attachments Collection

Parent object: Message object.

An object reference to an Attachments collection is returned from a call to the Attachments property of a Message object.

The Attachments collection is a child of a Message object and contains zero or more Attachment objects. Use the Attachments collection to add new Attachment objects to a message or to access the attachments that are already part of the current message. Table 15-6 and Table 15-7 list the properties and methods of the Attachments collection, respectively.

Table 15-6: Attachments Collection Properties

Property	Description
Count	An integer value that represents the number of Attachment objects in the Attachments collection. This property is read-only.
Item	Returns a reference to a single Attachment object in the collection. This property is read-only.

Table 15-7: Attachments Collection Methods

Method	Description
Add	Adds an Attachment object to the Attachments collection. You can add Attachment objects to an Attachments collection only for a message you are sending.
Delete	Removes *all* the Attachment objects from the current Attachments collection. Be cautious when using the Delete method of the Attachments collection, since it deletes every Attachment object in the collection. To remove a single Attachment object from a collection, use the Delete method of the Attachment object.

Folder Object

Parent object: Session object.

An object reference to a Folder object can be returned from a call to the GetDefaultFolder method or from the InBox or OutBox properties of a Session object.

The Folder object represents the Inbox or Outbox for the current session. Use the Folder object to access, add, or delete Message objects in the default Inbox or Outbox for the current messaging system and session. Table 15-8 and Table 15-9 list the properties and the single collection, respectively, of the Folder object.

Table 15-8: Folder Object Properties

Property	Description
Messages	Returns a pointer to the current Folder object's Messages collection
Name	A read-only string that represents the name of the folder

Table 15-9: Folder Object Collection

Collection	Description
Messages	Each Folder object has a child Messages collection. The Messages collection contains zero or more Message objects

Message Object

Parent object: Messages collection.

An object reference to a Message object is returned from a call to the Add method of a Messages collection.

Each Message object in the Messages collection contains a single email message or document. Each Message object is the child of a Messages collection. A Message object can contain embedded Attachment objects. Tables 15-10 through 15-12 list the properties, collections, and methods, respectively, of the Message object.

Table 15-10: Message Object Properties

Property	Description
Attachments	Points to either a single Attachment object or to the Message object's Attachments collection.
ContentBase	The Content-Base header of a MIME message content body.
ContentID	The Content-ID header of a MIME message content body.
ContentLocation	The Content-Location header of a MIME message content body.
HTMLText	A string value that represents the HTML version of the content body of the Message object.
Importance	An integer value that represents the priority of a Message object. This priority is used by the messaging system to schedule sending messages.
MessageFormat	An integer value that indicates whether the message is MIME encoded or simple text.
Recipients	An object pointer either to a single Recipient object for the current Message object or to the Recipients collection of the Message object.
Sender	The email address of the sender of the current Message object. This is an AddressEntry object.
Size	An integer value that represents the size in bytes of the Message object.
Subject	A string value representing the subject line that will be sent with the current Message object.
Text	A string value that contains the plain text of the message content body.
TimeReceived	A date/time value that represents the time and date when the current Message object was received into the Inbox.
TimeSent	A date/time value that represents the time and date when the current Message object was sent from the Outbox.

Table 15-11: Message Object Collections

Collection	Description
Attachments	Contains all the Attachment objects for the current message
Recipients	Contains all the Recipient objects for the current message

Table 15-12: Message Object Methods

Method	Description
Delete	Removes the current Message object from the Messages collection
Send	Sends the current Message object to all recipients represented in the current Message object's Recipients collection

Messages Collection

Parent object: Folder object.

An object reference to a Messages collection is returned from the Messages property of a Folder object.

The Messages collection contains all the Message objects in the current Folder object. Through the Messages collection, you can add Message objects to the current folder (Inbox only). Tables 15-13 and 15-14 list the properties and methods, respectively, of the Messages collection.

Table 15-13: Messages Collection Properties

Property	Description
Count	An integer value that represents the number of Message objects currently contained in the Messages collection
Item	An object pointer that allows you to retrieve a specific Message object from the Messages collection

Table 15-14: Messages Collection Methods

Method	Description
Add	Adds a Message object to the Messages collection
Delete	Removes all the Message objects currently in the Messages collection
GetFirst	Retrieves the first Message object in the Messages collection
GetLast	Retrieves the last Message object in the Messages collection
GetNext	Retrieves the next Message object in the Messages collection in relation to a specific Message object
GetPrevious	Retrieves the previous Message object in the Messages collection in relation to a specific Message object

NewMail Object

Parent object: None.

The NewMail object is an addition to the original CDO library specifically for adding messaging functionality to an application. It makes sending a mail message as simple as writing a few lines of code. The NewMail object was built solely to quickly generate messages from within an application. There is no user interaction allowed for the NewMail object, and there is no support for an interface for logging into a mail server.

None of the properties common to the other CDO library items are supported by the NewMail object. The properties of the NewMail object are write-only. If you add Recipient objects or Attachment objects to a NewMail object, those items cannot be removed.

You cannot access the properties of any of the other CDO objects from within a NewMail object. The NewMail object is not part of the CDO hierarchy but is instantiated by itself.

You cannot remove the NewMail object from memory until you explicitly set the NewMail object variable to Nothing.

All of the properties and methods of the NewMail object listed in Tables 15-15 and 15-16 are detailed in the "NewMail Object Properties Reference" and "Methods Reference" sections of this chapter.

Table 15-15: NewMail Object Properties

Property	Description
Bcc	A string value that represents the recipients that will receive a blind copy of the current message.
Body	A string value that represents the NewMail's content body text.
BodyFormat	An integer value that represents the text format for the message content body text.
Cc	A string value that represents the recipients who will receive a copy of the current message.
ContentBase	A string value that represents the base root URL for all URLs relating to the NewMail object's content.
ContentLocation	An absolute or relative path for all URLs relating to the NewMail object's content.
From	A string value containing the email address of the NewMail message sender.
Importance	An integer value that represents the priority of the NewMail message. It is used by the messaging subsystem in scheduling the delivery of the current message.
MailFormat	An integer value that represents the encoding method for the NewMail object message's content.
Subject	A string value containing the subject string for the current message.
To	A string value that represents the email address of the recipients of the NewMail object's message.
Value	A string property that allows you to add headers, such as File, Keywords, or Reference, to the current message. The messaging subsystem must recognize these headers or they will be ignored.
Version	A string value that represents the version of the CDO library.

Table 15-16: NewMail Object Methods

Method	Description
AttachFile	Attaches a file to the current message
AttachURL	Attaches a file to the current message and associates a URL with that attachment

Table 15-16: NewMail Object Methods (continued)

Method	Description
Send	Sends the current message to all the recipients listed in the To, Cc, and Bcc properties
SetLocaleIDs	Identifies the messaging user's locale

Recipient Object

Parent object: Recipients collection

Allows you to set and retrieve the properties for a specific recipient of your message. The properties and the single method of the Recipient object are shown in Tables 15-17 and 15-18, respectively.

Table 15-17: Recipient Object Properties

Property	Description
Address	A string value that represents the email address of the current message recipient
Name	A string value that represents the common name or alias for a specific recipient of the current message
Type	An integer value that represents the type of a specific recipient (To, Cc, or Bcc): cdoTo (1) = To cdoCc (2) = Cc cdoBcc (3) = Bcc

Table 15-18: Recipient Object Method

Method	Description
Delete	Deletes the current Recipient object from the Recipients collection.

Recipients Collection

Parent object: Message object

The Recipients collection contains all the Recipient objects, representing the receivers of the current message. Its properties and methods are listed in Tables 15-19 and 15-20, respectively.

Table 15-19: Recipients Collection Properties

Property	Description
Count	An integer value that indicates the number of Recipient objects currently contained in the collection
Item	An object property that returns a specific Recipient object in the collection

Collaboration Data Objects

Table 15-20: Recipients Collection Methods

Method	Description
Add	Adds a Recipient object to the collection
Delete	Removes all the current Recipient objects from the collection

Session Object

Parent object: None

The Session object is the top-level object in the CDONTS hierarchical object model. Unless you use the NewMail object, you must have an active Session object to send messages using the CDONTS library. The Session object's properties and methods are shown in Tables 15-21 and 15-22, respectively.

Table 15-21: Session Object Properties

Property	Description
InBox	A Folder object that represents the current Inbox of the current session
MessageFormat	An integer value that represents the default message encoding for any Message object instantiated within the current session
Name	A string value that represents the display name used to log into the mail system for this session
OutBox	A Folder object that represents the current Outbox of the current session
Version	A string value that represents the version of the CDO library

Table 15-22: Session Object Methods

Method	Description
GetDefaultFolder	Retrieves the default Folder object for the current session
Logoff	Closes the current session with the mail system and logs off from the system
LogonSMTP	Initializes the current session
SetLocaleIDs	Sets the default locale ID for messages sent or received during this session

NewMail Object Properties Reference

Bcc   *objNewMail*.Bcc = *strBCCRecipListString*

A string value containing a list of recipients who will receive a blind copy of the current message.

Parameters

strBCCRecipListString

A string containing one or more recipient email addresses separated by semi-colons (;)

Example

The following example demonstrates how to add a recipient to the Bcc list for the current message.

```
<%

' Dimension local variables.
Dim objNewMail
Dim strBCCRecipList

' Instantiate a NewMail object.
Set objNewMail = Server.CreateObject("CDONTS.NewMail")

' Set the Bcc property of the NewMail object to the following
' email addresses: (1) tom@execucom.com, (2) billw@firebird.com,
' and (3) helen@zoologyzine.com.
strBCCRecipList = _
    "tom@execucom.com;billw@firebird.com;helen@zoologyzine.com"

objNewMail.Bcc = strBCCRecipList

' Set the body string for the message.
objNewMail.Body = _
    "Wow, this message takes just a few lines of code."

' Send the message. For details about the Send method,
' see that section in this chapter.
objNewMail.Send , , "This is the subject",,cdoHigh

%>
```

Notes

As demonstrated in the example, the string you use to set the Bcc property of the NewMail object can contain a single email address or multiple email addresses separated by semicolons.

Body
objNewMail.Body = *strBody*

A string value that represents the body content text of the current mail message.

Parameters

strBody

A string value that contains the text you want sent as the body of your message

Example

The following example demonstrates how to set the Body property for the current message.

```
<%

' Dimension local variables.
Dim objNewMail

' Instantiate a NewMail object.
Set objNewMail = Server.CreateObject("CDONTS.NewMail")

' Set the body string for the message.
objNewMail.Body = _
   "Wow, this message takes just a few lines of code."

' Send the message. For details about the Send method,
' see that section in this chapter.
objNewMail.Send "me@here.com","you@there.com", _
   "This is the subject",,cdoHigh

%>
```

Notes

The string you use to set the value of the Body property can contain either text or HTML. If you wish to use HTML in the Body property, you must set the Body-Format property to reflect this content type. The possible values for BodyFormat are as follows:

Value	Description
0	The value in the Body property includes some HTML.
1	The value in the Body property includes only text.

BodyFormat   `objNewMail.BodyFormat = intFormatType`

An integer value that you can use to set whether the content of the current message is plain text or HTML.

Parameters

intFormatType

An integer that can be set to either of the following constants:

CdoBodyFormatHTML(0)
   The Body property represents HTML.

CdoBodyFormatText (1)
   The Body property represents plain text.

Example

The following example demonstrates how to set the BodyFormat property for the current message:

```
<%

' Dimension local variables.
Dim objNewMail
Dim strBodyContent

' Instantiate a NewMail object.
Set objNewMail = Server.CreateObject("CDONTS.NewMail")

' Set the body string for the message.
strBodyContent = _
   "<HTML><HEAD><TITLE>My HTML Content</TITLE></HEAD><BODY>"
strBodyContent = strBodyContent & _
   "Wow, this message takes just a few lines of code.</BODY>"

' Set the BodyFormat so that the NewMail object
' treats the body contents as HTML.
objNewMail.BodyFormat = cdoBodyFormatHTML
ojbNewMail.MailFormat = cdoMailFormatMIME

' Set the body content string for the NewMail object.
objNewMail.Body = strBodyContent

' Send the message. For details about the Send method,
' see that section in this chapter.
objNewMail.Send "me@here.com","you@there.com", _
   "This is the subject",,cdoHigh

%>
```

Notes

If you do not set the BodyFormat property, the default is cdoBodyFormatText.

Cc   objNewMail.Cc = strBCCRecipListString

A string value that contains a list of recipients who will receive a copy of the current message.

Parameters

strCCRecipListString

A string containing one or more recipient email addresses separated by semi-colons (;)

Example

The following example demonstrates how to add a recipient to the Cc list for the current message:

```
<%

' Dimension local variables.
Dim objNewMail
Dim strCCRecipList
```

```
' Instantiate a NewMail object.
Set objNewMail = Server.CreateObject("CDONTS.NewMail")

' Set the Bcc property of the NewMail object to the following
' email addresses: (1) billw@firebird.com and
' (2) helen@zoologyzine.com.
strCCRecipList = _
    "billw@firebird.com;helen@zoologyzine.com"

objNewMail.Cc = strCCRecipList

' Set the body string for the message.
objNewMail.Body = _
    "Wow, this message takes just a few lines of code."

' Send the message. For details about the Send method,
' see that section in this chapter.
objNewMail.Send , , "This is the subject",,cdoHigh

%>
```

Notes

As demonstrated in the example, the string you use to set the Cc property can contain a single email address or multiple email addresses separated by semicolons.

ContentBase   *objNewMail*.ContentBase = *strContentBase*

A string representing the base for all URLs referenced within the body of the message content. This property is used only for MIME HTML (for more information on MHTML, see RFC 2110). The ContentBase property represents the URL on which all relative URLs in the HTML section of the body are based.

Parameters

strContentBase

> A string containing a base URL for all URLs in the content HTML for the current message

Example

The following example demonstrates the use of the ContentBase property in conjunction with the ContentLocation property (see the entry for the ContentBase property):

```
<%

' Dimension local variables.
Dim objNewMail
Dim strBodyContent

' Instantiate a NewMail object.
Set objNewMail = Server.CreateObject("CDONTS.NewMail")
```

```
' Set the body string for the message.
strBodyContent = "<HTML><HEAD><TITLE>"
strBodyContent = strBodyContent & "My HTML Content"
strBodyContent = strbodyContent & "</TITLE></HEAD><BODY>"
strBodyContent = strBodyContent & "Here is an excellent image:"
strBodyContent = strBodyContent & "<BR>"
strBodyContent = strBodyContent & "<IMG SRC = "TodaysPic.jpg">"
strBodyContent = strBodyContent & _
    "<BR>I hope you like today's picture.</BODY>"

' Set the ContentBase and ContentLocation so the messaging
' system knows how to resolve the simple URL in the preceding
' image tag.
objNewMail.ContentBase = "http://www.MyPrimarySvr.com/"
objNewMail.ContentLocation = "graphics/dailypics/"

' Now the preceding img tag can be resolved to:
' www.MyPrimarySvr.com/graphics/dailypics/TodaysPic.jpg
' when it is displayed on the recipient's mail client.

' Set the BodyFormat so that the NewMail object
' treats the body contents as HTML.
objNewMail.BodyFormat = cdoBodyFormatHTML

' Set the body content string for the NewMail object.
objNewMail.Body = strBodyContent

' Send the message. For details about the Send method,
' see that section in this chapter.
objNewMail.Send "me@here.com","you@there.com", _
        "This is the subject",,cdoHigh

%>
```

Notes

The ContentBase and ContentLocation properties are useful only for message body content containing HTML.

The ContentBase property is to the URLs in the body HMTL content what the ContentBase argument of the AttachURL method is to URLs in attached HTML files.

ContentLocation *objNewMail*.ContentLocation = *strContentLocation*

A string property representing the absolute or relative path for all URLs referenced within the body of the message content.

Parameters

strContentLocation
> A string containing a relative or absolute path for all URLs in the content HTML for the current message

Example

See the example for the ContentBase property in the preceding section.

Notes

The ContentBase and ContentLocation properties are useful only for message body content containing HTML.

The ContentLocation property of the NewMail object is to the URLs in the body HMTL content what the ContentLocation argument of the AttachURL method is to URLs in attached HTML files.

From   objNewMail.From = strSenderAddr

A string value that represents the full messaging address of the sender of the current message.

Parameters

strSenderAddr

> A string value containing the messaging address of the person or process that is sending the current NewMail object. This address is not resolved (checked) before it is placed in the mail header sent with the NewMail object.

Example

This example demonstrates the use of the From property. It also shows that if you set the From property and also include a From string in the Send method call, the setting you used for the From property is ignored and only the string sent to the Send method is actually used.

```
<%

' Dimension local variables.
Dim objNewMail

' Instantiate a NewMail object.
Set objNewMail = Server.CreateObject("CDONTS.NewMail")

' Set the body string for the message.
objNewMail.Body = _
    "Wow, this message takes just a few lines of code."

' Set the From property to the sender's email address.
objNewMail.From = "sender@usacom.com"

' Send the message. For details about the Send method,
' see that section in this chapter.
' NOTE: Because we are including a value for the From
' parameter to the Send method call, the value here
' is actually sent to the message's recipient.
objNewMail.Send "me@here.com","you@there.com", _
        "This is the subject",,cdoHigh

%>
```

Notes

If you set the value of the From property and then also include a From parameter in your call to the NewMail object's Send method, the argument sent as a parameter to the Send method is the value actually placed in the message's mail header.

You cannot include more than one address in setting the From property, nor can you include a semicolon in the single address.

Importance   *objNewMail*.Importance = *intPriority*

An integer value that allows you to set the mail message's priority, which is used by the mail messaging system to schedule delivery of mail.

Parameters

intPriority
> An integer that can contain any of the following CDO constants:
>
> CdoLow (0)
>> Low. Schedule delivery during off-hours or times of low system use.
>
> CdoNormal (1)
>> Normal. Schedule delivery during regular delivery schedules for normal messages.
>
> CdoHigh (2)
>> High. Attempt to deliver immediately.

Example

```
<%

' Dimension local variables.
Dim objNewMail

' Instantiate a NewMail object.
Set objNewMail = Server.CreateObject("CDONTS.NewMail")

' Set the body string for the message.
objNewMail.Body = _
    "Wow, this message takes just a few lines of code."

' Set the importance for the message to high.
objNewMail.Importance = cdoHigh

' Send the message. For details about the Send method,
' see that section in this chapter.
objNewMail.Send "me@here.com","you@there.com", _
    "This is the subject",,cdoHigh

%>
```

Collaboration
Data Objects

Notes

If you do not set the Importance property, normal priority is assumed. If you set the Importance property explicitly, then later use the Importance argument in your call to the **Send** method, the second value (the argument to **Send**) is used and the earlier setting is ignored.

The underlying mail messaging system must support this feature or it is ignored.

Finally, you have no way of ascertaining how the recipient's mail messaging system will handle your priority settings.

MailFormat   *objNewMail.MailFormat = intFormatSetting*

An integer value that allows you to set whether the current message body is MIME encoded or simple text.

Parameters

intFormatSetting

> An integer value that can contain either of the following constants:

> CdoMailFormatMIME (0)
>> The contents of the current message will be in the MIME format.

> CdoMailFormatText (1)
>> The contents of the current message will be plain text. This is the default.

Example

This example demonstrates the use of the MailFormat property of the NewMail object.

```
<%

' Dimension local variables.
Dim objNewMail
Dim strRecipList

' Instantiate a NewMail object.
Set objNewMail = Server.CreateObject("CDONTS.NewMail")

' Set the MailFormat property to plain text (although
' this isn't strictly necessary since it's the default).
objNewMail.MailFormat = cdoMailFormatText

' Set the body string for the message.
objNewMail.Body = _
   "Wow, this message takes just a few lines of code."

' Send the message. For details about the Send method,
' that section in this chapter.
objNewMail.Send "me@here.com","you@there.com", _
   "This is the subject",,cdoHigh

%>
```

The value of the MailFormat property becomes the default setting for the *EncodingMethod* parameter of the NewMail object's AttachURL and AttachFile methods.

Subject   `objNewMail.Subject = strSubjectString`

The string that will be sent as the subject line for the current mail message.

Parameters

strSubjectString
> A string that holds the subject line to be sent with the message. This can be set to an empty string, but doing so defeats the purpose of the subject line.

Example

```
<%

' Dimension local variables.
Dim objNewMail
Dim strRecipList

' Instantiate a NewMail object.
Set objNewMail = Server.CreateObject("CDONTS.NewMail")

' Set the Subject property.
objNewMail.Subject = "RE: An important note for you"

' Set the body string for the message.
objNewMail.Body = _
   "Wow, this message takes just a few lines of code."

' Send the message. For details about the Send method,
' see that section in this chapter. Note that the
' subject parameter is not sent.
objNewMail.Send "me@here.com","you@there.com", _
   "This is the subject",,cdoHigh

%>
```

Notes

You should always set the Subject property of a NewMail object (or include a subject parameter in the call to the Send method for the current message).

If you set the Subject property of the NewMail property and also supply a subject argument when calling the Send method, the argument value is used and the Subject property setting is ignored.

To

A string value that contains a list of recipients who will receive the current message.

Parameters

strRecipListString

A string containing one or more recipient email addresses separated by semi-colons (;)

Example

The following example demonstrates how to add a recipient to the To list for the current message:

```
<%

' Dimension local variables.
Dim objNewMail
Dim strRecipList

' Instantiate a NewMail object.
Set objNewMail = Server.CreateObject("CDONTS.NewMail")

' Set the Newail object's To property to the following
' email addresses: (1) tom@execucom.com,
' (2) billw@firebird.com, and (3) helen@zoologyzine.com.
strRecipList = _
    "tom@execucom.com;billw@firebird.com;helen@zoologyzine.com"

objNewMail.To = strRecipList

' Set the body string for the message.
objNewMail.Body = _
    "Wow, this message takes just a few lines of code."

' Send the message. For details about the Send method,
' see the section on this chapter.
objNewMail.Send , , "This is the subject",,cdoHigh

%>
```

Notes

As the example shows, the string assigned to the To property can contain a single email address or multiple email addresses separated by semicolons.

Value

A string value that represents an additional header to be added to the mail message. The Value property allows you to set the value of this header.

Parameters

strHeaderName

> A string containing the name of the header you wish to add to your mail message

strHeaderValue

> A string containing the value of the header represented by *strHeaderName*

Example

The following example demonstrates how to use the Value property to add a new header to your current message.

```
<%

' Dimension local variables.
Dim objNewMail
Dim strRecipList

' Instantiate a NewMail object.
Set objNewMail = Server.CreateObject("CDONTS.NewMail")

' Set the Value property to add a ReplyTo header to
' the current message before it is sent.
objNewMail.Value("ReplyTo") = "Keyton<me@here.com>"

' Set the body string for the message.
objNewMail.Body = _
    "Wow, this message takes just a few lines of code."

' Send the message. For details on the Send method,
' see that ssection in this chapter
objNewMail.Send "me@here.com","you@there.com", _
    "This is the subject",,cdoHigh

%>
```

Notes

The Value property of the NewMail object should be used sparingly and only when you know with certainty that the receiving mail messaging system will process the added header(s) correctly.

You can set the value of a header more than once. However, this does not overwrite the first value, but rather adds a second header with the second value.

The header name you include must match exactly what the receiving mail messaging system expects, or your header will be ignored or misinterpreted. For example, the ReplyTo header added in the example is not the same as the popular Reply-To header, and would thus be misinterpreted.

Version

objNewMail.Version

A read-only string value holding the current version of CDONTS being used.

Parameters

None

Example

```
<%

' Dimension local variables.
Dim objNewMail
Dim strCDOVersion

' Instantiate a NewMail object.
Set objNewMail = Server.CreateObject("CDONTS.NewMail")

' The Version property for this version of CDONTS will
' always return the string "1.2".
strCDOVersion = objNewMail.Version

%>
```

Notes

The Version property is read-only. This property has limited functionality in typical applications.

Methods Reference

AttachFile

objNewMail.AttachFile (strSource
[, strFileName] [, lngEncodingSetting])

Embeds an attachment from a file into a mail message.

Parameters

strSource
> A string containing the pathname and filename of the file to embed

strFileName
> A string containing the name that will be displayed in the mail message to represent the embedded attachment

lngEncodingSetting
> A Long that can contain either of the following CDO constants:

> CdoEncodingUUEncode (0)
>> The attachment you embed in your message will be encoded in the UUEncode format. This is the default value.

> cdoEncodingBase64 (1)
>> The attachment you embed in your message will be encoded in the base 64 format.

Example

```
<%

' Dimension local variables.
Dim objNewMail
Dim strRecipList

' Instantiate a NewMail object.
Set objNewMail = Server.CreateObject("CDONTS.NewMail")

' Set the body string for the message.
objNewMail.Body = _
    "Wow, this message takes just a few lines of code."

' Attach a file in the current message.
objNewMail.AttachFile "c:\Data\Proposal.doc", _
                    "Proposal.Doc", cdoEncodingBase64

' Send the message. For details about the Send method,
' see that section in this chapter.
objNewMail.Send "me@here.com","you@there.com", _
    "This is the subject",,cdoHigh

%>
```

Notes

If you set the MailFormat property of the NewMail object, you do not have to include a *lngEncodingSetting* parameter in your call to the AttachFile method.

AttachURL *objNewMail*.AttachURL(*strSource* [, *strContentLocation*] _ [, *strContentBase*] [, *lngEncodingSetting*])

Associates a URL with the attachment embedded in your message.

Parameters

strSource
> A string containing the pathname and filename for the file that you want to embed in your message

strContentLocation
> A string containing a relative or absolute path for all URLs in the content HTML for the current message

strContentBase
> A string containing a base URL for all URLs in the content HTML for the current message

lngEncodingSetting
> A Long parameter that can contain either of the following CDO constants:

> CdoEncodingUUEncode (0)
>> The attachment you embed in your message will be encoded in the UUEncode format. This is the default value.

```
cdoEncodingBase64 (1)
```
The attachment you embed in your message will be encoded in the base 64 format.

Example

```
<%

' Dimension local variables.
Dim objNewMail
Dim strRecipList

' Instantiate a NewMail object.
Set objNewMail = Server.CreateObject("CDONTS.NewMail")

 ' Set the body string for the message.
objNewMail.Body = _
    "Wow, this message takes just a few lines of code."

' Attach an attachment to your file and associate a URL
' with it.
objNewMail.AttachURL "Proposal.htm", "htmdocs/april/", _
        http://www.mysvr.com/graphics/, cdoEncodingBase64

' Send the message. For details about the Send method,
' see tha section in this chapter.
objNewMail.Send "me@here.com","you@there.com", _
    "This is the subject",,cdoHigh

%>
```

Notes

The AttachURL method allows you to add an attachment and an associated URL. This is particularly important when the attachment internally references various images or hyperlinks containing only relative links. For example, an attached HTML document might contain the following hyperlink:

```
<A HREF = "Help.htm">Help Document</A>
```

When this attached document is opened by the message recipient, he will see the following hyperlink, assuming the sender used the syntax in the preceding example:

```
<A HREF = "http://www.mysvr.com/graphics/htmdocs/april/Help.htm">
Help Document
</A>
```

Send (NewMail Object)
objNewMail.Send strFrom [, strTo]
[, strSubject] [,strBody] _ [,intImportance]

Sends the current message to its recipients.

Parameters

strFrom

A string value containing the full messaging address of the message's sender. You cannot have semicolons in this string, nor can you specify multiple senders.

strTo

A string value containing the message's primary recipients. You can have multiple recipient addresses in this string, but each must be separated from the last using a semicolon.

strSubject

A string value containing the subject line for the message.

strBody

A string value containing the body content for the message.

intImportance

An integer value corresponding to the priority of the message. The possible values for this parameter are as follows:

CdoLow (0)

The importance is low. Schedule delivery during off-hours or times of low system use.

CdoNormal (1)

The importance is normal. Schedule delivery during regular delivery schedules for normal messages.

CdoHigh (2)

The importance is high. Attempt to deliver immediately.

Example

```
<%

' Dimension local variables.
Dim objNewMail
Dim strRecipList

' Instantiate a NewMail object.
Set objNewMail = Server.CreateObject("CDONTS.NewMail")

 ' Set the body string for the message.
objNewMail.Body = _
   "Wow, this message takes just a few lines of code."


' Send the message.
objNewMail.Send "me@here.com","you@there.com", _
   "This is the subject",_
   "This is the body of the message",cdoHigh

%>
```

Notes

The Send method does not require any arguments. However, if you include arguments, the values you include in your call override the values set using the corresponding property. For example, if you set the Importance property for your NewMail object to cdoHigh and then include an *intImportance* parameter of cdoLow in your call to the Send method, the message will be sent with low priority.

SetLocaleIDs (NewMail Object)

objNewMail.SetLocaleIDs(*lngCodePageID*)

Sets the message sender's locale. This locale setting controls how certain internal features of the message, such as dates, will be evaluated.

Parameters

lngCodePageID
> A required Long value that represents the code page identifier for the message

Example

```
<%

' Dimension local variables.
Dim objNewMail
Dim strRecipList
Dim lngChineseCodePage 950

' Instantiate a NewMail object.
Set objNewMail = Server.CreateObject("CDONTS.NewMail")

  ' Set the body string for the message.
objNewMail.Body = _
   "Wow, this message takes just a few lines of code."

  ' Set the LocaleID to that of Chinese for this message.
lngChineseCodePage = 950
objNewMail.SetLocaleIDs lngChineseCodePage
. . . [additional code]
%>
```

Notes

The LocaleID setting for a sender's message indicates how the sender's machine formats dates and times. It also dictates the character selection for the page. You can obtain the current CodePage for a WinNT system by calling the *GetCPInfo* API function.

If you do not use this method to set a LocaleID, your messaging system assumes that your message should use the value stored for this property in your system registry.

The SetLocaleIDs method will check the validity of your argument before setting the Locale ID for the current message.

CHAPTER 16

Content Linking Component

Webmasters attempting to reach a wider audience often model their web sites to fit a paradigm familiar to the site's clients. One popular paradigm is that of a book or a newspaper. Users unfamiliar with the web and the power of hyperlinking are often looking for just such a paradigm to help ease them from paper-based information to web-based information. The familiar context of a current page, previous page, and next page is very comfortable and easy to understand.

The links from page to page are simple and easy to navigate. Each page has only a link to the previous page (if it exists) and a link to the next page (if it exists). This simple theme has not only helped to reach a wider audience but also to present large quantities of information, such as that in a newspaper archive, for example.

The only problem with such a system is that maintenance, while simple, can be extremely tedious. For example, imagine that you have four pages and decide to remove the third, thus altering the Next link on the second page and the Previous link on the fourth. This change is a simple one. Now, imagine you have a thousand pages, and you must remove 90 of them from various places in the series. Such a task would be tedious and therefore error prone, to say the least. Thankfully, there is a better way.

Starting as an unsupported add-on, Microsoft introduced the Content Linking component. Using the Content Linking component, you can perform maintenance much more easily. Here's how it works: You instantiate a NextLink object from the Content Linking component in your ASP application. This NextLink object maintains the current, previous, and next documents in a stream of documents by reading each page's entry (and its surrounding entries) from a special text file called the Content Linking file. This file must reside in a virtual directory on your web site and be accessible from the page containing the instantiated NextLink object. The Content Linking file contains a list of URLs of web pages with a text description for each page. This file is detailed in the section "Content Linking List."

Using a NextLink object and a Content Linking file, maintenance of a long list of interlinked web pages is as simple as altering the text file. To remove a page from the stream of web pages, you simply remove its entry from the Content Linking file. To change a page, you simply open the Content Linking file and change the page's URL.

Content Linking Summary

Properties
>   None

Collections
>   None

Methods
>   GetListCount
>   GetListIndex
>   GetNextDescription
>   GetNextURL
>   GetNthDescription
>   GetNthURL
>   GetPreviousDescription
>   GetPreviousURL

Events
>   None

Accessory Files/Required DLL Files

Nextlink.DLL

The dynamic link library containing the Content Linking component. It must be registered on the web server before it can be instantiated in your web applications.

Content Linking List

The list of documents you wish to link one after another in your web site. For each entry in this list, there is a URL, a text description for the page, and an optional comment about the page. This file can reside anywhere on your server as long as it is within the directory structure of a virtual root. You can assign this file any legal filename.

Each line of the Content Linking file must match the following format:

```
DocumentURL  [DocumentDesc  [Comment]]
```

where each segment per line is separated by a single Tab character, and each line is separated from the next using a single carriage return/linefeed combination. The

---

first segment, the *DocumentURL*, is the only required segment. This and the other two segments are described here:

DocumentURL

A mandatory part of each content line in the list, it is a string value representing the full virtual or relative path to the web document. You cannot use physical paths, and you cannot use absolute URLs (those beginning with http://, //, or \\). If you do so and attempt to call one of the following methods, an error will be raised. When filling your Content Linking list file, ensure that each line is distinct and that you avoid any pages with a next or previous page that references the same URL.

DocumentDesc

An optional string describing the web page pointed to by the *DocumentURL* string. You can use it to display a name or other descriptive information for its link. You cannot have a tab within the *DocumentDesc* segment.

Comments

An optional string commenting the web page pointed to by the *DocumentURL* string. The user will not see this string, and it should be thought of only as a way to help the webmaster maintain this file. No method of the Content Linking component processes this segment of a line.

The following is a sample Content Linking list containing eight items:

```
/newinfo/headlines.asp     Headlines        New headline stories.
/newinfo/Page2header.htm   Human Interest   Variety section.
/Ad1/AdPage1.asp Advertisement Page1 First Ad Page.
/newinfo/Sports.asp        Sports Sports section.
/newinfo/OpEd.asp          Opinions         Editor opinion.
/Ad1/AdPage2.asp Advertisement Page2 Second Ad Page.
/Class1/Class1.asp         Classifieds
/Class2/Class2.asp         Classifieds
```

Though it is hard to distinguish where each segment begins and ends, the component looks for the Tab character. Notice that you do not have to have a comment. Also, a page can exist in more than one place in the file, as long as a loop does not arise from its improper placement. Finally, the document description field can be the same for more than one page listed in the Content Linking file.

Instantiating a Content Linking Object

To create an object variable containing an instance of the Content Linking component, use the Server object's CreateObject method. The syntax for the CreateObject method is as follows:

```
Set objMyObject = Server.CreateObject(strProgId)
```

where:

*   The *objMyObject* parameter represents the name of the Content Linking object.

*   The *strProgId* parameter represents the programmatic ID (ProgID) of the Content Linking component, which is MSWC.NextLink.

Example

```
<%

' The following code uses the CreateObject method of the
' Server object to instantiate a Content Linking object
' on the server.
Dim objNextLink

Set objNextLink = Server.CreateObject("MSWC.NextLink")

%>
```

For more details on the use of the CreateObject method, see its documentation in Chapter 9, *Server Object*.

Comments/Troubleshooting

Using the Content Linking component is simple. Remember to separate each field in the Content Linking file with a tab character and each line with a single carriage return/linefeed combination.

One excellent use of the Content Linking component that I have seen is to dynamically generate a table of contents for your site. For example, the following code reads the Content Linking list called *MyContentList.TXT* and from it generates a table of contents. For more details about the methods used, see the following Methods reference.

```
<%
' Dimension local variables.
Dim objNextLink
Dim intTotalCount
Dim intCounter

' Instantiate a NextLink object for this script.
Set objNextLink = Server.CreateObject("MSWC.NextLink")

' Retrieve a total count of items in the Content Linking
' file.
intTotalCount = _
   objNextLink.GetListCount("/MyContentList.TXT")

' Iterate through all the items in the Content Linking
' list and generate an entry in an ordered list.
%>
<OL>
<UL>
<%
For intCounter = 1 to intTotalCount
   strOutput = objNextLink.GetNthURL("/MyContentList.TXT", _
                                 intCounter)

%>
   <LI>
   <!-- Create a hyperlink to the URL for the current item -->
```

```
        <!-- in the list. -->
        <A HREF= "<%=strOutput%>">

        <!-- Retrieve the text description for that URL. -->
        <%=objNextLink.GetNthDescription("/MyContentList.TXT", _
            intCounter)%>
%>
        </A></LI>
<%
Next
%>
</UL>
</OL>
<%

    ' Release the memory held for the NextLink object.
    Set objNextLink = Nothing
%>
```

Methods Reference

GetListCount   *objNextLink*.GetListCount(*strContentLinkList*)

Retrieves an integer representing the total number of entries in the Content Linking list.

Parameters

strContentLinkList
> A string value representing the virtual or relative pathname and filename of your Content Linking file. You cannot use physical paths or absolute URLs (those beginning with http://, //, or \\) for this parameter.

Example

```
<%

    ' Dimension local variables.
    Dim objNextLink
    Dim intListCount

    ' Create an instance of the NextLink object.
    Set objNextLink = Server.CreateObject("MSWC.NextLink")

    ' Retrieve a count of the pages listed in the Content
    ' Linking list file.
    intListCount = _
        objNextLink.GetListCount("/Content/MyContentLinkList.txt")

    ' Free the memory consumed by the NextLink object.
    Set objNextLink = Nothing

%>
```

See the full example at the end of this chapter.

GetListIndex   `objNextLink.GetListIndex(`*`strContentLinkList`*`)`

Returns an integer containing the position (starting with position 1) of the current item in the Content Linking list. You can use this method to determine if you are at the last item in the content linking list or if there are more items to which to navigate.

Parameters

strContentLinkList

A string value representing the virtual or relative pathname and filename of your Content Linking file. You cannot use physical paths or absolute URLs (those beginning with http://, //, or \\) for this parameter.

Example

```
<HTML>
<HEAD>
<TITLE>Document List</TITLE>
<BODY>
<%

' Dimension local variables.
Dim objNextLink
Dim intCurrentPos

' Create an instance of the NextLink object.
Set objNextLink = Server.CreateObject("MSWC.NextLink")

' Retrieve a position of the current page listed in
' the Content Linking list file.
intCurrentPos = _
    objNextLink.GetListIndex("/Content/MyContentLinkList.txt")

' In this instance, calling GetListIndex will return the
' number 1 if this page is in the content linking list.
' Otherwise, it will return 0.

' Free the memory consumed by the NextLink object.
Set objNextLink = Nothing

%>
. . . [additional code]
```

Notes

The return value is zero (0) if the current page is not in the Content Linking list file.

In addition to the previous example, see the full example at the end of this chapter.

GetNextDescription

objNextLink`.GetNextDescription(`*strContentLinkList* `)`

Returns a string containing the description of the next document listed in the Content Linking list.

Parameters

strContentLinkList

A string value representing the virtual or relative pathname and filename of your Content Linking file. You cannot use physical paths or absolute URLs (those beginning with http://, //, or \\) for this parameter.

Example

```
<HTML>
<HEAD>
<TITLE>Document List</TITLE>
<BODY>
<%

  ' Dimension local variables.
Dim objNextLink
Dim strNextDesc

' Create an instance of the NextLink object.
Set objNextLink = Server.CreateObject("MSWC.NextLink")

' Retrieve a description text for the next item in the
' Content Linking list file.
strNextDesc = _
   objNextLink.GetNextDescription("/MyContentLinkList.txt")

  ' Display the next description to the client.
%>

<%= strNextDesc%>

<%
' Free the memory consumed by the NextLink object.
Set objNextLink = Nothing

%>
    . . . [additional HTML and code]
```

Notes

If the current document is not listed in the Content Linking list file, the description text for the last item in the list file is returned by default. If the current item is the last item in the list, calling GetNextDescription returns an empty string ("").

In addition to the previous example, see the full example at the end of this chapter.

GetNextURL   *objNextLink*.GetNextURL(*strContentLinkList*)

Returns a string containing the URL entry of the next document listed in the Content Linking list.

Parameters

strContentLinkList

> A string value representing the virtual or relative pathname and filename of your Content Linking file. You cannot use physical paths or absolute URLs (those beginning with http://, //, or \\) for this parameter.

Example

```
<%

' Dimension local variables.
Dim objNextLink
Dim strNextDesc
Dim strNextURL

' Create an instance of the NextLink object.
Set objNextLink = Server.CreateObject("MSWC.NextLink")

' Retrieve a description text for the next item in the
' Content Linking list file.
strNextDesc = _
    objNextLink.GetNextDescription("/MyContentLinkList.txt")

' Retrieve a URL for the next item in the Content Linking
' list file.
strNextURL = _
    objNextLink.GetNextURL("/MyContentLinkList.txt")

' Use strNextURL to create a link to the item whose
' description you retrieved using GetNextDescription.
%>

<A HREF = "<%= strNextURL %>"><%= strNextDesc%></A>

<%
' Free the memory consumed by the NextLink object.
Set objNextLink = Nothing

%>
    . . . [additional HTML and code]
```

Notes

If the current document is not listed in the Content Linking list file, the URL text for the last item in the list file is returned by default.

Using GetNextURL with a Content Linking file, you do not have to change the code within your HTML to update a "NEXT PAGE" hyperlink, for example. You have only to change the Content Linking list, and the component will automatically update this link for you.

In addition to the previous example, see the full example at the end of this chapter.

GetNthDescription

    objNextLink.GetNthDescription(*strContentLinkList*, *intItemIndex*)

Returns a string containing the description for the item in the Nth position (on the Nth line) in the Content Linking list.

Parameters

strContentLinkList

    A string value representing the virtual or relative pathname and filename of your Content Linking file. You cannot use physical paths or absolute URLs (those beginning with http://, //, or \\) for this parameter.

intItemIndex

    An integer indicating the index of the item whose description you wish to retrieve from the Content Linking list.

Example

```
<%
' Dimension local variables.
Dim objNextLink
Dim intTotalCount
Dim intCounter

' Instantiate a NextLink object for this script.
Set objNextLink = Server.CreateObject("MSWC.NextLink")

' Retrieve a total count of items in the Content Linking file.
intTotalCount = _
    objNextLink.GetListCount("/MyContentList.TXT")

' Iterate through all the items in the Content Linking
' list and generate an entry in an ordered list.
%>
<OL>
<UL>
<%
For intCounter = 1 to intTotalCount
%>
    <LI>
    <!-- Create a hyperlink to the URL for the current item -->
    <!-- in the list. -->
    <a href "<%=
    objNextLink.GetNthURL("/MyContentList.TXT", _
                        intCounter)%>">

    <!-- Retrieve the text description for that URL. -->
    objNextLink.GetNthDescription("/MyContentList.TXT", _
                        intCounter)
```

```
    </LI>
<%
Next
%>
</UL>
</OL>
<%

' Release the memory held for the NextLink object.
Set objNextLink = Nothing
%>
```

Notes

If there is not an item in the position sent in the *intItemIndex* parameter, an error results. To prevent this, you can compare the value to be supplied as the *intItemIndex* argument with the value returned by a call to the GetListCount method.

In addition to the previous example, see the full example at the end of this chapter.

GetNthURL

>   *objNextLink*.GetNthURL(*strContentLinkList*, *intItemIndex*)

Returns a string containing the URL for the item in the Nth position (on the Nth line) in the Content Linking list.

Parameters

strContentLinkList
> A string value representing the virtual or relative pathname and filename of your Content Linking file. You cannot use physical paths or absolute URLs (those beginning with http://, //, or \\) for this parameter.

intItemIndex
> The index of the item in the Content Linking list whose URL you wish to retrieve. This is an integer parameter.

Example

```
<%
' Dimension local variables.
Dim objNextLink
Dim intTotalCount
Dim intCounter

' Instantiate a NextLink object for this script.
Set objNextLink = Server.CreateObject("MSWC.NextLink")

' Retrieve a total count of items in the Content
' Linking file.
intTotalCount = _
    objNextLink.GetListCount("/MyContentList.TXT")
```

```
' Iterate through all the items in the Content Linking
' list and generate an entry in an ordered list.
%>
<OL>
<UL>
<%
For intCounter = 1 to intTotalCount
%>
    <LI>
    <!-- Create a hyperlink to the URL for the current -->
    <!-- item in the list. -->
    <a href ="<%=
    objNextLink.GetNthURL("/MyContentList.TXT", _
                        intCounter)%>">

    <!-- Retrieve the text description for that URL. -->
    objNextLink.GetNthDescription("/MyContentList.TXT", _
        intCounter)
    </LI>
<%
Next
%>
</UL>
</OL>
<%

' Release the memory held for the NextLink object.
Set objNextLink = Nothing
%>
```

Notes

If there is not an item in the position indicated by the *intItemIndex* parameter, an error results. To prevent this, you can compare the value to be supplied as the *intItemIndex* argument with the value returned by a call to the GetListCount method.

In addition to the previous example, see the full example at the end of this chapter.

GetPreviousDescription

`objNextLink.GetPreviousDescription(strContentLinkList)`

Returns an ASCII string containing the description of the previous document listed in the Content Linking list.

Parameters

strContentLinkList
A string value representing the virtual or relative pathname and filename of your Content Linking file. You cannot use physical paths or absolute URLs (those beginning with http://, //, or \\) for this parameter.

Example

```
<HTML>
<HEAD>
<TITLE>Document List</TITLE>
<BODY>
<%

' Dimension local variables.
Dim objNextLink
Dim strPrevDesc

' Create an instance of the NextLink object.
Set objNextLink = Server.CreateObject("MSWC.NextLink")

' Retrieve a description text for the previous item in
' the Content Linking list file.
strPrevDesc = _
    objNextLink.GetPreviousDescription("/MyContentLinkList.txt")

' Display the previous description to the client.
%>

<%= strPrevDesc%>

<%
' Free the memory consumed by the NextLink object.
Set objNextLink = Nothing

%>
```
. . . [additional HTML and code]

Notes

If the current page cannot be found in the Content Linking list file, the description text for the first item in the list file is returned by default. If the current item is the first item in the list, calling GetPreviousDescription will return an empty string (""").

In addition to the previous example, see the full example at the end of this chapter.

GetPreviousURL   `objNextLink.GetPreviousURL(strContentLinkList)`

Returns a string containing the URL entry of the previous document listed in the Content Linking list.

Parameters

strContentLinkList

A string value representing the virtual or relative pathname and filename of your Content Linking file. You cannot use physical paths or absolute URLs (those beginning with http://, //, or \\) for this parameter.

Example

```
<%

' Dimension local variables.
Dim objNextLink
Dim strPrevDesc
Dim strPrevURL

' Create an instance of the NextLink object.
Set objNextLink = Server.CreateObject("MSWC.NextLink")

' Retrieve a description text for the previous item in
' the Content Linking list file.
strPrevDesc = _
   objNextLink.GetPreviousDescription("/MyContentLinkList.txt")

' Retrieve a URL for the previous item in the Content
' Linking list file.
strPrevURL = _
   objNextLink.GetPreviousURL("/MyContentLinkList.txt")

' Use strNextURL to create a link to the item whose
' description you retrieved using GetPreviousDescription.
%>

<A HREF = "<%= strPrevURL %>"><%= strPrevDesc%></A>

<%
' Free the memory consumed by the NextLink object.
Set objNextLink = Nothing

%>
   . . . [additional HTML and code]
```

Notes

If the current page cannot be found in the Content Linking list file, the URL text
for the first item in the list file is returned by default.

Using GetPreviousURL with a Content Linking file, you do not have to change the
code within your HTML to update a "PREVIOUS PAGE" hyperlink, for example.
You only have to change the Content Linking list, and the component will automatically update this link for you.

In addition to the previous example, see the full example at the end of this
chapter.

Content Linking Component Example

The following example code demonstrates a complete Content Linking component example in one place to illustrate the overall mechanism of the Content
Linking component and its accessory content list file.

The scenario is simple. The following set of scripts demonstrates the dynamic construction of the first few pages of an online book introducing programming. There are five content files (*Content1.ASP* through *Content5.ASP*). For each file, you want to provide your users with an indicator of current page number (out of the total number of pages), a previous-page link, and a next-page link. You know the content files will change and pages will be inserted and removed often. This is a good example of a programming problem in which the Content Linking component can help.

The following script is the HTML version of the fourth page in our online book:

```
<HTML>
<HEAD><TITLE>Introduction to Programming: Lesson 4 Looping</TITLE></HEAD>
<BODY>
Welcome to the Introduction to Programming, Lesson 4:
Looping.<BR>

[TEXT ABOUT LOOPING AND LOOP STRUCTURES]

<!-- Begin navigation section construction -->
<HR>
You are currently viewing page # 4 of 5.<BR>
Use the following links to navigate:<BR>
<A HREF="Content3.asp">Previous: Lesson 3 Variables</A><BR>
<A HREF="Content1.asp">Home: Lesson 1 Introduction</A><BR>
<A HREF="Content5.asp">Next: Lesson 5 Pointers</A><BR>
<!-- End navigation section construction -->
</BODY>
</HTML>
```

This HTML page could be easily created by hand and kept up-to-date manually when pages are inserted and removed. However, you can see that with many pages, such upkeep would be tedious, at best. For example, suppose we had to insert a page (Lesson 3a: Advanced Variables) between lessons 3 and 4. To do this manually, everything in bold in the previous example would have to be changed by hand. If we removed the current home page and added a new one (with a different name and description), we would have to make even more changes.

The Content Linking component can help us here. We start by creating a Content Linking list, whose filename is ONLINE_CONTENT_LIST.TXT:

```
Content1.asp    Lesson 1 Background
Content2.asp    Lesson 2 Code Style
Content3.asp    Lesson 3 Variables
Content4.asp    Lesson 4 Looping
Content5.asp    Lesson 5 Pointers
```

The file contains one line for each of our five content pages. Each line consists of a filename and a file description, separated by a Tab character. We can now add the following code to the navigation section of each page in our online book:

```
<!-- Begin navigation section construction -->
<HR>
<%
Dim objContentLink
```

```
Set objContentLink = Server.CreateObject("MSWC.NextLink")

' Retrieve the index of the current page.
intCurrentPageNumber = _
    objContentLink.GetListIndex("ONLINE_CONTENT_LIST.TXT")

' Retrieve the total number of pages.
intTotalPageCount = _
    objContentLink.GetListCount("ONLINE_CONTENT_LIST.TXT")

' Retrieve the URL for the first page in the series.
strHomeURL = _
    objContentLink.GetNthURL("ONLINE_CONTENT_LIST.TXT")

' Retrieve the description for the first page in the series
strHomeDesc = objContentLink.GetNthDescription( _
        "ONLINE_CONTENT_LIST.TXT")

' If the current page index is greater than 1 (i.e., it
' is after the home page), then retrieve information
' about the previous page.
If intCurrentPageNumber > 1 Then
    ' Retrieve the URL for the first page in the
    ' series.
    strPrevURL = objContentLink.GetPreviousURL( _
                "ONLINE_CONTENT_LIST.TXT")

    ' Retrieve the description for the previous page in
    ' the series.
    strPrevDesc = objContentLink.GetPreviousDescription( _
                "ONLINE_CONTENT_LIST.TXT")
End If

' If the current page index is less than the total page
' count (i.e., it is before the last page), then retrieve
' information about the next page.
If intCurrentPageNumber < intTotalPageCount Then

    ' Retrieve the URL for the previous page in the series.
    strNextURL = objContentLink.GetNextURL( _
                "ONLINE_CONTENT_LIST.TXT")

    ' Retrieve the description for the next page in the series.
    strNextDesc = objContentLink.GetNextDescription( _
                "ONLINE_CONTENT_LIST.TXT")

End If

' Now use the preceding information to construct the
' navigation section of the current page.
%>

You are currently viewing page #
<%=intCurrentPageNumber%> of
```

```
<%=intTotalPageCount%>.<BR>
Use the following links to navigate:<BR>

<%If intCurrentPageNumber > 1 Then%>
<A HREF="<%=strPrevURL%>">Previous:
<%=strPrevDesc%></A><BR>
<%End If%>

<A HREF="<%=strHomeURL%>">Home: <%=strHomeDesc%></A><BR>

<%If intCurrentPageNumber < intTotalPageCount Then%>
<A HREF="<%=strNextURL%>">Next: <%=strNextDesc%></A><BR>
<%End If%>
<!-- End navigation section construction -->
```

If we were to replace the following code in bold:

```
<HTML>
<HEAD><TITLE>Introduction to Programming: Lesson 4 Looping</TITLE></HEAD>
<BODY>
Welcome to the Introduction to Programming, Lesson 4:
Looping.<BR>

[TEXT ABOUT LOOPING AND LOOP STRUCTURES]

<!-- Begin navigation section construction -->
<HR>
You are currently viewing page # 4 of 5.<BR>
Use the following links to navigate:<BR>
<A HREF="Content3.asp">Previous: Lesson 3 Variables</A><BR>
<A HREF="Content1.asp">Home: Lesson 1 Introduction</A><BR>
<A HREF="Content5.asp">Next: Lesson 5 Pointers</A><BR>
<!-- End navigation section construction -->
</BODY>
</HTML>
```

with the Content Linking component code segment preceding it, the result would be a navigation links section that stays current with the Content Linking list. All you would have to do to update the links is to update the Content Linking list file.

We could even go one step further and save the previous code as an include file (called *NavConstruct.INC*) and include it anywhere in the content pages for our online book:

```
<HTML>
<HEAD><TITLE>Introduction to Programming: Lesson 4 Looping
</TITLE></HEAD>
<BODY>
Welcome to the Introduction to Programming, Lesson 4:
Looping.<BR>

[TEXT ABOUT LOOPING AND LOOP STRUCTURES]

<!-- #INCLUDE FILE = NavConstruct.INC-->
</BODY>
```

Now suppose we must add a page between pages 3 and 4. All that we must do, after creating the page itself (and including our *NavConstruct.INC* include file), is to update the *ONLINE_CONTENT_LIST.TXT* Content Linking list file:

```
Content1.asp   Lesson 1    Background
Content2.asp   Lesson 2    Code Style
Content3.asp   Lesson 3    Variables
Content3a.asp  Lession 3a  Advanced Variables
Content4.asp   Lesson 4    Looping
Content5.asp   Lesson 5    Pointers
```

All the links constructed using the Content Linking list component are updated upon the code's execution and the links stay correct. You can avoid the task of going into each affected file and updating hardcoded links. It is all done for you.

CHAPTER 17

Content Rotator Component

More often than not, the greatest challenge facing a webmaster has little to do with the technology running her web site. The biggest challenge is providing enough different content quickly enough so that her clients keep coming back to the site and keep telling others about the site. Clients today have millions of sites to choose from—often several hundred on any given subject. Why frequent yours if the content doesn't change often enough to make the few clicks it takes to get there worth the effort?

One solution to this problem is to provide, on a regular basis, a small change to your web site or its more popular pages. This small change—if clever or original enough—can keep a user on the site just long enough for him to see something that he may not have seen before—even if the content in question has been present for some time. More important, for some sites this change could keep the user long enough to notice an advertisement and click on it.

If the change is really clever, the user may frequent your site (and see your content and view your sponsors' advertisements) just to see that small change in content.

Microsoft recognized this strategy as a common one and introduced an Active Server Pages component that makes rotating HTML content on an otherwise-unchanging document very easy. The server component is called the Content Rotator component. This component, in conjunction with a content schedule text file, allows you to set up a simple ASP script that retrieves a small bit of HTML. The component then displays this HTML snippet to the client without changing any part of your script's other functions and without the hassle of having to switch files on your web server in and out.

Accessory Files/Required DLL Files

Controt.DLL

Controt.DLL is the dynamic link library containing the Content Rotator component. It must be registered on the web server before it can be instantiated in your web applications. This DLL is *not* installed by default when you install IIS.

Content Schedule File

The content schedule file contains HTML snippets that the Content Rotator component retrieves and displays to the client. Each HMTL snippet is in the following format:

```
%% [#uintWeight]    [//Comment]
HTMLContentString
```

where:

`%%`

> Signals the beginning of an HTML snippet. Each entry must begin with the double percent sign or the Content Rotator component cannot distinguish it from the previous snippet.

`#uintWeight`

> A pound sign followed by an unsigned integer value (between 1 and 65,535) that represents the relative weight of the current HTML snippet. This optional parameter represents the relative probability that the Content Rotator component will select this HTML snippet from the list of snippets. The actual probability of this HTML snippet being selected by the Content Rotator component is `uintWeight` divided by the total of all the snippets' weights. For example, assume you have three snippets with weights of 33, 34, and 33. The first snippet would be selected 33% percent of the time, the second 34% percent, and the third 33% of the time. If a snippet's weight is zero, that snippet is never chosen. The default weight is 1.

//Comment

An optional string of comments describing the HTML snippet or its relevance. It is for your use in maintaining the content schedule file and is never displayed to the client. If a snippet requires more than one line of comments, start each comment with a double percent sign (%%) followed immediately with a double forward slash (//).

HTMLContentString

The actual HTML snippet that will be added to the client's display. This HTML can contain anything legal in HTML. However, you cannot have ASP script in the *HTMLContentString* parameter. The Content Rotator component identifies the beginning and end of an HTML snippet using the double percent signs. For this reason, you can have as many lines in your HTML snippet as you like.

The following is an example content schedule file containing five entries:

```
%% #33 // This identifies the first snippet of HTML.
%% // This is a second line of comments.
Click <A HREF = "http://www.movielines.com">here</A>
to learn where the following movie line originated:<BR>
<FONT SIZE = 3>"Most excellent."</FONT>

%% #5 // This is snippet two.
Click <A HREF = "http://www.horolines.com">here</A>
to learn today's horoscope.<BR>

%% #10 // This is snippet three.
This line came from a great movie:<BR>
"Humor. It is a difficult concept."

%% #27 // This is snippet four.
Comment your code; your replacement will appreciate
the work.<BR>

%% #450 // This is snippet five..
<IMG SRC="/images/coolimg.jpg">
```

The probabilities that each snippet in the example content schedule file will be selected are shown in the following table:

Snippet	Weight	Percentage
1	33/525	6%
2	5/525	1%
3	10/525	2%
4	27/525	5%
5	450/525	86%

Instantiating the Content Rotator Component

To create an object variable containing an instance of the Content Rotator component, use the Server object's CreateObject method. The syntax for the CreateObject method is:

```
Set objMyObject = Server.CreateObject(strProgId)
```

where:

- The *objMyObject* parameter represents the name of a Content Rotator object.
- The *strProgId* parameter represents the programmatic ID (ProgID) for the Content Rotator component, which is MSWC.ContentRotator.

Example

```
<%

' The following code uses the CreateObject method of the
' Server object to instantiate a Content Rotator object
' on the server.
Dim objContentRotator

Set objContentRotator = Server.CreateObject( _
          "MSWC.ContentRotator")

%>
```

For more details on the use of the CreateObject method, see its documentation in Chapter 9, *Server Object*.

Comments/Troubleshooting

The Content Rotator component is very simple to use. The few problems I've heard of have all stemmed from errors in the syntax of the content schedule file.

This component can be used for all sorts of "so-and-so-of-the-day" additions to any site. Creating a "Tip of the day" for your site is a very popular use for this component.

Methods Reference

ChooseContent

```
objContentRotator.ChooseContent(strContentSchedFile)
```

Selects an HTML snippet from the content schedule file. The snippet chosen by the Content Rotator component is selected from all the other snippets in the schedule file according to that snippet's weight relative to the other snippets. When you call the ChooseContent method, the component calls the MapPath method of the Server object to determine the physical path for the virtual path you pass as an argument to ChooseContent. The result of this method call is a small HTML snippet that can be placed in the HTML sent to the client.

Parameters

strContentSchedFile

A string value representing the virtual or relative pathname and filename of your content schedule file. You cannot use physical paths or absolute URLs (those beginning with http://, //, or \\) for this parameter.

Example

```
<HTML>
<HEAD>
<TITLE>Document List</TITLE>
<BODY>
<%

    ' Dimension local variables.
    Dim objContentRotr
    Dim strSelHTMLContent

    ' Create an instance of the Content Rotator object.
    Set objContentRotr = _
        Server.CreateObject("MSWC.ContentRotator")

    ' Retrieve a quotation from the Quote content schedule
    ' file for December.
    strSelHTMLContent = objContentRotr.ChooseContent( _
                        "/SchedFiles/DecemberQuotes.txt")

    ' Now you can add the content thus retrieved to the
    ' HTML sent to the client.
%>
Today's quote:<BR>
<%= strSelHTMLContent %>
. . . [additional HTML and code]
```

Notes

Obviously, the more snippets of HTML code you add to the content schedule file, the less likely any one will be selected more than once in a row, assuming all have the same weight.

You will receive an error if you attempt to call the ChooseContent method from within the *GLOBAL.ASA* file.

GetAllContent

objContentRotator.GetAllContent(*strContentSchedFile*)

Retrieves all the HTML snippets listed in the content schedule file. When you display the content from the call to GetAllContent, each snippet will be separated by a horizontal rule tag (<HR>) in the HTML.

Parameters

strContentSchedFile

A string value representing the virtual or relative pathname and filename of your content schedule file. You cannot use physical paths or absolute URLs (those beginning with http://, //, or \\) for this parameter.

Example

```
<HTML>
<HEAD>
<TITLE>Document List</TITLE>
<BODY>
<%

  ' Dimension local variables.
Dim objContentRotr
Dim strAllHTMLContent

' Create an instance of the Content Rotator object.
Set objContentRotr = _
    Server.CreateObject("MSWC.ContentRotator")

' Retrieve all the quotes from the Quote content
' schedule file for December. The call to GetAllContent
' will separate each HTML snippet from the Content
' Schedule file with an <HR> tag.
strAllHTMLContent = objContentRotr.GetAllContent( _
                    "/SchedFiles/DecemberQuotes.txt")

' Now you can add the content thus retrieved to the
' HTML sent to the client.
%>
All quotes:<BR>
<%= strAllHTMLContent %>
... [additional HTML and code]
```

Notes

The primary use for this method is for maintenance of the content schedule file.

CHAPTER 18

Counters Component

Chapter 4, *Application Object*, demonstrated how to instantiate an application-scoped variable and use it throughout your application. Such a variable maintains the same value for every user of your application and lasts until the last user session ends or until the web server is restarted. Such application-level variables can be very useful, but what happens when the application ends and restarts? The value of these application variables must be reinitialized. In that chapter, I suggested that you could save the application variables to a text file at the end of the application and reinitialize the variable using the saved value each time the application is restarted. If you have several application-level variables, this process can be problematic. Luckily, for numeric variables anyway, there is a better way. You can use a Counters component.

The Microsoft Counters component allows you to create, increment, decrement, store, and remove any number of unique counters. You declare one Counters component for your entire site in *GLOBAL.ASA*. A Counters object is instantiated once for your site (not once per application) and, from that time, is limitless in scope. No matter what session or application is available, the Counters component is *always* accessible from anywhere. You need only one Counters object for your entire site.

As you might guess, a Counters object allows you to create web-site-scoped counter variables that hold the same value for every user of every application on your site. For example, suppose you have two different applications defined by two separate virtual directories. If there is a Counters object instantiated for the site, a user of Application1 can add a counter to the Counters object and a user of Application2 can increment or decrement the same counter. The value of all the counters in the Counters object is saved to the web server's hard drive (in a file called *Counters.TXT*) so if the web server is restarted, you won't lose the value of your counter.

Accessory Files/Required DLL Files

Counters.DLL

The dynamic link library containing the Counters component. It must be registered on the web server before it can be instantiated in your web applications. This DLL is *not* installed by default when you install IIS.

Counters.TXT

A text file that contains the actual values of the counters that have been added to the site's Counters object, if one exists. This is a UTF8-encoded file. This file can contain any number of counters' values and should not be edited manually. The Counters component is hardcoded to look for this file, so don't rename it. Also, don't move it from its installation location, since this will cause the component to be unable to find it.

Instantiating the Counters Component

To create an object variable containing an instance of the Counters component, use the Server object's CreateObject method. The syntax for the CreateObject method is as follows:

```
Set objMyObject = Server.CreateObject(strProgId)
```

where:

- *objMyObject* represents the name of the Counters object

- *strProgId* represents the programmatic ID (ProgID) for the Counters component, which is `MSWC.Counters`

Example

```
<SCRIPT LANGUAGE = VBScript RUNAT SERVER>
' The following code uses the Server object's
' CreateObject method to instantiate a Counters
' component in the Application_OnStart event
```

```
' in the GLOBAL.ASA file.

Sub Application_OnStart
    Dim objCounter

    Set objCounter = Server.CreateObject("MSWC.Counters")
End Sub
</SCRIPT>
```

For more detail on the use of the CreateObject method, see its entry in Chapter 9, *Server Object.*

Comments/Troubleshooting

The Counters component provides a powerful way to keep track of counters that are the same throughout your site. It can contain as many counter variables as memory permits, and each counter name can contain any Unicode character.

The most important thing to remember about the Counters component is that it is scopeless. This component is basically a repository for "ultraglobal" variables and should be treated accordingly. Any script in any application that alters a counter's value changes that counter's value for every other script that uses that counter for the entire site.

One important use for this component is to store and display user vote tallies. For example, several sites have a quick survey on their home pages. You are asked a simple question with a few radio buttons for your vote and a Submit button that allows you to see the vote tallies for each item for which you can vote. This way, you can maintain the counts for each option indefinitely. The examples in this chapter demonstrate this concept.

If you are using Windows 9x with Personal Web Server for your development, be aware that a Counters object is instantiated in the *GLOBAL.ASA* file created by Personal Web Server by default. For this reason, you can treat the Counters component exactly as if it were a built-in object, like the Application, Session, or Server objects. Note also that although the SCOPE parameter of the OBJECT tag that you use to instantiate a Counters object has a value of Application, a Counters component is not limited to application scope.

The following shows how you instantiate a Counters object:

```
<OBJECT RUNAT="Server" SCOPE = "Application"
ID = "MyCounter" PROGID = "MSWC.Counters">
</OBJECT>
```

Methods Reference

Get   objCounter.Get(*strCounterName*)

Retrieves the current value of any counter held in the Counters component. If the counter name you provide is not yet stored by the Counters component, a new counter is added and given a value of zero (0).

Parameters

strCounterName

A string that represents the name of the counter variable you wish to manipulate. This name can contain any Unicode character.

Example

The following example assumes a Counters object already exists (see "Instantiating the Counters Component" earlier in this chapter) and demonstrates the use of the Get method. It assumes a Counters component (*gobjOptionCounter*) has been instantiated elsewhere.

```
<HTML>
<HEAD>
<TITLE>Favorite Games</TITLE>
<BODY>
<%

' Dimension local variables.
Dim intDoom
Dim intQuake
Dim intQuake2

' Initialize the preceding variables using the current
' values of the corresponding counters in the Counters
' object (instantiated elsewhere).
intDoom = gobjOptionCounter.Get("FavGameCounter_Doom")
intQuake = gobjOptionCounter.Get("FavGameCounter_Quake")
intQuake2 = gobjOptionCounter.Get("FavGameCounter_Quake2")

' Display the current vote tallies for favorite game.
%>
Here are the current vote counts for favorite game:<BR>
<TABLE WIDTH = 50%>
<TR>
    <TD WIDTH = 50%>
        Doom
    </TD>
    <TD WIDTH = 50%>
        <%= intDoom %>
    </TD>
</TR>
<TR>
    <TD WIDTH = 50%>
        Quake
    </TD>
    <TD WIDTH = 50%>
        <%= intQuake %>
    </TD>
</TR>

<TR>
    <TD WIDTH = 50%>
        Quake 2
```

```
        </TD>
        <TD WIDTH = 50%>
            <%= intQuake2 %>
        </TD>
    </TR>
    </TABLE>
    </BODY></HTML>
```

Notes

The value of a counter is limited to the range of an integer. Note that the number of counters held in the Counters component has little effect on the memory it holds on the web server, since the values of its counters are written to the hard drive.

Increment   *objCounter*.Increment(*strCounterName*)

Increments a counter in the Counters component. If you attempt to increment a counter that does not yet exist, the counter is created and its value is set to 1. The new value of the counter is returned.

Parameters

strCounterName

A string that represents the name of the counter variable you wish to manipulate. This name can contain any Unicode character.

Example

The following example assumes a Counters object (*gobjOptionCounter*) has been instantiated elsewhere (see "Instantiating the Counters Component" earlier in this chapter) and demonstrates the use of the Increment method.

```
<HTML>
<HEAD>
<TITLE>Favorite Games</TITLE>
<BODY>
<%

' The following line of code increments the
' FavGameCounter_Doom counter in the gobjOptionCounter
' object and returns the new value of the counter.
' Note that if FavGameCounter_Doom does not yet exist
' in the gobjOptionCounter object, the returned value
' is 1.
%>
You are user number
<%= gobjOptionCounter.Increment("FavGameCounter_Doom") %>
to vote for Doom as your favorite game.<BR>

%>
. . . [additional HTML and code]
```

Remove   `objCounter.Remove(strCounterName)`

Removes a counter from the Counters component and deletes its entry from the *Counters.TXT* file. This method has no return value.

Parameters

`strCounterName`
> A string that represents the name of the counter variable you wish to remove. This name can contain any Unicode character.

Example

The following example demonstrates the use of the Remove method of the Counters object. This example assumes a Counters object (*gobjOptionCounter*) has been instantiated elsewhere.

```
<%

' The following code removes the FavGameCounter_Wolf3D
' counter from the gobjOptionCounter object.
gobjOptionCounter.Remove("FavGameCounter_Wolf3D")

%>
```

Notes

See the explanation of the Get method earlier in this chapter.

Set   `objCounter.Set(strCounterName, intCounterValue)`

The Set method allows you to create a counter in the Counters component and add its entry to the *Counters.TXT* file. The new counter's value is returned.

Parameters

`strCounterName`
> A string that represents the name of the counter variable you wish to manipulate. This name can contain any Unicode character.

`intCounterValue`
> An integer that represents the new value of the counter variable you wish to set.

Example

The following example demonstrates the use of the Set method. This example assumes a Counters object (*gobjOptionCounter*) has been instantiated elsewhere.

```
<%
' The following code sets the value of the
' FavGameCounter_Unreal counter to an arbitrary number
' (high) to inflate its perceived popularity. If it does
' not already exist, it is created and initialized to the
' value 987.
gobjoptionCounter.Set("FavGameCounter_Unreal", 987)

%>
```

CHAPTER 19

File Access Component

In addition to the native ASP objects (Request, Response, etc.) and the various installable components (Ad Rotator, Browser Capabilities, etc.), you also have access to a third group of objects. These objects are instantiated directly from the Microsoft Scripting Runtime DLL (*scrrun.dll*). This DLL contains functionality that is neither in the native ASP objects nor in the VBScript runtime (*vbscript.dll*) itself. From the scripting DLL, you can instantiate objects that provide your application with extensive file-manipulation capabilities. (From this DLL, you also can create a Dictionary object that provides you with a way to perform collection-type functions without true collections.)

All file manipulation is performed by the FileSystemObject object. Your application will have only one of these, and it represents your application's "window" onto the system's file structures. With this object, you are able to perform some simple functions such as opening and closing files, but the real strength of this object is that through it you are able to instantiate the other file manipulation objects: Drive, Folder, and File. Through these objects, your application has almost all the power over the file system that you have through a command-line interface.

Accessory Files/Required DLL Files

Scrrun.DLL
> The dynamic link library that contains all the scripting objects. This DLL is installed by default when you install IIS 4.0 on your web server.

Instantiating Installable Components

To create an object variable containing an instance of the FileSystemObject component, use the CreateObject method of the Server object. The syntax for the CreateObject method is as follows:

```
Set objMyObject = Server.CreateObject(strProgId)
```

where:

- *objMyObject* represents the name of the FileSystemObject variable.

- *strProgId* represents the programmatic identifier (ProgID) for the FileSystemObject component, which is `Scripting.FileSystemObject.`

Example

```
<%

' The following code uses the CreateObject method of
' the Server object to instantiate a FileSystemObject.
Dim fsFileSystemObject
Set fsFileSystemObject = _
    Server.CreateObject("Scripting.FileSystemObject")

%>
```

For more details on the use of the CreateObject method, see its entry in Chapter 9, *Server Object.*

Comments/Troubleshooting

The file access components of *scrrun.dll* are straightforward to use. When errors occur, the various properties and methods all return error messages that are in accordance with what you would expect if you were to perform a given file operation through the command line. For example, if you attempt to write or read files on the floppy drive on your computer, but you have no disk in the drive, you will receive a "disk not ready" error.

Object Model

The diagram in Figure 19-1 illustrates the hierarchical object model representing the file system and all its constituents. (Figure 19-1 offers a simplified view of the model. Each collection is in fact made up of its constituent objects; the Folders collection, for example, contains individual Folder objects that, in turn, have Files collections of their own.) The following sections list each object in the model, along with its properties, collections, and methods. Items marked with an asterisk are documented in detail in the Properties Reference and the Methods Reference in this chapter.

Drive Object

The Drive object represents a physical drive. This drive can exist on your machine, or it can be a drive shared by another machine. The Drive object's properties are listed in Table 19-1. Except for VolumeName, the properties in Table 19-1 are all read-only.

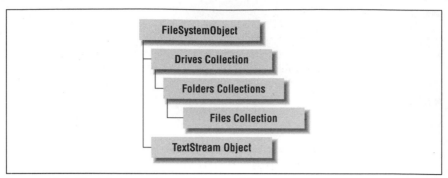

Figure 19-1: The FileSystemObject object model

Table 19-1: Drive Object Properties

Property	Description
AvailableSpace*	Indicates the amount of space (in bytes) left on the drive or network share represented by the Drive object.
DriveLetter	A string value representing the physical drive letter or share name for the Drive object.
DriveType	One of the following integer values representing the type of drive: 0—Unknown 1—Removable 2—Fixed 3—Network 4—CD-ROM 5—RAM Disk
FileSystem*	A string value representing the file system used to format the drive represented by the Drive object. Some possible return values are FAT, FAT32, NTFS, and CDFS.
FreeSpace	A long integer representing the number of bytes of space available on the drive. This is the same value as that for the AvailableSpace property unless the drive represented by the Drive object supports quotas.
IsReady*	A Boolean value that indicates whether the drive represented by the Drive object is ready for operation.
Path	The physical path of the drive represented by the Drive object.
RootFolder	Returns the Folder object (described later in this chapter) that is the root folder for the drive represented by the Drive object. The RootFolder property has a Folders property that returns a Folders collection which serves as the gateway to the drive's file system
SerialNumber	A decimal number that represents a uniquely identifying number for the drive represented by the Drive object.
ShareName	A string value that represents the network share name of the drive represented by the Drive object, if it's shared.

Table 19-1: Drive Object Properties (continued)

Property	Description
TotalSize	A long integer that represents the total size in bytes (used and unused) of the drive represented by the Drive object.
VolumeName	A string value representing the file system volume name of the drive represented by the Drive object.

Drives Collection

The Drives collection contains Drive objects representing the collection of all the drives on the current machine. This collection includes both physical drives and drives shared by other machines. This is a read-only collection; you cannot use this collection to add or remove a drive. The Drives collection's properties are shown in Table 19-2.

Table 19-2: Drives Collection Properties

Property	Description
Count	An integer that represents the total number of Drive objects in the collection.
Item	Returns a specific Drive object from the Drives collection. It works exactly as does the Item property of the Contents collection of the Application or Session objects. You can retrieve a specific Drive object by index (`Drives(1)`) or by name (`Drives("C")`).

File Object

The File object represents a given file on the local machine or on a network share. This object makes all the properties of that file accessible to your code. The File object's properties and methods are listed in Table 19-3 and Table 19-4, respectively.

Table 19-3: File Object Properties

Property	Description
Attributes*	The operating system attributes for that file. Depending on the specific file attribute, this property could be either read/write or read-only.
DateCreated*	The date the file was created.
DateLastAccessed*	The date a user last accessed the file.
DateLastModified*	The date the file was last modified.
Drive*	The drive letter of the drive that holds the current file.
Name	A string value that contains the name of the file.
ParentFolder*	The name of the folder in which the file resides.
Path	The physical path of the file.
ShortName	The 8.3 format name of the file.
ShortPath	The 8.3 format physical path of the file.

Table 19-3: File Object Properties (continued)

Property	Description
Size	The size in bytes of the current file.
Type	The file's type, as determined using your machine's file associations (if one exists). For example, on a machine with Microsoft Word installed, the file *test.doc* would have a Type property of "Microsoft Word Document."

Table 19-4: File Object Methods

Method	Description
Copy*	Copies the file from one location to another
Delete*	Deletes the file
Move*	Moves the file from one location to another
OpenAsTextStream*	Opens the file for reading, writing, or appending

Files Collection

The Files collection represents the collection of all the files in a Folder object. Its properties are shown in Table 19-5.

Table 19-5: Files Collection Properties

Property	Description
Count	The total number of files in the collection.

Item	Retrieves a particular file from the collection. Again, the Item property is similar to the same property of the Application and Session Contents collections. You can retrieve a specific File object using its index in the collection or its name. For example, either of the following two lines will work:
	`Set filObj1 = Files(1)`
	`Set filObj2 = Files("help.txt")`

FileSystemObject Object

The FileSystemObject object is the top-level object through which all access to a file system occurs. Table 19-6 lists its single collection, while Table 19-7 lists its methods. Note that many of these methods are only parsing functions and have no real correlation with the underlying file system.

Table 19-6: FileSystemObject Object Collections

Property	Description
Drives	Returns the Drives collection containing all the drives accessible through the current FileSystemObject.

Table 19-7: FileSystemObject Object Methods

Method	Description
BuildPath	Appends a folder name or a relative path to a path. For example, you could append the folder name *Documents* to the path *C:\MyStuff\Personal*. The result would be *C:\MyStuff\Personal\Documents*. The extra backslash is automatically provided, if necessary.
CopyFile	Copies a file from one location to another. This method is similar to the File object's Copy method, but no File object is required.
CopyFolder	Copies a folder and all its contents from one location to another.
CreateFolder*	Creates a new folder.
CreateTextFile	Creates a new text file.
DeleteFile	Deletes a specific file. This method is similar to the File object's Delete method, but no File object is required.
DeleteFolder	Deletes a folder and all its contents.
DriveExists	Determines whether a specific drive exists on your machine. It does not, however, guarantee that the drive is available.
FileExists	Determines whether the specified file exists.
FolderExists	Determines whether the specified folder exists.
GetAbsolutePathName	Determines the physical path from the root of a specific file or folder.
GetBaseName*	Determines the last element in a physical path string minus any file extension, if one exists.
GetDrive	Retrieves the Drive object for a given file or folder.
GetDriveName	Retrieves the name of the drive associated with a particular file or folder.
GetExtensionName	Retrieves the file extension for the last element in a file specification, if one exists.
GetFile	Retrieves a File object associated with a specified file.
GetFileName	Retrieves the name of the last element of a file path. For example, given the argument *C:\docs\mystuff\ test.txt*, you would retrieve *test.txt*.
GetFileVersion	Returns the version of an executable file or dynamic link library; otherwise, returns a null string.
GetFolder	Retrieves a Folder object associated with a specified folder.
GetFolderName	Retrieves the name of the last folder in a physical path. For example, given the argument *C:\docs\ mystuff*, you would retrieve the string *mystuff*.
GetParentFolderName*	Retrieves the name of the parent folder for the file or folder you specify as an argument.

Table 19-7: FileSystemObject Object Methods (continued)

Method	Description
GetSpecialFolder*	Retrieves the physical path for any of the special Windows-related folders: *Windows, Windows\System,* or the *Temp* folder. You can use this method on any Windows platform.
GetStandardStream	Returns a reference to a TextStream object representing the standard input, standard output, or standard error stream.
GetTempName	Generates a random temporary file or folder for those methods that require one. This method only returns a temporary filename but does not create the actual file.
MoveFile	Moves a specific file from one location to another. This method is similar to the File object's Move method, but no File object is required.
MoveFolder*	Moves a folder and all its contents from one location to another
OpenTextFile	Opens a specified text file. You can then read from, write to, or append to this file.

Folder Object

A Folder object represents an actual file folder on the current machine. Its properties, collections, and methods are listed in Tables 19-8 through 19-10, respectively.

Table 19-8: older Object Properties

Property	Description
Attributes*	The operating system attributes for that folder. Depending on the specific folder attribute, this property could be either read/write or read-only.
DateCreated*	The date the folder was created on the current drive.
DateLastAccessed*	The date a user last accessed the folder.
DateLastModified*	The date the folder was last modified.
Drive*	A string value containing the drive letter of the drive that holds the current folder.
IsRootFolder*	A Boolean value indicating whether the current Folder object represents the root folder on a specific drive.
Name	A string value representing the name of the folder.
ParentFolder*	Returns a reference to the current Folder object's parent folder.
Path	A string value representing the full physical path of the current folder.
ShortName	The 8.3 format name of the folder.
ShortPath	The 8.3 format physical path of the folder.
Size	The size in bytes of all of the current folder's contents.

Table 19-9: Folder Object Collections

Collection	Description
Files	The collection of Files within the current folder only. It does not represent files existing in subfolders of the current folder.
SubFolders	The collection of subfolders (retrieved through the SubFolders property of a Folder object) within the current Folder object.

Table 19-10: Folder Object Methods

Method	Description
Copy*	Copies the folder and its contents from one location to another
CreateTextFile	Opens a new text file
Delete*	Deletes the folder and all its contents
Move*	Moves the folder and all its contents from one location to another

Folders Collection

The Folders collection represents all the folders that exist within the current folder on a particular drive. To retrieve information from subfolders, you must access the Folders collection returned from a call to the SubFolders property of a Folder object. The Folders collection's properties are shown in Table 19-11, while its single method appears in Table 19-12.

Table 19-11: Folders Collection Properties

Property	Description
Count	The total number of folders in the current collection.
Item	Returns a reference to a particular folder in the collection. The Item property is similar to the same property of the Application and Session Contents collections. You can retrieve a specific Folder object using its index in the Folders collection or its name.

Table 19-12: Folders Collection Methods

Method	Description
Add	Adds a new folder to the Folders collection

TextStream Object

The TextStream object allows you to access text files sequentially. This allows you to read, write, or append characters or lines to a text file. The TextStream object's properties and methods are listed in Table 19-13 and Table 19-14, respectively.

Table 19-13: TextStream Object Properties

Property	Description
AtEndOfLine*	A Boolean value that indicates whether the current position within the file is at the end of a line
AtEndOfStream*	A Boolean value that indicates whether the current position within the file is at the end of the text file
Column	An integer value that indicates the column number of the current position in a line of text
Line	An integer value that indicates the line number within a text file

Table 19-14: TextStream Object Methods

Method	Description
Close*	Closes the current text file. Once closed, the file must be reopened before you can read from or write to it.
Read	Reads a specified number of characters from an open text file.
ReadAll	Reads all the characters from an open text file into a string.
ReadLine*	Reads an entire line of text from an open text file.
Skip	Skips over a specified number of characters in an open text file. In conjunction with the Read method, the Skip method allows you to read a number of characters starting at a specific position.
SkipLine	Skips over a specified number of lines in an open text file.
Write*	Writes a specified string to an open text file.
WriteBlankLines	Writes a specified number of newline characters to an open text file.
WriteLine*	Writes an entire line of text to an open text file. You specify the string to be written, and the method will include a newline character at the end of the line.

Properties Reference

AtEndOfLine (TextStream Object)   `tsObj.AtEndOfLine`

A Boolean value that indicates whether the file pointer is at the end of the current line. This is a read-only property.

Parameters

None

Example

The following code instantiates a FileSystemObject and a TextStream object. It then uses the Read method to read one character at a time until the end of the line is reached. Notice that the use of the AtEndOfStream and AtEndOfLine properties are identical.

```
<%

' Set up constants.
Const constForReading      = 1
Const constTristateFalse   = 0

' Dimension local variables.
Dim fsoObject      ' FileSystemObject
Dim tsObject       ' TextStream Object
Dim strReturned    ' String variable to hold file contents

' Instantiate the FileSystemObject variable.
Set fsoObject = Server.CreateObject( _
                "Scripting.FileSystemObject")
' Using the OpenTextFile method of fsoObject,
' create a text file.
Set tsObject = _
    fsoObject.OpenTextFile("d:\docs\test.txt", _
    constForReading, constTristateFalse)

' Read one character at a time until the end of the
' line has been reached.
Do While Not tsObject.AtEndOfLine
    StrReturned = strReturned & tsObject.Read(1)
Loop
. . . [additional code]
%>
```

Notes

If you attempt to use the AtEndOfLine property with a text file opened for any purpose other than reading, you will receive an error.

The AtEndOfLine property will not inform you that you have reached the end of the file.

AtEndOfStream (TextStream Object)   `tsObj.AtEndOfStream`

A Boolean value that indicates whether you have reached the end of the current text file. This is a read-only property.

Parameters

None

Example

The following code instantiates a FileSystemObject and a TextStream object. Then it uses the Read method to read one character at a time until the end of the file is reached. Notice that the use of the AtEndOfStream and AtEndOfLine properties are identical.

```
<%
    ' Set up constants.
    Const constForReading    = 1
    Const constTristateFalse = 0

    ' Dimension local variables.
    Dim fsoObject        ' FileSystemObject
    Dim tsObject         ' TextStream Object
    Dim strReturned    ' String variable to hold file contents.

    ' Instantiate the FileSystemObject variable.
    Set fsoObject = Server.CreateObject( _
                    "Scripting.FileSystemObject")
    ' Using the OpenTextFile method of fsoObject, create
    ' a text file.
    Set tsObject = _
        fsoObject.OpenTextFile("d:\docs\test.txt", _
        constForReading, constTristateFalse)

    ' Read one character at a time until the end of the
    ' file has been reached
    Do While Not tsObject.AtEndOfStream
        StrReturned = strReturned & tsObject.Read(1)
    Loop
    . . . [additional code]
%>
```

Notes

If you attempt to use the AtEndOfStream property with a text file opened for any purpose other than reading, you will receive an error.

Attributes (File Object, Folder Object)

Obj.Attributes [= *intNewAttributes*]

An integer containing a combination of values representing various file system attributes. This property is read-only or read/write depending on the specific file attribute in question.

The following table lists the values that the Attributes property can contain. To determine whether a File or Folder object has a particular value, use the bitwise **And** operator to compare the Attributes property value and the specific constant in which you're interested. If the result is **True**, then that specific attribute is **True**. See the following examples.

Attributes Constant	Value	Description
Normal	0	No attributes are set.
ReadOnly	1	Read-only. This attribute is read/write.
Hidden	2	Hidden. This attribute is read/write.

Attributes Constant	Value	Description
System	4	System file. This attribute is valid only for File objects and is read/write.
Volume	8	The drive's volume label. This attribute is read-only.
Directory	16	Directory. This attribute is read-only.
Archive	32	Archived. This attribute is read/write.
Alias	64	A link or shortcut for another file. This attribute is valid only for File objects and is read-only.
Compressed	128	Compressed. This attribute is valid only for File objects and is read-only.

Parameters

intNewAttributes

An integer containing the sum of a file's or folder's attributes. For example, if you wanted to set the Archived and Hidden attributes to **True**, *intNewAttributes* would have a value of **Hidden** + **Archive**, or 34 (2 + 32). When assigned to the Attributes property, this integer would set these two attributes to **True**.

Example

The following code uses the Attributes property first with a File object, and then with a Folder object.

```
<%

' Dimension local variables.
Dim fsoObject     ' FileSystemObject
Dim filObject     ' File Object
Dim fdrObject     ' Folder Object

' Declare constants.
Const Hidden = 2
Const Archive = 32

' Instantiate the FileSystemObject variable.
Set fsoObject = Server.CreateObject( _
                "Scripting.FileSystemObject")
' Using the GetFile method of fsoObject, initialize the
' File object.
Set filObject = fsoObject.GetFile("d:\docs\test.txt")

' Set the Hidden (value = 2) and Archive (value = 32)
' attributes for the Test.TXT file.
filObject.Attributes = (Hidden + Archive)

' Using the GetFolder method of fsoObject, initialize
' the Folder object.
Set fdrObject = fsoObject.GetFolder("d:\docs")
```

```
' Determine whether the folder is itself hidden.
If (fdrObject.Attributes And Archive) Then
    ' Folder is hidden.
Else
    ' Folder is NOT hidden.
End If
. . . [additional code]
%>
```

Notes

If you attempt to use the read-only attributes that deal only with File objects with a Folder object, the result is always a **False** value. However, if you attempt to set any of the read-only attributes for File or Folder objects, the result is an error.

Note that you must explicitly declare constants for use with the File Access components.

AvailableSpace (Drive Object)   *drvObj*.AvailableSpace

The number of bytes of space left on the current drive. It is inaccurate for drives with over 2GB of available space. This is a read-only property.

Parameters

None

Example

```
<%
' Dimension local variables.
Dim fsoObject       ' FileSystemObject
Dim drvObject       ' Drive Object
Dim lngAvailBytes   ' Number of bytes available

' Instantiate the FileSystemObject variable.
Set fsoObject = Server.CreateObject( _
                "Scripting.FileSystemObject")
' Using the GetDrive method of fsoObject, initialize a
' Drive object.
Set drvObject = fsoObject.GetDrive("\\PublicDocs")
' Retrieve the amount of space (in bytes) available
' on the drive.
lngAvailBytes = drvObject.AvailableSpace
. . . [additional code]
%>
```

Notes

The only time the value for the AvailableSpace property and the value for the FreeSpace property will be different is if the drive supports quotas. For all practical purposes, you can use these two properties interchangeably.

DateCreated (File Object, Folder Object)   *Obj*`.DateCreated`

A date value that represents the date the file or folder was created. This is a read-only value controlled by the operating system.

Parameters

None

Example

```
<%

' Dimension local variables.
Dim fsoObject      ' FileSystemObject.
Dim fdrObject      ' Folder object.
Dim datCreated     ' Date variable.

' Instantiate the FileSystemObject variable.
Set fsoObject = Server.CreateObject( _
               "Scripting.FileSystemObject")
' Using the GetFolder method of fsoObject, initialize
' a Folder object
Set fdrObject = fsoObject.GetFolder("c:\Docs")
' Retrieve the date the folder was created.
datCreated = fdrObject.DateCreated
. . . [additional code]
%>
```

Notes

The value of this property indicates the date the file was created, *not* the date the file was written to the current drive.

Drive (File Object, Folder Object)   *Obj*`.Drive`

Returns a Drive with which the File or Folder object is associated. This property is read-only.

Parameters

None

Example

```
<%

' Dimension local variables.
Dim fsoObject      ' FileSystemObject
Dim filObject      ' File Object
Dim objDrive       ' Drive name

' Instantiate the FileSystemObject variable.
Set fsoObject = Server.CreateObject( _
               "Scripting.FileSystemObject")
' Using the GetFile method of fsoObject, initialize
```

```
' a File object.
Set filObject = fsoObject.GetFile("PublicDocs.txt")
' Retrieve the drive name with which the File object
' is associated.
Set objDrive = filObject.Drive
' Note that this drive is actually the current drive
' in this case.
. . . [additional code]
%>
```

Notes

The Drive property can represent either a physical, local, or mapped drive or a network share.

Because the Drive object's default property is Path, you can assign the drive name to a string as follows:

```
strDrive = filObject.Drive
```

This is really a shorthand version of:

```
strDrive = filObject.Drive.Path
```

If you wish to manipulate the Drive object, though, you must use the Set statement to assign the reference to an object variable. For example:

```
Set objDrive = filObject.Drive
```

FileSystem (Drive Object)   drvObj.FileSystem

A string value that represents the file system type used to format the current drive. The recognized file system types are CDFS, NTFS, FAT, and FAT32. This is a read-only property.

Parameters

None

Example

```
<%

' Dimension local variables.
Dim fsoObject      ' FileSystemObject
Dim drvObject      ' Drive Object
Dim strFileSys     ' File system of drive

' Instantiate the FileSystemObject variable.
Set fsoObject = Server.CreateObject( _
                "Scripting.FileSystemObject")
' Using the GetDrive method of fsoObject, initialize
' a Drive object.
Set drvObject = fsoObject.GetDrive("\\PublicDocs")
' Retrieve the file system for the drive. This value
' will contain one of the following strings:
' NTFS, FAT, or CDFS.
```

```
strFileSys = drvObject.FileSystem
. . . [additional code]
%>
```

Notes

You can rely on the value of the FileSystem property of a Drive object to reflect cluster sizes and security features available for the current drive.

IsReady (Drive Object)   drvObj.IsReady

A Boolean value representing whether the current drive is available for reading or writing. Use this property, for example, to determine whether a floppy disk or CD has been placed in a drive. This is a read-only property.

Parameters

None

Example

```
<%

' Dimension local variables.
Dim fsoObject       ' FileSystemObject
Dim drvObject       ' Drive Object

' Instantiate the FileSystemObject variable.
Set fsoObject = Server.CreateObject(
                "Scripting.FileSystemObject")
' Using the GetDrive method of fsoObject, initialize a
' Drive object.
Set drvObject = fsoObject.GetDrive("\\PublicDocs")
' Check to see if the drive is ready.
If drvObject.IsReady Then
    ' Drive is ready for read/write.
Else
    ' Drive is not ready.
End If
. . . [additional code]
%>
```

Notes

It is a good idea to use the IsReady property before attempting to do any drive access. It can be used to determine the readiness of removable-media drives (floppy and CD-ROM drives) and fixed-media drives.

IsRootFolder (Folder Object)   fdr.IsRootFolder

A Boolean value that allows you to determine if the current folder is the root folder. This is a read-only property.

Parameters

None

Example

```
<%

    ' Dimension local variables.
    Dim fsoObject      ' FileSystemObject
    Dim fdrObject      ' Folder Object

    ' Instantiate the FileSystemObject variable.
    Set fsoObject = Server.CreateObject( _
                "Scripting.FileSystemObject")
    ' Using the GetFolder method of fsoObject, initialize a
    ' File object.
    Set fdrObject = fsoObject.GetFolder("PublicDocs.txt")
    ' Determine whether the current folder is a root folder
    ' or if it is nested.
    If fdrObject.IsRootFolder Then
        ' Folder is located directly off the drive letter
        ' or share name.
    Else
        ' The folder is nested within at least one other
        ' folder.
    End If
    . . . [additional code]
%>
```

Notes

The Microsoft documentation shows how to use this property to determine to how many levels the current folder is nested. For convenience, the following code demonstrates this:

```
<%

    ' Dimension local variables.
    Dim fsoObject      ' FileSystemObject
    Dim fdrObject      ' Folder Object
    Dim intNestedLevel ' Level to which the folder is nested

    ' Instantiate the FileSystemObject variable.
    Set fsoObject = Server.CreateObject( _
                "Scripting.FileSystemObject")
    ' Using the GetFolder method of fsoObject, initialize a
    ' File object.
    Set fdrObject = fsoObject.GetFolder("PublicDocs.txt")
    ' Determine whether the current folder is a root folder
    ' or if it is nested.
    If fdrObject.IsRootFolder Then
        ' Folder is located directly off the drive letter or
        ' share name.
    Else
        ' For more on the ParentFolder property of the
```

```
    ' Folder object, see the following.
    Do Until fdrObject.IsRootFolder
        Set fdrObject = fdrObject.ParentFolder
        intNestedLevel = intNestedLevel + 1
    Loop
End If
. . . [additional code]
%>
```

ParentFolder (File Object, Folder Object)   *Obj*.ParentFolder

Returns a Folder object representing the folder in which the file or folder is located. This is a read-only property.

Parameters

None

Example

The following code demonstrates the use of the ParentFolder property when used with a File object and then with a Folder object. Note that, because Name is the default property of a Folder object, the code in the ASP page appears to treat the value returned by the ParentFolder property as a string.

```
<%

' Dimension local variables.
Dim fsoObject           ' FileSystemObject
Dim filObject           ' File Object
Dim fdrObject           ' Folder Object
Dim strFileParent       ' Parent folder of file object
Dim strFolderParent     ' Parent folder of folder object

' Instantiate the FileSystemObject variable.
Set fsoObject = Server.CreateObject( _
                "Scripting.FileSystemObject")
' Using the GetFile method of fsoObject, initialize the
' File object.
Set filObject = fsoObject.GetFile("d:\docs\test.txt")

' Retrieve the name of the folder containing the file Test.TXT.
' In this example, the value of strFileParent is "docs".
strFileParent = filObject.ParentFolder
' Using the GetFolder method of fsoObject, initialize
' the Folder object.
Set fdrObject = fsoObject.GetFolder("d:\mystuff\docs")

' Retrieve the name of the folder that contains the
' folder "docs". In this example, the value of
' strFileParent is "mystuff".
strFolderParent = fdrObject.ParentFolder
. . . [additional code]
%>
```

Methods Reference

Close (TextStream Object)
<code>tsObj.Close</code>

Closes a text file that has been opened as a TextStream object.

Parameters

None

Example

```
<%

    ' Dimension local variables.
    Dim fsoObject    ' FileSystemObject
    Dim tsObject     ' TextStream Object

    ' Instantiate the FileSystemObject variable.
    Set fsoObject = Server.CreateObject( _
                 "Scripting.FileSystemObject")
    ' Using the OpenTextFile method of fsoObject, initialize
    ' the File object.
    Set tsObject = fsoObject.OpenTextFile( _
                 "d:\docs\test.txt", ForReading, False)

    ' Read into the string the contents of the text file.
    strContents = tsObject.ReadAll
    ' Close the open text file.
    tsObject.Close
    . . . [additional code]
%>
```

Notes

You can have only a limited number of open files in your application (similar to the use of open files in Visual Basic), so it is important to close all open text files after you are finished with them.

Copy (File Object, Folder Object)
<code>obj.Copy strDestination [, blnOverWrite]</code>

Copies a file from one location to another.

Parameters

strDestination
    A string value that represents the full path of the location to which you wish to copy the current file.

blnOverWrite
    A Boolean value that indicates whether a file of the same name as the file to be copied will be overwritten. The default is **True**.

Example

```
<%

' Dimension local variables.
Dim fsoObject    ' FileSystemObject
Dim filObject    ' File Object

' Instantiate the FileSystemObject variable.
Set fsoObject = Server.CreateObject( _
                "Scripting.FileSystemObject")
' Using the GetFile method of fsoObject, initialize
' the File object.
Set filObject = fsoObject.GetFile("d:\docs\test.txt")

' Copy the file to a temporary directory.
filObject.Copy "e:\storage\temp\test_copy.txt", True
. . . [additional code]
%>
```

Notes

The Copy method performs exactly the same function as the CopyFile and Copy-Folder methods of the FileSystemObject object. However, it is important to note that the CopyFile and CopyFolder methods will allow you to copy more than one file or folder at a time.

CopyFolder (FileSystemObject Object)

```
fsoObj.CopyFolder strSource, strDestination [, blnOverWrite]
```

Allows you to copy a folder and all of its contents from one location to another.

Parameters

strSource

   A string value that represents the full path of the location from which you wish to copy a folder or folders. *strSource* can include wildcard characters.

strDestination

   A string value that represents the full path of the location to which you wish to copy the folder or folders designated by *strSource*.

blnOverWrite

   A Boolean value that indicates whether a file of the same name as the file to be copied will be overwritten. The default is **True**.

Example

```
<%

' Dimension local variables.
Dim fsoObject    ' FileSystemObject
' Instantiate the FileSystemObject variable.
Set fsoObject = Server.CreateObject( _
                "Scripting.FileSystemObject")
' Use the FileSystemObject object's CopyFolder method
```

```
' to copy the Temp directory and all its contents from
' the C drive to the D drive, overwriting if necessary.
fsoObject.CopyFolder "c:\temp", "d:\temp", True
...[additional code]
%>
```

Notes

If an error is raised when calling CopyFolder, the method stops immediately and does not reverse any actions already performed.

The CopyFolder method is as fast as copying the folder using the command line.

CreateFolder (FileSystemObject Object)

fsoObj.CreateFolder(*strFolderName*)

Creates a folder in a specified location.

Parameters

strFolderName
> A string value that represents the full physical path of the folder you want to create

Example

```
<%

' Dimension local variables.
Dim fsoObject     ' FileSystemObject
' Instantiate the FileSystemObject variable.
Set fsoObject = Server.CreateObject( _
                "Scripting.FileSystemObject")
' Create a new directory.
fsoObject.CreateFolder("e:\storage\newdir")
...[additional code]
%>
```

Notes

If you attempt to create a folder that already exists, an error will be raised.

Delete (File Object, Folder Object)

Obj.Delete *blnForce*

Deletes a file or folder.

Parameters

blnForce
> A Boolean value that indicates whether to delete files or folders, even if they are marked as read-only

Example

```
<%

' Dimension local variables.
```

```
Dim fsoObject    ' FileSystemObject
Dim filObject    ' File Object

' Instantiate the FileSystemObject variable.
Set fsoObject = Server.CreateObject( _
                "Scripting.FileSystemObject")
' Using the GetFile method of fsoObject, initialize the
' File object.
Set filObject = fsoObject.GetFile("d:\docs\test.txt")

' Delete the TEST.TXT file—even if the file is marked
' as read-only.
filObject.Delete True
. . . [additional code]
%>
```

Notes

The Delete method of the File and Folder objects is functionally the same as the DeleteFile and DeleteFolder methods of the FileSystemObject object. If you use the Delete method of a Folder object, that folder and all of its contents will be deleted. The method will not warn you if you attempt to delete a directory that contains files.

GetBaseName (FileSystemObject Object)

<code>fsoObj.GetBaseName(strPath)</code>

Extracts the name of a file—minus any file extension—from a full file path.

Parameters

strPath

A string representing the full file path of a given file whose base name you want to retrieve

Example

```
<%

' Dimension local variables.
Dim fsoObject    ' FileSystemObject
' Instantiate the FileSystemObject variable.
Set fsoObject = Server.CreateObject( _
                "Scripting.FileSystemObject")
' Using the GetBaseName method, retrieve the base
' names of several path strings.
' This example returns "searchstart" as the base name.
Response.Write fsoObject.GetBaseName( _
               "/apps/search/searchstart.asp")
' This example returns "search" as the base name.
Response.Write fsoObject.GetBaseName("/apps/search/")
' This example returns "search" as the base name.
Response.Write fsoObject.GetBaseName("/apps/search")
```

```
' This example returns "nofile" as the base name—even
' though the nofile.txt file does not exist.
fsoObject.GetBaseName("/apps/search/nofile.txt")
... [additional code]
%>
```

Notes

GetBaseName attempts to retrieve the base name for a file from a path string. If the last element in the path string is a folder, the folder name is returned—even if you include a closing slash (/) or backslash (\) character. The path string is not checked for its validity or its existence as a real path on the server. The method just looks at the path as a string. For this reason, the association of this method with the FileSystemObject object is deceiving, since no file manipulation actually occurs.

GetParentFolderName (FileSystemObject Object)

`fsoObj.GetFolderName (strPath)`

Determines the name of the last parent folder in a given path string.

Parameters

strPath
:   A string representing the full file path of a given file or folder whose parent folder name you are attempting to retrieve

Example

```
<%

' Dimension local variables.
Dim fsoObject    ' FileSystemObject
' Instantiate the FileSystemObject variable.
Set fsoObject = Server.CreateObject(
                "Scripting.FileSystemObject")
' Using the GetParentFolderName method, retrieve the
' parent folder names of several path strings.
' This example returns "search" as the parent folder
' name.
Response.Write fsoObject.GetParentFolderName( _
                "/apps/search/searchstart.asp")
' This example return "apps" as the parent folder name
Response.Write fsoObject.GetParentFolderName ("/apps/search/")
' This example also returns "apps" as the parent folder
' name.
Response.Write fsoObject.GetParentFolderName ("/apps/search")
' This example returns "nofile" as the parent folder
' name—even though nofile.txt does not exist.
Response.Write fsoObject.GetParentFolderName( _
                "/apps/search/nofile.txt")
... [additional code]
%>
```

Notes

Like the GetBaseName method of the FileSystemObject object, the GetParentFolderName method acts only on the path string itself. The path string argument is not checked for validity or existence.

GetSpecialFolder (FileSystemObject Object)

fsoObj.GetSpecialFolder (*intSpecialFolderType*)

Retrieves the full physical path of a special folder on the web server.

Parameters

intSpecialFolderType
An integer that represents the type of special folder whose full physical path you wish to retrieve. The possible values for this parameter are as follows:

Constant	Value	Description
WindowsFolder	0	The Windows or WinNT folder into which your operating system was installed
SystemFolder	1	The System folder into which libraries and device drivers are installed
TemporaryFolder	2	The Temp folder as it is declared in the environment variables

Example

```
<%

' Dimension local variables.
Dim fsoObject    ' FileSystemObject
' Declare file constants.
Const WindowsFolder   = 0
Const SystemFolder    = 1
Const TemporaryFolder = 2

' Instantiate the FileSystemObject variable.
Set fsoObject = Server.CreateObject( _
                "Scripting.FileSystemObject")
' Use GetSpecialFolder to retrieve the physical path
' for the Windows, System, and Temp directories.
' This example returns something similar to "C:\WINNT".
fsoObject.GetSpecialFolder(WindowsFolder)
' This example returns something similar to
' "C:\WINNT\SYSTEM32".
fsoObject.GetSpecialFolder(SystemFolder)

' This example returns something similar to
' "C:\WINNT\TEMP"
fsoObject.GetSpecialFolder(TemporaryFolder)
. . . [additional code]
%>
```

Notes

Note that you must explicitly declare constants for use with the file access components.

MoveFolder (FileSystemObject Object)

> *fsoObj*.MoveFolder *strSourcePath*, *strDestinationPath*

Moves a folder and all its contents from one location to another.

Parameters

strSourcePath
> A string representing the path to the folder or folders you wish to move. You can include wildcard characters in the *strSourcePath* argument in the last segment of the path only.

strDestinationPath
> A string representing the path to which you wish to move the folders referenced in the *strSourcePath* parameter. The *strDestinationPath* parameter cannot contain any wildcard characters.

Example

```
<%

' Dimension local variables.
Dim fsoObject    ' FileSystemObject
' Instantiate the FileSystemObject variable.
Set fsoObject = Server.CreateObject( _
                "Scripting.FileSystemObject")
' Using the MoveFolder method, move all the folders
' under C:\APPS to the D: drive.
fsoObject.MoveFolder "C:\APPS\*.*", "D:\"
. . . [additional code]
%>
```

Notes

If you attempt to move a folder to a destination that is already a filename, you will receive an error. If the destination you provide represents the name of a preexisting folder, you will receive an error unless the source argument ends with a wildcard or a backslash (\). In this case, the source folder (or folders) and all its contents will be moved to the destination folder. For example, the following code results in an error:

```
<%
' Assume FileSystemObject object is instantiated
'already. Also assume that D:\ apps already exists.
fsoObject.MoveFolder "C:\apps", "d:\apps"
%>
```

whereas the following code would not result in an error:

```
<%
' Assume FileSystemObject object is instantiated
```

```
' already. Also assume that D:\ apps already exists.
fsoObject.MoveFolder "C:\apps\*.*", "d:\apps"
' This last line create an apps folder in the D:\apps
' folder (making D:\apps\apps)
%>
```

Note that if the web server experiences an error when calling MoveFolder, all actions stop without any rollback of previous actions. For example, if you attempt to move a series of three folders with all their contents and an error occurs on the third folder to be moved, the first two folders remain moved even though the third is not. You must include your own code to check for which files and folders were actually moved and which were not.

If you attempt to move folders between volumes, the underlying operating system must support this, and user security on the web server must allow for this.

OpenAsTextStream (File Object)

```
tsObject = filObj.OpenAsTextStream [intAccessMode][, intFormat]
```

Opens a file and creates a TextStream object that you can use to read or modify the text file. The method returns a TextStream object.

Parameters

intAccessMode
> An integer that indicates the input/output mode in which you wish to open the text file. Possible values for this parameter are as follows:

Constant	Value	Description
ForReading	1	The file will be opened as read-only and cannot be modified by the current TextStream object.
ForWriting	2	The file will be opened for writing. If the file already exists when you call the OpenAsTextStream method, the original file is overwritten.
ForAppending	8	The file is opened for appending only. You can only add characters to the end of this file.

intFormat
> An integer that indicates the format of the file to be opened as a TextStream object. The possible values for this parameter are thought of as a single tristate value. The file is Unicode, ASCII, or whichever is the system default. Possible values for this parameter are:

Constant	Value	Description
TristateUseDefault	−2	The file format will be the same as the default for the web server (Unicode or ASCII).
TristateTrue	−1	The file format will be Unicode.
TristateFalse	0	The file format will be ASCII.

Example

```
<%

    ' Dimension local variables.
    Dim fsoObject    ' FileSystemObject
    Dim filObject    ' File Object
    Dim tsObject     ' TextStream object

    ' Declare File Access constants.
    Const ForAppending = 8
    Const TristateTrue = -1

    ' Instantiate the FileSystemObject variable.
    Set fsoObject = Server.CreateObject( _
                  "Scripting.FileSystemObject")
    ' Using the GetFile method of fsoObject, initialize the
    ' File object.
    Set filObject = fsoObject.GetFile("d:\docs\test.txt")

    ' Use the OpenAsTextStream method to open the file for
    ' appending and in Unicode format.
    Set tsObject = filObject.OpenAsTextStream(ForAppending, TristateTrue)
%>
```

Notes

The OpenAsTextStream method is virtually equivalent to the OpenTextFile method of the FileSystemObject object. The only difference is that the OpenAsTextStream method also can be used to create a new text file if one does not already exist.

Note that you must explicitly declare constants for use with the File Access components.

ReadLine (TextStream Object)   `tsObj.ReadLine`

The ReadLine method is similar to the Read method of the TextStream object in that it allows you to read from a text file into a string variable or compare the results of such a read to another entity. However, unlike the Read method, which uses an argument to determine how many characters to read, the ReadLine method reads all characters from the current pointer location to the next newline character.

Parameters

None

Example

```
<%

    ' Dimension local variables.
    Dim fsoObject    ' FileSystemObject
    Dim filObject    ' File Object
    Dim tsObject     ' TextStream object
```

```
Dim strBuffer     ' Holding buffer

' Declare file access constants.
Const ForReading = 1
Const TristateFalse = 0

' Instantiate the FileSystemObject variable.
Set fsoObject = Server.CreateObject( _
              "Scripting.FileSystemObject")
' Using the GetFile method of fsoObject, initialize the
' File object.
Set filObject = fsoObject.GetFile("d:\docs\test.txt")

' Use the OpenAsTextStream method to open the file for
' reading and in ASCII format.
Set tsObject = filObject.OpenAsTextStream(ForReading, TristateFalse)
' Use the ReadLine method to read the next line of text
' from the text file into the strBuffer variable.
strBuffer = tsObject.ReadLine
%>
```

Notes

After calling the ReadLine method, the current location of the pointer within the file is the character immediately after the last newline character or at the end of file marker.

Note that you must explicitly declare constants for use with the File Access components.

Write (TextStream Object) *tsObj*.Write(*strWriteString*)

Writes a specified string to an open text file at the current location of the file pointer.

Parameters

strWriteString
   A string that represents the text you wish to write to the open file

Example

```
<%

' Dimension local variables.
Dim fsoObject     ' FileSystemObject
Dim filObject     ' File Object
Dim tsObject      ' TextStream object
Dim strEnding
' Declare file access constants.
Const ForAppending = 8
Const TristateFalse = 0

' Initialize string variable. This string will be
' written to the end of the file opened next.
```

```
strEnding = "This is the end, my only friend, the end..."
' Instantiate the FileSystemObject variable.
Set fsoObject = Server.CreateObject( _
                "Scripting.FileSystemObject")
' Using the GetFile method of fsoObject, initialize the
' File object.
Set filObject = fsoObject.GetFile("d:\docs\test.txt")

' Use the OpenAsTextStream method to open the file for
' appending and in Unicode format.
Set tsObject = filObject.OpenAsTextStream(ForAppending, TristateFalse)
' Write a short string to the end of the opened file.
tsObject.Write strEnding
. . . [additional code]
%>
```

Notes

The Write method does not place any characters at the beginning or end of each written string. For this reason, if you use the Write method to add to a file, make sure that you include any desired characters (like spaces or newline characters) at the beginning or end of the strings you write to the file.

WriteLine (TextStream Object) tsObj.WriteLine([strWriteString])

Writes a string's value into an open file at the location of the pointer within the file. This method also writes a newline character to the end of the added string. Otherwise, it is exactly the same as the Write method.

strWriteString

A string that represents the text you wish to write to the open text file

Example

```
<%

' Dimension local variables.
Dim fsoObject    ' FileSystemObject
Dim filObject    ' File Object
Dim tsObject     ' TextStream object
Dim strEnding
' Declare file access constants.
Const ForAppending = 8
Const TristateFalse = 0

' Initialize a string variable that will be written to
' the end of the file opened next.
strEnding = "This is the end, my only friend, the end..."
' Instantiate the FileSystemObject variable.
Set fsoObject = Server.CreateObject( _
                "Scripting.FileSystemObject")
' Using the GetFile method of fsoObject, initialize the
' File object.
Set filObject = fsoObject.GetFile("d:\docs\test.txt")
```

```
' Use the OpenAsTextStream method to open the file for
' appending and in Unicode format.
Set tsObject = filObject.OpenAsTextStream(ForAppending, TristateFalse)
' Write a short string plus a newline character to the
' end of the opened file.
tsObject.WriteLine strEnding
. . . [additional code]
%>
```

Notes

After calling the WriteLine method, the file pointer will point to the character located immediately after the newline character added to the file.

CHAPTER 20

Logging Utility Component

Introduced with Active Server Pages 3.0 and IIS 5.0, the Logging Utility component allows you to programmatically access the IIS web or FTP server log. This allows you to create ASP scripts (or Visual Basic components) that construct reports based on data extracted from the log files. You could also use the Logging Utility Component to extract information from the log that could be stored elsewhere, such as in a database.

Additionally, you can use the Logging Utility component to read records from one log file and write them into another log file.

Accessory Files/Required DLL Files
logscrpt.dll
> The dynamic link library for the Logging Utility component. This DLL is installed by default.

Instantiating the Logging Utility Component

To create an object variable containing an instance of the Logging Utility component, use the CreateObject method of the Server object. The syntax for the CreateObject method is as follows:

    Set objMyObject = Server.CreateObject(strProgId)

where:

- *objMyObject* represents the name of a Logging Utility object.

- *strProgId* represents the programmatic identifier (ProgID) for the Utility component; its ProgID is MSWC.IISLog.

Logging Utility Summary

Properties

BytesReceived
BytesSent
ClientIP
Cookie
CustomFields
DateTime
Method
ProtocolVersion
Referer
ServerIP
ServerName
ServerName
ServerPort
ServiceName
TimeTaken
URIQuery
URIStcm
UserAgent
UserName
Win32Status

Methods

AtEndOfLog
CloseLogFiles
OpenLogFile
ReadFilter
ReadLogRecord
WriteLogRecord

Example

```
<%

' The following code uses the CreateObject method of the
' Server object to instantiate a Logging Utility object on
' the server.
Dim objLogUtil

Set objLogUtil = _
    Server.CreateObject("MSWC.IISLog")

%>
```

For more details on the use of the CreateObject method see its documentation in Chapter 9, *Server Object*.

For several of the methods of the Logging Utility component, you can use constants instead of the long or integer values (for example, the ForReading constant for the OpenLogFile method). To enable the use of these constants, you must set a reference to the Logging Utility component's type library by adding the following code to *GLOBAL.ASA* or within the <HEAD> tag of your script:

```
<!-- METADATA TYPE="typelib" FILE="c:\WINNT\system32\inetsrv\logscrpt.
dll" -->
```

Note that the METADATA code from an individual ASP page does not show up in the response sent to the client.

Comments/Troubleshooting

Once you've instantiated the Logging Utility component, reading a log file record consists of the following steps:

1. Open the log file you wish to read by calling the OpenLogFile method. Optionally, set a filter to limit the accessible records by calling the ReadFilter method.

2. Check whether there are any valid records left to read by calling the AtEndOfLog method. (Typically, this operation is performed at the beginning of a Do loop.)

3. Navigate to a log record by calling the ReadLogRecord method. This updates the component's property values with the current record's field values.

4. Perform the desired operation(s) on data from the current record.

5. Repeat steps 2–4 as needed.

When you are done, you should close the log file by calling the CloseLogFiles method.

The use of the Logging Utility component is straightforward. The only restriction on its use is that the user accessing the script containing the use of the Logging Utility component must be authenticated and have either administrator writes over the machine running the web server or be an operator of the site (configured in IIS). If a client using only anonymous access attempts to use a Logging Utility script, the component will not function properly and the web server log files cannot be succesfully accessed.

Properties Reference

BytesReceived   *objLogUtil*.BytesReceived

The size of the user's HTTP request in bytes. This includes both the HTTP request itself and any data submitted.

Parameters

None

Example

See the example at the end of this chapter.

BytesSent
<code>objLogUtil.BytesSent</code>

The total number of bytes returned to the client in response to an HTTP request.

Parameters

None

Example

See the example at the end of this chapter.

ClientIP
<code>objLogUtil.ClientIP</code>

The IP address of the client's machine or the client's proxy server.

Parameters

None

Example

See the example at the end of this chapter.

Notes

You can only rarely assume this IP address represents the actual IP address of the client making the HTTP request. More often, it is either the address of a host (as is the case when the client is using an ISP) or the address of a proxy server (as is usually the case when the client is connecting from work).

Cookie
<code>objLogUtil.Cookie</code>

The complete contents of any cookies sent with the client's HTTP request.

Parameters

None

Example

See the example at the end of this chapter.

Notes

This property is equivalent to the Request.Cookies collection, except that it returns the cookie as a single string (as opposed to requiring that you iterate a collection).

CustomFields   `objLogUtil.CustomFields`

This is an array of the custom headers and their values (in name/value pairs) sent in the HTTP request header.

Parameters

None

Example

See the example at the end of this chapter.

Notes

This property will only hold a value if the client is using a customized browser or browser-like application that allows custom HTTP request headers. Most browsers do not send any custom HTTP request headers.

DateTime   `objLogUtil.DateTime`

The date and time of the client HTTP request.

Parameters

None

Example

See the example at the end of this chapter.

Notes

The format of the DateTime property is Greenwich Mean Time (GMT).

Method   `objLogUtil.Method`

The type of operation performed in the client's HTTP request (i.e., GET or POST).

Parameters

None

Example

See the example at the end of this chapter.

ProtocolStatus   `objLogUtil.ProtocolStatus`

The status message sent to the client from the server. For example, if the request was served successfully, the web server would send a Status header of 200 OK.

Parameters

None

Example

See the example at the end of this chapter.

Notes

This property can be read regardless of how you handle errors generated in building your HTTP responses and is initiated by the web server itself.

ProtocolVersion *objLogUtil*.`ProtocolVersion`

The specific version of the protocol used in the client request. For example, HTTP/1.0.

Parameters

None

Example

See the example at the end of this chapter.

Referer *objLogUtil*.`Referer`

The URL of the page from which the client made the HTTP request (i.e., the URL of the page containing a link to the current page), if available.

Parameters

None

Example

See the example at the end of this chapter.

Notes

This is only available if the current request came as a result of a user clicking a link or submitting a form into the server. If the user entered a URL into the browser's address line, this property has no value.

ServerIP *objLogUtil*.`ServerIP`

The web server's IP address.

Parameters

None

Example

See the example at the end of this chapter.

Notes

This property is very useful in multiserver environments in which logging is coordinated among multiple servers.

ServerName `objLogUtil.ServerName`

The name of the web server.

Parameters

None

Example

See the example at the end of this chapter.

Notes

This property is very useful in multiserver environments in which logging is coordinated among multiple servers.

ServerPort `objLogUtil.ServerPort`

The specific port through which the client's request came, such as Port 80 or 8080.

Parameters

None

Example

See the example at the end of this chapter.

Notes

Most web traffic comes into a web server through port 80 and into an FTP server through port 21. Any requests coming through another port—especially one not set up on the web server—should be considered carefully in terms of a possible security breach.

ServiceName `objLogUtil.ServiceName`

The name of the server service being requested by the client. For example, MSFTPSVC or W3SVC.

Parameters

None

Example

See the example at the end of this chapter.

TimeTaken

The total time (in milliseconds) taken by the server to receive the HTTP request from the client and to return the completed HTTP response.

Parameters

None

Example

See the example at the end of this chapter.

Notes

This property is very valuable to ASP developers. Using a Logging Utility component in an admin script combined with the TimeTaken property will allow you to determine which scripts are taking a long time to execute.

URIQuery

`objLogUtil.URIQuery`

The query string appended to the URL specified in the client HTTP request, if applicable.

Parameters

None

Example

See the example at the end of this chapter.

Notes

This is the same as the QueryString property of the Request object taken, except that it returns a single string (as opposed to requiring that you iterate the collection's property/value pairs).

URIStem

`objLogUtil.URIStem`

The complete URL (minus any query string) specified in the client HTTP request.

Parameters

None

Example

See the example at the end of this chapter.

UserAgent

`objLogUtil.UserAgent`

The user agent string sent with the client request. This usually reflects the browser used by the client.

Parameters

None

Example

See the example at the end of this chapter.

Notes

The UserAgent property in the log record comes from the User Agent HTTP header sent with all HTTP requests. This is the same HTTP header used by the BrowserCap component to determine the abilities of the browser used by the client.

UserName   *objLogUtil*.UserName

The user name of the client as sent in the HTTP request.

Parameters

None

Example

See the example at the end of this chapter.

Notes

This is only useful if the current site is not accessible through anonymous access. If the access is anonymous, no UserName is sent in the HTTP header.

Win32Status   *objLogUtil*.Win32Status

The Win32 status code returned to the server once the client request has been successfully processed and the response sent to the client.

Parameters

None

Example

See the example at the end of this chapter.

Methods Reference

AtEndOfLog   *blnResult* = *objLogUtil*.AtEndOfLog( )

The AtEndOfLog method returns a **True** or **False** value depending on whether the last record read is the last in the log file. Used in conjunction with the Read-LogRecord method.

Parameters

None

Example

See the example at the end of this chapter.

Notes

The AtEndOfLog method allows you to stop iterating the records in a log file once you've reached the end of the file.

CloseLogFiles   `objLogUtil.CloseLogFiles lngIOMode`

Closes all log files currently open in the IO mode specified in the `intIOMode` parameter.

Parameters

`lngIOMode`
> The mode of the files you want to close. Its value can be any *one* of the following constants (from the type library) or its corresponding Long value:

> `ForReading (1)`
>> Closes those files that have been opened for read-only access.

> `ForWriting (2)`
>> Closes those files that have been opened for read/write access.

> `AllOpenFiles (32)`
>> Closes all open files.

Example

See the example at the end of this chapter.

Notes

It is very important to close whatever log files you open before the end of your script. Holding log files open takes memory from the server and, although this memory should be released at the end of the script, there is no guarantee that this will happen.

OpenLogFile   `objLogUtil.OpenLogFile(strFilename, [lngIOMode],` `[strServiceName], [strServiceInstance], [intOutputLogFileFormat])`

Allows you to open a web or FTP log file for reading.

Parameters

`strFileName`
> This is the full filename and path to the log file. The name of the file is specific to the Extended Logging Properties set. This file is located, by default, in the *c:\ winnt\system32\logfiles* directory. The web server logs are in the subdirectory

W3SVC1 and the FTP server log files are in the subdirectory *\MSFTPSVC1*. The following filenames are possible name formats for the web server log file itself:

exyymmddhh.log
> Hourly log files.

exyymmdd.log
> Daily log files.

exyymmww.log
> Weekly log files.

exyymm.log
> Monthly log files.

extend#.log
> Unlimited file size and specific file size log files. The "#" is replaced with a specific number starting with 1.

lngIOMode
> Optional. The mode with which you wish to open the log file. It can be one of the following constants or its corresponding Long value:

ForReading (1)
> Opens *strFileName* for read-only access. This is the default value.

ForWriting (2)
> Opens *strFileName* for read/write access.

strServiceName
> Optional. Allows you to specify a server service. For example, you can view those records that have as their service a specific name, such as W3SVC or MSFTPSVC.

strServiceInstance
> Optional. There can be multiple instances of each type of server running on the server. This argument allows you to specify the specific instance running (1, 2, etc). On most servers, this value should be 1.

lngOutputLogFileFormat
> Optional. The format of the log file to which you will be writing, if applicable.

Example

See the example at the end of this chapter.

Notes

As mentioned previously, the *strFileName* argument must be a complete physical path to the log file desired. I reiterate this because in both the Microsoft documentation and in other published sources, it is stated that this argument is simply the filename (and not the full path) of the log file. This did not work with the several example servers on which I tested this code.

If the name of the file submitted is incorrect or the file doesn't exist, this method will fail. Unfortunately, however, you are not given a reason for its failure. The call will simply result in an internal server error with no mention in the error notice about the log file named in the *strFileName* argument not existing.

ReadFilter

`objLogUtil.ReadFilter( [dtStart], [dtEnd])`

Allows you to limit the records to be read from an already opened log file. Using ReadFilter, you can limit the records you view by date range.

Parameters

dtStart
> The beginning date/time of the date range to which you wish to limit your record access. This date/time is specific to the server (as opposed to GMT).

dtEnd
> The ending date/time of the date range to which you wish to limit your record access. This date/time is specific to the server (as opposed to GMT).

Example

See the example at the end of this chapter.

Notes

Log files for even the most modest web sites can be very large. As a result, the ReadFilter method is imperative to reduce the number of records visible in the log file.

ReadLogRecord

`objLogUtil.ReadLogRecord`

Reads in the next record in the currently open log file (opened using OpenLogFile).

Parameters

None

Example

See the example at the end of this chapter.

Notes

In a Logging Utility component, there is only one current record being accessed. The ReadLogRecord method reads in the next record in the log file. You can then access the various properties of the record currently read. It is very similar to the current record in a recordset accessed through ActiveX Data Objects.

WriteLogRecord

`objLogUtil.WriteLogRecord objLogUtilWrite`

Allows you to write a log record from one open log file to another log file. You can only write a log record that already exists in a separate log file.

Parameters

objLogUtilWrite
> The Logging Utility object whose current record you wish to write to a second log file (accessed through *objLogUtil*).

Example

See the example at the end of this chapter.

Notes

The WriteLogRecord method allows you to iterate through one log file and add specific records that match some criterion to another log file. This is very important for reporting on very large sites. For example, you could create a script that iterates through all records in a log file and flags those whose security is questionable by recording them in another log file, then uses the new log file to generate a report.

Logging Utility Component Example

The following script demonstrates the use of several of the Logging Utility object's properties and methods.

This script opens the entire extended log file filtering for today's date. Then the script iterates through all the records that match the filter and displays the information from the records that represent large-sized HTTP requests.

Note that you must set your extended logging so that BytesReceived is captured or this example will not work.

```
<HTML>
<HEAD>
<TITLE>Logging Utility Example</TITLE>
<!-- METADATA TYPE="typelib" FILE="c:\WINNT\system32\inetsrv\logscrpt.
dll" -->
</HEAD>
<BODY>
<%
' Instantiate a Logging Utility object to read the
' records from the standard log file.
Set objLogUtil = Server.CreateObject("MSWC.IISLog")

' Open the standard log file for reading.
objLogUtil.OpenLogFile _
        "c:\winnt\system32\logfiles\W3SVC1\extend1.log", ForReading,
"W3SVC", 1, 0

' Filter the log file's entries for today's activity.
objLogUtil.ReadFilter Date(), Date()

%>
<TABLE>
    <TR>
        <TH>Date</TH>
        <TH>Client IP</TH>
        <TH>User Name</TH>
        <TH>Bytes Received</TH>
    </TR>
<%
' Iterate through the records.
```

```
Do While Not objLogUtil.AtEndOfLog
    ' Read in the next record.
    objLogUtil.ReadLogRecord

    ' If the record's corresponding bytes received
    ' are greater than 2000, display the record in today's report.
    If objLogUtil.BytesReceived > 2000 Then
%>
<TR>
<TD><% = objLogUtil.DateTime %></TD>
<TD><% = objLogUtil.ClientIP %></TD>
<TD><% = objLogUtil.UserName %></TD>
<TD><% = objLogUtil.BytesReceived %></TD>
</TR>
<%
    End If
Loop

objLogUtil.CloseLogFiles(AllOpenFiles)
%>

</TABLE>
</BODY>
</HTML>
```

CHAPTER 21

MyInfo Component

The MyInfo component allows you to maintain an encapsulated list of named string values that you use often throughout your site. This component was ostensibly designed (according to the documentation) for use with Personal Web Server (PWS), but it is also useful within Internet Information Server (IIS) ASP applications.

Each site can have only a single MyInfo component, and this component can contain as many values as you wish. This component helps you maintain this information by giving you a convenient, easy-to-use interface. Each value you store using the MyInfo object is stored in a text file on the web server. To access the value, you simply refer to the name of the object, followed by the dot operator, followed by the name of the value—exactly as if your value were another property of the MyInfo object.

Assuming your site has a single MyInfo object called *myinfoObj* defined with application-level scope, you can retrieve any of its values (custom or not) using simply the syntax *ObjName.PropertyName* that you have used repeatedly. The example code at the end of this chapter demonstrates this.

Accessory Files/Required DLL Files

myinfo.dll
> The dynamic link library for the MyInfo component. It is installed with IIS.

myinfo.xml
> The file in which your MyInfo component stores its values. (Note: You cannot change this filename. The component is hardcoded to look in this file.) This is a standard XML file.*

---

* The latest XML specification can be found at *http://www.w3.org/TR/REC-xml.*

MyInfo Summary

Properties
   Background
   CommunityLocation
   CommunityName
   CommunityPopulation
   CommunityWords
   CompanyAddress
   CompanyDepartment
   CompanyName
   CompanyPhone
   CompanyWords
   Guestbook
   HomeOccupation
   HomePhone
   HomeWords
   Messages
   OrganizationAddress
   OrganizationName
   OrganizationPhone
   OrganizationWords
   PageType
   Personal Address
   PersonalMail
   PersonalName
   PersonalPhone
   PersonalWords
   SchoolAddress
   SchoolDepartment
   SchoolName
   SchoolPhone
   SchoolWords
   Style
   Title
   URL
   URLWords

Collections
   None

Methods
   None

Events
   None

Here is an example of a *myinfo.xml* file on an IIS web server:

```
<XML>
<PersonalName>A. Keyton Weissinger</>
<PersonalAddress>Addr1</>
<PersonalPhone>Phone1</>
<PersonalMail>Mail1</>
<PersonalWords>Words1</>
<CompanyName>CompName1</>
<CompanyAddress>CompAddr1</>
<MyInfo1></>
<AdRot1></>
<Addr1></>
<Phone1></>
<Mail1></>
<Words1></>
<CompName1></>
<CompAddr1></>
<objprop></>
</XML>
```

Here is an example of a *myinfo.xml* file on a Personal Web Server (mine):

```
<XML>
<theme>journal</>
<ranWizard>-1</>
<sync></>
<guestbook>0</>
<messages>-1</>
<title>Keyton's Home Homepage</>
<name>Keyton Weissinger</>
<Email>keyton@home.com</>
<Phone>555-1000</>
<faxPhone>555-1001</>
<Department>AtHome Books</>
<Address1>123 Main Street</>
<Address2>USA</>
<Address3></>
<Address4></>
<Heading1>Here's a little about me:</>
<Words1>I enjoy spending time with my family,
programming, reading Patrick O'Brian novels,
and Age of Sail history.</>
<Heading2></>
<Words2></>
<Heading3></>
<Words3></>
<Heading4></>
<Words4></>
<intUrl>1</>
<checkEmail></>
<url1>http://www.avault.com</>
<urlWords1>Adrenaline Vault</>
<urlWords0>null</>
<url0>null</>
<favoriteLinks>-1</>
</XML>
```

Finally, note that *MyInfo.XML* is only updated by PWS upon a reboot. Simply stopping and restarting PWS will not accomplish the task.

Comments/Troubleshooting

The MyInfo component is useful for storing and maintaining the many administrative values that correspond to properties of your web site in general. You may use items like the name of the webmaster, her phone number, and her email address in your applications repeatedly. You could simply declare them all as application-level variables, but this is problematic, since you must save these values through code if you want them maintained through the course of a restart on your web server, for example.

There are two points to remember when using the MyInfo component:

- Once a property has been created, it is in the *MyInfo.XML* file forever. You must edit this file by hand to remove it. As this is a small text file, this isn't a huge problem, but it's worth mentioning.

- You should have only one MyInfo object per site (i.e., you should instantiate just one object per application) because there is only one *MyInfo.XML* file. This file could conceivably be in flux due to the actions of one MyInfo object while you are attempting to read or change a value from a second object. Contrary to the Microsoft documentation, your MyInfo object should have application-level, not session-level scope.

You can use either of the following two pieces of code to instantiate a MyInfo object. The first uses *Global.asa* to call the Server.CreateObject method:

```
[FROM GLOBAL.ASA]
<%
' Declare local variables.
Dim appMyInfo

' Instantiate a MyInfo object with Application level scope
Set Application("appMyInfo") = _
                Server.CreateObject("MSWC.MyInfo")

' You can now initialize the values
Application("appMyInfo").PersonalName = _
                    "A. Keyton Weissinger"
. . . [additional code]
%>
```

The second uses the <OBJECT> tag:

```
[FROM GLOBAL.ASA]
<OBJECT
RUNAT = SERVER
SCOPE = APPLICATION
ID = appMyInfo
PROGID = "MSWC.MyInfo">
</OBJECT>
```

MyInfo

Properties Reference

[All Properties]   `infoObject.PropertyName [ = strPropertyValue]`

The meaning of the default properties is shown in Table 21-1.

Parameters

PropertyName

> The name of the desired property. If the property does not exist and you are attempting to retrieve its value, an empty string is the result. If, however, you use a nonexistent property name and include a value, that property is created and initialized to the designated value. Although you can add as many property names to a MyInfo object as you like, the properties shown in Table 21-1 are set up by default by Personal Web Server (those marked with an asterisk are also set up by Microsoft Internet Information Server).

Table 21-1: Property Name and Description

Property Name	Description
Background	A string representing the background image for the site.
CommunityLocation	A string representing the location of the web site's community.
CommunityName	A string representing the name of the web site's community.
CommunityPopulation	A string representing the population of the web site's community.
CommunityWords	A string describing the web site's community.
CompanyAddress*	The address of the web site's company.
CompanyDepartment	The department within the web site's company.
CompanyName*	The name of the web site's company.
CompanyPhone	The phone number of the web site's company.
CompanyWords	A string representing any additional text associated with the web site's company.
Guestbook	A string indicating whether the guest book (from PWS) should be available on the site.
HomeOccupation	The occupation of the web site's owner.
HomePhone	The webmaster's home phone number.
HomeWords	A string representing any additional text associated with the web site's owner.
Messages	Personal Web Server stores information about your personalized home page (if it is created through the wizard) using a MyInfo component. One option you have on your personal home page is a drop box that allows the user of your PWS web site to send you a personal message. The Messages property of the MyInfo component is a string that reflects whether this Messages form should appear on your home page.

Table 21-1: Property Name and Description (continued)

Property Name	Description
	The value is "" by default (before you build your web page using the wizard), −1 if you have chosen to have the Messages form, and 0 if you have chosen not to have the Messages form
OrganizationAddress	A string representing the address of the web site's organization.
OrganizationName	A string representing the name of the web site's organization.
OrganizationPhone	A string representing the phone number of the web site's organization.
OrganizationWords	Any additional text associated with the web site's organization.
PageType	This property is also a reflection of information you choose through the use of the Personal Web Server Home Page Wizard. However, it is from the older version (3.0) of PWS and is not the Home Page wizard for PWS 4.0. This property's value is a number that represents whether the current site is (1) About My Company, (2) About My Life, (3) About My School, (4) About My Organization, or (5) About My Community.
PersonalAddress*	A string representing the address of the web site's owner.
PersonalMail*	The email address of the web site's owner.
PersonalName*	A string representing the name of the web site owner.
PersonalPhone*	A string representing the phone number of the web site's owner.
PersonalWords*	The additional text associated with the web site's owner.
SchoolAddress	The address of the web site's school.
SchoolDepartment	The department of the web site's school.
SchoolName	A string representing the name of the web site's school.
SchoolPhone	The phone number of the web site's school.
SchoolWords	A string representing any additional text associated with the web site's school.
Style	A string representing the relative URL of a style sheet for the web site.
Title	A string representing the user-defined title for the home page.
URL(N)	A string representing the Nth user-defined URL. This collection allows you to store multiple user-defined URLs for easy access.
URLWords(N)	A string representing the description of the Nth user-defined URL. This collection allows you to store the descriptions for the URLs in the URL collection.

strPropertyValue

A string that represents the new value for a given property. If the property name does not exist, it is created and initialized with the value of *strPropertyValue.*

Example

The following example code demonstrates both the instantiation of a MyInfo object and its use. First, a MyInfo object named *appMyInfo* is instantiated in *GLOBAL.ASA*:

```
[FROM GLOBAL.ASA]
<%
' Declare local variables.
Dim appMyInfo

' Instantiate a MyInfo object with application-level scope.
Set Application("appMyInfo") = _
    Server.CreateObject("MSWC.MyInfo")
...[additional code]
%>
```

The following is from elsewhere in the ASP application and shows how to assign values to and retrieve values from the MyInfo object:

```
<%

' You can set the default values.
Application("appMyInfo").PersonalName = _
            "A. Keyton Weissinger"

' You can also create (or set) new values.
Application("appMyInfo").MyNewProp = _
            "Custom Property Value"
...[additional code]
' Now you can use these values as you would any other
' application-level values.
%>

The value of the PersonalName property is
<%= Application("appMyInfo").PersonalName %><BR>

The value of the MyNewProp property is
<%= Application("appMyInfo").MyNewProp %><BR>
```

Notes

The only properties whose values are in any way unusual are the URL and URLWords collections. These allow you to create a collection of URLs for later use in your site. The following demonstrates the use of these properties:

```
<%

' Set the URL for the first URL in the collection.
Application("appMyInfo").URL(1) = _
            "/Apps/HomeDir/Home.asp"
```

```
' Set the description for the first URL in the
' collection.
Application("appMyInfo").URLWords(1) = _
          "My Site's Home Page"
    .

    .

    .
' Now you can use these values to create a link (with a
' descriptive name) to a particular URL.
%>

<A HREF = "Application("appMyInfo").URL(1)">
<%=Application("appMyInfo").URLWords(1)%>
</A>
```

CHAPTER 22

Page Counter Component

There was a time that I'm sure many of you remember (not that long ago) when a page counter on a web site's home page was a novelty. Back then, adding a page counter required—or so it seemed—far more work than it was worth, involving at least a CGI application or maybe a Java applet.

The alternative was easier but fraught with difficulties of its own. It involved using a counter service. This involved adding an <IMG> tag to your site that referenced a CGI application on the counter service-maintained server. The service maintained the counter for you. The problem was that such services often were out of commission for long periods of time and would go down completely under heavy loads. Because counter services were problematic, many developers decided to create their own, often simply reinventing the wheel.

Now, however, the web is beginning to show signs that it has moved from infancy to its toddler years, and such mundane items as page counters have become everyday occurrences. There are now at least a dozen easily obtainable versions of the ever-present page counter. Microsoft has its own version; its Page Counter component is the topic of this chapter.

Microsoft's version of the Page Counter is a simple component that stores the current page count for a specific page to a text file. Code on your active server page increases the counter and retrieves the current count programmatically through calls to methods of the Page Counter object.

Accessory Files/Required DLL Files
pagecnt.dll
> The dynamic link library for the Page Counter component. This DLL comes with the IIS installation media but is not installed by default. You must register this DLL by hand before you can use it.

Hit Count Data File
> The hit count data file contains the current hit count for every page for which the Page Counter object is being used. Microsoft suggests that you do not

Page Counter Summary

Properties
    None
Collections
    None
Methods
    Hits
    PageHit
    Reset
Events
    None

modify this file by hand. However, doing so does not adversely affect the page counter's functionality unless the format of the entries is changed. The name and location of this file is specified by the `File Location` value entry in the registry key `HKEY_CLASSES_ROOT\MSWC.PageCounter`. The default name for this page count file is *hitcnt.cnt*.

Note that the Page Counter object will save the current hit count for a page if the count rises above a certain number. This number is located in the `Save_Count` value (under the same registry key as the `File_Location` value). The default number for this setting is 25.

Instantiating the Page Counter Component

To create an object variable containing an instance of the Page Counter component, use the CreateObject method of the Server object. The syntax for the CreateObject method is as follows:

```
Set objMyObject = Server.CreateObject(strProgId)
```

where:

- *objMyObject* represents the name of a Page Counter object.

- *strProgId* represents the programmatic identifier (ProgID) for the Page Counter component; its ProgID is `MSWC.PageCounter`.

Example

```
<%

' The following code uses the CreateObject method of the
' Server object to instantiate a Page Counter object on
' the server.
Dim objPgCounter

Set objPgCounter = _
    Server.CreateObject("MSWC.PageCounter")

%>
```

For more details on the use of the CreateObject method see its documentation in Chapter 9, *Server Object*.

Comments/Troubleshooting

The Page Counter component uses an internal object called a Central Management object that is part of the IIS architecture. This object is what actually counts the number of times each page has been hit.

What if you want to create an application-wide counter, rather than just a page-level counter? Unfortunately, the Page Counter component cannot help you. You must use either the Counters component or an application-scoped variable that is saved on the system manually.

The other limitation of the Page Counter component is that there is no way to prevent the page count from being artificially incremented by the user's clicking the Refresh button or reloading the page repeatedly.

The Page Counter component is simple to use and works as documented.

Methods Reference

Hits   `objPgCntr.Hits([strPathInfo])`

Retrieves a Long from the Page Counter hits file representing the total number of times a given page has been requested.

Parameters

strPathInfo

> The virtual path and filename for the page whose hit count you wish to retrieve. If you do not include a *strPathInfo* argument, the Page Counter object will retrieve the number of times the current page has been requested.

Example

```
<%

' Declare local variables.
Dim objPgCntr
Dim lngHitCount

' Instantiate a Page Counter object.
Set objPgCntr = Server.CreateObject( _
                "MSWC.PageCounter")

' Retrieve the hit count for the home page.
lngHitCount = objPgCntr.Hits("/Apps/Homepage.asp")
%>

The home page has been served <%= lngHitCount %> times.
```

Notes

As explained earlier, a page's hit count is updated automatically (assuming that page contains a Page Counter object) any time a user requests it. This number

shows both "new" requests and those produced from simply clicking on the
Refresh button.

PageHit

Increments the hit counter for the current web page.

Parameters

None

Example

```
<%
Set MyPageCounter = Server.CreateObject("MSWC.PageCounter")
    MyPageCounter.PageHit

lHits = MyPageCount.Hits
If lHits > 0 Then
    Response.Write "This web page has been viewed " & lHits & " times."
End If
%>
```

Reset

objPgCntr`.Reset([`*strPathInfo*`])`

Resets the page counter for a web page. Once called, the page count for the page
is reset to zero in the Page Count hits file.

Parameters

strPathInfo

A string value that represents the virtual path and filename for the page
whose hit count you wish to reset. If you do not include a *strPathInfo*
argument, the Page Counter object will reset the count for the current page to
zero.

Example

```
<%

' Declare local variables.
Dim objPgCntr
Dim lngHitCount

' Instantiate a Page Counter object.
Set objPgCntr = Server.CreateObject( _
                "MSWC.PageCounter")

' Reset the hit count for the home page.
objPgCntr.Reset("/Apps/Homepage.asp")
. . . [additional code]
%>
```

Notes

If the hits file becomes corrupted or is deleted, the hit counts for all pages are
essentially reset.

CHAPTER 23

Permission Checker Component

One of the benefits of using Microsoft's Internet Information Server is its close connection to Windows NT and its security model. The Permission Checker component allows you to utilize this connection to determine whether a user on your web site has permission to view a given file stored on an NTFS volume. This allows you to customize your site's pages according to the permissions granted a given user. For example, you could use the Permission Checker component to check whether a user has access to a certain downloadable file before creating a link to the file. This way, if the user does not have access to the file, she does not even see the link to it. Conceivably, you could use this strategy to prevent unauthorized users from ever seeing any indication that files to which they do not have access exist.

There are two requirements for using the Permission Checker component. The first is that your site must be running on Windows NT or Windows 2000. (Personal Web Server for Windows 95/98 will *not* work.) Second, your web site must not rely exclusively on anonymous connections and the (low-level) security such an access method provides. You must have either Basic Clear Text or Windows NT Challenge Response authentication selected as a security option for your web site. These authentication methods provide the Permission Checker object with a security context in which to test for various permissions. If you do not have Basic or NT Challenge Response, the Permission Checker is unable to distinguish between one anonymous user and another.

 Note that this chapter documents the Permission Checker component 2.0 (Beta 3) that can be downloaded from Microsoft's web site.

Permission Checker Summary

Properties
    None

Collections
    None

Methods
    HasAccess

Events
    None

Accessory Files/Required DLL Files

permchk.dll

> The dynamic link library for the Permission Checker component. This DLL comes with the IIS installation media but is not installed by default. You must register this DLL by hand before you can use it.

Instantiating the Permission Checker

To create an object variable containing an instance of a Permission Checker object, use the Server object's CreateObject method. The syntax for the CreateObject method is as follows:

```
Set objMyObject = Server.CreateObject(strProgId)
```

where:

- *objMyObject* represents the name of the Permission Checker object.

- The *strProgId* parameter represents the programmatic ID (ProgID) for the Permission Checker component, which is MSWC.PermissionChecker.

Example

```
<%

' The following code uses the CreateObject method of the
' Server object to instantiate a Permission Checker
' object on the server.
Dim objPermChkr

Set objPermChkr = _
    Server.CreateObject("MSWC.PermissionChecker")

%>
```

For more details on the use of the CreateObject method see its documentation in Chapter 9, *Server Object*.

Comments/Troubleshooting

Suppose that your web site consists of several pages that must be accessible to all users—even anonymous users. It also contains several pages that require that the user use a specific account or be a member of a specific group. To allow for both types of users on your site, select the Anonymous option and either the Basic Clear Text or Windows NT Challenge Response using the Internet Information Server Management Console. Then set the file permissions on the restricted files so that anonymous users are forbidden access. Alternatively, you could check the LOGON_USER element of the Request object's ServerVariables collection and, if it's blank, set the Status property of the Response object to 401 Unauthorized. This will force the user to log on to the site using a valid username and password.

Note that Basic Clear Text authentication is by no means secure. However, Windows NT Challenge Response, though more secure, is supported only by Microsoft's Internet Explorer. Also, it may not work when your users are connecting to your site (and providing security information) through a proxy server. In my experience, the typical result in this latter case is that you receive two empty strings for the username and password.

Even if you exclusively use anonymous access to your site, the Permission Checker component still has a useful purpose. In attempting to determine the security on a given file, the Permission Checker object must determine if the file exists. Although there are other ways to determine this information, this may be the easiest.

Methods Reference

HasAccess   *objPermChkr*.HasAccess(*strPath*)

Determines whether the current user has access to the file specified in the *strPath* argument. The return value is a Boolean.

Parameters

strPath

A string value that represents the relative path to the file to which you are determining accessibility. This path can be a virtual or a physical path.

Example

```
<%

' Declare local variables.
Dim objPermChkr
Dim blnPermission

' Instantiate a Permission Checker object.
Set objPermChkr = Server.CreateObject( _
                        "IISSample.PermissionChecker")

' Determine whether the current user has access to the
' security page using a virtual path.
```

```
blnPermission = objPermChkr.HasAccess("/Apps/SecPage.asp")

' Determine whether the current user has access to the
' security page using a physical path.
blnPermission = objPermChkr.HasAccess( _
                "c:\inetpub\wwwroot\Apps\SecPage.asp")
...[addition code]
' You can then use the results of these tests to determine
' whether or not to create a hyperlink to the restricted
' page
If blnPermission Then
%>
    Congratulations, you have access to the security page.
    <A HREF = "/Apps/SecPage.asp">Security Page</A>
<%
End If
%>
```

Notes

If the file does not exist, the call to HasAccess returns a value of False.

CHAPTER 24

Tools Component

The Tools component is an installable component that provides several useful utility functions to your Active Server Page scripts.

Tools Summary

Properties
> None

Collections
> None

Methods
> FileExists
> PluginExists
> ProcessForm
> Owner
> Random

Events
> None

Accessory Files/Required DLL Files

tools.dll
> The dynamic link library for the Tools component. This DLL is installed by default.

Instantiating the Tools Component

To create an object variable containing an instance of the Tools component, use the CreateObject method of the Server object. The syntax for the CreateObject method is as follows:

```
Set objMyObject = Server.CreateObject(strProgId)
```

where:

- *objMyObject* represents the name of a Tools object.

- *strProgId* represents the programmatic identifier (ProgID) for the Tools component; its ProgID is MSWC.Tools.

Example

```
<%

' The following code uses the CreateObject method of the
' Server object to instantiate a Tools object on
' the server.
Dim objTools

Set objTools = _
    Server.CreateObject("MSWC.Tools")

%>
```

For more details on the use of the CreateObject method see its documentation in Chapter 9, *Server Object.*

Comments/Troubleshooting

The Tools component allows you to call several utility functions easily, but does not provide much flexibility in some cases. The most notable example of this is the ProcessForm method. This method, while excellent in theory, is less useful in practice, since it is not robust enough to use for high-volume sites. This is the case with many of the methods of the Tools component. The PluginExists method is an exception to this, but it only works when writing ASP scripts for the Personal Web Server for Apple computers. Unfortunately, ASP on the Apple platform does not provide the same robust platform (due to the limitations of the ASP implementation, not the platform itself) as ASP written for use in a Microsoft-based operating system platform.

Methods Reference

FileExists   objTools.FileExists(strPath)

The FileExists method, as its name implies, allows you to determine whether a given file exists on the server. This method returns –1 if the file exists and the URL represents a published directory. It returns a 0 otherwise.

Parameters

strPath

The relative URL of the file whose existence you are testing.

Example

```
<HTML>
<HEAD><TITLE>Latest Submitted Stories</TITLE></HEAD>
<BODY>
Below is a link to the latest science fiction story submitted to our
site:<BR>
<%
' This script assumes that elsewhere in the site, users are allowed to '
' submit stories which are then written as a file to a published
directory.

' Check for existence of file first, before writing the link.
Set objTools = Server.CreateObject("MSWC.Tools")
If objTools.FileExists("/userstories/story.html") = -1 Then
%>
<A HREF="/userstories/story.html">Latest Science Fiction Story</A>
<%
Else
%>
Sorry. No story available.
<%
End If
%>
</BODY>
</HTML>
```

Notes

This method is useful if you need to create a link on the fly to a file that may or may not exist. For example, if your website allows users to add content (through some template or otherwise) and that content is stored on the server, you may want to determine whether that file exists before creating a link to it.

Note that this method is functionally equivalent to the FileExists method of the FileSystemObject component.

Owner   objTools.Owner()

The Owner method returns −1 if the name and password submitted in the HTTP request header matches that of the site's administrator. Otherwise Owner returns 0.

Parameters

None.

Example

```
<HTML>
<HEAD><TITLE>Site Tools</TITLE></HEAD>
<BODY>
```

```
Please select one of the following tools:<BR>
<A HREF="update.asp">Update Page</A>
<A HREF="comments.asp">Comments Page</A>
<A HREF="search.asp">Search Page</A>
<%
Dim objTools
Set objTools = Server.CreateObject("MSWC.Tools")

' Determine if the current user is the site administrator.
' If so, display a link to the admin tools.
If objTools.Owner = -1 Then
%>
<A HREF="admin.asp">Admin Page</A>
<%
End If
%>
</BODY>
</HTML>
```

Notes

This method is implemented only for users of Personal Web Server for Macintosh. For all other server platforms, this method always returns 0.

PluginExists   objTools.PluginExists(*strPluginName*)

This method allows Macintosh server ASP developers to determine whether a specific server plugin is installed on the server. If it is installed, PluginExists returns −1. If not, PluginExists returns 0. This method always returns 0 on non-Macintosh web servers.

Parameters

strPluginName
> The name of valid Macintosh server plugin.

Example

```
<%
Set objTools = Server.CreateObject("MSWC.Tools")

If objTools.PluginExists("MyPlugin") Then
%>

<%
End If
%>
```

ProcessForm   objTools.ProcessForm(*strOutputURL,*
                                   strTemplateURL, [strInsertionPoint])

The ProcessForm method of the Tools component allows you to generate a file on your server in response to data entered by a client through an HTML form. The format of the output file is retrieved at runtime by using a template file. The name of the template file and the name of the new output file are provided in the call to the method.

Parameters

strOutputURL

> The relative URL of the file to which ProcessForm will write its resulting text after processing an HTML form using the template specified in the *strTemplateURL* argument.

strTemplateURL

> The relative URL of the file ProcessForm will use to create the output file. This file contains the script for processing the HTML form contents.

strInsertionPoint

> Optional. The insertion point within the file specified by the *strOutputURL* argument where the ProcessForm will insert the results of its processing. This argument has not been implemented in the most recent edition of the Tools component and will be ignored if supplied.

Example

```
****** BEGIN INITIAL CLIENT FORM *******
<HTML>
<HEAD><TITLE>Form to Process</TITLE></HEAD>
<BODY>

<H1>ProServices Employee Suggestion Box</H1>
<FORM ACTION="ProcessForm.asp" METHOD="POST">
Suggestion Category:
<SELECT NAME="lstCategory">
        <OPTION SELECTED VALUE="all">General
        <OPTION VALUE="projmgmt">Project Mgmt
</SELECT><BR>
First Name: <INPUT TYPE="TEXT" NAME="txtFName"><BR>
Last Name: <INPUT TYPE="TEXT" NAME="txtLName"><BR>
Email Address: <INPUT TYPE="TEXT" NAME="txtEmailAddress"><BR>
Suggestion: <INPUT TYPE="TEXT" NAME="txtSuggestion" SIZE=50></TEXT><BR>
<INPUT TYPE="SUBMIT">
</FORM>

</BODY>
</HTML>
****** END INITIAL CLIENT FORM *******


****** BEGIN FORM PROCESSING SCRIPT *******
<HTML>
<HEAD><TITLE>Form Processed</TITLE></HEAD>
<BODY>
<%
Dim objTools
Set objTools = Server.CreateObject("MSWC.Tools")

If Request.Form("lstCategory") = "all" Then
      objTools.ProcessForm "OutputAll.asp", "ProcessForm_TemplateAll.asp"
```

```
Else
      objTools.ProcessForm "OutputPM.asp", "ProcessForm_TemplateProjMgmt.
asp"
End If
%>
Your form's contents have been processed.
</BODY>
</HTML>
****** END FORM PROCESSING SCRIPT *******


****** BEGIN GENERAL TEMPLATE *******
<HTML>
<HEAD><TITLE>Generated Output File</TITLE></HEAD>
<BODY>

<%
' This ASP code is NOT executed until the final output
' file is executed in response to a client request for
' the page.
Dim strFirstName
Dim strLastName
Dim strSuggestion

' The script in the next three lines containing the value
' for the variable initialization IS executed when the
' ProcessForm method of the Tools component is executed.
strFirstName = "<%% = Request.Form("txtFName") %%>"
strLastName = "<%% = Request.Form("txtLName") %%>"
strSuggestion = "<%% = Request.Form("txtSuggestion") %%>"

' This ASP code is NOT executed until the final output
' file is executed in response to a client request for
' the page.
Response.Write "<H1>General Suggestion</H1>"
Response.Write strFirstName & " " & strLastName
Response.Write " suggested:<BR>"
Response.Write strSuggestion & "<BR><BR>"
%>

</BODY>
</HTML>
****** END GENERAL TEMPLATE *******


****** BEGIN PROJ MGMT TEMPLATE *******
<HTML>
<HEAD><TITLE>Generated Output File</TITLE></HEAD>
<BODY>

<%
' This ASP code is NOT executed until the final output
' file is executed in response to a client request for
' the page.
```

Tools

```
Dim strFirstName
Dim strLastName
Dim strSuggestion


' The script in the next three lines containing the value
' for the variable initialization IS executed when the
' ProcessForm method of the Tools component is executed.
strFirstName = "<%% = Request.Form("txtFName") %%>"
strLastName = "<%% = Request.Form("txtLName") %%>"
strSuggestion = "<%% = Request.Form("txtSuggestion") %%>"


' This ASP code is NOT executed until the final output
' file is executed in response to a client request for
' the page.
Response.Write "<H1>Project Management Suggestion</H1>"
Response.Write strFirstName & " " & strLastName
Response.Write " suggested:<BR>"
Response.Write strSuggestion & "<BR><BR>"
%>


</BODY>
</HTML>
****** END PROJ MGMT TEMPLATE *******
```

Notes

In the preceding example, there is an HTML form page that allows users to enter a comment on either the company in general or the project management team specifically. Once submitted, the form's contents are processed using the Tools component's ProcessForm method and the appropriate template file.

In most cases, the use of a database to store user entries is more efficient than using the ProcessForm and text files on the server. However, the ProcessForm method does have its uses. For example, you could create an admin tool using the ProcessForm method of the Tools component that would let you update the contents of a specific web page online. This would allow you to update your web content for a specific page easily over the web using without the need of a complex content management system or a database.

Finally, it is important to stress the point made earlier about the *strInsertionPoint* argument to the ProcessForm method. This argument is completely ignored. The consequence of this is that your output file is overwritten every time, making the ProcessForm method useful only in very limited circumstances, such as the content control example described previously.

Random   objTools.Random( )

This method returns a random integer between –32768 and 32767.

Example

```
<%
' Generate a random integer between 0 and 100 using the Tools Component's
' Random function and the VBScript Mod function.
```

```
Dim objTools
Dim intRndm

Set objTools = Server.CreateObject("MSWC.Tools")
intRndm = (objTools.Random() Mod 101)
%>
```

Notes

The VBScript *Rnd* function is used more often than the Tools component's Random method, since *Rnd* is more flexible.

PART IV

Appendixes

The appendixes treat such diverse topics as migrating from CGI to WinCGI to ASP, configuring IIS for ASP applications, and running ASP applications on web servers other than Microsoft's Internet Information Server. The appendixes consist of the following:

Appendix A, *ASP Intrinsic Objects Member Summary*

Appendix B, *Converting CGI/WinCGI Applications into ASP Applications*

Appendix C, *ASP on Alternative Platforms*

Appendix D, *Configuration of ASP Applications on IIS*

APPENDIX A

ASP Intrinsic Objects Member Summary

The following table lists the collections, properties, methods, and events of the seven ASP built-in objects, along with the object to which they apply and the chapter in which they are documented:

Member	Object(s)	Chapter(s)
Abandon method	Session	10
AddHeader method	Response	8
AppendToLog method	Response	8
ASPCode property	ASPError	5
ASPDescription property	ASPError	5
BinaryRead method	Request	7
BinaryWrite method	Response	8
Buffer property	Response	8
CacheControl property	Response	8
Category property	ASPError	5
Charset property	Response	8
Clear method	Response	8
ClientCertificate collection	Request	7
CodePage property	Session	10
Column property	ASPError	5
Contents collection	Application, Session	4, 10
ContentType property	Response	8
Cookies collection	Request, Response	7, 8
CreateObject method	Server	9
Description property	ASPError	5

Member	Object(s)	Chapter(s)
End method	Response	8
Execute method	Server	9
Expires property	Response	8
ExpiresAbsolute property	Response	8
File property	ASPError	5
Flush method	Response	8
Form collection	Request	7
GetLastError method	Server	9
HTMLEncode method	Server	9
IsClientConnected property	Response	8
LCID property	Session	10
Line property	ASPError	5
Lock method	Application	4
MapPath method	Server	9
Number property	ASPError	5
OnEnd event	Application, Session	4, 10
OnStart event	Application, Session	4, 10
OnTransactionAbort event	ObjectContext	6
OnTransactionCommit event	ObjectContext	6
PICS property	Response	8
QueryString collection	Request	7
Redirect method	Response	8
ScriptTimeout property	Server	9
ServerVariables collection	Request	7
SessionID property	Session	10
SetAbort method	ObjectContext	6
SetComplete method	ObjectContext	6
Source property	ASPError	5
StaticObjects collection	Application, Session	4, 10
Status property	Response	8
Timeout property	Session	10
TotalBytes property	Request	7
Transfer method	Server	9
Unlock method	Application	4
URLEncode method	Server	9
Write method	Response	8

All ASP collection objects have the following standard members:

Member	Description
Count	Returns the number of items in the collection
Item	Allows you to reference a particular item in the collection either by its key or by its ordinal position
Key	Allows you to retrieve and in some cases to change the key value of an item at a particular ordinal position in the collection

In addition, the Contents collection of the Application and Session objects has the following additional members:

Member	Description	Chapter
Remove	Removes an item from the collection	4
RemoveAll	Removes all items from the collection	4

APPENDIX B

Converting CGI/WinCGI Applications into ASP Applications

Complete coverage of how to convert a CGI application (standard or WinCGI) would require an entire book to itself. However, this appendix should provide a starting point for your conversion.

The CGI Application

In this example, I will convert a simple CGI application to an ASP. I have written this application in two forms: one version in Perl and one in Visual Basic. Each version provides exactly the same functionality. It retrieves the user's name and programming language preference from a posted HTML form, then saves this information into a Microsoft Access database using ActiveX Data Objects. Figure B-1 shows the CGI application in a browser window.

Figure B-1: The HTML interface for our CGI application

The HTML code for the form in Figure B-1 is straightforward and is shown in Example B-1.

Example B-1: HTML Source for the Sample CGI Application

```
<HTML>
<HEAD>
<TITLE>Sample Form</TITLE>
</HEAD>
<BODY bgcolor = #cccccc>
<form action="XXXXXXXX SEE BELOW XXXXXXXXXX" method="POST">
<center>
<h2>Welcome to the Programming Language Survey.</h2>
<h3>Please enter your name and your programming language preference below.</
h3>
<TABLE WIDTH = 40%>
    <TR VALIGN = TOP>
        <TD WIDTH = 40%>
            <font face="Arial" size="+2">Name:</font>
        </td>
        <TD WIDTH = 60%>
            <input type="Text" name="UsrName" size="20"
                maxlength="80"><BR><BR>
        </TD>
    </tr>
    <TR VALIGN = TOP>
        <TD WIDTH = 40%>
            <font face="Arial" size="+2">Language:</font>
        </td>
        <TD WIDTH = 60%>
            <select name="ProgLang">
                <option value="Perl">Perl
                <option value="Python">Python
                <option value="Visual Basic">Visual Basic
            </select>
        </TD>
    </tr>
</TABLE>
<BR><BR>
<input type="Submit" name="Submit" value="Submit Form" align="MIDDLE">
</form>
</center>

</BODY>
</HTML>
```

I will use the same form with three separate values for the <FORM> tag's ACTION attribute, as shown in Table B-1.

Table B-1: Values for the ACTION Attribute

Server Method	ACTION Parameter Value	Description
CGI/Perl	*/cgi-shl/LangForm/Post_CGI.cgi*	CGI script written in Perl 5
CGI/VB	*/cgi-win/VB_CGI_32.exe*	Visual Basic executable written using CGI32.BAS (from O'Reilly's CGI framework for Visual Basic programmers)
ASP	*/LangPref/SavePref.ASP*	Active Server Pages version

The Microsoft Access database consists of one table, `LangPrefStorage`, with two text fields, `Name` and `LangPref`. The database's data source name (DSN) in this example is `LangPref`. All three server solutions will perform the same steps to add the submitted information to the database:

1. Instantiate an ADO connection to the database.

2. Construct a `SQL INSERT` statement based on the name and language preference submitted by the user (retrieved from the server).

3. Execute the SQL statement.

4. Return a "Thank You" message in an HTML page back to the user, which will allow him to return to the form.

The Perl CGI Script

Our first CGI script, which is shown in Example B-2, is written in Perl. I used ActivePerl (from *http://www.ActiveState.com*) on a Windows 2000 Workstation machine. The Perl 5 CGI script is very straightforward. Read the comments (those lines starting with a # character) to understand the code line by line.

Example B-2: The Perl Version of the CGI Script

```
# Use the CGI and OLE perl modules.
use CGI qw(:standard);
use OLE;

# Instantiate an ADO Connection object and open the database.
$conn = CreateObject OLE "ADODB.Connection" || die "CreateObject: $!";
$conn->Open('LangPref');

# Retrieve the Name and Language Preference of the user.
$Name = param("UsrName");
$LangPref = param("ProgLang");

# Construct the SQL INSERT statement.
$sql = "INSERT INTO LangPrefStorage (Name, LangPref) VALUES (\'$Name\', \
'$LangPref\')";

# Execute the SQL INSERT statement and close the ADO connection.
$conn->Execute($sql);
$conn->Close();
```

Example B-2: The Perl Version of the CGI Script (continued)

```
# Print out the "Thank You" message in an HTML
# form to the user.
print header,start_html("Language Preference Storage"),h1("Thank you, $Name.
");
print p("Click <A HREF = '/~wsdocs/langform/formsample.htm'>here</a> to reset
the form.<BR>");
print end_html;
```

Once the user has entered her name and programming language preference and clicked on the Submit button, this script will save the information to the database and send the response shown in Figure B-2 back to the user.

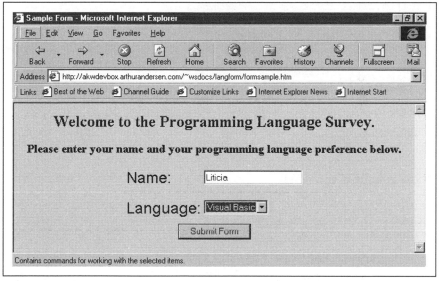

Figure B-2: The CGI reply

The Perl code is straightforward. First the script imports code from the OLE and CGI Perl modules. The Active Data Object (ADO) connection object is created and initialized. Next, the user's input is retrieved from the submitted HTTP request. The information is inserted into the database. Finally, the response is written back to the user.

The Visual Basic CGI Application

I wrote the second CGI application using Microsoft Visual Basic 6.0. I used O'Reilly's Windows CGI framework for Visual Basic Programmers (which comes with O'Reilly's WebSite Pro 2.0), which is defined by the *CGI32.BAS* code module. This code module does much of the CGI work for you by retrieving all of the CGI environment variables (among other things) from the temporary file created on the server when the user submits the HTML form. For more information on the WinCGI specification or on O'Reilly's CGI framework for Visual Basic programmers, see the "Creating Dynamic Content" section of the documentation for

WebSite Pro 2.0. For more information on CGI variables (and their mapping to ASP variables), see the second half of this appendix.

Example B-3 shows the Visual Basic code for our CGI application.

Example B-3: The Visual Basic Version of the CGI Script

```
' +------------------------------------+
' | Force variable declarations.       |
' +------------------------------------+
Option Explicit
Sub Inter_Main()

        ' +-------------------------------------+
        ' | If a user of the web server machine |
        ' | inadvertently attempts to run       |
        ' | this program as a standalone        |
        ' | application, let them know it is a  |
        ' | CGI app.                            |
        ' +-------------------------------------+
        MsgBox "This is a Windows CGI program."

End Sub

Sub CGI_Main()

        ' +-------------------------------------+
        ' | Local variable declarations.        |
        ' +-------------------------------------+
        Dim strUserName As String
        Dim strPrefLang As String
        Dim adoCon As Object
        Dim strSQL As String

        ' +-------------------------------------+
        ' | Create the ADO Connection object.   |
        ' +-------------------------------------+
        Set adoCon = CreateObject("ADODB.Connection")
        adoCon.Open "LangPref"

        ' +-------------------------------------+
        ' | Retrieve the name and preference    |
        ' | field values from the posted form.  |
        ' +-------------------------------------+
        strUserName = GetSmallField("UsrName")
        strPrefLang = GetSmallField("ProgLang")

        ' +-------------------------------------+
        ' | Create the INSERT statement.        |
        ' +-------------------------------------+
        strSQL = "INSERT INTO LangPrefStorage (Name, "
        strSQL = strSQL & "LangPref) VALUES ('"
        strSQL = strSQL & strUserName & "', '"
        strSQL = strSQL & strPrefLang & "')"
```

```
' +-------------------------------------+
' | Execute the SQL statement and close |
' | the ADO connection.                 |
' +-------------------------------------+
adoCon.Execute strSQL
adoCon.Close


' +-------------------------------------+
' | Send the HTTP request header and    |
' | HTML page back to the client.       |
' +-------------------------------------+
Send ("Content-type: text/html")
Send ("")
Send ("<HTML><HEAD><TITLE>")
Send ("Language Preference Storage</TITLE>")
Send ("</HEAD><BODY>")
Send ("<H1>Thank you, " & strUserName & ".</H1>")
Send ("Click <A HREF = _
'/~wsdocs/langform/formsample.htm'>here</a> to reset the form.<BR>")
Send ("</BODY></HTML>")

End Sub
```

Even if you are not familiar with Visual Basic, this code is very simple. The `Option Explicit` statement simply forces the developer to declare variables. The *Inter_Main* subroutine is called any time a user mistakenly attempts to execute this application in a standalone context (i.e., not as a CGI application). The next code block retrieves the user's submitted information from the temporary file created by the web server (the real work is constructed in the *GetSmallField* function in the *CGI32.BAS* module). Next, the information is stored into the database (for more on the ActiveX Data Objects code, see Chapter 12, *ActiveX Data Objects 2.6*). Finally, the *CGI32.BAS* subroutines for sending HTML back to the client are called to return a response to the user.

The Active Server Pages

The Active Server Pages equivalent to the earlier CGI applications, which is shown in Example B-4, is perhaps the simplest of the three applications. First I'll show you the code, then I'll discuss it a bit.

Example B-4: The ASP Equivalent of the CGI Application

```
<HTML>
<HEAD>
<TITLE>Language Preference Storage</TITLE>
</HEAD>
<BODY>
<%
' +-------------------------------------+
' | Local variable declarations.        |
' +-------------------------------------+
```

```
Dim strUserName
Dim strPrefLang
Dim adoCon
Dim strSQL


' +-------------------------------------+
' | Create the ADO Connection object.   |
' +-------------------------------------+
Set adoCon = Server.CreateObject("ADODB.Connection")
adoCon.Open "LangPref"


' +-------------------------------------+
' | Retrieve the name and preference    |
' | field values from the posted form.  |
' +-------------------------------------+
strUserName = Request.Form("UsrName")
strPrefLang = Request.Form("ProgLang")


' +-------------------------------------+
' | Create the INSERT statement.        |
' +-------------------------------------+
strSQL = "INSERT INTO LangPrefStorage (Name, "
strSQL = strSQL & "LangPref) VALUES ('"
strSQL = strSQL & strUserName & "', '"
strSQL = strSQL & strPrefLang & "')"


' +-------------------------------------+
' | Execute the SQL statement and close |
' | the ADO connection.                 |
' +-------------------------------------+
adoCon.Execute strSQL
adoCon.Close
%>
<H1>Thank you, <%=strUserName%>.</h1>
Click
<A HREF = '/~wsdocs/langform/formsample.htm'>
here</a> to reset the form.<BR>

</BODY>
</HTML>
```

Example B-4 is written using VBScript only because all the code samples in this book are written in VBScript (and because it is relatively easy to read). However, as always with ASP, you can use any scripting language you like.

The ASP equivalent to our CGI application is very similar to the Visual Basic CGI application, with the only significant difference coming in how we retrieve the information from the HTML form. Instead of retrieving the information from a temporary file created by the server (by calling the *GetSmallField* function from the *CGI32.BAS* module), as I did in the VB application, I was able to retrieve the information from the ASP Request object's Form collection. The only other real

---

difference from a code perspective is that the final response display is written as straight HTML in the ASP, whereas we were forced to rely on some functions in the VB application.

Behind the scenes, there are some fundamental differences in how ASP retrieves information. For more on this, see Chapter 1, *Active Server Pages: An Introduction*, and Chapter 2, *Active Server Pages: Server-Side Scripting*.

Converting Environment Variables

CGI applications often make use of information residing in environment variables. These variables contain information about the web server itself or about the HTTP request sent by the client browser. In CGI written in Perl, these variables' values are retrieved from the %ENV associative array. In WinCGI written using O'Reilly's CGI framework for Visual Basic programmers, these values are retrieved from the contents of global variables made available by the *CGI.BAS* or *CGI32.BAS* code modules.

Active Server Pages applications also make use of these variables. In ASP, this information is retrieved from the Request object's ServerVariables collection. Table B-2 will help you convert your CGI environment variables to ASP, while Table B-3 will aid in converting WinCGI to ASP. Note that the general syntax required to retrieve the ASP variable is:

```
varname = Request.ServerVariables("ASP_Variable")
```

Note also that there are other environment-type variables available to ASP applications that are not available to CGI or WinCGI.

Table B-2: Converting CGI Environment Variables to ASP Variables

CGI Environment Variable	ASP Variable	Description
AUTH_TYPE	AUTH_TYPE	Authentication method used to validate user.
CONTENT_LENGTH	CONTENT_LENGTH	Length of the query data (in bytes or number of characters) passed through standard input to the CGI application.
CONTENT_TYPE	CONTENT_TYPE	The media type of the query data (for example "text/html") sent to the CGI application.
DOCUMENT_ROOT	APPL_PHYSICAL_PATH	Directory from which web pages are served. This directory is the root parent for your web site.
GATEWAY_INTERFACE	GATEWAY_INTERFACE	The version of CGI running on your web server.
HTTP_ACCEPT	HTTP_ACCEPT	List of media types the user's browser can accept.

CGI Environment Variable	ASP Variable	Description
HTTP_COOKIE	HTTP_COOKIE	List of cookies on the client machine defined for the particular URL.
HTTP_FROM	HTTP_FROM	Email address of user sending HTTP request (rarely supported).
HTTP_REFERER	HTTP_REFERER	URL of document from which user accesses CGI application.
HTTP_USER_AGENT	HTTP_USER-AGENT	Browser used by user. Note: You must use a hyphen instead of an under-score for this one. See Chapter 6 and the discussion of the ServerVariables collection of the Request object for more details.
PATH_INFO	PATH_INFO	Any extra path information sent with the CGI request.
PATH_TRANSLATED	PATH_TRANSLATED	Physical path represented by PATH_INFO variable.
QUERY_STRING	QUERY_STRING[a]	Query passed to the CGI application. This consists of all character data following the "?" at the end of the URL.
REMOTE_ADDR	REMOTE_ADDR	Remote IP address of the sender of the HTTP request. This could be the address of the user or a proxy server.
REMOTE_HOST	REMOTE_HOST	Remote hostname from which the CGI request is being sent.
REMOTE_IDENT	NA	Username of user making the request.
REMOTE_USER	LOGON_USER	Authenticated name of user sending the request to CGI (if one exists).
REQUEST_METHOD	REQUEST_METHOD	Method used by user's browser in sending CGI request (for example GET, POST, etc.).
SCRIPT_NAME	SCRIPT_NAME	Virtual path of currently executing CGI script.
SERVER_NAME	SERVER_NAME	Server's hostname or IP address.

CGI Environment Variable	ASP Variable	Description
SERVER_PORT	SERVER_PORT	Number of the port on the host on which the server is running.
SERVER_PROTOCOL	SERVER_PROTOCOL	Name/revision of the information protocol by which the CGI request was sent.
SERVER_SOFTWARE	SERVER_SOFTWARE	Name/version information for the web server software.

a A better way to manipulate the information in the QueryString HTTP request information is to use the Request object's QueryString collection. See Chapter 7, *Request Object*, for more details.

Table B-3: Converting WinCGI Environment Variables to ASP Variables

WinCGI Environment Variable	ASP Variable	Description
CGI_AcceptTypes	HTTP_ACCEPT	List of media types the user's browser can accept.
CGI_AuthPass	NA	Password of authenticated user, if supported on the web server.
CGI_AuthRealm	NA	Realm or domain of authorized user, if supported.
CGI_AuthType	AUTH_TYPE	Authentication method used to validate user.
CGI_AuthUser	LOGON_USER	Authenticated name of user sending request to CGI (if one exists)..
CGI_ContentFile	NA	Full pathname of the file created by the web server that contains any attached data (i.e., any POSTed information).
CGI_ContentLength	CONTENT_LENGTH	Total length in bytes or number of characters of the user's CGI request.
CGI_ContentType	CONTENT_TYPE	MIME type of the request data POSTed.
CGI_DebugMode	NA	CGI tracing flag from the web server.
CGI_ExecutablePath	SCRIPT_NAME	Path of CGI application being executed.
CGI_ExtraHeaders	NAa	Any extra HTTP headers sent by the browser.

Table B-3: Converting WinCGI Environment Variables to ASP Variables

WinCGI Environment Variable	ASP Variable	Description
CGI_FormTuples	NA[b]	Name=Value pairs sent in the form data of the CGI request, if any exist.
CGI_From	HTTP_FROM	Email address of user sending HTTP request (rarely supported).
CGI_GMTOffset	NA	Number of seconds +/– from GMT.
CGI_HugeTuples	NA[b]	Large Name=Value pairs in the form data sent with the CGI request.
CGI_LogicalPath	SCRIPT_NAME	Logical path or extra path information for the CGI application being executed.
CGI_NumAcceptTypes	NA[c]	Number of accepted media types of the user's browser.
CGI_NumExtraHeaders	NA[c]	Number of extra HTTP headers sent by the browser.
CGI_NumFormTuples	NA[c]	Number of Name=Value pairs submitted through a form with the CGI request sent by the user.
CGI_NumHugeTuples	NA[c]	Number of large Name=Value pairs in the form data sent with the CGI request.
CGI_OutputFile	NA	Full pathname of the file in which the web server expects to find the results of the CGI application's execution.
CGI_PhysicalPath	NA[d]	Physical path represented by the logical path.
CGI_QueryString	QUERY_STRING	Query passed to the CGI application. This consists of all character data following the "?" at the end of the URL.
CGI_Referer	HTTP_REFERER	URL of document from which user accesses CGI application.

Table B-3: Converting WinCGI Environment Variables to ASP Variables

WinCGI Environment Variable	ASP Variable	Description
CGI_RemoteAddr	REMOTE_ADDR	Remote IP address of the sender of the HTTP request. This could be the address of the user or a proxy server.
CGI_RemoteHost	REMOTE_HOST	Remote hostname from which the CGI request is being sent.
CGI_RequestMethod	REQUEST_METHOD	Method used by user's browser in sending CGI request (for example GET, POST, etc).
CGI_RequestProtocol	SERVER_PROTOCOL	Name and version of the request protocol used in the query to the CGI application.
CGI_ServerAdmin	NA[e]	Email address of the web server admin, if available.
CGI_ServerName	SERVER_NAME	Server's hostname or IP address.
CGI_ServerPort	SERVER_PORT	Number of the port on the host on which the server is running.
CGI_ServerSoftware	SERVER_SOFTWARE	Name and version of the web scrver software.
CGI_Version	GATEWAY_INTERFACE	Version of the CGI running on the web server.

[a] You can retrieve all HTTP headers sent by the user with ALL_HTTP.

[b] You can retrieve this information from the Form collection of the Request object. See Chapter 7 for more details.

[c] You can retrieve this information programmatically.

[d] You can derive this using the Server object's MapPath method in conjunction with the Request.ServerVariables ("SCRIPT_NAME") variable. See Chapter 9, *Server Object*, for more information on the MapPath method.

[e] You could use the MyInfo component to define a similar property. See Chapter 21, *MyInfo Component*, for more details.

APPENDIX C

ASP on Alternative Platforms

Throughout this book, I have discussed ASP in terms of its use on Microsoft web servers (Internet Information Server, Peer Web Services, and Personal Web Server) using servers running Microsoft operating systems. However, as ASP applications gain in popularity, there is increasing demand for this web application development platform. Several third-party vendors are beginning to answer this demand by providing solutions that range in maturity from beta to full-strength production-quality software.

In this appendix, I will briefly describe the few available options for developing ASP on non-Microsoft platform products.

Chili!ASP from Chili!Soft

Chili!Soft's Chili!ASP product is the most popular alternative environment available for running your ASP applications. It is a functional and syntactic equivalent of Microsoft's Active Server part of IIS, allowing developers to build ASP applications that run on many web servers on both Windows NT and Sun Solaris. See Table C-1 for details. Chili!Soft is also beginning development of ASP 3.0 support.

Table C-1: Platforms Supported by Chili!ASP

Operating System	Web Server	Status
Windows NT 4.0, SP3	Apache 1.3.4, 1.3.6, 1.3.9, 1.3.11	Available
	Netscape (iPlanet) Enterprise 3.51, 3.6, 4.0 Netscape FastTrack 3.01	Available
	O'Reilly Website Pro	Available
Sun Solaris 2.5.1, 2.6, 2.7	Netscape Enterprise 3.51, 3.6, 4.0 Netscape FastTrack 3.0	Available

Table C-1: Platforms Supported by Chili!ASP (continued)

Operating System	Web Server	Status
IBM AIX 4.3.1, 4.3.2, 4.3.3	Apache 1.2.6 (Solaris 2.5.1 and 2.6 only) 1.3.3, 1.3.4, 1.3.6, 1.3.9 (Solaris 2.5.1 and 2.6 only)	Available
	Apache 1.2.6, 1.3.3, 1.3.4, 1.3.6, 1.3.9	Available
	Netscape (iPlanet) Enterprise 3.51, 3.6, 4.0 Netscape FastTrack 3.01	Available
	IBM HTTP Server 1.3.3.1	Available
	Lotus Domino Go 4.6	Available
HP-UX 11.0	Apache 1.3.6, 1.3.9	Available
	Netscape (iPlanet) Enterprise 4.0, SP2	Available
RedHat Linux 6.0, 6.1	Apache 1.2.6, 1.3.3, 1.3.4, 1.3.9, 1.3.11	Available

Comments

Chili!Soft's implementation of ASP is the most mature of the non-Microsoft alternatives. My experience with their products was good. The products installed as their instructions suggested they would, and I was able to write for my Windows NT server and then run the same code on another platform.

Chili!Soft's Chili!ASP is a complete production-quality ASP solution for large firms looking to write ASP on high-volume servers. However, if you have only a small number of users or a small bandwidth connection, the cost of Chili!ASP is somewhat prohibitive.

Contact Information

> Chili!Soft
> 2700 Richards Road
> Suite 103
> Bellevue, WA 98005
> Phone: (425) 957-1122
> Fax: (425) 562-9565
> *http://www.chilisoft.com*

Instant ASP (iASP) from Halcyon Software

Halcyon Software's Instant ASP (iASP) is another alternative. Their implementation is less mature than Chili!Soft's, but runs on a very wide range of platforms.

iASP was developed in Java™ as a Java servlet. As such, Halcyon claims, you will be able to use it on most web servers that implement Java runtimes. See Table C-2 for the advertised list of web servers. Furthermore, Halcyon claims that it will provide developers with the capability to use not only ActiveX (including Active Data Objects), but also Enterprise JavaBeans or CORBA-compliant objects. Finally, iASP will also support JavaServer Pages and remote debugging.

Multiplatform ASP

Halcyon's iASP runs on a very wide range of servers, as mentioned above. As such, it is more important to know whether your platform choice has been tested by Halcyon. As this testing is still going on, please refer to Halcyon's documentation for the latest test results. For now, refer to the following URL for an extensive table listing supported platforms:

http://www.halcyonsoft.com/asp-doc/docs/config/main.html

Comments

Building ASP through the use of a Java servlet promises to allow for the most extensive support of platforms. However, adding ASP and Java on the server may result in slow performance under large loads. It is imperative to test any application you write for iASP for the expected user load.

Contact Information

Halcyon Software
50 W San Fernando St. #1015
San Jose, CA 95113
Phone: (408) 998-1998
http://www.halcyonsoft.com

OpenASP from the ActiveScripting Organization

The ActiveScripting Organization, started in August of 1998, is a group within Summit Software Company. This group is constructing Open Source software solutions that will allow developers to host ASP applications on several non-Microsoft web servers. Currently this project's focus is the creation of ASP support for the Apache web server. See Table C-2 for details.

Reviewing the ActiveScripting site in preparation for writing the second edition of this book, there appears to have been little development on OpenASP for non-Win32 platforms since writing the first edition.

Table C-2: Platforms Supported by OpenASP

Operating System	Web Server	Status
Windows NT	Apache 1.3.0 - 1.3.6	Beta
	Netscape (running as NSAPI)	Beta
Sun Solaris	Apache	In development?
Linux	Apache	In development?

Comments

Like many authors at O'Reilly, I'm a big supporter of additions to the free software arena. I'm very excited about OpenASP. Currently, however, this is a very immature product in terms of support for ASP. Table C-3 (from the *readme.txt* file from OpenASP for Apache) reports the level of support for various ASP features.

Table C-3: OpenASP's Support for ASP Functionality

Feature	Supported
ASPError Object	No
ObjectContext Object	No
Request	Partial (collection must be specified)
Request.ClientCertificate	No
Request.QueryString	Yes
Request.Form	Yes
Request.Cookies	Yes
Request.ServerVariables	Yes
Request.TotalBytes	No
Request.BinaryRead	No
Response	Partial
Response.Buffer	Yes
Response.CacheControl	No
Response.Charset	No
Response.ContentType	Yes
Response.Expires	Yes
Response.ExpiresAbsolute	No (almost supported)
Response.IsClientConnected	No
Response.Pics	No
Response.Status	No
Response.AddHeader	Yes
Response.AppendToLog	Yes
Response.BinaryWrite	Yes
Response.Clear	Yes
Response.End	Yes
Response.Flush	Yes
Response.Redirect	Yes
Response.Write	Yes
Server	Partial
Server.CreateObject	Yes
Server.Execute	No
Server.GetLastError	No
Server.HTMLEncode	Yes
Server.MapPath	Yes
Server.ScriptTimeout	No
Server.Transfer	No
Server.URLEncode	Yes
Session	Yes
Session.Abandon	Yes

Table C-3: OpenASP's Support for ASP Functionality (continued)

Feature	Supported
Session.CodePage	No
Session.Contents	Yes
Session.Contents.Remove	No
Session.Contents.RemoveAll	No
Session.LCID	No
Session.SessionID	Yes
Session.StaticObjects	No
Session.Timeout	Yes
Session_OnStart	Yes (though not as part of *GLOBAL.ASA*) [a]
Session_OnEnd	No
Application	Yes
Application.Contents	Yes
Application.Contents.Remove	No
Application.Contents.RemoveAll	No
Application.Lock	Yes
Application.Unlock	Yes
Application.StaticObjects	No
Application_OnStart	Yes (though not as part of *GLOBAL.ASA*) [a]
Application_OnEnd	No
Standard Base Components	No
GLOBAL.ASA	No

[a] Note that OpenASP does not support the *GLOBAL.ASA* file. Handling of the Application_ OnStart and Session_OnStart events must be handled on individual pages currently.

Contact Information

http://www.activescripting.org

APPENDIX D

Configuration of ASP Applications on IIS

To cover all aspects of configuration for Internet Information Server is beyond the scope of this book. However, it is important to understand, at an introductory level, how information for IIS is stored and how to configure your virtual directories for your ASP applications

Microsoft Management Console and the Metabase

Microsoft's Management Console (MMC) allows you to configure and administer several server applications in your enterprise, from SQL Server 7.0 to Site Server to Transaction Server to Internet Information Server. This console application allows you to administer several aspects of your enterprise that previously required you to master several separate applications without a consistent interface. Microsoft's goal is that MMC eventually be used to control all segments of Microsoft BackOffice.

It is important to note, however, that MMC itself is not actually doing anything. MMC is simply a container for administration programs called snap-ins. The interface of the MMC is published, and third parties can write their own snap-ins in addition to those provided by Microsoft.

The snap-in for administration of Internet Information Server is similar to all other snap-ins. Each snap-in consists of two panes (see Figure D-1). The left pane, called the scope pane, displays a hierarchical view of all the items that can be administered by this snap-in. As you would expect, administering high-level items in this pane affects those items located hierarchically below them. For example, if you administer the properties of the web server itself, all the web sites located under it also are affected.

This simplification of IIS administration is not the only thing to change since IIS 3.0. Also changed is the location where information about your web server's administration is stored. In IIS 3.0, this information was stored in the system registry; now it is stored in the metabase.

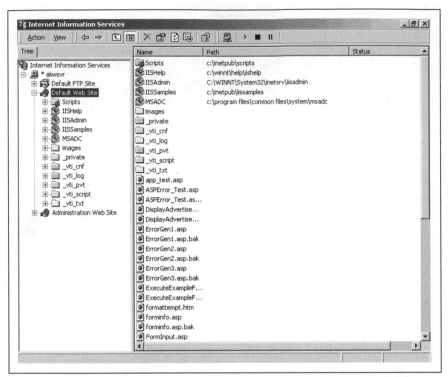

Figure D-1: The Microsoft Management Console

The metabase is a memory-resident data store that was designed to be faster and more flexible than the registry. You use a snap-in called IIS Admin Objects to administer the metabase directly. This makes direct manipulation of the metabase more complex than manipulation of the registry. It is important to note that when you are changing the properties of various items in IIS, you are actually changing IIS Admin Objects behind the scenes. After changes have been made, the IIS snap-in writes them to the metabase. Finally, the metabase is stored to your server's drive upon exiting IIS. It is loaded into memory each time you open the IIS snap-in.

The metabase can also be backed up and restored using a Windows Script Host (WSH) script that is included in the IIS samples directory when you install WSH. You must have WSH installed to use these scripts.

Similar to the registry in architecture, information in the metabase is stored in metabase keys that correspond to the various items in IIS. Each key has corresponding metabase properties. These metabase properties have values that change to reflect your administration of the item in question. Almost all the properties from IIS that were stored in the registry in IIS 3.0 are now stored in the metabase.

For more information on the metabase, visit *http://www.microsoft.com*.

ASP Application Configuration

Before you can create an ASP application, you must create a virtual directory. To create a virtual directory on your web server, follow these steps (see Figure D-2):

1. Right-click the web server on which you wish to create a virtual directory.
2. From the pop-up menu, select New → Virtual Directory.
3. Select a name for your virtual directory.
4. Select a physical directory to which your virtual directory is mapped.
5. Leave the default access (Allow Read Access and Allow Script Access) for ASP applications.

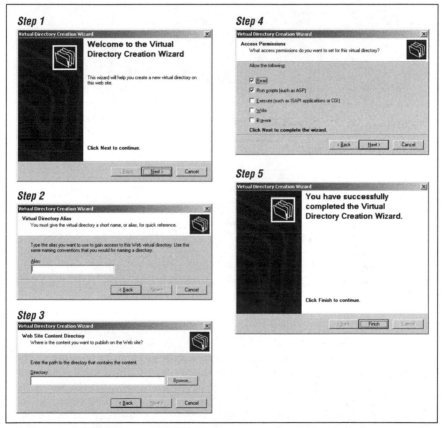

Figure D-2: Configuring a virtual directory

Now that you have created your virtual directory, you must configure it for your ASP application. To do this, right-click your virtual directory and select Properties from the pop-up menu to open the Properties dialog shown in Figure D-3.

From this Virtual Directory tab, you can configure several features of your virtual directory. Before discussing those properties that affect ASP, let's briefly go over what the other tabs on this dialog do. The Documents tab allows you to set the

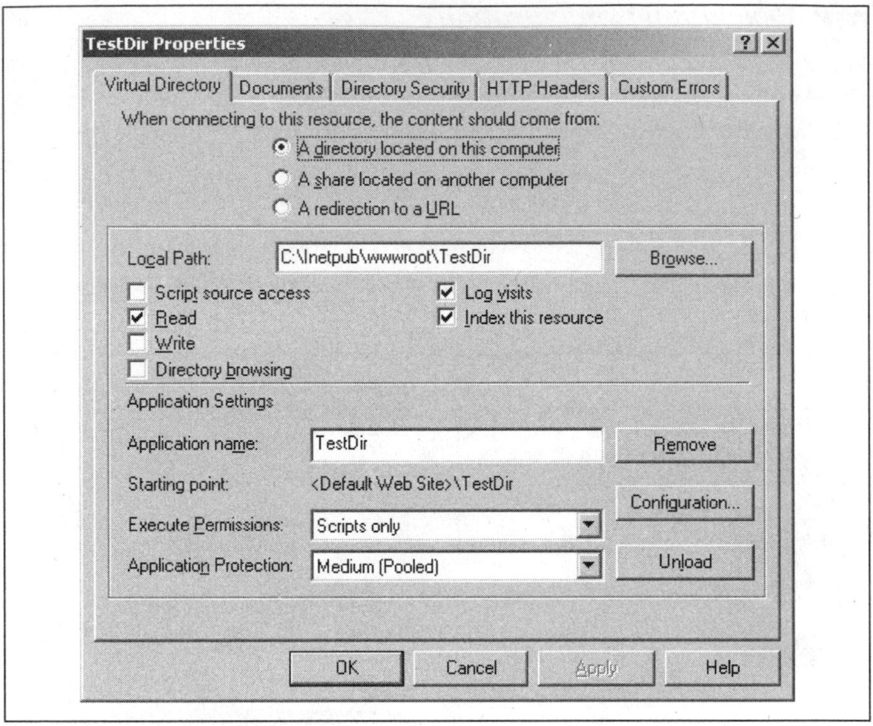

Figure D-3: The Virtual Directory Properties page

default document for your virtual directory and/or enable document footers. The Directory Security tab, as its name implies, allows you to set various security settings for the virtual directory, including NT rights to the underlying physical directory. The HTTP Headers tab allows you to enable content expiration, add custom HTTP headers, edit your Content Rating settings, or edit your MIME Map. Finally the Custom Errors tab allows you to set the paths to custom error files that the web server will use instead of its default files.

Use the Virtual Directory tab shown in Figure D-3 to configure your ASP settings. At the top of the page, you can define where the content for your virtual directory should come. This is straightforward. The bottom allows you to set various properties, such as the physical directory, access (read/write) settings for your directory, logging settings, and whether you want your virtual directory indexed. It also allows you to set the permissions (Read/Script/Execute) for your virtual directory. If you are only going to be using ASP (and not CGI) within your virtual directory, then leave the default setting (Script).

Finally, this page allows you to define whether you want your ASP application to run in the same memory space as the web server (the default) or in a separate memory space. Leaving the default allows for faster execution time for your script, but running your application in its own memory space avoids bringing down the web server if your application commits a critical error. The choice is yours.

Also from the page shown in Figure D-3, you can click on the Configuration button to configure the application options for your application. The first settings that you can configure from this page are the application mappings. The App

Mappings tab, which is shown in Figure D-4, allows you to map file extensions to the ISAPI filters that IIS will use to execute or read that file. For example, for .ASP files, IIS uses *c:\WINNT\SYSTEM32\INETSRV\ASP.DLL*. If you want to use Perl scripts in your virtual directory, you would use this tab to map the Perl file extensions (.PL or .PLX) to your Perl executable or your PerlIS DLL.

Application Configuration

App Mappings | App Options | App Debugging

☑ Cache ISAPI applications

Application Mappings

Extension	Executable Path	Verbs
.htw	C:\WINNT\System32\webhits.dll	GET,HEAD,...
.ida	C:\WINNT\System32\idq.dll	GET,HEAD,...
.idq	C:\WINNT\System32\idq.dll	GET,HEAD,...
.asp	C:\WINNT\System32\inetsrv\asp.dll	GET,HEAD,...
.cer	C:\WINNT\System32\inetsrv\asp.dll	GET,HEAD,...
.cdx	C:\WINNT\System32\inetsrv\asp.dll	GET,HEAD,...
.asa	C:\WINNT\System32\inetsrv\asp.dll	GET,HEAD,...
.htr	C:\WINNT\System32\inetsrv\ism.dll	GET,POST
.idc	C:\WINNT\System32\inetsrv\httpodbc.dll	OPTIONS,G...
.shtm	C:\WINNT\System32\inetsrv\ssinc.dll	GET,POST
.shtml	C:\WINNT\System32\inetsrv\ssinc.dll	GET,POST
.stm	C:\WINNT\System32\inetsrv\ssinc.dll	GET,POST

Add | Edit | Remove

OK | Cancel | Apply | Help

Figure D-4: The App Mappings tab

The App Options tab, which is shown in Figure D-5, allows you to configure various application options. From here, you can enable or disable the use of session state and define how long session information is saved on the server. You can control whether you want all ASP output buffered before it is sent. (See Chapter 8, *Response Object*, for more on buffering.) You can determine whether to allow your ASP applications access to information in parent directories using relative paths (the "../" syntax). If you leave this set to `True`, make sure the parent directories of the current ASP directories have their Execute permission set to `False`. Otherwise, an ASP script could execute an application on the server using this syntax.

This page also allows you to set the default scripting language to any supported language. Not surprisingly, VBScript is the default. Finally, this page allows you to set the ASP script timeout in seconds. If you do not want any script in your virtual directory to be executed on the server for longer than 30 seconds, set this value to 30, for example.

App Debugging, the final tab in the Application Configuration dialog, is shown in Figure D-6; it allows you to set up debugging. If your development environment supports server-side debugging, you can enable it here. The client-side debugging checkbox is ignored by the server. The last option on this page is whether to send

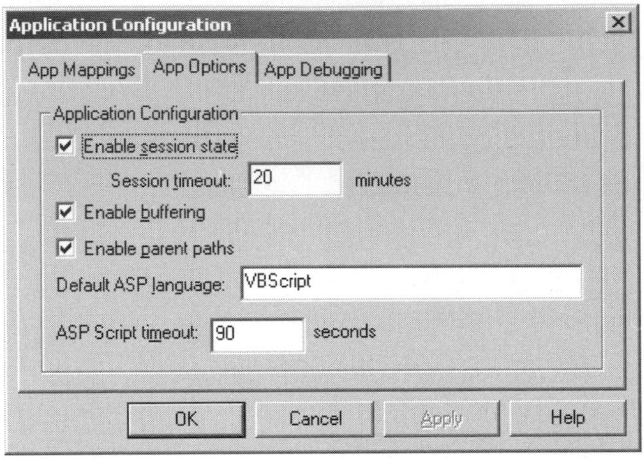

Figure D-5: The App Options tab

your users detailed ASP error information or a custom message. Often, for security reasons, it may be best to create a detailed custom message. Otherwise, your web server could reveal details about the script that you might want to keep secret.

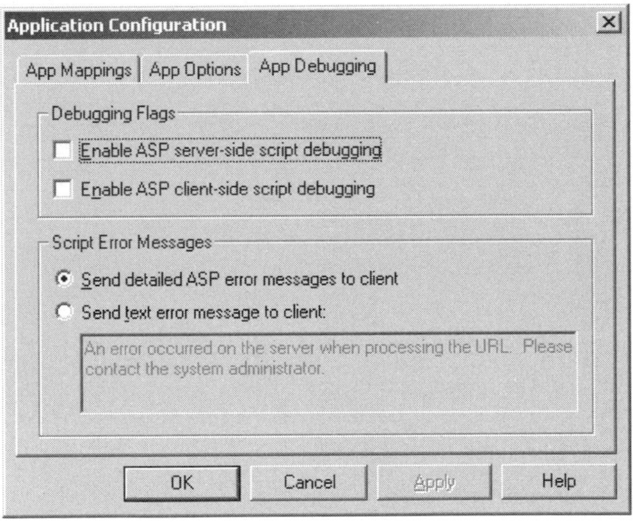

Figure D-6: The App Debugging tab

Unloading ASP Applications

Once you have configured your application, it is important to know how to unload it from IIS. Unloading an application from IIS closes all currently active user sessions and removes all currently instantiated objects (including built-in objects and their properties) from memory. You may want to unload your application for any of the following reasons:

- To reset all Application and Session-scoped variables for all users.

- To remove a custom server component from memory so that it can be replaced by a more recent vesion.

- To close all connections with client machines.

To unload your application, perform the following steps (see Figure D-3):

1. In the Internet Information Services management console, right-click your application and select Properties.

2. In the Virtual Directory tab, in the lower-right corner, click on the Unload button.

You may also want to stop that application to prevent other users from connecting to it. Once unloaded, you can then load your more recent version of your server component or whatever else you wish to do.

ASP Error Handling Configuration

As mentioned in Chapter 5, *ASPError Object*, IIS5.0 and later redirects the user's browser to a custom error page, *500-100.ASP*, any time an error occurs in your application (unless you have inserted into your code the On Error Resume Next statement). The server's redirection (through an internal call to the Transfer method of the Server object) occurs in reaction to a custom application error, which is a specific version of the generic Internal Server Error (HTTP Response Status 500). Similar redirections occur within the server for all errors (see Figure D-7).

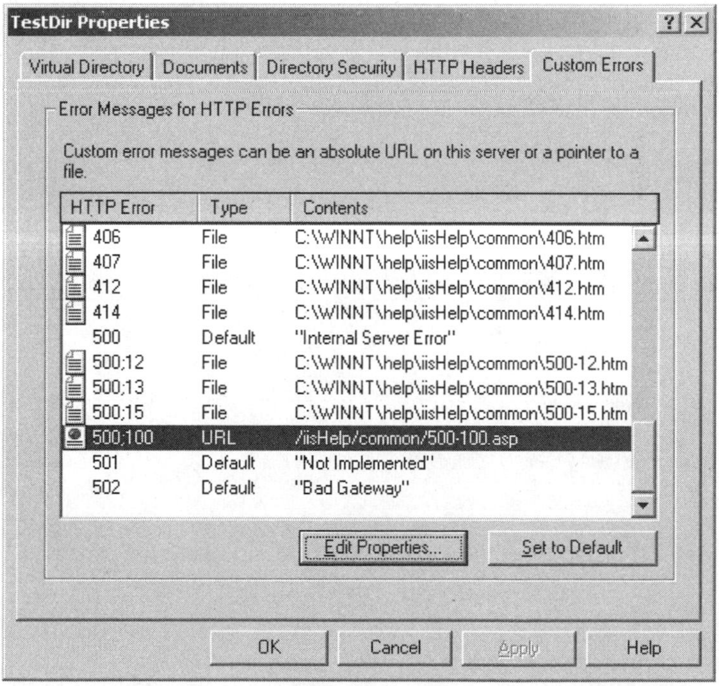

Figure D-7: Custom Errors tab of the Properties page

You can change the page to which IIS transfers execution in response to an error in your application, by performing the following steps:

1. Right-click the application whose error page you want to change and select Properties.

2. Click on the Custom Errors tab of the Properties page (see Figure D-7).

3. Select the error whose Error Page you wish to change and click the Edit Properties button (see Figure D-8).

4. Enter a new URL for the page you wish IIS to execute in response to the selected error type and click on the OK button.

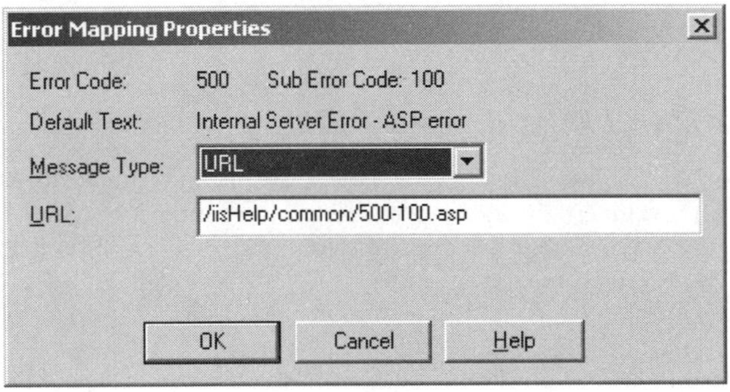

Figure D-8: Error Mapping Properties dialog

Once changed, the server will redirect execution to the selected URL. You can also further customize the server's error display by customizing the file located at the URL you've entered, as detailed in Chapter 5.

Index

ReadFilter method (Logging
  Utility), 395
ReadFromFile method
  (Attachment), 302
reading
  from HTTP requests, 101–102
  text files, 380
ReadLine method (TextStream), 362,
  380
ReadLogRecord method (Logging
  Utility), 395
ReadText method (Stream), 207
reason phrase, 74
recipient information (CDO), 307, 318
Recipient object, 307
Recipients collection (Message), 304,
  307
Recipients property (Message), 304
Record object (ADO), 189, 200
record source, 239
RecordCount property (Recordset), 204,
  236–237
records
  creating new, 241–244
  deleting all, 247–250
  fields, 197
    refreshing, 265–267
  moving pointer within
    recordset, 254–258
  resulting from queries
    based on recordset
      position, 208–210
    counting in recordset, 236–237
    retrieving new recordset, 258–259
    viewing subset of
      recordset, 228–231
  saving changes, 270–272
Recordset object (ADO), 202–208
recordsets, 202–208
  closing, 246
  counting records in, 236–237
  cursor type for creating,
    retrieving, 222–224
  deleting, 247–250
  determining if at end, 212–213,
    226–228
  duplicating, 244–246
  feature support testing, 267–270

moving pointer within, 254–258
opening, 261–264
refreshing all record fields, 265–267
retrieving next, 258–259
returning records based on
  position, 208–210
saving changes, 270–272
source of records in, 239
update modes, 243
viewing record subset, 228–231
RecordType property (Record), 201
Redirect method (Response), 128
redirecting requests, 128
redirection file (Ad Rotator), 274, 283
reexecuting database queries, 264
Referer property (Logging Utility), 389
refreshing record fields, 265–267
relative directory notation, 142
Remote Data Services (RDS), 188
REMOTE_ADDR environment
  variable, 436, 439
REMOTE_ATTR element
  (ServerVariables), 100
REMOTE_HOST element
  (ServerVariables), 100
REMOTE_HOST environment
  variable, 436, 439
REMOTE_IDENT environment
  variable, 436
REMOTE_USER environment
  variable, 436
Remove method
  Contents collection, 35, 37, 38
  Counters component, 353
RemoveAll, Contents collection, 38
RemoveAll method, Contents
  collection, 156–161
Requery method (Recordset), 206, 264
Request object, 10, 76–102
  BinaryRead method, 101–102
  collections reference, 78–101
  HTTP requests and, 74–75
  TotalBytes property, 77
request types, 71
request-line, 73
REQUEST_METHOD element
  (ServerVariables), 100
REQUEST_METHOD environment
  variable, 436, 439

About the Author

Keyton Weissinger is currently the Director for Enterprise Solutions at a start-up company in Atlanta. Before that he worked as the Manager of the Software Architecture Group for MarchFIRST (formerally known as USWeb/CKS and Whittman-Hart). He also spent time at Arthur Andersen, where he was a senior engineer for the worldwide knowledge management system, the KnowledgeSpace.

Colophon

Our look is the result of reader comments, our own experimentation, and feedback from distribution channels. Distinctive covers complement our distinctive approach to technical topics, breathing personality and life into potentially dry subjects.

The animal appearing on the cover of *ASP in a Nutshell, 2nd Edition* is an asp, which is a term applied to various venomous snakes, including the depicted asp viper (*Vipera aspis*) of Europe as well as the Egyptian cobra (*Naja haje*), thought to have been the means of Cleopatra's suicide.

Needing to eat at least 5–6% of their body weight in food per week, European asp vipers hunt by lying in wait for approaching prey. After grabbing and biting a small rodent or other prey, they release it and wait several minutes for it to stop moving; the generally sluggish viper rarely chases prey. Vipers know their home territory very well, which allows quick escape from their asp-kicking natural enemies, serpent eagles and hedgehogs. This trick hasn't helped them escape from their greatest threat, the expansion of human civilization, which frequently wipes out large sections of their territory.

The chemical composition of asp viper venom can vary from one population to the next, hampering initial antivenin development until 1896, but few viper bite fatalities occur in Europe today.

Jeffrey Holcomb was the production editor for *ASP in a Nutshell, 2nd Edition*. Claire-marie Fisher O'Leary was the copyeditor. Nancy Kotary was the production manager, providing production support and quality control. Maeve O'Meara also provided production support. Mike Sierra provided tools support. Brenda Miller wrote the index.

Edie Freedman designed the cover of this book using a 19th-century engraving from the Dover Pictorial Archive. Emma Colby produced the cover layout with Quark-XPress 4.1 using the ITC Garamond font. Whenever possible, our books use RepKover™, a durable and flexible lay-flat binding. If the page count exceeds RepKover's limit, perfect binding is used.

Alicia Cech and David Futato designed the inside layout, based on a series design by Nancy Priest. Mike Sierra implemented the design in FrameMaker 5.5.6. The text and heading fonts are ITC Garamond Light and Garamond Book. The illustrations that appear in the book were created in Macromedia Freehand 8.0 and screen shots were created in Adobe Photoshop 5.0 by Robert Romano and Rhon Porter. This colophon was written by Nancy Kotary.

More Titles from O'Reilly

In a Nutshell Quick References

VB & VBA in a Nutshell: The Languages

By Paul Lomax
1st Edition October 1998
656 pages, ISBN 1-56592-358-8

For Visual Basic and VBA programmers, this book boils down the essentials of the VB and VBA languages into a single volume, including undocumented and little documented areas essential to everyday programming. The convenient alphabetical reference to all functions, procedures, statements, and keywords allows VB and VBA programmers to use this book both as a standard reference guide to the language and as a tool for troubleshooting and identifying programming problems.

Visual Basic Controls in a Nutshell

By Evan S. Dictor
1st Edition July 1999
762 pages, ISBN 1-56592-294-8

This quick reference covers one of the crucial elements of Visual Basic: its controls, and their numerous properties, events, and methods. It provides a step-by-step list of procedures for using each major control and contains a detailed reference to all properties, methods, and events. Written by an experienced Visual Basic programmer, it helps to make painless what can sometimes be an arduous job of programming Visual Basic.

Microsoft Exchange Server in a Nutshell

By Mitch Tulloch
1st Edition April 1999
404 pages, ISBN 1-56592-601-3

This resource guides experienced sysadmins through implementing and configuring Microsoft Exchange Server 5.5, whether they're setting up a single Exchange server or a multisite rollout with connectivity to foreign mail systems. The heart of the book is an alphabetical reference for the Exchange directory objects, the GUI tools, and the command-line tools.

Windows 98 in a Nutshell

By Tim O'Reilly, Troy Mott & Walter Glenn
1st Edition August 1999
642 pages, ISBN 1-56592-486-X

From the authors of the bestselling *Windows 95 in a Nutshell* comes this easy-to-use quick reference for all serious users of Windows 98. It summarizes differences between Windows 95 and Windows 98, covers almost every Windows 98 command and utility available, gives advice for using the Registry, includes short-hand instructions on many important Win98 tasks, and much more.

Windows NT in a Nutshell

By Eric Pearce
1st Edition June 1997
364 pages, ISBN 1-56592-251-4

Anyone who installs Windows NT, creates a user, or adds a printer is an NT system administrator (whether they realize it or not). This book features a new tagged callout approach to documenting the 4.0 GUI as well as real-life examples of command usage and strategies for problem solving, with an emphasis on networking. *Windows NT in a Nutshell* will be as useful to the single-system home user as it will be to the administrator of a 1,000-node corporate network.

Windows 95 in a Nutshell

By Tim O'Reilly & Troy Mott
1st Edition June 1998
528 pages, ISBN 1-56592-316-2

A comprehensive, compact reference that systematically unveils what serious users of Windows 95 will find interesting and useful, capturing little known details of the operating system in a consistent reference format.

O'REILLY®

TO ORDER: **800-998-9938** • **order@oreilly.com** • **http://www.oreilly.com/**
OUR PRODUCTS ARE AVAILABLE AT A BOOKSTORE OR SOFTWARE STORE NEAR YOU.
FOR INFORMATION: **800-998-9938** • **707-829-0515** • **info@oreilly.com**

In a Nutshell Quick References

UML in a Nutshell

By Sinan Si Alhir
1st Edition September 1998
290 pages, ISBN 1-56592-448-7

The Unified Modeling Language (UML), for the first time in the history of systems engineering, gives practitioners a common language. This concise quick reference explains how to use each component of the language, including its extension mechanisms and the Object Constraint Language (OCL). A tutorial with realistic examples brings those new to the UML quickly up to speed.

How to stay in touch with O'Reilly

1. Visit Our Award-Winning Web Site

http://www.oreilly.com/

★ "Top 100 Sites on the Web" —*PC Magazine*
★ "Top 5% Web sites" —*Point Communications*
★ "3-Star site" —*The McKinley Group*

Our web site contains a library of comprehensive product information (including book excerpts and tables of contents), downloadable software, background articles, interviews with technology leaders, links to relevant sites, book cover art, and more. File us in your Bookmarks or Hotlist!

2. Join Our Email Mailing Lists

New Product Releases
To receive automatic email with brief descriptions of all new O'Reilly products as they are released, send email to:
listproc@online.oreilly.com
Put the following information in the first line of your message (*not* in the Subject field):
subscribe oreilly-news

O'Reilly Events
If you'd also like us to send information about trade show events, special promotions, and other O'Reilly events, send email to:
listproc@online.oreilly.com
Put the following information in the first line of your message (*not* in the Subject field):
subscribe oreilly-events

3. Get Examples from Our Books via FTP

There are two ways to access an archive of example files from our books:

Regular FTP
* ftp to:
  ftp.oreilly.com
  (login: anonymous
  password: your email address)
* Point your web browser to:
  ftp://ftp.oreilly.com/

FTPMAIL
* Send an email message to:
  ftpmail@online.oreilly.com
  (Write "help" in the message body)

4. Contact Us via Email

order@oreilly.com
To place a book or software order online. Good for North American and international customers.

subscriptions@oreilly.com
To place an order for any of our newsletters or periodicals.

books@oreilly.com
General questions about any of our books.

software@oreilly.com
For general questions and product information about our software. Check out O'Reilly Software Online at **http://software.oreilly.com/** for software and technical support information. Registered O'Reilly software users send your questions to: **website-support@oreilly.com**

cs@oreilly.com
For answers to problems regarding your order or our products.

booktech@oreilly.com
For book content technical questions or corrections.

proposals@oreilly.com
To submit new book or software proposals to our editors and product managers.

international@oreilly.com
For information about our international distributors or translation queries. For a list of our distributors outside of North America check out:
http://www.oreilly.com/www/order/country.html

5. Work with Us

Check out our website for current employment opportunites:
www.jobs@oreilly.com
Click on "Work with Us"

O'Reilly & Associates, Inc.
101 Morris Street, Sebastopol, CA 95472 USA
TEL   707-829-0515 or 800-998-9938
        (6am to 5pm PST)
FAX   707-829-0104

International Distributors

UK, EUROPE, MIDDLE EAST AND AFRICA (EXCEPT FRANCE, GERMANY, AUSTRIA, SWITZERLAND, LUXEMBOURG, LIECHTENSTEIN, AND EASTERN EUROPE)

INQUIRIES
O'Reilly UK Limited
4 Castle Street
Farnham
Surrey, GU9 7HS
United Kingdom
Telephone: 44-1252-711776
Fax: 44-1252-734211
Email: information@oreilly.co.uk

ORDERS
Wiley Distribution Services Ltd.
1 Oldlands Way
Bognor Regis
West Sussex PO22 9SA
United Kingdom
Telephone: 44-1243-779777
Fax: 44-1243-820250
Email: cs-books@wiley.co.uk

FRANCE

INQUIRIES
Éditions O'Reilly
18 rue Séguier
75006 Paris, France
Tel: 33-1-40-51-52-30
Fax: 33-1-40-51-52-31
Email: france@editions-oreilly.fr

ORDERS
GEODIF
61, Bd Saint-Germain
75240 Paris Cedex 05, France
Tel: 33-1-44-41-46-16 (French books)
Tel: 33-1-44-41-11-87 (English books)
Fax: 33-1-44-41-11-44
Email: distribution@eyrolles.com

GERMANY, SWITZERLAND, AUSTRIA, EASTERN EUROPE, LUXEMBOURG, AND LIECHTENSTEIN

INQUIRIES & ORDERS
O'Reilly Verlag
Balthasarstr. 81
D-50670 Köln
Germany
Telephone: 49-221-973160-91
Fax: 49-221-973160-8
Email: anfragen@oreilly.de (inquiries)
Email: order@oreilly.de (orders)

CANADA (FRENCH LANGUAGE BOOKS)

Les Éditions Flammarion ltée
375, Avenue Laurier Ouest
Montréal (Québec) H2V 2K3
Tel: 00-1-514-277-8807
Fax: 00-1-514-278-2085
Email: info@flammarion.qc.ca

HONG KONG

City Discount Subscription Service, Ltd.
Unit D, 3rd Floor, Yan's Tower
27 Wong Chuk Hang Road
Aberdeen, Hong Kong
Tel: 852-2580-3539
Fax: 852-2580-6463
Email: citydis@ppn.com.hk

KOREA

Hanbit Media, Inc.
Chungmu Bldg. 201
Yonnam-dong 568-33
Mapo-gu
Seoul, Korea
Tel: 822-325-0397
Fax: 822-325-9697
Email: hant93@chollian.dacom.co.kr

PHILIPPINES

Global Publishing
G/F Benavides Garden
1186 Benavides Street
Manila, Philippines
Tel: 632-254-8949/637-252-2582
Fax: 632-734-5060/632-252-2733
Email: globalp@pacific.net.ph

TAIWAN

O'Reilly Taiwan
No. 3, Lane 131
Hang-Chow South Road
Section 1, Taipei, Taiwan
Tel: 886-2-23968990
Fax: 886-2-23968916
Email: taiwan@oreilly.com

CHINA

O'Reilly Beijing
Room 2410
160, FuXingMenNeiDaJie
XiCheng District
Beijing, China PR 100031
Tel: 86-10-66412305
Fax: 86-10-86631007
Email: beijing@oreilly.com

INDIA

Computer Bookshop (India) Pvt. Ltd.
190 Dr. D.N. Road, Fort
Bombay 400 001 India
Tel: 91-22-207-0989
Fax: 91-22-262-3551
Email: cbsbom@giasbm01.vsnl.net.in

JAPAN

O'Reilly Japan, Inc.
Yotsuya Y's Building
7 Banch 6, Honshio-cho
Shinjuku-ku
Tokyo 160-0003 Japan
Tel: 81-3-3356-5227
Fax: 81-3-3356-5261
Email: japan@oreilly.com

ALL OTHER ASIAN COUNTRIES

O'Reilly & Associates, Inc.
101 Morris Street
Sebastopol, CA 95472 USA
Tel: 707-829-0515
Fax: 707-829-0104
Email: order@oreilly.com

AUSTRALIA

Woodslane Pty., Ltd.
7/5 Vuko Place
Warriewood NSW 2102
Australia
Tel: 61-2-9970-5111
Fax: 61-2-9970-5002
Email: info@woodslane.com.au

NEW ZEALAND

Woodslane New Zealand, Ltd.
21 Cooks Street (P.O. Box 575)
Waganui, New Zealand
Tel: 64-6-347-6543
Fax: 64-6-345-4840
Email: info@woodslane.com.au

LATIN AMERICA

McGraw-Hill Interamericana
Editores, S.A. de C.V.
Cedro No. 512
Col. Atlampa
06450, Mexico, D.F.
Tel: 52-5-547-6777
Fax: 52-5-547-3336
Email: mcgraw-hill@infosel.net.mx

O'REILLY®